# SELECTED QUESTIONS IN
# ACCOUNTING

# SELECTED QUESTIONS IN
# ACCOUNTING

## II—INTERMEDIATE

*Edited by:*

**K C DICKINSON** B.COM., M. COMPT., CA(SA), C.F.A.
*Senior Lecturer in Accounting, University of Witwatersrand*

*and*

**F A SANDERS** CA(SA)
*Senior Tutor in Accounting, University of Witwatersrand*

*Seventh Edition*

## JUTA & CO. LTD
CAPE TOWN    WETTON    JOHANNESBURG

First published ................................. November 1955
Fourth edition ................................... January 1976
Fifth edition .................................... February 1989
Sixth edition .................................... November 1990
Seventh edition .................................. September 1993

© Juta & Co, Ltd 1955

PO Box 14373, Kenwyn 7790

*This book is copyright under the Berne Convention. In terms
of the Copyright Act, No 98 of 1978, no part of this book may
be reproduced or transmitted in any form or by any means,
electronic or mechanical, including photocopying, recording
or by any information storage and retrieval system, without
permission in writing from the Publisher.*

ISBN 0 7021 2622 5

PRINTED AND BOUND IN THE REPUBLIC OF SOUTH AFRICA
BY CREDA PRESS (PTY) LTD, EPPINDUST 2

# PREFACE TO FIRST EDITION

Every teacher of accounting realizes how essential it is for his students to have the opportunity of attempting a large number of practical problems illustrating the application of the various theories he has discussed with his class. To provide the necessary number of suitable questions is, however, an arduous task.

The prime object of compiling this book is to meet the needs of the first-year students at this University, but it is, of course, hoped that teachers of accounting at other universities and other institutions will find it of value.

The book contains questions set by many different individuals over a number of years. Special thanks for permission to reprint questions of which they are the owners of the copyright are due to the South African Accountants' Societies' General Examining Board, the University of the Witwatersrand and Messrs. R. Brownlee, J. Ramsay Thomson and G. Thurley.

<table>
<tr><td>University of the Witwatersrand</td><td>B. J. S. WIMBLE</td></tr>
<tr><td>Milner Park</td><td>T. CAIRNS</td></tr>
<tr><td>Johannesburg</td><td></td></tr>
<tr><td>7 August 1952</td><td></td></tr>
</table>

# PREFACE TO SEVENTH EDITION

In this new edition we have endeavoured to incorporate many of the constructive suggestions which have been made to us. In addition, we have taken the opportunity to revise existing questions and introduce new questions to the sections. The revision of the Companies Act has also been taken into account in the questions. New sections covering hire purchase transactions, deferred taxation and financial leases have been introduced in order to ensure that this book meets the requirements for a second-year syllabus in financial accounting at university.

As in the past any constructive comments or suggestions from users would be more than welcome to assist us in improving future editions.

<table>
<tr><td>JOHANNESBURG</td><td>K C DICKINSON</td></tr>
<tr><td></td><td>F A SANDERS</td></tr>
<tr><td>JULY 1993</td><td></td></tr>
</table>

# CONTENTS

## SECTION A
# REVISION

**A1**

The following are the entries in the bank columns of the cash book of the ABC
Company for the month of August 19x3:

| Aug. | 3 | Deposit | R95,55 | Aug. | 1 | Balance | R275,65 |
|---|---|---|---|---|---|---|---|
| " | 8 | " | 142,06 | | | Cheque received | |
| " | 13 | " | 87,38 | | | from A Brown and | |
| " | 18 | " | 50,00 | | | deposited in July | |
| " | 22 | " | 41,55 | | | now returned | |
| " | 27 | " | 63,18 | | | unpaid by the bank | 10,00 |
| " | 31 | " | 125,00 | " | 3 | Cheque No. 36 | 7,50 |
| " | 31 | " | 15,75 | " | 4 | Cheque No. 37 | 11,60 |
| | | Balance carried | | " | 8 | Cheque No. 38 | 75,00 |
| | | forward | 85,15 | " | 8 | Cheque No. 39 | 5,20 |
| | | | | " | 9 | Cheque No. 40 | 12,50 |
| | | | | " | 11 | Cheque No. 41 | 10,57 |
| | | | | " | 15 | Cheque No. 42 | 8,30 |
| | | | | " | 16 | Cheque No. 43 | 19,55 |
| | | | | " | 22 | Cheque No. 44 | 22,50 |
| | | | | " | 23 | Cheque No. 45 | 37,80 |
| | | | | " | 24 | Cheque No. 46 | 16,80 |
| | | | | " | 25 | Cheque No. 47 | 82,50 |
| | | | | " | 27 | Cheque No. 48 | 10,00 |
| | | | | " | 30 | Cheque No. 49 | 27,50 |
| | | | | " | 31 | Cheque No. 50 | 72,65 |
| | | | R705,62 | | | | R705,62 |

The entries on the bank statement for the corresponding period were as
follows:

### Deposits

| August | 1 | R50,00 |
|---|---|---|
| " | 4 | 95,55 |
| " | 9 | 142,06 |
| " | 13 | 87,38 |
| " | 19 | 50,00 |
| " | 23 | 41,55 |
| " | 29 | 63,18 |
| " | 31 | 125,00 |

### Cheques, etc., paid

| Cheque | No. 36 | R7,50 |
|---|---|---|
| " | No. 40 | 12,50 |
| " | No. 43 | 19,55 |
| " | No. 37 | 11,60 |
| " | No. 39 | 5,20 |
| " | No. 38 | 75,00 |
| " | No. 41 | 10,57 |
| " | No. 45 | 37,80 |
| " | No. 42 | 8,30 |
| " | No. 44 | 22,50 |

# A1 CONTINUED

Cheques, etc., paid

| | |
|---|---|
| Cheque No. 30 | 10,00 |
| "    No. 46 | 16,80 |
| "    No. 49 | 27,50 |
| Bank charges | ,60 |

At 31 August 19x3 the bank statement reflected a credit balance of R63,65.

<u>YOU ARE REQUIRED TO:</u>

prepare the bank reconciliation statement at 31 August 19x3.

## A2

M Lategan purchases goods from W Wakefield.   Lategan balances his ledger on the last day of each month but Wakefield balances his on the 15th of each month and prepares statements of account on that date.

These statements (which contain errors) as at 15 June and 15 July appeared thus:

<u>Statement at 15 June 19x3</u>

| | | |
|---|---:|---:|
| Account rendered (debit balance) | | R300 |
| Received 2 June | R185 | |
| Discount 2 June | <u>15</u> | |
| | | <u>200</u> |
| | | 100 |
| Invoice 24 May | 50 | |
| Invoice 12 June | <u>100</u> | |
| | | <u>150</u> |
| | | 250 |
| Credit note 31 May | <u>10</u> | |
| | | <u>10</u> |
| | | R230 |
| | | === |

<u>Statement at 15 July 19x3</u>

| | | |
|---|---:|---:|
| Account rendered (debit balance) | | R240 |
| Received 20 June | R97 | |
| Discount 20 June | 3 | |
| Received 1 July (net) | <u>50</u> | |
| | | <u>150</u> |
| | | 90 |
| Invoice 18 June | R70 | |
| Invoice 24 June | <u>130</u> | |
| | | <u>200</u> |
| | | 290 |
| Debit note for discount over-deducted in June statement - 2 June | | <u>10</u> |
| | | R280 |
| | | === |

The following further information is obtained:

1. The cheque for R185 was sent on 29 May.
2. The credit note for R10 was received and entered on 3 June.
3. The cheque for R50 was sent on 30 June.
4. The debit note for R10 was received and entered on 2 July
5. The invoice of 24 June was for R230, not R130.

Show W Wakefield's account in M Lategan's ledger for the month of June 19x3 in full detail.

# A3

A Beeton, a retail merchant, consistently marks up his cost price by 75% to arrive at the selling price.   He informs  you that he allows a 20% trade discount on sales made to other retailers but that he does not allow any trade discount to other customers.

During the year Beeton took home goods which had cost R500 for his own use. His bookkeeper had made and posted the following journal entry in respect of the goods he had taken:

| | |
|---|---|
| Drawings | R500 |
| Sales - customers other than retailers | R500 |

At 3 June 19x3 Beeton presents you with the following figures and asks you to estimate the value of his stock, assuming that there have been no stock shortages and that the expected profit has been realised.

| | |
|---|---|
| Purchases for year | R80 000 |
| Stock at 30 June 19x2 | 5 000 |
| Sales for year - to customers other than retailers | 70 500 |
|         - to retailers | 49 000 |
| Returns outwards for year | 1 000 |

## A4

P Graham, a merchant, shows you the following trading account prepared by his
bookkeeper:

TRADING ACCOUNT FOR THE YEAR ENDED 31 MARCH 19X3

| | | | |
|---|---|---|---|
| Stock on hand at 31 March 19x2 | R1 000 | Sales | R4 500 |
| Purchases | 3 600 | Stock on hand at 31 March 19x3 | 1 300 |
| Gross profit | 1 200 | | |
| | R5 800 | | R5 800 |
| | ===== | | ===== |

Graham tells you he consistently adds 50% to the cost of his goods to arrive
at their selling price and that it has been unnecessary to reduce the price
of any goods during the year.

Does the trading accounting reflect the results you would expect?  If not,
what explanations occur to you to account for any discrepancy?

## A5

On 1 September 19x3 O Snoek, a wholesale merchant, purchased 1 000 articles in London for R2 each less 25% trade discount.

He paid the following charges on the 1 000 articles:

| | |
|---|---:|
| Freight and marine insurance | R100 |
| Clearing agent's charges | 30 |
| Customs duty | 300 |

The consignment was landed at East London and 100 articles were railed to Snoek's branch in Kimberley at a cost of R27. The balance of the consignment was railed to his head office in Johannesburg at a cost of R333.

By 31 December 19x3 60 articles had been sold in Kimberley at R4,25 each and 868 articles had been sold in Johannesburg at R4,50 each.  Snoek donated two of the articles railed to Johannesburg to an orphanage to be sold at their annual fete on 15 December 19x3.

Prepare a statement showing the gross profits realised on the articles sold in Kimberley and Johannesburg respectively.

## A6

J Waite of Johannesburg imported 200 articles from England for R30 each f.o.b.
Liverpool.   The goods were consigned to Durban.

The importing charges paid by J Waite were:

|                                    |       |
|------------------------------------|-------|
| Freight and marine insurance       | R180  |
| Clearing agent's charges           |  20   |
| Customs duty on 100 articles       | 300   |

100 articles were railed 'in bond' to Johannesburg.  Railage charges on these
articles amounting to R50 were paid.

By 31 March 19x3 the end of Waite's financial year, the following transactions
had taken place in Durban:

50 articles were sold to wholesalers at a price which would give a profit of
50% on turnover.
40 articles were sold to retailers at the wholesale selling price plus 50%.
1 article was given to J Waite's father as a present.

By 31 March 19x3 70 of the articles sent to Johannesburg were sold 'in bond'
at cost plus 100%.

You are required to prepare a statement showing:

(1)   the profit made on the articles sold;
(2)   the cost of the stock on hand at 31 March 19x3.

J Cheetham, a trader, employs a general manager, R Maclew, and a sales manager, K Viljoon.

Maclew is entitled to a salary of R15 000 per annum and a commission of 5% on the total profits after charging all expenses and commissions, including his own.

Viljoon is entitled to a salary of R10 000 per annum and a commission of 1/2% on turnover plus 2 1/2% of the total profits after charging all expenses and commissions, including his own.

From the following information in respect of the year ended 31 August 19x3, calculate the commission due to each

| | |
|---|---|
| Turnover for the year | R1 000 000 |
| Cheetham certifies that the stock sold during the year was marked up to realise a profit of 30% on turnover | |
| Income from investments for the year | 20 000 |
| Expenses for the year other than Maclew's and Viljoon's salaries and commissions | 157 990 |

# A8

VIP Valiant trading as Rebel Stores informs you that a fire occurred in the store on the night of Sunday, 5 November 19x6 and requests you to assist him in preparing his claim from the insurance company.

The fire insurance policy indicates the following compensation will be paid:

> Stock destroyed by fire - at cost
> Fixtures and fittings - at book value at end of calendar month preceding the fire
> Cash - at face value.

The following information is available:

1. **Fixtures and fittings**
   (a)  The fixtures and fittings were completely destroyed by the fire.
   (b)  All the fixtures and fittings were acquired when the business was started on 1 January 19x2 for R6 000, with the exception of a new showcase which was purchased on 1 October 19x5 for R360.
   (c)  The fixtures and fittings have been depreciated at the rate of 10% per annum on cost.

2. **Stock**

|   |   |   |
|---|---|---|
| (a) | Stock at 1 July 19x6 | R14 000 |
| (b) | Purchases, 1 July 19x6 to 4 November 19x6 | 42 000 |
| (c) | Sales, 1 July 19x6 to 4 November 19x6 | 48 000 |
| (d) | Stock salvaged | 1 200 |

   (e)  Goods have always been marked up by 50% to arrive at the normal selling prices.
   (f)  All goods were sold at the marked selling prices except during September 19x6 when a 'spring sale' was held.
   (g)  During the 'spring sale' all marked prices were reduced by 50%.
   (h)  The turnover during the 'spring sale' was R12 000. This is included in the figure for sales given in (c) above.

3. **Cash**
   (a)  The cash box had been completely destroyed.
   (b)  The cashier remembered that at the close of business on 4 November the cash box had contained:

| | |
|---|---|
| Notes | R960 |
| Cheque in favour of creditor, D Odge | 140 |
| Cheque for October salary to employee who was on leave | 180 |
| Cheques from debtors totalling | 720 |
| | R2 000 |

4. **General**
   The financial year of Rebel Stores ends on 30 June.

<u>YOU ARE REQUIRED TO:</u>

prepare a statement detailing the amount to be claimed from the insurance company.

Collins and Davis are in partnership as tea and coffee merchants sharing profits and losses in the ratio 4:1. Collins is entitled to a salary of R10 000 per annum and Davis R5 000 per annum, and both must be credited with interest on their capital accounts at the rate of 5% per annum. No interest is charged on drawings.

The following trial balance was extracted at 30 September 19x3:

| | | |
|---|---:|---:|
| Bank | R14 000 | |
| Advertising | 10 400 | |
| Creditors | | R10 000 |
| Capital - Collins at 30 September 19x2 | 50 000 | |
|        - Davis at 30 September 19x2 | 60 000 | |
| Debtors | 40 000 | |
| Drawings - Collins | 12 000 | |
|        - Davis | | 9 000 |
| General expenses | 2 000 | |
| Purchases - tea | 120 000 | |
|        - coffee | | 150 000 |
| Rent | 9 000 | |
| Salaries | 25 600 | |
| Sales - tea | 150 000 | |
|      - coffee | | 240 000 |
| Stock on hand at 30 September 19x2 - tea | 30 000 | |
|                   - coffee | | 75 000 |
| Travellers' commission | 13 000 | |
| | R510 000 | R510 000 |

Tea is sold at cost plus 25% and coffee at cost plus 33 1/3%.

Stock was not taken at 30 September 19x3 but when it was taken on 31 October 19x3 it was found that the expected rates of gross profit had been realised.

Prepare the balance sheet at 30 September 19x3, and the income statement for the year ended on that date. Selling expenses should be allocated to departments in proportion to turnover, and other expenses should be divided equally.

# A10

In the audit of a certain firm you discovered that as soon as orders for goods of R200, R350 and R1 200 had been completed and the goods made ready for dispatch, the purchasers had been debited with the amounts, although the goods still remained on the firm's premises. The stock-takers, unaware of these facts, included the goods in stock at 10% below selling prices. You further discovered that invoices received for R170, R190 and R210 had been dated forward to the next year's account, but that the goods had been taken into stock. On  the accounts as submitted to you for audit the profit shown was R2 700. What adjustments, if any, do you consider necessary before certifying the final accounts and what effect would they have on the balance sheet?

# A11

The following is the income and expenditure account of the Tipplers Club for the year ended 31 December 19x3:

| | | | | |
|---|---|---|---|---|
| Salaries | R6 000 | Subscriptions | | R5 000 |
| Sundry expenses | 820 | Bar sales | R12 000 | |
| Debenture interest | 330 | Cost of sales | 6 200 | 5 800 |
| Assessment rates | 120 | Unredeemed coupons | | |
| Secretary's bonus | 100 | forfeited | | 150 |
| Depreciation of furniture | 440 | Profit on sale of furniture | | 50 |
| Unsaleable bar stock written off | 140 | Interest on fixed deposit | | 60 |
| Excess of income over expenditure | 3 110 | | | |
| | R11 060 | | | R11 060 |
| | ====== | | | ====== |

The following are the balance sheets of the club at 31 December 19x2 and 31 December 19x3 respectively:

| | 19x2 | 19x3 | | | 19x2 | 19x3 |
|---|---|---|---|---|---|---|
| Accumulated funds | | | Land and buildings | | | |
| Balance at 1 January | R6 405 | R8 655 | at cost | | R10 000 | R10 000 |
| Entrance fees received | 100 | 60 | Furniture at | | | |
| Excess of income over | | | 1 January | | R2 000 | R2 000 |
| expenditure | 2 150 | 3 110 | Sales at book | | | |
| | 8 655 | 11 825 | value | | - | 200 |
| Debentures | 6 000 | 5 000 | | | 2 000 | 1 800 |
| Coupons | 1 200 | 1 100 | Additions | | 500 | 400 |
| Subscriptions received | | | | | 2 500 | 2 200 |
| in advance | 150 | 180 | Deprecia- | | | |
| Creditors for - | | | tion | 500 | 2 000 | 440 | 1 760 |
| Bar purchases | 500 | 600 | Glassware at valuation | | 200 | 250 |
| Salaries | 100 | 50 | Bar stock | | 3 000 | 3 200 |
| Secretary's bonus | 75 | 100 | Debtors for coupons sold | | 50 | 60 |
| Debenture interest | 180 | 150 | Subscriptions outstanding | | 20 | 30 |
| | | | Fixed deposit | | 1 000 | 2 000 |
| | | | Interest accrued on | | | |
| | | | fixed deposit | | 20 | 40 |
| | | | Cash at bank | | 420 | 1 445 |
| | | | Cash on hand | | 230 | 200 |
| | R16 860 | R19 005 | | | R16 860 | R19 005 |
| | ====== | ====== | | | ====== | ====== |

The glassware account for 19x3 is as follows:

| 19x3 | | | | 19x3 | | | |
|---|---|---|---|---|---|---|---|
| Jan. 1 | Balance | | R200 | Dec. 31 | Sundry expenses | | R130 |
| Dec. 31 | Cash | | 180 | " 31 | Balance | | 250 |
| | | | R380 | | | | R380 |
| | | | === | | | | === |

Coupons are sold on credit and for cash.    Coupons only are accepted in the bar.
Prepare a receipts and payments account for the year 19x3.    The balances at the beginning and end of the account should be made up of cash on fixed deposit, cash at bank and cash on hand.

# A12

The balances in the books of the Bachelors' Club at 31 March 19x4 were as follows:

| | |
|---|---:|
| Furniture at cost less depreciation to 31 March 19x3 | R1 730 |
| Furniture bought on 31 March 19x4 | 610 |
| Fixtures and fittings at cost less depreciation to 31 March 19x3 | 670 |
| Billiard table and accessories at cost less depreciation to 31 March 19x3 | 930 |
| Glassware, cutlery and linen at valuation at 31 March 19x3 | 800 |
| Purchases of glassware, cutlery and linen | 2 760 |
| Stock in restaurant, at 31 March 19x3 | 50 |
| Stock in bar, at 31 March 19x3 | 870 |
| Restaurant takings | 25 140 |
| Bar takings | 26 050 |
| Billiard room takings | 3 270 |
| Membership subscriptions | 5 250 |
| Interest on deposit account | 170 |
| Purchases - restaurant | 15 740 |
| Purchases - bar | 16 000 |
| Rent and rates | 3 490 |
| Wages | 9 240 |
| Fuel and light | 2 700 |
| Sundry expenses | 2 300 |
| Cash in hand, at 31 March 19x4 | 250 |
| Cash at bank, at 31 March 19x4 | 3 900 |
| Cash on deposit at 31 March 19x4 | 5 860 |
| Debtors, at 31 March 19x4 | 1 790 |
| Creditors, at 31 March 19x4 | 2 600 |
| Accumulated funds, at 31 March 19x3 | 7 210 |

You are required to prepare an income and expenditure statement for the year ended 31 March 19x4, and a balance sheet at that date taking into account the following:

(a)  Stocks on hand at 31 March 19x4 - restaurant R40, bar R890 and glassware, cutlery and linen R800.

(b)  During the year meals from the restaurant and cigarettes and drinks from the bar costing R4 000 and R1 000 respectively were supplied free to members of the staff.

(c)  Depreciation (which in respect of the items below is to be calculated to the nearest R1) is to be provided for as follows:

| | |
|---|---|
| Furniture | 10% per annum |
| Fixtures and fittings | 5% per annum |
| Billiard table and accessories | 15% per annum. |

# A13

The following items appear in the ledger accounts stated, before any closing
or adjusting entries have been made at 30 September 19x9:

(a)    in the payments in advance account:
       1 October 19x8 a balance brought forward of R352.

(b)    in the insurance account:
       1 November 19x8 payment of R192 in respect of policy CD97531 for the
       period 1 November 19x8 to 31 October 19x9.
       15 January 19x9 payment of R800 in respect of policy CD86421 for the
       period 1 January to 31 December 19x9.
       1 April 19x9 payment of R72 in respect of policy CD98542 for the period
       1 May 19x9 to 30 April 19y0.

(c)    in the assessment rates account:
       5 March 19x9 payment  of R480  in  respect of rates  for  the  period
       1 January to 30 June 19x9.
       4 September 19x9 payment of R480 in respect of rates for the period
       1 July to 31 December 19x9.

(d)    in the rent received account:
       4 October 19x8 receipt of R720 for the quarter ended 31 October 19x8.
       1 November 19x8 receipt of R720 for the quarter ended 31 January 19x9.
       2 February 19x9 receipt of R960 for the quarter ended 30 April 19x9.
       3 May 19x9 receipt of R960 for the quarter ended 31 July 19x9.
       5 August 19x9 receipt of R960 for the quarter ended 31 October 19x9.

<u>YOU ARE REQUIRED TO STATE</u>:

(a)    the amount by which the payments in advance would increase or decrease
       at 30 September 19x9.

(b)    the amount for rent received which would be disclosed in the income
       statement for the year ended 30 September 19x9.

# A14

Ace Wholesalers Limited sells to Zenos Traders. Ace Wholesalers Limited closes off its sales records on the 25th of the month and its cash book on the last day of the month. Cash discount of 2 1/2% is allowed on all purchases (other than those carrying a trade discount) paid for and received by them by the last day of the month following the month in which the invoice appeared on the statement.

Zenos Traders close off their books on the last day of the month. They allow a 5% cash discount on purchases paid within 1 month after date of statement on which the invoice appeared.

Zenos Traders received a statement from Ace Wholesalers dated 30 November 19x9

showing a balance of R1 885 owing by Zenos Traders.

On comparing the statement with the ledger account for Ace Wholesalers Limited in the creditors' ledger, the bookkeeper of Zenos Traders found the following discrepancies:

(i)    The statement balance at 31 November includes the full statement balance at 30 October for the following reasons:

    a)    No adjustments had been made for the overcast error of R10 in the debit column in the October statement.

    b)    A credit note in respect of invoice 41 for R35 in respect of goods which were incorrectly supplied and subsequently returned had not yet been passed by Ace Wholesalers Limited. This amount has never been debited nor credited in the ledger.

    c)    A payment of R273 in respect of October purchases after allowing the 2 1/2% discount had not been received by Ace Wholesalers Limited by 30 November 19x9.

(ii)    The following invoices did not appear on the statement:

| Invoice No. | Amount | Date | Date of goods received note |
|---|---|---|---|
| 89 | R165 | 27 November | 29 November |
| 93 | R190 | 28 November | 30 November |
| 99 | R225 | 29 November | 30 November |

(iii)    Invoice No. 10 for R87 had been entered in the purchases book as R78 and to Acme Wholesalers Limited in the creditors ledger.

(iv)    The statement recorded invoice No. 12 which showed a charge for 100 units at R8,00 each whereas Zenos Traders had only received 90 units. The purchase order stated that 100 units had been ordered at a price of R8,00 less 10% trade discount.

# A14 CONTINUED

(v)   During the month of November, Ace Wholesalers Limited purchased goods
      listed at R140 from Zenos Traders and agreed that the amount should be
      set off against purchases from them.  Zenos Traders had debited R140 in
      their creditors ledger, but the set off was not reflected on the
      statement.  It was agreed that discount would be allowed on this
      amount.

(vii) Invoice No. 70 for R51 had been recorded in the purchases journal
      correctly but entered in the creditors ledger as if it was a credit
      note for R15.

      Assuming Zenos Traders wishes to claim the discount allowed by Ace
      Wholesalers Limited for prompt settlement of the account, but only
      wishes to pay those invoices which have been entered on statements

(a)   Prepare a reconciliation statement to accompany the cheque to be sent
      to Ace Wholesalers Limited to reach them before 31 December 19x9 in
      settlement of the November statement.

(b)   Prepare the necessary journal entries to correct the mistake in Zenos
      Traders books in respect of Ace Wholesalers Limited's account and to
      record the cheque payment in settlement of account.  Control accounts
      are maintained.

(c)   State the balance on Ace  Wholesalers  Limited's  account after the
      corrections have been made and the payment for the November statement
      recorded.

# A15

You received a statement for A Jack, a wholesaler, dated 30 September 19x9.
On comparing the statement with his account in your books you found that:

(i)     His account in your ledger had a debit balance of R139,73.
(ii)    His credit note No. 51 for R20 was correctly entered in the returns
        outwards and allowances book, but had been posted to the wrong side of
        his account in your ledger.
(iii)   His invoice No. 201 for R32,25 had been entered in the purchases book
        as R32,52.
(iv)    His invoice No. 324 for R42,70 had been entered on his statement
        as R4,27.
(v)     His invoice No. 431 had been shown gross on his statement whereas the
        invoice from which the books had been entered reflected 25% trade
        discount amounting to R10.
(vi)    His statement showed an amount of R100 owing to him brought forward
        from August.  His August statement had been overcast by R1 and the
        balance after deducting discount of R6 had been paid by you on 29
        September, but his receipt was dated 2 October.  Discount was
        disallowed due to late payment but no entry has been made to correct
        this.
(vii)   You had charged him R80 for goods, but this amount was not shown on his
        statement.  This was the only sale to Jack during September.
(viii)  The credit side of Jack's account in your ledger had been undercast by
        R200.
(ix)    All purchases made from Jack, except those carrying trade discount, are
        subject to 5% cash discount if paid by the 25th of the following month.
        Jack is entitled to 2 1/2% cash discount on goods he purchases from
        you.


WHAT AMOUNT SHOULD BE PAID TO JACK TO SETTLE HIS ACCOUNT ON 10 OCTOBER 19X9?

# A16

In the trial balance taken out from the books of the Magic Ruby Trading Company Limited at 31 December 19x4, the debits exceeded the credits by R7 260. Instead of looking for the error or errors the bookkeeper put through the journal entry:

```
19x4
Dec.  31              X                                   -
                 Suspense                         R7 260
                 Amount credited to suspense
                 to balance books
```

He then discovered that the list of debtors did not agree with balance on the debtors control account and he put through the journal entry:

```
            Debtors control                   R1 330
                 Debtors suspense                        R1 330
            Amount debited to debtors control
            to make that account agree with
            the list of debtors
```

He also found that the creditors control did not agree with the list of creditors so he put through the journal entry.

```
            Creditors suspense                 R10
                 Creditors control       R10
            Amount credited to creditors
            control to make the account agree
            with the list of creditors
```

The following are summaries of the debtors and creditors control accounts as they appear in the books of the company at 31 December 19x4.

### Debtors control

| 19x4 | | | | 19x4 | | | |
|---|---|---|---|---|---|---|---|
| Jan | 1 | Balance | R24 300 | Dec 31 | Cash | | R197 360 |
| Dec | 31 | Sales | 215 910 | | Bills receivable | | 20 300 |
| | | Cash - refund | | | Cash - bills dis- | | |
| | | to a debtor | 100 | | counted with bank | | 8 000 |
| | | Discount allowed | 3 810 | | Bad debts | | 150 |
| | | | | | Amounts set off | | |
| | | | | | against debts due to | | |
| | | | | | creditors | | 630 |
| | | | | | Balance | | 17 680 |
| | | | R244 120 | | | | R244 120 |
| | | | ======= | | | | ======= |

# A16 CONTINUED

Creditors control

| 19x4 | | | | 19x4 | | | |
|---|---|---|---|---|---|---|---|
| Dec. 31 | Returns outwards | R1 210 | | Jan. 1 | Balance | R17 650 | |
| | Cash | 89 210 | | Dec. 31 | Purchases | 95 430 | |
| | Bills payable | 18 670 | | | | | |
| | Discount received | 930 | | | | | |
| | Amount set off against debts due by debtors | 360 | | | | | |
| | Balance | 2 700 | | | | | |
| | | R113 080 | | | | R113 080 | |
| | | ======= | | | | ======= | |

The following mistakes are discovered:

(a)    The sales book was undercast by R1 000.

(b)    An amount of R320 was not posted from the sales book to the debit of G Hall's account in the debtors ledger.

(c)    Bills payable had been posted from the bills payable book to the creditors control account as R18 670 instead of R18 760.

(d)    The list of creditors was overcast by R100.

Show by means of journal entries how you would adjust these mistakes and any others which you can discover from a scrutiny of the control accounts and draw up a statement showing whether the mistakes account for the amount by which the books are out of balance.

# A17

A bookkeeper took out a trial balance at 28 February 19x7 which did not balance.    He transferred the difference to a general ledger difference account.

On checking the books he then discovered the following mistakes:

1.    He had posted the total of the returns inwards book of R10 420 to the credit of purchases.    The posting to debtors control had been made correctly.

2.    He had posted the total of the returns outwards book of R7 609 to the debit of sales as R6 790.    The posting to the creditors control had been made correctly.

3.    The stationery column in the purchases book had been overcast by R1 000.    The analysis columns did not cross cast.

4.    A bill receivable of R42 000 which had been dishonoured was debited to bills receivable account from the cash book.

5.    An amount of R426 had been posted from the debit side of the cash book to the wrong side of telephone account.

6.    A cheque for R6 581 in payment of creditor A's account had been posted to his account in the creditors ledger, but had not been entered in the cash book.    This error was discovered during preparation of the bank reconciliation statement.

    These were the only mistakes in the books.

Prepare the adjusting journal entries.

# A18

A bookkeeper took out a trial balance at 31 December 19x1 which did not balance. Instead of looking for the difference he entered R25,10 on the debit side of a suspense account in order to make the debit side agree with the credit side.

Immediately afterwards he extracted a list of debtors balances and a list of creditors balances. He discovered that the list of debtors balances did not agree with the debtors control account, the list of debtors balances being R32,10 larger than the debtors control account. He made a journal entry crediting the debtors control account and debiting the debtors suspense account with R31,20. The balance on the creditors control account was larger than the list of creditors balances by R50,60. He made a journal entry debiting the creditors control account and crediting a creditors suspense account with this amount.

Thereafter the following mistakes were found:

1. A debtor, Adams, who owed R25,60, had been omitted from the list of debtors balances.

2. An amount of R6,30 received from G Botha had been posted from the cash book to the wrong side of his account in the debtors ledger.

3. An amount of R12,60 for delivery outwards had been posted to the debit side of purchases.

4. The bills payable book for November 19x1 had been undercast by R10.

5. An amount of R15,20 in the purchases book had been posted twice to the credit side of C Cohen's account in the creditors ledger.

6. An amount of R30 owing by a creditor, D Donn, should have been set off against the balance owing to him in the creditors ledger. No adjustment had been put through in respect of this.

7. The debit side of the trial balance had been overcast by R10.

8. Advertising R50 had been entered on the credit side of the trial balance instead of the debit side.


<u>YOU ARE REQUIRED TO</u>:

i. draft all the journal entries necessary to adjust the above, and

ii. show the debtors and creditors suspense accounts and the general ledger suspense account after all the entries in (i) have been posted.

# A19

**PART A**

X Co. was incorporated with a capital of 200 000 shares of no par value.

The subscribers to the memorandum subscribed for 10 000 shares and paid R10 000.  90 000 shares were offered to the public at R1,20 per share. The offer was fully subscribed.

Preliminary and share issue expenses amounting to R4 000 were paid in cash.

During the first year the company made a net income after taxation of R35 000. At the end of the first year the directors decided to write off the preliminary and share issue expenses but they required that the distributable reserve be maintained at the maximum amount.

Two years later the company agrees to offer a further 50 000 shares to the public.

WHAT IS the minimum price at which these shares can be issued to the public without a special resolution?

**PART B**

Hoe Limited was incorporated on 1 June 19x4 with the following share capital:

    100 000 10% preference shares of R1 each
    200 000 ordinary shares of R1 each.

The following issues and allotments were made:

| | | |
|---|---|---|
| 1 June 19x4 | - | Subscribers to memorandum - 5 000 ordinary shares at par. |
| 30 November 19x4 | - | 25 000 preference shares at a premium of 5% and 50 000 ordinary shares at par. Share issue expenses amounted to R7 500. |
| 1 July 19x5 | - | 50 000 ordinary shares at a premium of 10%. Share issue expenses amounted to R2 500. |

On 1 June 19x7 the ordinary shares were converted into shares of no par value and on 30 June 19x7 the remaining unissued ordinary shares were issued at R1,75 per share.

On 1 December 19x7 R50 000 12% debentures were issued at a discount of 10%.

The policy of the company has been to write off share issue expenses during the financial year in which they were incurred in such a way as to leave distributable reserves at the maximum amount possible.  This policy has been carried out since incorporation and the company has made substantial profits each year ending 28 February.

What was the balance on the stated capital account at 28 February 19x8?

## A20

Boz (Pty) Limited manufactures a single type of article which is sold by its sales centre.   The factory and sales centre are operated as two separate departments and relevant costing and trading records are maintained.

Manufactured articles are delivered by the factory to the sales centre on internal invoices and are charged at factory cost of production plus 10%. Undelivered manufactured articles in the factory and unsold stock in the sales centre are valued on the same basis.   Movements of stock in both the factory and sales centre are recorded by the first-in-first-out method.   The sales centre sells only articles manufactured by the factory.

The manager of the sales centre receives a salary of R10 000 per annum and is entitled to a commission of 5% of the net profit of the sales centre after allowing for all expenses of that department and after allowing for his salary and commission.

The following information relates to the transactions in the financial year ended 30 September 19x7, but nothing has been charged to the sales centre in respect of the manager's commission:

| FACTORY | QUANTITY | VALUE |
|---|---|---|
| Stocks - | | |
|   raw materials at 30 September 19x6 | | R23 500 |
|   raw materials at 30 September 19x7 | | 22 400 |
|   manufactured articles at 30 September 19x6 | 420 | 13 860 |
|   manufactured articles at 30 September 19x7 | 390 | |
| Purchases - Raw materials | | 116 600 |
| Factory wages earned | | 44 400 |
| Factory overheads incurred | | 32 140 |
| Number of articles delivered to sales centre | 6 100 | |

| SALES CENTRE | QUANTITY | VALUE |
|---|---|---|
| Stocks - | | |
|   manufactured articles at 30 September 19x6 | 300 | 9 900 |
| Sales | 5 900 | 309 144 |
| Manufactured articles scrapped - 19 April 19x7 | 100 | |
| Articles stolen on 25 September 19x7 (uninsured) | 20 | |
| Selling expenses | | 30 048 |
| Salary - manager | | 10 000 |

| GENERAL | | |
|---|---|---|
| Total administration expenses | | 35 600 |

# A20 CONTINUED

<u>NOTES</u>

(1)    The actual loss incurred in respect of the 100 articles scrapped and the 20 articles stolen is not to be regarded as a charge against the factory or the sales centre.   The amounts involved are to be written off in the income statement.

(2)    All manufactured articles undelivered and unsold at 30 September 19x6 were sold within the first two months of the current year.

<u>YOU ARE REQUIRED TO PREPARE</u>:

(a)    Manufacturing statement for the factory for the year ended 30 September 19x7.

(b)    Trading statement for the sales centre for the year ended 30 September 19x7.

(c)    Income statement for the company for the year ended 30 September 19x7.

# A21

The T.T.C. Club has been left R10 000 in the will of a former member.  It has
embarked on an expansion programme which will involve expenditure of R5 000
on 31 August and a further R6 000 on 31 October 19x5.  As the legacy can be
expected only late in December 19x5 and the club executive are anxious to know
whether they will have to raise additional funds to meet expenditure before
31 December  they ask your advice:

The following information is available:

1.   <u>INCOME AND EXPENDITURE ACCOUNT FOR THE YEAR ENDED 30 JUNE 19x5</u>

| | | | | | |
|---|---|---|---|---|---|
| Assessment rates | | R200 | Bar sales | R12 000 | |
| Bar salaries | | 2 160 | Cost of sales | 6 000 | R6 000 |
| Breakage of glassware | | 100 | Subscriptions | | 4 520 |
| Debenture interest | R300 | | | | |
| Debenture premium accrued | 25 | 325 | | | |
| Depreciation furniture | | 450 | | | |
| (at 5% per annum on cost) | | | | | |
| General expenses | | 1 296 | | | |
| Wages | | 2 400 | | | |
| Excess of income over expenditure | | 3 589 | | | |
| | | R10 520 | | | R10 520 |
| | | ====== | | | ====== |

BALANCE SHEET AT 30 JUNE 19x5

| | | | | | | |
|---|---|---|---|---|---|---|
| ACCUMULATED FUNDS | | | FIXED ASSETS | | | |
| Balance 1 July 19x4 | | R33 848 | Land and buildings, | | | |
| Entrance fees | | 3 600 | at cost | | | R40 990 |
| | | 37 448 | Furniture, at cost | R9 000 | | |
| Excess of income over | | | Accumulated depre- | | | |
| expenditure | | 3 589 | ciation | | 2 900 | 6 100 |
| | | 41 037 | Glassware, at valuation | | | 500 |
| | | | | | | 47 590 |
| SIX PER CENT DEBENTURES | R5 000 | | | | | |
| Debenture premium | | | | | | |
| accrued | 119 | 5 119 | CURRENT ASSETS | | | |
| CURRENT LIABILITIES | | | Bar stock | R300 | | |
| Interest accrued on | | | Bank | 1 081 | | |
| debentures | R225 | | Cash on hand | 20 | | 1 401 |
| Subscriptions received | | | | | | |
| in advance | 2 000 | | | | | |
| Bar creditors | 500 | | | | | |
| Creditors for general | | | | | | |
| expenses | 110 | 2 835 | | | | |
| | | R48 991 | | | | R48 991 |
| | | ====== | | | | ====== |

# A21 CONTINUED

2. The following information relates to membership:

 (a) The club had a membership of 177 at 30 June 19x5 and there was a considerable waiting list of prospective members.

 (b) Members pay an entrance fee of R100 and a subscription of R20 per annum or part thereof.  Subscriptions are due on 1 July or on date of admission.

 (c) The committee has decided to admit 45 members on 1 July 19x5 in addition to those mentioned  in the next sub-paragraph.

 (d) There are approximately three resignations per month which are always filled  on the first day of the following month.

 (e) All members pay their subscriptions on or before due date.

3. The admission of the 45 additional members will have an immediate effect on bar turnover (in direct proportion to the increase in membership) but no effect on expenses.  Bar salaries have been increased by R50 per month from 1 July 19x5.

4. 500 6% debentures of R10 each were issued on 1 October 19x0.  They are redeemable ten years after issue at a premium of 5%.  Interest is payable on 30 September each year.

5. An order for R364 glassware was  placed  in  May  19x5  and a bill at 3 months/sight for this amount was accepted on 15 July 19x5.

6. Assessment rates are payable on 15 March and 15 September for the six months ended 30 June and 31 December respectively.  (No increase in assessment rates has taken place for a number of years and no increase is expected).

7. The bar creditors must be paid at the end of the month following the month in which the purchase was made.

8. Other expenses are not expected to increase.

9. Except where otherwise stated, all income and expenditure is earned or incurred evenly throughout the year.

<u>REQUIRED</u>:

(a) Prepare a statement to show whether the club is likely to have to raise additional funds before 31 December 19x5 and

(b) If you consider funds will be required to state (with reasons) how you advise these funds should be raised.

**A22**

The L & P Society organises study groups and lectures and publishes a quarterly journal. The following is a summary of the receipts and payment of the society for the year 19x8.

<u>Receipts and payments account</u>

| | | | | | |
|---|---|---:|---|---|---:|
| Balance at bank 1/1/x8 | | R915 | Salaries | | R2 460 |
| Annual membership subscriptions | | | Rent | | 700 |
|   For 19x7 | R63 | | Lecture fees and expenses | | 528 |
|   "  19x8 | 3 680 | |   Cost of printing quarterly | | |
|   "  19x9 | <u>104</u> | 3 847 |   journal | | 2 130 |
| Sales and subscriptions - | | | Stationery and postages | | 416 |
|   quarterly journal | | 1 873 | General expenses | | 896 |
| Income from investments | | 480 | New office equipment | | 800 |
| Proceeds from sale of investments | | 1 071 | Balance at bank 31/12/x8 | | 754 |
| Legacy | | <u>500</u> | | | |
| | | R8 686 | | | R8 686 |
| | | ===== | | | ===== |

You are given the following information:

(1)    At 31/12/19x7, membership subscriptions and subscriptions for the quarterly journal had been received in advance as follows:

       Membership subscriptions for 19x8               R126
       Journal subscriptions for 19x8 issue of journal    740
       Journal subscriptions for 19x9 issue of journal     16

(2)    The subscriptions for the quarterly journal received in 19x8 included R671 for 19x9 issues and R24 for 19x10 issues.

(3)    Amounts owing to the printers of the quarterly journal were:

       At 31/12/x7                  R490
       At 31/12/x8                  R560

(4)    One quarter of the cost of stationery and postages was on account of the quarterly journal.

(5)    The balance sheet of the society at 31/12/x7 included:

    (a)    Lecture endowment R1 018 representing a legacy of R1 000 the income from which was to finance an annual lecture and R18 unspent income.
    (b)    Investments at cost R9 000 of which R1 000 represented investments held on account of the lecture endowment.
    (c)    Office furniture and equipment, at cost R1 500.

(6)    The cost of the investments sold in 19x8 (none of which were held on account of the lecture endowment) was R1 200.

# A22 CONTINUED

(7)    R50 of the investment income received in 19x8 was on account of the lecture endowment and R46 of the lecture fees and expenses were in respect of the relevant lecture.

(8)    No special conditions were attached to the legacy of R500 received in 19x8.

<u>YOU ARE REQUIRED</u>:

to prepare an income statement for the quarterly journal for the year 19x8, a general income and expenditure account for the year 19x8 (to which the profit or loss on the quarterly journal should be transferred) and a balance sheet at 31/12/x8.

Show your detailed calculations for the balance on the accumulated fund at 31/12/x7.

There were no subscriptions in arrear at 31/12/x8.

Ignore taxation and depreciation.

**A23**

The constitution of the YOUNG CRICKETERS CLUB stipulates that an unaudited
cash flow statement must be presented to the board every six months.  The
treasurer of the club hands to you the following information, and asks you to
draw up the cash flow statement for the six months ended 31 December 19x0.

<u>INCOME AND EXPENDITURE ACCOUNT FOR THE SIX MONTHS ENDED 31 DECEMBER 19X0</u>

<u>INCOME</u>

| | |
|---|---:|
| Bar takings - gross | R1 000 |
| Entrance fees | 5 000 |
| Subscriptions | 10 000 |
| Interest on deposit | 240 |
| | R16 240 |

<u>EXPENDITURE</u>

| | |
|---|---:|
| Salaries and wages | R2 400 |
| Bookkeepers costs | 200 |
| Maintenance of grounds | 1 000 |
| Depreciation | 1 200 |
| | 4 800 |
| Surplus | 11 440 |
| | R16 240 |

Once you have perused his figures and supporting schedules the following
information comes to light:

(1)     One month's interest of R240, was received on 1 October 19x0 and
        represented a quarterly payment made by the building society on monies
        invested with them on a 3 year fixed deposit of 12% p.a.  The club had
        made the investment on 1 September 19x0.   The building society pays
        interest on 1 October, 1 January, 1 April and 1 July each year.

(2)     Bar prices are determined by consistently marking up stock by 25% on
        cost.   Stock control in the bar is maintained by using the imprest
        system.   At the end of each month stocks are replenished to the float
        amount.

(3)     The constitution of the club stipulates that entrance fees are to be
        taken directly to the credit of the accumulated funds accounts.

(4)     The figure for subscriptions in the income and expenditure account is
        cash received only and does not take into account any of the following
        items:

        (a)   Debtors for subscriptions 1 July 19x0                     R500
              Debtors for subscriptions 31 December 19x0                 400
              Subscriptions received in advance 1 July 19x0            1 000
              Subscriptions received in advance 31 December 19x0         600
              Bad debts for subscriptions 1 July to 31 December 19x0     100

## A23 CONTINUED

(5)     Bookkeeper's costs do not take into account your fees which you estimate will be R210.

(6)     The bank balance at 31 December 19x0 is less than that at 1 July 19x0 by the amount deposited in the building society.

(7)     The club had granted bursaries to deserving candidates to attend universities in the U.K. to further their cricketing talent.   The bank drafts and cash grants amounted to R13 000.   The board had authorised this expenditure due to the significant balance on Accumulated Funds and the liquidity of the club.

(8)     Bar creditors had increased from 1 July 19x0 to 31 December by R1 160.


<u>YOU ARE REQUIRED TO</u>:

Prepare the cash flow statement for the period 1 July 19x0 to 31 December 19x0.

Give supporting schedules necessary to comply with the requirement of good presentation.

# A24

The following information has been extracted from the books of the Old Boys
Club at 31 May 19x4:

CASH FLOW STATEMENT FOR THE YEAR ENDED 31 MAY 19x4

| | | | |
|---|---:|---|---:|
| Excess of revenue over | | Land and buildings - | |
| expenditure before charging | | additions | R1 000 |
| depreciation of R200 | R600 | Sports equipment purchased | 400 |
| Entrance fees received | 150 | Cash on deposit | 200 |
| Loans increased | 500 | | |
| Increase in creditors for wages | 10 | | |
| Increase in creditors for | | | |
| assessment rates | 10 | | |
| Increase in creditors for | | | |
| additions to Club House | 300 | | |
| Increase in creditors for | | | |
| interest on loan | 5 | | |
| Decrease in debtors for | | | |
| subscriptions | 5 | | |
| Net decrease in bank | 20 | | |
| | R1 600 | | R1 600 |
| | ===== | | ===== |

The balance sheet and revenue and expenditure account in abridge form are as
follows:

BALANCE SHEET AT 31 MAY 19x4

| | | | |
|---|---:|---|---:|
| Accumulated funds | | Land and buildings, at cost | R4 000 |
| Balance 31 May 19x4 | R2 950 | Sports equipment at cost | |
| Loan | 2 500 | less depreciation | 1 200 |
| Creditors for wages | 60 | Debtors for subscriptions | 30 |
| Creditors for assessment rates | 50 | Cash on deposit | 500 |
| Creditors for additions to | | Cash at bank | 160 |
| Club House | 300 | | |
| Creditors for loan interest | 30 | | |
| | R5 890 | | R5 890 |
| | ===== | | ===== |

REVENUE AND EXPENDITURE ACCOUNT FOR THE YEAR ENDED 31 MAY 19x4

| | | | |
|---|---:|---|---:|
| Salaries and wages | R1 250 | Subscriptions | R1 540 |
| Assessment rates | 90 | Billiard room revenue | 578 |
| General expenses | 45 | Interest on deposit | 7 |
| Bad debts - subscriptions | 15 | | |
| Depreciation - sports | | | |
| equipment | 200 | | |
| Interest on loan | 125 | | |
| Excess of revenue over | | | |
| expenditure | 200 | | |
| | R2 125 | | R2 125 |
| | ===== | | ===== |

<u>YOU ARE REQUIRED TO</u>:

prepare a receipts and payments account for the year ended 31 May 19x4.

# A25

From the receipts and payments account presented by the treasurer of the Old Boys' Club, you are required to prepare an income and expenditure account and balance sheet.  After investigation you are able to construct the following opening statement.

<u>STATEMENT</u>

| 30 JUNE 19x2 | | | |
|---|---|---|---|
| Creditors for tea room supplies | R50 | Buildings | R4 000 |
| Bond on building | 2 000 | Furniture | 800 |
| Subscriptions paid in advance | 20 | Crockery, etc. | 100 |
| Balance - accumulated funds | 3 130 | Tea room stock | 80 |
| | | Subscriptions unpaid | 90 |
| | | Cash at bank | 130 |
| | R5 200 | | R5 200 |
| | ===== | | ===== |

You ascertain that at 30 June 19x2

(i)   Tea room stock was R120.
(ii)  Subscriptions unpaid amounted to R100 for the current year and R12 had been paid in advance.
(iii) Creditors for supplies were R60 and a final balance of R400 is due to a building contractor for club-house extensions completed in December.
(iv)  Interest is due on the bond for 6 months at 6% p.a.
(v)   Depreciation is calculated on the balance remaining at the end of the year at the following rates:
      buildings        2 1/2%
      furniture        10%

      Crockery etc. is valued at R105 on 30 June 19x2.
(vi)  Furniture sold during the year stood in the books at R200 on 30 June 19x1.

<u>RECEIPTS AND PAYMENTS ACCOUNT</u>

<u>For the year ended 30 June 19x2</u>

| Opening balance | R130 | Creditors (tea room) | R2 190 |
|---|---|---|---|
| Subscriptions | 1 480 | Furniture | 300 |
| Tea room sales | 2 600 | Crockery etc. | 40 |
| Building Society (final balance | | Wages | 600 |
| on bond 2.1.9x2) | 600 | Dance expenses | 70 |
| Furniture sold | 140 | Bond interest to 31.12.19x1 | 60 |
| Dance tickets sold | 120 | General expenses | 780 |
| Entrance fees | 20 | Payments to builder | 800 |
| Donation for new building | 100 | Closing balance | 350 |
| | R5 190 | | R5 190 |
| | ===== | | ===== |

## A26

The secretary/treasurer of the Rockport Club has requested that you assist him
in the preparation of the balance sheet at 30 September 19x8 and the necessary
supporting accounts for the year ended on that date.

The club consists of an indoor recreational centre where light refreshments,
club badges and ties are sold, a bowling section, a tennis section, and
licensed bar.

The following information is available:

1.      Balances in the balance sheet at 30 September 19x7:

        Accumulated funds                                              R8 280
        Land and improvements - at cost less amounts written off       18 230
        Sports equipment, furniture and fittings - at nominal value         1
        Five per cent debentures of R10 each                           12 800
        Bank                                                            2 453
        Bar till float                                                     60
        Municipal deposits                                                 64
        Stock - bar                                                       772
              - club badges and ties                                     293
        Creditors for bar purchases                                      793

2.      During the year 34 debentures were redeemed

3.      From the summary of the duplicate deposit slips it can be ascertained
        that R13 356 was banked.

        This amount comprises:

        Subscriptions - bowling section                                R2 049
        Subscriptions - tennis section                                  1 639
        Share of profit on sale of refreshments                           372
        Sale of club badges and ties                                       44
        Bar sales                                                       7 649
        Sundry revenue - bowling section                                  866
                       - tennis section                                   651
        Entrance fees                                                      86
                                                                       R13 356
                                                                       ======

# A26 CONTINUED

4.     From the cheque stubs you are to make the following summary:

| | |
|---|---:|
| Bar purchases | R3 820 |
| Bar expenses | 482 |
| Expenses - club | 1 254 |
|        - bowling section | 287 |
|        - tennis section | 120 |
| Honoraria - club | 170 |
|        - bowling section | 210 |
|        - tennis section | 100 |
| Maintenance - club | 808 |
|        - bowling greens | 571 |
|        - tennis courts | 57 |
| Wages | 2 766 |
| Tennis balls | 316 |
| Alterations to clubhouse | 1 304 |
| Sundry debenture holders | 304 |
| | R12 605 |

5.     It is the usual practise of the club to allocate wages, to the nearest rand, as follows:

| | |
|---|---:|
| Bowling section | 60% |
| Tennis section | 20% |
| Club | 10% |
| Bar | 10% |

6.     The bank statement has a credit balance of R3 325, but upon inspection you find that cheques amounting to R163 have not yet been presented for payment and R42 in respect of bank cheques had been debited to the account.

7.     You ascertain that the debenture interest is chargeable against the bar profits. The amount of R634, in respect of the interest for the year ended 30 September 19x8, has not yet been paid to the debenture holders.

8.     From an examination of the available records you are able to determine that R1 135 is owing in respect of bar purchases and R80 is owing in respect of wages.

9.     At 30 September 19x8 the bar stocks amounted to R537 and the stock of club badges and ties to R249.

10.    Certain alterations to the club house have recently been started. The contract price was R500. No payment has yet been made.

It is usual for the club to have columnar accounts for the bowls and tennis sections and a separate account for the bar.

<u>YOU ARE REQUIRED</u>:

to prepare the balance sheet as at 30 September 19x8 together with the detailed supporting accounts for the year ended on that date.

# A27

A fire occurred in the offices and a showroom of Beta Limited on 15 April 19x9, which destroyed all their stock, except for R8 000 worth of goods at cost which were salvaged in good condition.

The only accounting record which was saved was the general ledger which had been written up to March 31 19x9.

The following additional information was obtained:

(1)　General ledger balances -

The following relevant balances at 31 March 19x9 were extracted

|  | Dr | Cr |
|---|---|---|
| Debtors | R54 000 | |
| Sales | | R165 800 |
| Purchases | 84 000 | |

(2)　The bank statements and paid cheques for April obtained from the bank disclosed:

(i)　Payments

| | |
|---|---|
| Creditors for goods purchased in March | R11 400 |
| Creditors for goods purchased 1 - 15 April | 4 000 |
| Expenses | 7 800 |

(ii)　Deposits

| | |
|---|---|
| Payments by debtors | R20 400 |
| Refund by creditor in respect of goods returned between 1 - 15 April | 900 |

(3)　Creditors were circularised and it was established that purchases amounting to R17 000 made between 1 - 15 April had not been recorded, and that these included goods in transit at 15 April 19x9 amounting to R2 700.

(4)　Debtors acknowledged indebtedness of R55 200 at 15 April 19x9, and it was reliably estimated that a further R1 600 was owing but not acknowledged, and, which due to the loss records, would never be recovered. Of the amounts of R55 200 it was considered that R1 200 was bad and would be irrecoverable.

(5)　The insurance company agreed that the value of the stock destroyed in the fire should be calculated on the assumption that the gross profit achieved during the two previous financial years ended 31 December 19x8 was also achieved in the period to the date of the fire. The stock had been insured for R82 500 and was subject to "average".

# A27 CONTINUED

(6)  The financial statements of the company for the two previous years
     reflected the following relevant information:

| Years ended 31 December | 19x7 | 19x8 |
|---|---|---|
| Net sales | R550 000 | R650 000 |
| Net purchases | 355 500 | 394 500 |
| Stock at beginning of year | 70 000 | 90 000 |
| Stock at end of year | 90 000 | 100 000 |

<u>YOU ARE REQUIRED TO PREPARE</u>:

(a)  A schedule showing the gross  profit for the two years ended 31
     December 19x7 and 19x8.

(b)  A schedule showing the computation of the value of stock at 15 April
     19x9 and the amount of the claim payable by the insurance company and
     the treatment of any loss caused by under-insuring.

A fire occurred in the offices and a showroom of Beta Limited on 15 April
19x9, which destroyed all their stock, except for R8 000 worth of goods  at
cost  which were salvaged in good condition.

The only accounting record which was saved was the general ledger  which had
been written up to March 31 19x9.

The following additional information was obtained:

(1)  General ledger balances -

     The following relevant balances at 31 March 19x9 were extracted

|  | Dr | Cr |
|---|---|---|
| Debtors | R54 000 | |
| Sales | | R165 800 |
| Purchases | 84 000 | |

(2)  The bank statements and paid  cheques for April obtained from the bank
     disclosed:

     (i)   <u>Payments</u>

| | |
|---|---|
| Creditors for goods purchased in March | R11 400 |
| Creditors for goods purchased 1 - 15 April | 4 000 |
| Expenses | 7 800 |

     (ii)  <u>Deposits</u>

| | |
|---|---|
| Payments by debtors | R20 400 |
| Refund by creditor in respect of goods returned between 1 - 15 April | 900 |

# A27 CONTINUED

(3)  Creditors were circularised and it was established that  purchases amounting to R17 000 made between 1 - 15 April had not been recorded, and that these included goods in transit at 15 April 19x9 amounting to R2 700.

(4)  Debtors acknowledged indebtedness of R55 200 at 15 April 19x9, and it was reliably estimted that a further R1 600 was owing but not acknowledged, and, which due to the loss records, would never be recovered. Of the amounts of R55 200 it was considered that R1 200 was bad and would be irrecoverable.

(5)  The insurance company agreed that the value of the stock destroyed in the fire should be calculated on the assumption that the gross profit achieved during the two previous financial years ended 31 December 19x8 was also achieved in the period to the date of the fire. The stock had been insured for R82 500 and was subject to "average".

(6)  The financial statements of the company for the two previous years reflected the following relevant information:

| Years ended 31 December | 19x7 | 19x8 |
|---|---|---|
| Net sales | R550 000 | R650 000 |
| Net purchases | 355 500 | 394 500 |
| Stock at beginning of year | 70 000 | 90 000 |
| Stock at end of year | 90 000 | 100 000 |

YOU ARE REQUIRED TO PREPARE:

(a)  A schedule showing the gross profit for the two years ended 31 December 19x7 and 19x8.

(b)  A schedule showing the computation of the value of stock at 15 April 19x9 and the amount of the claim payable by the insurance company and the treatment of any loss caused by under-insuring.

# SECTION B

# PARTNERSHIP

# B1

X and Y were in partnership sharing profits/losses in the ratio 2 : 1.  On 1 January 19x8 they admitted Z to the partnership. Z was to pay R24 000 into the business bank account and become entitled to a one-third share in the partnership.  X and Y were to continue to share profits/losses between themselves in the same ratio as before.  X, Y and Z would each be entitled to a salary at the rate of R8 000 per annum. At 1 January 19x8 it was agreed that the assets and liabilities of the partnership of X and Y were fairly valued except goodwill which stood in the books at R4 000.  At the same date there was a reserve of R10 800.

The summarised balance sheet of X, Y and Z at 30 June 19x8 was as follows:

| | | | | |
|---|---:|---|---:|---|
| Capital X | R24 400 | Goodwill | | R4 000 |
| Y | 12 000 | Furniture at cost less | | |
| Z | 17 200 | depreciation | | 8 000 |
| Reserve | 18 000 | Current assets | | 69 600 |
| Creditors | 10 000 | | | |
| | R81 600 | | | R81 600 |

<u>Notes</u>:

1. The net profit for the six months ended 30 June 19x8 amounted to R28 800 after allowing for partners salaries but before making the transfer to the reserve.
2. An amount of R7 200 was transferred to the reserve.
3. Partners drawings were:

    X R10 800;  Y R7 600;  Z R9 600


<u>YOU ARE REQUIRED TO</u>:

Calculate the value placed on goodwill on 1 January 19x8 upon Z's admission to the partnership.

Aron, Leon and Martin have been in partnership for many years. The partnership agreement stated that:

(i)    Profits and losses would be shared in proportion to their fixed capital accounts.
(ii)   Profits would accumulated during the year and be apportioned annually on 28 February or on death or retirement of the partners.
(iii) Drawings would be treated as debtors and carry interest on the daily balance at bank overdraft rates.
      (The partners, in practice, limit their drawings to their share of the profits and only make one withdrawal once the profits have been established.)

An interim balance sheet was prepared at 31 May 19x3, the date Aron retired for health reasons.

BALANCE SHEET AT 31 MAY 19x3

| | | |
|---|---:|---:|
| Capital | | R18 000 |
|   Leon | 9 000 | |
|   Martin | 6 000 | |
|   Aron | <u>3 000</u> | |
| Accumulated profits | | 10 800 |
| Creditors | | <u>1 800</u> |
| | | R30 600 |
| | | ====== |
| | | |
| Goodwill at cost | | R5 000 |
| Fixed assets at cost less depreciation | | 14 000 |
|   Equipment | R10 000 | |
|   Vehicles | <u>4 000</u> | |
| Bank | | <u>11 600</u> |
| | | R30 600 |
| | | ====== |

**Additional information:**

1.     The three partners agree that Aron's share of the business is R4 500 (including his share of goodwill). Leon and Martin pay him from their private bank accounts in the ratio they share profits (such payment to be reflected in the books).

2.     On Aron's retirement Leon and Martin admit Stella who is to have a one-sixth share of profits with effect from 1 June 19x3 while Leon and Martin retain their original profit sharing ratios. For the purposes of the admission of Stella the following is agreed upon:

    (a)   Goodwill (which is no longer to appear in the books) is worth R5 000.
    (b)   Vehicles are revalued at R6 000 but equipment is worth only R6 200. (These assets are to be shown at their new values.)

# B2 CONTINUED

     (c)    Stella must pay R5 400 into the partnership for her share of profits (including goodwill).  This amount is to be retained in the partnership.

<u>YOU ARE REQUIRED TO</u>:

(i)    Draw up the partners' capital accounts, in columnar form, to reflect the transactions negotiated following
    (a)    Aron's retirement
    (b)    Stella's admission.

(ii)   Draft an explanation to Aron detailing why his payout on retirement was R4 500 whereas Stella was required to pay in R5 400.

WORK TO THE NEAREST RAND.

**B3**

Franks and Goldman are in partnership sharing profits and losses in the ratio of 3 : 2.

Franks is entitled to a salary of R15 000 per annum and they are both entitled to interest on capital at the rate of 5% per annum, no interest being charged on drawings.

At 31 December 19x4 their balance sheet was as follows:

| | | | | | |
|---|---|---|---|---|---|
| Capital - Franks | | R10 000 | Stock on hand | | R75 000 |
| Goldman | | 50 000 | Debtors | R50 000 | |
| Creditors | R60 000 | | Provision | | |
| Bills payable | 20 000 | 80 000 | for bad debts | 5 000 | 45 000 |
| | | | Bank | | 20 000 |
| | | R140 000 | | | R140 000 |
| | | ======= | | | ======= |

They did not keep proper books, but you are able to ascertain:

(a)    They purchased a piece of land on 28 February 19x5 for R50 000 which was mortgaged for R30 000, which amount was owing with interest accrued amounting to R250 on 30 June 19x5.

(b)    Stock was not taken on 30 June 19x5, but the firm consistently realises 33 1/3% gross profit on turnover.

(c)    Debtors at 30 June 19x5  totalled R40 000, but as bad debts totalling R5 000 had been written off during the half-year a provision of only R3 000 was necessary at 30 June 19x5.

(d)    Cash collected from debtors for the half-year amounted to R95 000 and all of them, without exception, had been allowed 5% cash discount.

(e)    Cash sales totalled R85 000.

(f)    Purchases of stock for the half-year totalled R100 000.

(g)    Creditors at 30 June 19x5 totalled R20 000 and bills payable R10 000.

(h)    At the same date they had an overdraft according to the bank's books of R5 000, but cheques totalling R1 000 had not been presented.

(i)    An unexpected liability of R5 000 had arisen and had been paid, but, as it applied to a date before Goldman became a partner, the whole amount had to be borne by Franks.

(j)    During the six months Franks had drawn R10 000 and Goldman R6 000.


Prepare the partners' capital accounts for the six months.

## B4

F Flynn and G Grim are in partnership sharing profits and losses in the ratio
2 : 1.  Their balance sheet is as follows:-

| Capital:  Flynn | R19 200 | Vehicles | R 5 200 |
| "        Grim | 9 000 | Shop equipment | 3 600 |
| General reserve | 2 700 | Stock | 15 410 |
| Sundry creditors | 5 500 | Debtors | 12 000 |
| | | Bank | 190 |
| | R36 400 | | R36 400 |
| | ====== | | ====== |

They decide to adjust their balance sheet.

a.     Shop equipment is to be written down to R2 700.

b.     Vehicles are to be revalued at R4 600.

c.     A bad debts provision of 6% is to be created.

d.     General reserve will be written off.

e.     They agree that goodwill is valued at R5 000 but should not be shown in
       the books.

f.     Profits will in future be shared by Flynn and Grim in the ratio 3 : 2
       and Grim is to pay in extra cash to make the capitals proportionate.

Journalise the above adjustments and prepare the adjusted balance sheet in
vertical format.

# B5

A, B and C are in partnership. The partnership agreement contains the following provisions:

a.  Profits or losses on the realisation of investments are shared equally by A and B.

b.  Trading profits or losses are shared A - 1/2, B - 3/10, and C - 1/5.

c.  The following rates of depreciation are to be written off the assets including any additions during the year:

        Property - 2 percent.        Furniture - 10 percent

d.  The following salaries must be credited to the partners and charged to the trading profits:

        A - R1 000.        B - R2 000.        C - R1 500.

e.  Interest is allowed at 5 percent per annum on capital but is not charged on drawings.

The following is their balance sheet at 30 September 19x1:

| | | | | |
|---|---|---|---|---|
| Capital - A | R12 000 | Property | | R12 500 |
| - B | 6 000 | Furniture | | 2 500 |
| - C | 5 000 | Investments | | 5 000 |
| Creditors | 6 000 | Stock | | 7 000 |
| | | | | |
| Bank | 4 000 | Debtors | | R6 500 |
| | | Provision for | | |
| | | bad debts | 500 | 6 000 |
| | R33 000 | | | R33 000 |
| | ====== | | | ====== |

They did not keep a complete set of books, but the following information is available:

(i)    The investments were sold during the year for R12 000.
(ii)   Stock was not taken at 30 September 19x2.
(iii)  The firm consistently realises 20 percent gross profit on turnover.
(iv)   R500 was spent during the year on furniture and cash paid for purchases of stock amounted to R25 000.
(v)    Debtors outstanding at 30 September 19x2 totalled R8 000, of which R500 was bad and R500 doubtful. Of the doubtful debts, it is expected that R300 will be collected.
(vi)   Cash sales for the year totalled R3 000.
(vii)  Cash collected from debtors amounted to R25 500.
(viii) Creditors outstanding at 30 September 19x2 totalled R8 000.
(ix)   At the same date there was R750 cash in the bank. Sundry expenses were all paid in cash.

**B5 CONTINUED**

(x)     During the year A had drawn R2 000, B had drawn R1 500 and C had drawn
        R1 000.
(xi)    An unexpected claim of R2 000 had been paid during the year.  As the
        cause of this arose before C was admitted to the partnership, it had to
        be borne 5/8 by A and 3/8 by 8.

49

<u>YOU ARE REQUIRED TO</u>:

Prepare the partners' capital accounts for the year ended 30 September 19x2.

**B6**

Rod and Reel were in partnership sharing profits and losses in the ratio 2 : 1. On 1 January 19x1 they admitted Trout to the partnership. Trout was to contribute the following assets to the new partnership: debtors R10 000, stock R11 250 and cash R10 000 for a one third share in the partnership. Trout's assets are considered to be fairly valued except for debtors where it is considered that a provision for doubtful debts of 5% should be provided. Rod and Reel would relinquish the one third share of the business acquired by Trout equally.

Rod, Reel and Trout would each be entitled to a salary at the rate of R10 000 per annum. At 1 January 19x1 it was agreed that the assets and liabilities of the partnership were fairly valued except for

(a)  goodwill which stood in the books at R6 000
(b)  the surrender value of life insurance policies for R10 000 on the lives of Rod and Reel. Premiums paid on these policies have been charged to the income statement in full each year. On 1 January 19x1 the surrender value of these policies amounted to R3 000. A similar policy on the life of Trout was taken out on 1 January 19x1 and it was agreed to continue writing off premiums on all the policies in the income statement in full each year.

At the same date there was a reserve of R12 000.

The summarised balance sheet of Rod, Reel and Trout at 30 June 19x1 was as follows:

| | | | | |
|---|---|---|---|---|
| Capital Rod | R25 500 | Goodwill | | R6 000 |
| Reel | 13 600 | Equipment, at cost less | | |
| Trout | 21 450 | depreciation | | 16 000 |
| Reserve | 16 900 | Stock | | 21 000 |
| Creditors | 8 850 | Debtors | R26 400 | |
| | | Provision for | | |
| | | doubtful debts | 500 | 25 900 |
| | | Bank | | 17 400 |
| | R86 300 | | | R86 300 |

NOTES:

1.  The net income for the six months ended 30 June 19x1 amounted to R32 300 after allowing for partners' salaries but before making the transfer to the reserve and before allowing for the life insurance premiums on the partners' lives.
2.  An amount of R4 900 was transferred to the reserve.
3.  The life insurance premiums on the partners' lives for the period 1 January 19x1 to 31 December 19x1 amount to R6 200 and are payable semi-annually on 31 March and 30 September.
4.  Partners drawings were: Rod R12 400; Reel R9 200; Trout R8 900.

<u>YOU ARE REQUIRED TO</u>:


(1)    prepare the capital accounts of the partners in columnar form for the
       period 1 January to 30 June 19x1.
(2)    determine the value placed on goodwill on 1 January 19x1 upon Trout's
       admission to the partnership.
(3)    show how  Rod and Reel  determined the cost to Trout of the one third
       share of the partnership acquired on 1 January 19x1.

**B7**

The following is the balance sheet of two skiers Anton and Johann, who were
in partnership and who shared profits and losses in the ratio 2:3.

<u>ANTON AND JOHANN</u>

trading as

<u>SKIERS SUPREME</u>

<u>BALANCE SHEET AT 30 SEPTEMBER 19x7</u>

| Capital | | | Land and buildings | R80 000 |
|---|---|---|---|---|
| Anton | | R66 020 | Furniture | 8 000 |
| Johann | | 110 020 | Equipment | 10 000 |
| | | 176 040 | Motor vehicles | 60 000 |
| | | | | 158 000 |
| Current account | | | Listed investments | 20 000 |
| Anton | | 12 000 | Bank | 4 040 |
| Current account | | | Johann | 60 000 |
| | | R188 040 | | R188 040 |
| | | ======= | | ======= |

The accounts of Skiers Supreme have been maintained on a cash basis.  No year-
end adjustments have been made in the preparation of the financial statements.

The following additional information is available:

(i)    Net income for the year ended 30 September 19x7, using the cash basis
       of accounting, amounted to R100 000.   This amount included gross
       rentals from land and buildings of R9 600 and income from investments
       of R2 200.    The only property expenses incurred and paid during the
       year were rates of R2 100 and repairs of R960.

(ii)   The partners, Anton and Johann, had occupied their ski shop (i.e. part
       of the partnership's land and buildings) rent free and it was agreed
       that a fair rental was R12 000 p.a.

(iii)                                          30 September      30 September
                                                   19x7              19x6

       Creditors not recorded                    R13 600*           R8 600

       *All creditors relate to ski stores except for an amount of R1 600
       outstanding in respect of equipment purchased during September 19x7.

(iv)   All fixed assets other than land and buildings were acquired during the
       year ended 30 September 19x7.

# B7 CONTINUED

(v)

|  | 30 September 19x7 | 30 September 19x6 |
|---|---|---|
| Debtors not recorded | R22 800 | R17 800 |
| Ski stores on hand | R8 000 | R5 600 |

(vi)  Depreciation, which had been ignored in the preparation of the above balance sheet, is to be provided for on closing balances of the fixed assets at 30 September 19x7 as follows:

|  |  |
|---|---|
| Furniture | 10% |
| Equipment | 25% |
| Motor vehicles | 20% |

In addition a provision for doubtful debts of R1 560 has to be created at 30 September 19x7.

On 1 October 19x7 Anton and Johann decided to admit Wolfgang to the partnership.   It was agreed that the above balance sheet should be adjusted to reflect balance sheet values arrived at by using the accrual basis of accounting.

It was further agreed that:

(a)  Anton would take over listed investments at R28 000. Johann would take over land and buildings at R90 000.  All other assets (including CASH) and liabilities were to be taken over by the new partnership.
(b)  Goodwill, which was to appear in the books of the new partnership, was to be equal to one-half of the previous year's net income from professional work only, determined on an accrual basis.
(c)  Wolfgang's capital account was to be equal to one-third of the combined capital of Anton and Johann after making all the adjustments.  He was to be allowed to contribute as part of his capital his car valued at R10 000 and furniture valued at R6 000.   The balance due by him was to be paid in cash.  Wolfgang had never skied before and was regarded as contributing no goodwill to the partnership.


<u>YOU ARE REQUIRED</u>:

(a)  To calculate the net income according to the accrual basis of accounting.

(b)  To calculate the goodwill.

(c)  Show the journal entries for the opening of the new partnership books.

**B8**

Douglas and Eaton are in partnership as furniture manufacturers.  At 30 June 19x4 their balance sheet is as follows:

| Capital-Douglas | .. | R150 000 | Plant and machinery at cost | | |
|---|---|---|---|---|---|
|       Eaton | .. | 100 000 |   less depreciation .. | .. | R 80 000 |
| General reserve | .. | 50 000 | Stock on hand | | |
| Creditors | .. | 20 000 | Raw materials | .. | R100 000 |
| | | | Manufactured | | |
| | | |    goods | .. .. | 50 000 |
| | | | | | 150 000 |
| | | | Debtors | .. | 40 000 |
| | | | Bills receivable | .. | 30 000 |
| | | | Bank | .. .. | 20 000 |
| | | R320 000 | | | R320 000 |

The partnership deed provides:

(a)   Douglas receives a salary of R15 000 per annum and Eaton R10 000.

(b)   Interest is allowed on capital at 6% per annum, but no interest is charged on drawings.

(c)   Profits thereafter are divided equally.

(d)   At the end of each financial year, 10% of the profits, after allowing for salaries and interest, is to be credited to a reserve account until this account amounts to R50 000.  (This state of affairs had been attained in 19x1).

(e)   Their capital accounts are to remain at R150 000 and R100 000 respectively and, at the end of each year, cash must be drawn or brought in to achieve this purpose.

(f)   A joint non-profit life policy is to be taken out for R200 000 and the premiums charged against profits.  (This has been done.)

(g)   In the event of the death of one of the partners, he is to be paid out:

      (i)   his interest in the business;

      (ii)   his share of the profits (including salary and interest) to date of death, based on the average of the last two years' profits;

      (iii) his share of goodwill based on two years' purchase of the average income he has received from the business during the three previous years.

Douglas died on 31 August 19x4.  The profits, before allowing the partners' salaries and interest on capital, were as follows:

```
Year ended 30 June 19x2   R61 000
  "    "      "   "   19x3    76 000
  "    "      "   "   19x4    91 000
```

Show, in the form of journal entries, the adjustments affecting Douglas's account that would have to be made as a result of his death,  He had drawn R2 000 per month in July and August 19x4.

**B9**

O Oliver and T Twist are partners with capitals respectively of R20 000 and R15 000.  Profits and losses were shared pro rata to capital.

They decided to take out the following life policies:

(a)    Each insured the life of the other.  The premiums were charged to drawings.  The policy in each case was for the amount of the other's capital.

(b)    Each partner's life was also insured for the amount of his capital, and the premiums were charged to profit and loss account.

(c)    A joint policy was taken out for R21 000 and the premiums were charged to profit and loss account.

Premiums payable were:  Oliver 2 1/2%;  Twist 3%; and for the joint policy 4%.

Oliver died on 15 May.  What journal entries will arise out of the above policies following Oliver's death.

# B10

<u>PART A</u>

Julius and Fulvio had been trading as equal partners for many years.  On
1 September 19x1 Julius relinquished half of his share in favour of Gaius who
paid him a personal cheque of R17 150.  All assets other than goodwill were
fairly valued.

The new partnership traded for 6 months but the shortage of money in the
economy and the surcharge on foreign imports resulted in their franchise
operation no longer being viable.  They decided to liquidate the partnership
and place the money on call individually until such time as a new venture
presented itself.

The balance sheet at the date of liquidation (28 February 19x2) showed:

| CAPITAL EMPLOYED | | |
|---|---|---|
| Capital - Julius | R9 725 | |
|       - Fulvio | 32 750 | |
|       - Gaius | <u>23 025</u> | R65 500 |
| Reserve | | <u>22 500</u> |
| | | R88 000 |

| EMPLOYMENT OF CAPITAL | | |
|---|---|---|
| Fixed assets | | |
|   Goodwill at cost | R5 000 | |
|   Furniture at cost less depreciation | <u>10 000</u> | |
| | | 15 000 |
| Net current assets | | 73 000 |
|   Current assets | | |
|     Stock | R30 000 | |
|     Debtors | 40 000 | |
|     Cash | <u>17 000</u> | |
| | R87 000 | |
|   Current liabilities | | |
|     Creditors | R14 000 | |
| | | R88 000 |

During the six months ended 28 February 19x2:

(i)    Each partner was entitled to a salary of R1 000 per month.
(ii)   The net income for the six months available for distribution after
       allowing for salaries was R16 000.
(iii) An amount of R7 500 was transferred from the reserve on 1 February
       19x2.
(iv)  The partners had withdrawn their salaries monthly.  These were the
       only drawings.


<u>YOU ARE REQUIRED TO:</u>

Determine the value placed on goodwill on the admission of Gaius.  (It is
suggested that your workings show the partners' capital accounts in columnar
form, but in any case they must be clearly shown).

# B10 CONTINUED

<u>PART B</u>

The assets of the partnership of Julius, Fulvio and Gaius were realised as follows:

| <u>Date realised</u> | <u>Assets</u> | <u>Book value</u> | <u>Net proceeds</u> |
|---|---|---|---|
| By 31.3.x2 | Stock | R15 000 | R26 000 |
| | Debtors | 30 000 | 29 025 |
| By 31.5.x2 | Stock | 15 000 | 20 000 |
| | Debtors | 10 000 | 5 000 |
| | Furniture | 10 000 | 8 000 |

The partnership had signed a twelve month lease on 1 September 19x1 and were committed to pay R1 000 per month.  On advising the lessor of their intention to dissolve the partnership, the lessor agreed to accept three months notice from 28 February 19x2 provided new tenants could be found.  The partnership was advised on 15 May 19x2 that the premises had been let.

All creditors were paid within 30 days of statement and a uniform 2 1/2% discount was deducted.

Due to an oversight certain invoices had not been accrued at the year end, 28 February 19x2, but were settled in March for R4 875 (net of 2 1/2%).

<u>YOU ARE REQUIRED TO</u>:

Determine the maximum "safe payment" to be made to the partners on 31 March 19x2.

It is suggested that your workings show the capital accounts in columnar form, but in any case they must be clearly shown.

Joe, Amy and Beth were in partnership sharing profits and losses in the ratio:
5 : 3 : 2 respectively except for the profits or losses on investments which
are shared equally between only Joe and Amy.

Their balance sheet at 31 December 19x7 was as follows:

CAPITAL EMPLOYED

| | |
|---|---:|
| Capital - Joe | R130 000 |
|         - Amy | 80 000 |
|         - Beth | 14 000 |
| General reserve | 20 000 |
| Loan - Beth | 12 000 |
| Long-term loans | 80 000 |
| | R336 000 |

EMPLOYMENT OF CAPITAL

Fixed assets
  Land and buildings and
    plant and machinery     R156 000
Investments - listed shares     80 000
Net current assets     100 000
Current assets
  Stock     R60 000
  Debtors     45 000
  Cash     15 000
    120 000

Current liabilities
  Creditors     R20 000

    R336 000

Contingent liability
  Discounted bill not yet matured     R3 000

<u>Additional information</u>:

(1)    The partners have agreed to dissolve the partnership due to the ill
health of Beth. It was agreed  to distribute the cash received from the
sale of assets immediately in such a way that, while maximum
distribution was to be made to the partners, under no circumstances
would a partner be required to refund to the partnership any amount he
had received.

(2)    The general reserve arose in 19x5 before the partnership speculated in
investments.  The partnership agreement provides that on the insolvency
of any partner, the remaining partners will share in the profit sharing
ratio.

(3)   The partner's loan account is to be transferred to her capital account.

(4)   The partnership had taken out an insurance policy on the life of the partners.  The surrender value of R15 000 was paid to the partnership on 12 January 19x8.

(5)   The discounted bill was honoured on 15 January 19x8.

(6)   The assets were sold for cash as follows:

|  |  | Book value | Proceeds |
|---|---|---|---|
| 3 January | Investments | R80 000 | R94 000 |
| 12 January | Fixed assets | 156 000 | 130 000 |
| 30 January | Debtors and stocks | 105 000 | 110 000 |

(7)   Liquidation expenses in respect of sale of stocks of R2 000 were incurred on 30 January and paid by the firm.

YOU ARE REQUIRED TO PREPARE:

(a)   the cash account.

(b)   cash distribution statements up to 30 January 19x8.

# B12

The following is the balance sheet of A, B, and C who share profits
respectively in the ratio 5: 3: 2.

| | | | |
|---|---|---|---|
| Capital A | R6 000 | Assets | R15 800 |
| B | 4 800 | | |
| C | 2 100 | | |
| Loan - C | 2 000 | | |
| Creditors | 900 | | |
| | R15 800 | | R15 800 |
| | ====== | | ====== |

It is decided to terminate the partnership.

Assets standing in the books at R8 000 are sold for R9 000, realisation
expenses amounting to R1 500.

It is decided to retain R500 for contingencies and distribute the balance of
R7 000.

It is doubtful whether the remaining assets can be realised for some
considerable time.

How should the R7 000 be distributed?   Show your workings.

# B13

Jones, Brown and Smith are partners sharing profits and losses in the ratio
of 6 : 5 : 3 respectively.  They decide to dissolve the partnership and their
balance sheet is as follows:

CAPITAL

| | | | |
|---|---|---|---|
| Jones | | | R27 000 |
| Brown | | | 25 500 |
| Smith | | | 14 500 |
| | | | R67 000 |

FIXED ASSETS                                                     22 250

| | | | |
|---|---|---|---|
| Property at cost | | R17 500 | |
| Furniture at cost | R2 200 | | |
| Less depreciation | 200 | 2 000 | |
| Vehicles at cost | 4 750 | | |
| Less depreciation | 2 000 | 2 750 | |

NET CURRENT ASSETS                                              44 750

CURRENT ASSETS

| | |
|---|---|
| Stock | 34 000 |
| Debtors | 29 750 |
| | R63 750 |

CURRENT LIABILITIES

| | |
|---|---|
| Creditors | 11 500 |
| Bank overdraft | 7 500 |
| | R19 000 |

                                                                R67 000

The property is sold for R38 000 and the furniture is sold for R1 000.
Brown takes over one vehicle at R1 500 and the other is sold for R2 000.
Smith takes over certain stock at R12 000 and all the debtors at R23 000.
The remaining stock realises R25 400.  All the creditors are paid, discount
of R850 being allowed.  It is further agreed that Smith is to be allowed R250
for his services in connection with the realisation and that the partners
shall bring in cash, if necessary, to square their accounts.

You are required to draw up the realisation account and to show the partners'
capital accounts and the cash account.

# B14

Adams, Benade and Cohen were in partnership.  The partnership deed provided:

(a)   Profits and losses on share transactions were to be divided equally between Adams and Benade.

(b)   All other profits and losses were to be shared:

   Adams   one-half   Benade   two-fifths   Cohen one-tenth

(c)   Any deficiency arising from the insolvency of a partner was to be borne by the other partners equally.

Their balance sheet at 30 June 19x4 was:

| | | | |
|---|---|---|---|
| Capital - Adams | R12 000 | Goodwill at cost | R 2 500 |
| Benade | 8 000 | Land and buildings at cost | 5 500 |
| Cohen | 1 000 | Furniture at cost less | |
| Sundry creditors | 3 000 |   depreciation | 1 000 |
| | | Stock | 8 000 |
| | | Debtors | 5 000 |
| | | Gold mining shares at cost | 500 |
| | | Bank | 1 500 |
| | R24 000 | | R24 000 |

The partners quarrelled in August 19x5 and it was decided to dissolve the partnership.  Proper books had not been kept but you are able to ascertain that between 1 July 19x4 and 31 August 19x5:

(a)   Adams had drawn R1 800.  Benade had drawn R1 500.  Cohen had drawn R1 000.

(b)   Shares in certain diamond mining companies had been bought for R1 200 and were sold afterwards for R1 400.

(c)   The gold mining shares included in the 19x4 balance sheet had been sold for R1 000.

On 31 August 19x5 the furniture and stock were put up for auction and realised altogether R5 500 net.  This sum was banked on the same day.  All book debts at the date they stopped trading were sold outright for R6 000 and the cheque in settlement was received and banked on 24 August 19x5.  The cash in the bank at 31 August 19x5 amounted to R13 500 and, at the same date, there were creditors outstanding of R2 000.

As the property market was depressed it was decided not to sell the land and buildings, but to let them from 1 September 19x5 at a rent of R50 per month net.

## B14 CONTINUED

YOU ARE REQUIRED TO:

(a)    Prepare a balance sheet at 31 August 19x5.

(b)    State how the amount in the bank at 31 August 19x5 should be distributed.

(c)    State how the amount received for rent (assuming there were no expenses) should be distributed at the end of the first six months.

## B15

The following balances were extracted from the books of the Retail Company at
31 May 19x9:

| | | |
|---|---|---:|
| Administration expenses | | R21 600 |
| Capital accounts at 31 May 19x8: | Able | 20 000 |
| | Baker | 16 000 |
| | Cain | 12 000 |
| Cash at bank | | 8 000 |
| Creditors | | 5 000 |
| Debtors | | 15 800 |
| Delivery vehicles at cost less depreciation at 31 May 19x9 | | 14 400 |
| Drawings:  Able | | 16 100 |
| Baker | | 13 000 |
| Cain | | 3 500 |
| Estate late Able | | 20 400 |
| Furniture and fittings at cost less depreciation at 31 May 19x9 | | 3 800 |
| Goodwill at 31 May 19x8 | | 12 000 |
| Gross profit for the year ended 31 May 19x9 | | 78 000 |
| Life insurance policy - proceeds | | 24 000 |
| Selling expenses | | 8 400 |
| Stock at 31 May 19x9 | | 18 000 |

<u>NOTES:</u>

1.  The partnership agreement of Able, Baker and Cain, who have been in
    partnership for many years trading as the Retail Company, stated that:

    (i)   Each partner would receive a salary at the rate of R12 000 per
          annum.
    (ii)  Thereafter profits and losses would be shared in the ratio 3:3:2.
    (iii) An insurance policy would be taken out on the lives of the
          partners and all premiums would be written off against profits.
    (iv)  In the event of the death of one of the partners his share of the
          profits would be based on the profits for the previous year and
          an independent assessor would value the assets of the
          partnership.

2.  On 31 August 19x8 Able died.  The valuation of the assets revealed that
    all, except goodwill, were fairly valued in the books.

3.  The proceeds of the insurance policy maturing on Able's death were
    credited to a life insurance policy account.

4.  The final amount due by the partnership to Able's estate was calculated
    and paid.  The only entry recorded in the books was the payment which
    was debited to "Estate late Able".

5.  The partnership agreement of Baker and Cain who continued trading as
    the Retail Company stated that:

    (i)   Each partner would receive a salary at the rate of R12 000 per
          annum.
    (ii)  Thereafter profits would be shared equally.

## B15 CONTINUED

6.  Baker and Cain wish goodwill to appear in the books of their
    partnership at its valuation on 31 August 19x8.

7.  Profits (before allowing for partners' salaries) for the year ended 31
    May 19x8 were R52 000 and had accrued evenly throughout the year.

8.  The amounts drawn for salaries by the partners have been debited to
    their drawings accounts.

9.  You may assume that gross profit is earned and expenses are incurred
    evenly throughout the year.

<u>YOU ARE REQUIRED TO:</u>

1.  Draw up a detailed statement showing the amount paid to the estate of
    Able.
2.  Draw up the balance sheet of Baker and Cain at 31 May 19x9 (the
    detailed capital accounts should be shown in columnar form).

Dicky, Evans and Fox are in partnership sharing trading profits and losses equally.   Profits and losses on the realisation of investments are shared as follows:

        Dicky - one-half and
        Evans and Fox each one-quarter.

Their balance sheet is:

```
Capital
  Dicky                                        R12 000
  Evans                                          4 000
  Fox                                            9 000
                                               R25 000
                                               ======


Investments - listed at cost                            R10 000
Net current assets                                       15 000
Current assets
  Stock                                        16 000
  Cash                                          2 000
                                               R18 000
                                               ======


Current liabilities
  Creditors                                    R3 000
                                               =====
                                                        R25 000
                                                        ======
```

They agree to dissolve partnership and the total stock is put up for auction and realises R7 300 net.

They wish to pay out all cash on hand, but they do not want to receive any cash which they may subsequently have to refund.


How should the cash on hand be distributed?

In the event of any partner having a deficit on his capital account, the deficit should be borne equally by the other parties.

# B17

You have been requested to assist in winding up the affairs of the partnership of Able, Baker and Charlie.  The information available is as follows:

1.      The partners share profits and losses
        Able 1/2; Baker 3/10; Charlie 1/5

2.      The trial balance at 30 September 19x8 is as follows:

| | | |
|---|---:|---:|
| Capital - Able | | R46 900 |
|     "      - Baker | | 31 500 |
|     "      - Charlie | | 22 050 |
| Creditors | | 11 900 |
| Debtors | R15 400 | |
| Cash | 4 200 | |
| Plant | 69 300 | |
| Stock | 9 800 | |
| Loan Able | 8 400 | |
| Loan Charlie | 5 000 | |
| | R112 350 | R112 350 |

3.      As from the date of the trial balance all trading ceased.

4.      The assets were sold as follows:

| | |
|---|---:|
| 15 October   : Plant | R51 000 |
| 20 November : Stock | 7 000 |
| 17 December : Debtors | 12 000 |
| | R70 000 |

<u>YOU ARE REQUIRED TO</u>:

prepare a cash distribution statement to 17 December 19x8, showing the cash as distributed.  (All cash is to be distributed  as soon as it becomes available in such a way that no partner will be required to pay in cash at a later date).

# B18

Exe, Wye and Zed share profits and losses 5:3:2. They dissolve partnership when their balance sheet is as follows:

BALANCE SHEET

| Capital: | | Property | R33 000 |
|---|---|---|---|
| Exe | R22 800 | Vehicles | 3 100 |
| Wye | 14 200 | Furniture | 800 |
| Zed | 9 800 | Stock | 13 600 |
| Mortgage bond | 15 000 | Debtors | 15 900 |
| Creditors | 4 600 | | |
| | R66 400 | | R66 400 |

Exe takes over certain stock at R4 800 and all the debtors at R9 200, Exe also buys the goodwill for R3 600.

The property is sold to Zed for a total of R35 200.    Zed takes over the mortgage bond.

Wye takes over one vehicle for R1 000.    The others are sold for R1 440.

The furniture is sold for R560.    The remaining stock fetches R8 160.

The creditors are paid, discount of R340 being received.

It is agreed that Exe be allowed R500 for his services in connection with the realisation.    Other realisation expenses are R800.

Draw up the realisation account, bank account and capital accounts.

**B19**

Lindsay, Miles and Nelson were in partnership sharing profits and losses in the proportion 7 : 4 : 3.

Their balance sheet was as follows:

| | |
|---|---|
| Capital | |
|   Lindsay | R8 595 |
|   Miles | 5 730 |
|   Nelson | 1 000 |
| | R15 325 |
| | ====== |
| | |
| Current assets | |
|   Sundry assets | 16 875 |
|   Bank | 2 252 |
| | 19 400 |
| | |
| Current liabilities | |
|   Creditors | 4 075 |
| | R15 325 |
| | ====== |

The sundry assets were sold for R10 000.
The realisation took place because Nelson had been declared insolvent.
His estate paid no dividend.

The expenses of realisation amounted to R125.

(a)    Give the journal entries closing the partnership books assuming that the partnership agreement provided that in the event of a partner being unable to contribute towards the deficiency on his capital account, that deficiency was to be borne by the other partners in the ratio 13 : 12, the larger share to be borne by that partner with the greater capital at the date of the entry is made.

(b)    If the partnership agreement is silent as to how a partner's deficiency is to be dealt with, give the journal entries dealing with the transfer of the deficiency

        (i)    assuming that the rule of Garner v. Murray applies, and
        (ii)   assuming it does not apply.

# B20

Alphonse, Baptista and Camero were in partnership sharing profits and losses in the ratio 6:3:1.

Their balance sheet at 31 December 19x6 was as follows:

Capital employed

| Capital | - | Alphonse | R9 000 |
| | - | Baptista | 1 000 |
| | - | Camero | 9 000 |
| | | | R19 000 |
| | | | ====== |

Employment of capital

| Sundry assets | R20 000 |
| Cash | 1 000 |
| | 21 000 |
| Creditors | 2 000 |
| | R19 000 |
| | ====== |

Contingent liability

A bill due 1 July 19x7, discounted at the bank, R2 000.

It was agreed to dissolve the partnership and distribute the cash received from the sale of the assets immediately it was received.  This was to be done in such a way that, while maximum distribution was to be made to the partners, under no circumstances would a partner be required to refund to the partnership any amount he had received.

It was also agreed that if the situation arose the rule of GARNER vs MURRAY was to be used.

Creditors were paid on 31 January 19x7.

Assets were sold for cash as follows:-

| 31 January | 19x7 | assets of book value | R 6 000 | for | R 8 000 |
| 28 February | 19x7 | "    "    "    " | 10 000 | " | 2 000 |
| 31 March | 19x7 | "    "    "    " | 4 000 | " | 8 000 |
| | | | R20 000 | | R18 000 |
| | | | ====== | | ====== |

All expenses of selling the assets had been deducted in determining the net proceeds from sales above.  No further expenses would be incurred in dissolving the partnership.

Distributions were made on 31 January, 28 February and 31 March 19x7.


<u>YOU ARE REQUIRED TO</u>:
to show the capital accounts of the partners, the realisation account and bank account for the period 1 January to 31 March 19x7 with balances brought down at 31 March 19x7.

Arthur, Brian and Charles share profits and losses in the ratio 3 : 2: 1.

On 1 January 19x9 they decided to dissolve their partnership and realise the assets.

Their balance sheet at that date was as follows:

<u>ABC ENTERPRISES</u>

<u>Balance sheet at 1 January 19x9</u>

| Capital : A | R90 000 | Land and buildings | | R66 755 |
|---|---|---|---|---|
| B | 11 040 | Motor vehicle | | |
| C | 45 000 |   - Cost | R20 000 | |
| Creditors | 78 750 |   - Accumulated | | |
| | |     depreciation | (<u>5 000</u>) | 15 000 |
| | | Debtors | | 75 000 |
| | | Work-in-progress | | 45 750 |
| | | Bank | | <u>22 285</u> |
| | <u>R224 790</u> | | | <u>R224 790</u> |
| | ======= | | | ======= |

The partnership decided to distribute cash received from the realisation of the assets on the last day of each month, but do it in such a way that under no circumstances would a partner be called upon to refund any cash he had received. In the event of any partner having a deficit on his capital account, the deficit should be borne by the other partners in their profit sharing ratio.

The following transactions occurred during January 19x9:

(a)    Brian took over the work-in-progress at a discounted price of 33 1/3% less than its book value.

(b)    Half the debtors settled their accounts after claiming a cash discount for early payment of 5%.

(c)    An amount of R18 000, being the surrender value on a partnership life policy, was received.

(d)    Land and buildings were sold for book value. A payment of R30 000 was received immediately, the balance was paid on completion of the transfer of the property.

# B21 CONTINUED

The following transactions occurred during February 19x9:

(a)    The remaining debtors paid in full.

(b)    Transfer of the property was completed.

(c)    The motor vehicle was sold for R875 less than book value.

(d)    Brian contributed sufficient cash to make up the deficit on his capital
       account.

<u>YOU ARE REQUIRED TO PREPARE</u>:

(a)    the cash account

(b)    schedules of safe payments for January and February 19x9.

Workings to the nearest R.

**B22**

Berks, Robbie, Mills and Gibbons are partners in 702 Promotions and share
profits 5:3:1:1.  Berks decided to retire on 31 December 19x0. At that date
their balance sheet was:-

<u>CAPITAL EMPLOYED</u>

CAPITAL
    Berks                                 R60 000
    Robbie                               40 000
    Mills                                30 000
    Gibbons                         <u>10 000</u>        R140 000
GENERAL RESERVE                                    <u>20 000</u>
                                                R160 000
                                              =======

<u>EMPLOYMENT OF CAPITAL</u>
FIXED ASSETS (at cost less accumulated depreciation)         R120 000
NET CURRENT ASSETS                                 <u>40 000</u>
  CURRENT ASSETS
    Stock                                   R30 000
    Debtors                     R15 000
    Provision for bad debts       <u>3 000</u>    12 000
    Bank                                 <u>18 000</u>
                                               R60 000
                                              ======

  CURRENT LIABILITIES                       <u>20 000</u>
    Creditors                            R20 000
                                            ======

                                              R160 000
                                              =======

The following additional information requires consideration

1.    The life of each partner is separately insured for R50 000.  The
    insurance premiums paid to date have been charged against profits.  The
    insurance company has agreed to pay the partnership R20 000 which is
    the surrender value of the policy on Berks' life.  The surrender value
    of the remaining insurance policies is estimated to be 10% of their
    value.

2.    The partners agreed that the assets of the partnership, except for
    goodwill, are fairly valued.  The partners calculated that Berks should
    be paid out R101 000 for his share of the partnership's assets.

3.    Berks agreed to take over a vehicle at its book value of R10 000 in
    partial payment of the amount owing to him, the balance outstanding is
    to be paid to him in two equal annual payments.

4.      Robbie, Mills and Gibbons agree to share profits equally and do not
        wish goodwill, the general reserve or the value of the insurance
        policies to be reflected in the books.

On 8 January 19x1 the partners decided to dissolve the partnership as clients
had indicated that they had lost confidence in the partnership.

During January 19x1 the following transactions took place:

a.      The insurance company paid the amount owing to the partnership in
        respect of the policy on Berks' life.  The insurance company agreed to
        pay the surrender value of R15 000 on the remaining life policies in
        February.

b.      Fixed assets, book value, were R39 000 sold for R33 000.

c.      All the stock was sold at an auction sale for R27 000.  Auctioneers'
        fees of R600 were paid.

d.      R12 000 was collected from debtors.  Discounts of R600 were allowed.
        The partners consider that the remaining debtors balances are
        irrecoverable.

During February 19x1 the following transactions took place:

(i)     The insurance company paid the surrender values on the remaining
        insurance policies.

(ii)    Fixed assets, book value R35 000, were sold for R50 000.


<u>ADDITIONAL INFORMATION</u>

1.      The partnership agreement provides that any shortfall on the insolvency
        of a partner will be borne equally by the remaining partners.

2.      The partners wish to retain R3 000 in the bank to meet any unexpected
        liquidation expenses.


The partners wish to receive the maximum cash possible but wish to ensure that
they will not be required to refund any distribution to the partnership.

<u>YOU ARE REQUIRED TO</u>:

a.   Calculate the value placed on goodwill at 31 December 19x0.

b.   Prepare the journal entries necessary to record Berks' retirement from the partnership.

c.   Prepare the realisation account and bank account in the books of the partnership for January and February 19x1.

d.   Prepare the cash distribution statements of the partnership at 31 January and 28 February 19x1.

# SECTION C

# CONVERSION OF PARTNERSHIP TO COMPANY

# C1

A Brown decides to form a company, A Brown and Company Limited, to take over his business.  The total price is to be R125 000 payable  R25 000 in  cash, R50 000 in 8% mortgage debentures, and R50 000 in shares of R1 each at par.

The tangible assets taken over by the company are:

|  | Brown's book value | Purchase price |
|---|---|---|
| Plant and machinery | R15 000 | R18 000 |
| Stock | 32 000 | 34 000 |
| Bills receivable | 5 000 | 5 000 |
| Debtors | 18 000 | 17 000 |
| Land and buildings | 25 000 | 49 000 |

Brown had no provision for bad debts in his books.  The company undertakes to pay the following liabilities:

| | |
|---|---|
| Creditors | R4 000 |
| Bills payable | 15 000 |

Record, by means of journal entries, the above transaction in the books of A Brown and in the books of the company.

# C2

A, B and C are partners sharing profits and losses in the ratio 3:2:1 respectively.   Their balance sheet at 31 December 19x4 is as follows:

CAPITAL EMPLOYED

| | |
|---|---:|
| Capital - A | R3 000 |
|        - B | 2 500 |
|        - C | 2 000 |
| | R7 500 |

EMPLOYMENT OF CAPITAL

Fixed assets
  Equipment at cost less depreciation — R3 600

Net current assets — 3 900

| Current assets | | |
|---|---:|---:|
|   Stock | R3 250 | |
|   Debtors | 6 100 | |
| | R9 350 | |
| | | |
| Current liabilities | | |
|   Creditors | R4 000 | |
|   Bills payable | 650 | |
|   Bank overdraft | 800 | |
| | R5 450 | |
| | | R7 500 |

On 30 November 19x4 the Investment Company Limited is formed with an authorised share capital of R15 000 in R1 shares.   The whole of the share capital is taken up.

The company takes over the business of the partnership as a going concern for the sum of R10 000, payable in cash on 1 January 19x5.   Of this, R5 000 was paid for the equipment, the stock and debtors being taken over at book value.

<u>YOU ARE REQUIRED TO</u>:

(a)    to prepare the balance sheet of the company at 1 January 19x5;  and
(b)    to prepare the partners' capital accounts showing the distribution to each partner

# C3

The Maxwell Company Limited was formed to purchase the business of Max &
Wells, who share profits two-thirds and one-third respectively, and whose
balance sheet at 30 June 19x4 was as follows:

BALANCE SHEET

CAPITAL EMPLOYED

| | | | |
|---|---|---|---|
| Capital | | | |
| - Max | | R65 000 | |
| - Wells | | 35 000 | R100 000 |
| Loan | | | |
| Max | | | 25 000 |
| | | | R125 000 |

EMPLOYMENT OF CAPITAL

| | | | |
|---|---|---|---|
| Fixed assets | | | |
| Land an buildings at cost | | R75 000 | |
| Plant and machinery at cost | R40 000 | | |
| Accumulated depreciation | 4 000 | 36 000 | R111 000 |
| Net current assets | | | 14 000 |
| Current Assets | | | |
| Stock | | 20 000 | |
| Debtors | | 19 000 | |
| Provision for bad debts | 1 000 | 18 000 | |
| Cash | | 7 000 | |
| | | R45 000 | |
| Current liabilities | | | |
| Creditors | | R22 000 | |
| Bills payable | | 9 000 | |
| | | R31 000 | |
| | | | R125 000 |

The company takes over the assets, including cash, at book values.   The firm
discharged the loan by Max of R25 000 and the company takes over the remaining
liabilities.

The purchase consideration is R155 000 payable as follows:
     R90 000 in debentures.
     R30 000 in fully paid up ordinary shares and the balance in cash.

Max and Wells agree to divide the purchase consideration as follows:

(a)    The balance of cash, after paying off Max's loan account, to be share
       equally.
(b)    The debentures and shares in the proportions which their capital
       accounts bear to one another after transferring any profit or loss on
       realisation, and after debiting the balance of cash which they share
       equally as in (a) above.

Show the ledger accounts closing the firm's books and the journal entries
opening the company's books.  Ignore dates.

# C4

The following is the balance sheet at 30 June 19x4 of Jenks and Kemp, who
share profits and losses 3:1 respectively.

BALANCE SHEET AT 30 JUNE 19X4

CAPITAL EMPLOYED

| | | |
|---|---:|---:|
| Capital | | |
| - Jenks | R6 000 | |
| - Kemp | 3 000 | R9 000 |
| General reserve | | 3 000 |
| | | R12 000 |

EMPLOYMENT OF CAPITAL

| | |
|---|---:|
| Current assets | |
| Stock | 7 500 |
| Debtors | 4 000 |
| Bank | 2 500 |
| | 14 000 |
| Current liabilities | |
| Creditors | 2 000 |
| | R12 000 |

The assets of the business except cash, are sold to Wits Traders Ltd, stock
being taken over for R8 000 and debtors at book value.

The purchase consideration is satisfied by the issue of

(a)    30 000 ordinary shares of 25c each at a premium of 5c per share.
(b)     6 000 preference shares of R1 each at par.
(c)       200 debentures of R10 each at a discount of 3%.

Jenks and Kemp paid the creditors R1 950 in full settlement of their accounts
and they also incurred expenses of realisation amounting to R210.

A debtor whose account of R250 had been written off as bad two years ago paid
his account together with interest of R30 to Wits Traders Ltd.   By mutual
agreement Wits Traders Ltd immediately paid the amount received to Jenks and
Kemp.

The partners decide to distribute the shares and debentures in the following
manner:

(i)    Ordinary shares - equally.
(ii)   Preference shares - in the ratio of the balances on the capital
       accounts
       as per the above balance sheet.
(iii)  Debentures - in the ratio in which profits are shared.

Record the above transactions in the books of Jenks and Kemp in the form of
ledger accounts which show a complete record of all the decisions relating to
the sale of the business and subsequent distribution of the purchase
consideration and cash.

Give the journal entries in the books of the company.

# C5

A, B and C were partners shaing profits and losses in the ratio of 4:3:3 respectively.   At 30 June 19x4, as they had been trading at a loss for some time, they dissolved partnership when their balance sheet read:

CAPITAL EMPLOYED

| | |
|---|---:|
| Capital | |
| - A | R55 000 |
| - B | 37 000 |
| | 92 000 |
| - C (debit balance) | (10 800) |
| | R81 200 |

EMPLOYMENT OF CAPITAL

| | | |
|---|---:|---:|
| Fixed assets | | |
| Property at cost | | R30 000 |
| | | |
| Investments - unlisted | | |
| 10 000 shares of R1 each in XY Ltd, at cost | | 12 000 |
| | | |
| Net current assets | | 39 200 |
| Current assets | | |
| Stock | R40 000 | |
| Debtors | 25 000 | |
| | R65 000 | |
| | | |
| Current liabilities | | |
| Creditors | R18 000 | |
| Expenses accrued | 800 | |
| Bank overdraft | 7 000 | |
| | R25 800 | |
| | | R81 200 |

The investments were taken over by A at R1 per share.   The remaining assets were sold to XY Ltd on that date, the purchase price of R80 000 being settled by the issue at par of 40 000 fully paid shares of R1 each in XY Ltd plus a cash payment of R40 000.

The old firm paid all the liabilities, plus realisation expenses amounting to R3 000.

As C was insolvent, A and B bore the resulting loss, in terms of the partnership agreement, in their normal profit-sharing ratio.

Of the shares issued to the partnership by XY Ltd, A took over 25 000 at par, and B the balance at par.

YOU ARE REQUIRED:

(a)   To close the books of the partnership - give ledger accounts only.
(b)   To show the opening journal entries in the books of XY Ltd, assuming that the stock and debtors purchased were entered at their book values. Journalise any cash transactions.

# C6

Hook, Line and Sinker are partners sharing profits and losses in the ratio 4:3:2 respectively.   At 30 June 19x4 the balance sheet is:

<u>BALANCE SHEET</u>

CAPITAL EMPLOYED

Capital
- Hook                                                    R40 000
- Line                                                     40 000
- Sinker                                                   <u>30 000</u>
                                                          R110 000
                                                          =======

EMPLOYMENT OF CAPITAL

Fixed assets
  Property at cost                                         R60 000

Net current assets                                         50 000
  Current assets
    Stock                              R18 000
    Debtors                            <u>36 000</u>
                                       R54 000
                                       ======

  Current liabilities
    Creditors                          R4 000
                                       =====
                                                          <u>R110 000</u>
                                                          =======

A new company, Maasbankers Limited, with an authorised capital of 100 000 9% cumulative preference shares of R1 each, and 200 000 ordinary shares of 50c each, is formed to take over the business at that date.

The following agreements are reached:

1.    The company takes over all assets and liabilities for R128 000.
2.    The property is a shop on freehold stand No. 123 Kingklip.   It is considered to be worth R80 000 and stock is considered to be worth R19 000.
3.    A provision for bad debts amounting to R3 000 is to be created.
4.    The purchase price payable is made up as follows:
      (a)   By the issue of 36 000 preference shares, at par.
      (b)   By the issue of 180 000 ordinary shares, at par.
      (c)   By the payment of the balance due in cash.
5.    The partners divide the preference and ordinary shares among themselves in the profit-sharing ratio, and they pay in or withdraw cash to settle their capital accounts.
6.    A further 44 000 preference shares are issued at par to W Snoek, who pays cash for them.
7.    The expenses of revaluation of the assets and the flotation of the company are paid by the company and amount to R2 000.   Of this, R600 is in respect of share issue expenses.

<u>YOU ARE REQUIRED TO PREPARE</u>:

(a)   The realisation and capital accounts of the partnership.
(b)   The opening balance sheet of the new company.

## C7

Fisher and Cramer are in business as equal partners and their balance sheet at 31 December 19x4 is as follows:

CAPITAL EMPLOYED

| | | |
|---|---|---|
| Capital | | |
| - Fisher | R46 540 | |
| - Cramer | 22 730 | R69 270 |
| Loan - G Considine secured by | | |
|   first mortgage over fixed property | | 55 250 |
| | | R91 810 |

EMPLOYMENT OF CAPITAL

| | | |
|---|---|---|
| Fixed assets | | |
|   Land and buildings at cost | | R27 140 |
|   Furniture at cost | R10 000 | |
|   Accumulated depreciation | 1 440 | 8 560 |
| | | 35 700 |
| Investments - unlisted, at cos | | 9 500 |
| | | |
| Net current assets | | 46 610 |
|   Current assets | | |
|     Stock | R28 920 | |
|     Debtors | 14 190 | |
|     Bank | 14 290 | |
| | R57 400 | |
| | | |
|   Current liabilities | | |
|     Creditors | R10 790 | |
| | | R91 810 |

Sunken Investments Ltd was formed in 19x4 to take over the business as a going concern from 1 January 19x5 on the following terms:

Land and buildings are taken over at R30 000, furniture at R7 000, stocks at R25 000 and investments at R7 200.

Debtors and creditors are taken over at their balance sheet value.

The company was formed with an authorised share capital of R200 000 divided into 400 000 shares of 50c each.  The purchase consideration is R70 000 and is satisfied by the issue of fully paid shares in the company.

To enable the company to extend its operations, the directors offer the unissued shares for public subscription at par.  Applications are received for 300 000 shares and allotment is made in proportion to the number of shares applied for by each applicant.  Excess application money is refunded to unsuccessful applicants.

Show, by means of journal entries, how the above transactions would be recorded in the books of the partnership and the company.  All cash transactions should be journalised.

# C8

North and South are in business as equal partners and their balance sheet at 30 September 19x4 is as follows:

BALANCE SHEET AT 30 SEPTEMBER 19X4

CAPITAL EMPLOYED

| | | |
|---|---:|---:|
| Capital | | |
| - North | R90 000 | |
| - South | <u>50 000</u> | R140 000 |
| Distributable reserves | | <u>20 000</u> |
| | | R160 000 |
| | | ======= |

EMPLOYMENT OF CAPITAL

| | | | |
|---|---:|---:|---:|
| Fixed assets | | | |
|   Goodwill at cost | | | R10 000 |
|   Land and buildings at cost less depreciation | | | 45 000 |
|   Furniture and fixtures at cost less depreciation | | | <u>15 000</u> |
| | | | 70 000 |
| Investments - unlisted, at cost | | | 10 000 |
| Net current assets | | | 80 000 |
|   Current assets | | | |
|     Stock | | | 56 000 |
|     Debtors | R30 000 | | |
|     Provision for bad debts | <u>2 000</u> | 28 000 | |
|     Bank | | <u>16 000</u> | |
| | | R100 000 | |
| | | ======= | |
|   Current liabilities | | | |
|     Creditors | | R20 000 | |
| | | ====== | |
| | | | R160 000 |
| | | | ====== |

A company, Equator Ltd, is formed in July 19x4 with a share capital of R500 000 divided into 100 000 9% preference shares of R1 each and 400 000 ordinary shares of R1 each to take over the business as from 1 October 19x4 on the following terms:

Land and buildings are taken over at R50 000, furniture and fixtures at R12 000, investments at R8 000, stock at R54 000 and debtors at R30 000. Bank is taken over and the company assumes responsibility for the liabilities of the partnership.

The purchase price agreed upon is R170 000, which is to be settled by the issue of 65 000 9% preference shares of R1 each at par and 100 000 ordinary shares of R1 each at a premium of 5c per share.

The subscribers to the memorandum subscribe for 50 000 ordinary shares at a premium of 5c per share and pay for them in full.

In terms of the purchase agreement 65 000 9% preference shares and 100 000 ordinary shares are allotted to North and South in settlement of the purchase price.

# C8 CONTINUED

The remaining preference shares and ordinary shares are offered to the public
for subscription as follows:

    Preference shares at R1.
    Ordinary shares at R1,05.

45 000 9% preference shares are applied for and 35 000 are allotted.

375 000 ordinary shares are applied for and 250 000 are allotted.

Journalise the above transactions in the books of the company.

Note: Dates are to be ignored, but entries must be made in their proper
sequence.

# C9

Martha and Mary are in partnership sharing profits in the proportion of two-thirds to one-third.   Their balance sheet at 31 December 19x4 is as follows:

CAPITAL EMPLOYED

```
Capital
- Martha                                          R28 400
- Mary                                             19 600    R48 000
Loan                                                          100 000
                                                             R148 000
                                                             =======
```

EMPLOYMENT OF CAPITAL

```
Fixed assets
  Goodwill at cost                                            R30 000
  Land and buildings at cost less depreciation                93 000
                                                              123 000
Net current assets                                             25 000
  Current assets
    Stock                                         R12 700
    Debtors                                        47 200
    Bank                                            3 000
                                                  R62 900
                                                  ======

  Current liabilities
    Creditors                                     R23 200
    Bills payable                                  14 700
                                                  R37 900
                                                  ======
                                                             R148 000
                                                             =======
```

They dispose of their business to a newly formed company, Fashion Fair Limited, with an authorised share capital of 200 000 9% cumulative preference shares of R1 each, and 1 000 000 ordinary shares of 25c each.

It is agreed that the new company will take over all the assets and liabilities of the firm except bank.

The assets are taken over at the following valuations:

```
        Goodwill              R45 000
        Land and buildings    R155 000
        Stock                 At book value
        Debtors               After making a provision for bad debts of R4 700
```

Certain expenses amounting to R2 350 are to be paid by the partnership.

It is also agreed that Fashion Fair Limited will, upon taking transfer of the property, immediately pay off the loan.

# C9 CONTINUED

The purchase consideration received by the partnership is payable as follows:

(1)    R60 000 by the issue at par of fully paid preference shares.
(2)    R55 000 by the issue at par of fully paid ordinary shares.
(3)    The balance by cash.

In paying out the partners, it is agreed that Martha shall receive all the preference shares, together with ordinary shares to make up the balance due to her.

The capital of the company is fully subscribed by the directors of the company, the preference shares being issued to them at par, and the ordinary shares at a premium of 5c per share.

Show: (1)    Ledger  accounts of the partnership showing the results of the dissolution.
     (2)    The balance sheet of Fashion Fair Limited.

All calculations to be made to nearest R10.

Any essential information may be supplied from your imagination.

# C10

During June 19x9 Light and Dark who were in partnership sharing profits and losses equally entered into an agreement with Daylight (Proprietary) Limited in terms of which the company was to take over the assets of the partnership at 30 June 19x9 other than cash at bank, and its liabilities  at that date other than Light's loan.

Tangible fixed assets were taken over at:

|  |  |
|---|---|
| Land and buildings | R54 000 |
| Fixtures and fittings, which had been depreciated at 5% per annum on cost, at a value arrived at had depreciation been written off at the rate of 6% per annum on cost | |
| Motor cars | 1 145 |

Current assets and current liabilities were taken over at the figures shown in an audited balance sheet of the partnership at 30 June 19x9, except that an allowance of 5% was deducted from the cost of stock on hand to cover possible obsolescence.

The company assumed the responsibility of paying for the costs of dissolving the partnership.

The following were issued in full settlement of the amount owing to the partners under the agreement:

(i)   21 000 seven per cent preference shares of R1 each, at par.
(ii)  15 000 six per cent debentures of R1 each, at par.
(iii) 37 400 ordinary shares of R1 each, at par.

The following is a summary of the audited balance sheet of the partnership at 30 June 19x9:

| | | | | | |
|---|---:|---:|---|---:|---:|
| Capital accounts | | | Goodwill at valuation | | R2 000 |
| Light | R16 460 | | Land and buildings at | | |
| Dark | 9 370 | R25 830 | cost | | 35 000 |
| General reserve | | 8 000 | Fixtures and fittings | | |
| Loan - Light | | 10 000 | at cost | R2 500 | |
| Creditors | | 5 840 | Accumulated depreciation | 1 800 | 700 |
| | | | Motor cars at cost | 4 000 | |
| | | | Accumulated depreciation | 2 400 | 1 600 |
| | | | Stock | | 5 900 |
| | | | Debtors | 3 400 | |
| | | | Provision for bad debts | 250 | 3 150 |
| | | | Bank | | 1 320 |
| | | R49 670 | | | R49 670 |
| | | ====== | | | ====== |

# C10 CONTINUED

Light had been paid interest at 8% per annum annually in arrear on his loan, which he had advanced to the firm on 1 July 19x7 and which had remained unchanged since that date.  It was agreed by the partners on 30 June 19x9 that a fair rate of interest would have been 6% per annum and, therefore, the amounts of excessive interest paid be treated as repayments of the principal owing on the loan account.

The shares and debentures in the company were divided between the partners as follows:

> Debentures:  firstly to settle Light's loan and the remainder equally.
> Ordinary shares:  equally.
> Preference shares:  two-thirds to Light and one-third to Dark.
> The cost involved in dissolving the partnership amounted to R210.

<u>YOU ARE REQUIRED TO</u>:

(1)     show the realisation account and partners' capital accounts.

(2)     give the journal entries in the company's book in respect of the foregoing.  (Cash transactions are to be journalised.)

# C11

Walsh and Collier Limited was incorporated on 1 July 19x5, with an authorised share capital consisting of 200 000 shares of no par value.

Walsh and Collier each subscribed for 1 000 shares and each paid the company R1 000 on 10 July 19x5.   The shares were allotted on the same day.

The company purchased from the partnership of Walsh and Collier certain assets and liabilities under a contract which was ratified on 10 July 19x5.   The assets and liabilities taken over were the following:

| | | |
|---|---:|---:|
| Land and buildings - at sworn valuation | | R90 000 |
| Furniture and equipment - at cost | R30 000 | |
|         - accumulated depreciation | 10 000 | 20 000 |
| Motor vehicles - at cost | 25 000 | |
|         - accumulated depreciation | 10 500 | 14 500 |
| Stock | | 100 000 |
| Debtors | 80 000 | |
| Provision for bad debts | 2 000 | 78 000 |
| | | 302 500 |
| Creditors | | 80 500 |
| | | R222 000 |

The purchase consideration which had been agreed at R252 000 was settled by the issue of 125 000 shares of no par value to Walsh and Collier on 15 July 19x5.

A further 50 000 shares were privately placed by Barston Merchant Bank Limited during August 19x5 at the lowest amounts for which the shares could be allotted in terms of the Companies Act 1973 without a special resolution. In terms of the agreement between the company and the merchant bank the latter received a commission of R2 000 for their services.

On 25 August 19x5 the bank paid the net amount due to the company and an allotment was made in terms of a directors resolution dated 30 August 19x5.

<u>YOU ARE REQUIRED</u>:

(a)   To prepare journal entries for all the above transactions (including cash transactions).

(b)   To discuss the disclosure requirements in so far as the income statement and balance sheet are concerned should the directors resolve to write off the issue expenses while still maximising distributable reserves.

# C12

Zimbabwe Limited was formed on 1 January 19x5 to take over a partnership operated by Bob and Josh (in which profits and losses were shared equally) and a business run by Ian, with effect from that date. The company's authorised share capital consisted of 400 000 ordinary shares of 50c each and 50 000 9% cumulative preference shares of R1 each.

On December 19x4, the ledgers of the two businesses taken over contained the following balances:

|  | Bob & Josh | Ian |  | Bob & Josh | Ian |
|---|---|---|---|---|---|
| Capital - Bob | R34 000 | - | Goodwill | - | R1 000 |
| - Josh | 24 000 | - | Land and buildings | R80 000 | - |
| - Ian | - | R34 000 | Fixtures and fittings |  |  |
| Reserve | 10 000 | - | at cost | 14 000 | - |
| Accumulated depr. |  |  | Stock | - | 35 000 |
| - fixture and fittings | 6 000 |  | Accounts receivable | 26 000 | - |
| Accounts payable | 40 000 | 16 000 | Bills receivable | - | 8 000 |
| Bank overdraft | 6 000 | - | Bank | - | 6 000 |
|  | R120 000 | R50 000 |  | R120 000 | R50 000 |

(a)   The company purchased the two businesses on the following terms:

(i)   The assets of Bob and Josh were taken over at the following values:

| | | |
|---|---|---|
| Land and building | - | at book value |
| Fixtures and fittings | - | for R5 000 |
| Accounts receivable | - | at book value subject to a provision for doubtful debts of R3 000 |
| Goodwill | - | for R20 000 |

The company assumed responsibility for the accounts payable but the partners agreed to settle the bank overdraft personally. In payment of the purchase consideration the company issued 160 000 of its ordinary shares to the partners.

(ii)  The company took over Ian's assets at book value, except for goodwill which was agreed to be worth R7 000, and assumed responsibility for the accounts payable. The purchase consideration was settled by the issue to Ian of ordinary shares at par. Ian was also given the option to subscribe for a further 20 000 ordinary shares at par on or before 31 December 19x8.

Bob and Josh were appointed the company's first directors and, in terms of the company's Articles of Association, the directors have the general power to issue the unissued shares provided this power is confirmed annually by the company in general meeting. Bob and Josh decided that the transactions of the company should be recorded in the ledger and journals which they had been using for their partnership.

REQUIRED:

Entries in general journal form to record the conversion of the partnership into a limited company and the terms of the above business purchase agreements. (Ignore narrations.)

# C13

A company, Atlantic Limited, was formed on 1 January 19x8.   The promoter of the company was A Count who operated a small business as a sole trader.   On 1 January 19x8 the company took over Count's business and that of D Urban and A L Goa who operated as a partnership and shared profits and losses in the ration of 3:2 respectively.

On 31 December 19x7 the balance sheets of the business taken over contained the following items:

| | A Count | D Urban and A L Goa | | A Count | D Urban and A L Goa |
|---|---|---|---|---|---|
| Capital - A Count | R100 000 | - | Goodwill | - | R80 000 |
| D Urban | - | R80 000 | Land and buildings | - | 100 000 |
| A L Goa | - | 160 000 | Fixtures and fittings | R30 000 | - |
| Mortgage bond | - | 50 000 | Stock | 40 000 | 20 000 |
| Accumulated depreciation - F.F. | 10 000 | - | Accounts receivable | 20 000 | 40 000 |
| Accounts payable | 30 000 | 10 000 | Bank | 40 000 | 60 000 |
| | R130 000 | R300 000 | | R130 000 | R300 000 |

In terms of the agreements the company took over the businesses on the following terms:

(1)    A Count's <u>tangible assets</u> were valued by the company as follows:

| | |
|---|---|
| Fixtures and fittings | R23 000 |
| Stock | 35 000 |
| Accounts receivable and bank at book value. | |

The company assumed responsibility for the accounts payable as well as a contingent liability of R12 000 in respect of unmatured bills discounted with the bank.   When determining the purchase price of R120 000 to be settled by an issue of 200 000 ordinary 50c shares.   The contingent liability was taken into account as the likelihood of the drawee honouring the bills was slim.

(2)    The assets and liabilities of Urban and Goa were taken over at book value except for:

- goodwill which was valued at R100 000
- land and buildings which were valued at R150 000
- the mortgage bond which was paid by Goa from his private bank account.

The purchase price was settled by an issue of 600 000 ordinary 50c shares.

It was decided that the company would continue to use the same ledger and journals which had been used by A Count.

# C13 CONTINUED

The company issued its shares as payment on 1 January 19x8.


<u>REQUIRED</u>:

(a)  Entries to record the transactions of conversion and purchase in terms
     of the agreements in the journal of Atlantic Ltd.
(b)  Journal entries to dissolve the partnership of Urban and Goa.

# C14

Alpha Limited entered into contracts for the acquisition of two businesses as follows:

1.(i)      To acquire all the assets and take over all liabilities of X (Proprietary) Limited with effect from 1 MARCH 19x8.

(ii)      To acquire only the fixed assets and stocks of the partnership of A and B with effect from 1 MARCH 19x8.

(iii)      Goodwill in respect of X (Pty) Ltd and the partnership was to be valued at two years' purchase of the average profits of the last three financial years subject to the adjustments mentioned in note (2) below.

(iv)      The purchase considerations were to be paid in ordinary R1 shares of Alpha Limited to be issued at R1,25 per share. In computing the number of shares to be issued for each business the following factors were to be taken into account:

    (a)    Land and buildings and plant and machinery were to be taken over at values placed on them by an independent valuer.

    (b)    Stocks were to be taken over at book values subject to a deduction of R1 200 from the stocks of A and B for obsolete stock.

    (c)    In the case of X (Pty) Ltd, debtors, creditors and the bank balance were to be taken over at book values less R1 500 in respect of a doubtful debt.

v)      Immediately after the contracts were completed X (Pty) Ltd was to be liquidated and the partnership of A and B dissolved.

2.      Goodwill of the two businesses was to be calculated after making allowances for the following adjustments:

X (Pty) Ltd:

(i)      Directors' remuneration paid in respect of the last three financial years was to be reduced by R2 000 per annum.

(ii)      Depreciation which has been provided on plant and machinery at the rate of 10% per annum by the reducing balance method was to be substituted with depreciation calculated at the rate of 10% per annum by the fixed instalment method.

Partnership A and B:

(i)      Partners' salaries were to be increased by R2 500 per annum for each partner in respect of the last three financial years.

(ii)      An abnormal item of expense amounting to R3 000 incurred in 19x6 is to be added back.

3. The summarised balance sheets of the three businesses at 28 February 19x8 were as follows:

|  | ALPHA LTD | X (PTY) LTD | A AND B |
|---|---|---|---|
| Ordinary shares of R1 | R500 000 | R100 000 | - |
| Capital - A | - | - | R38 500 |
| Capital - B | - | - | 30 500 |
| Retained income | 88 000 | 38 049 | - |
| Creditors | 72 000 | 42 000 | 8 000 |
|  | R660 000 | R180 049 | R77 000 |
|  | ======= | ======= | ====== |
| Land and buildings at cost | R150 000 | R50 000 | R20 000 |
| Plant and machinery - at cost less depreciation | 294 000 | 59 049 | 26 000 |
| Stock | 140 000 | 21 000 | 10 200 |
| Debtors | 60 000 | 45 000 | 12 800 |
| Bank | 16 000 | 5 000 | 9 000 |
|  | R660 000 | R180 049 | R77 000 |
|  | ======= | ======= | ====== |

4. The independent valuations at 28 February 19x8 were:

|  | X (PTY) LTD | A AND B |
|---|---|---|
| Land and buildings | R70 000 | R30 000 |
| Plant and machinery | R50 000 | R24 000 |

5. The profits for the last three financial years ended 28 February were as follows:

|  | X (PTY) LTD | A AND B |
|---|---|---|
| 19x6 | R12 200 | R 8 500 |
| 19x7 | 13 062 | 10 500 |
| 19x8 | 15 137 | 11 000 |

6. The plant and machinery shown in the above balance sheet of X (Pty) Ltd had all been acquired on 1 March 19x4.  X (Pty) Ltd had, however, disposed of certain plant and machinery at book value on 28 February 19x8.  This plant and machinery had been purchased on 1 March 19x6 at a cost of R5 000.

7. The authorised share capital of Alpha Limited is 1 000 000 ordinary shares of R1 each.

8. The debtors of A and B paid the full amount owing by them (R12 800) and the  partnership was dissolved.  The shares in Alpha Limited were divided equally between them.  A and B share profits and losses equally.

# C14 CONTINUED

<u>YOU ARE REQUIRED</u>:

(a)    To state the number of shares issued to the shareholders of X (Pty) Ltd and to the partnership of A and B by Alpha Limited in settlement of the purchase consideration.

(b)    To prepare the balance sheet of Alpha Limited on 1  March 19x8 in summarised form after completion of the acquisitions.  Notes to the balance sheet are NOT required.

(c)    Prepare the capital accounts of A and B in columnar form, showing the shares and cash distributed to them on dissolution of the partnership.

# C15

Senty and Meeters were in partnership sharing profits and losses in the following ratio, Senty, three-fifths, Meeters, two-fifths.  The following was the summarised balance sheet of the partnership:

<u>CAPITAL EMPLOYED</u>

| | | |
|---|---|---|
| CAPITAL - SENTY | R7 516 | |
|       - MEETERS | <u>4 408</u> | R11 924 |
| LOAN   - SENTY | | <u>3 000</u> |
| | | R14 924 |

<u>EMPLOYMENT OF CAPITAL</u>

| | | |
|---|---|---|
| FIXED ASSETS | | R8 400 |
|   Land and buildings, plant and machinery and motor cars | | |
| INVESTMENTS | | 3 200 |
| NET CURRENT ASSETS | | 3 324 |
|   CURRENT ASSETS | | |
|     Stock | R4 000 | |
|     Debtors | <u>3 500</u> | |
| | R7 500 | |
|   CURRENT LIABILITIES | | |
|     Creditors | R2 580 | |
|     Bank overdraft | <u>1 596</u> | |
| | R4 176 | |
| | | <u>R14 924</u> |

<u>Notes</u>:

1. Senty and Meeters, wishing to dissolve the partnership, accepted the offer of Metrication Ltd to purchase the business.  The company agreed:
   (a) to take over  stock, land and buildings and plant and machinery, with the exception of two motor cars whose book values were R800 and R400 respectively, and
   (b) that the consideration, R20 000, was to be satisfied by a cash payment of R11 000 and the balance by the issue to the partners of 21 000 no par value shares valued at R9 000.

2. Senty took over the motor car with  a book value  of R800 at a valuation of R850 and Meeters  the other  at a valuation of R350.

3. Senty's loan, together with the interest accrued thereon, R80, which is included in creditors, was to be transferred to his capital account.

4. The investments were sold for cash for R2 800.   The debtors realised R3 300 and the creditors were settled in full paying R2 400.

5. Costs of dissolution paid by partnership were R150.

# C15 CONTINUED

6.      The partnership agreed to divide the ordinary shares in proportion to the balances on their capital accounts after the realisation profit or loss has been transferred to their capital accounts and Senty's loan had been transferred to his capital account.   The final balances were settled in cash.

7.      Metrication Ltd valued the land and buildings at R10 000, the plant and machinery at R6 000 and the stock at R2 500.

<u>YOU ARE REQUIRED TO PREPARE</u>:

(i)    (a)   The realisation account,
       (b)   The bank account, and
       (c)   Partners' capital accounts after  books of partnership had been closed.

(ii)   The journal entries in the books of Metrication Ltd regarding the above.

# C16

A company, Delvers Limited was formed on 1 March 19X9 to take over the partnership operated by Charlotte and Anne and a business run by Branwell with effect from that date.   Charlotte and Anne shared profits and losses in the ratio 2:1.   The newly formed company's authorised share capital consisted of 500 000 ordinary shares of R1,00 each.

On 28 February 19X9 the balance sheets of the partnership and sole trader taken over contained the following items:

|  | Charlotte & Anne | Branwell |
|---|---|---|
| Goodwill | - | R 3 000 |
| Land and buildings | R65 000 | 28 000 |
| Furniture and fittings | 18 000 | - |
| Motor vehicles | 32 000 | 25 000 |
| Stock | 40 000 | 14 000 |
| Debtors | 35 000 | 17 000 |
| Bank | 16 000 | 3 000 |
|  | R206 000 | R90 000 |
|  |  |  |
| Capital - Charlotte | R80 000 | - |
| - Anne | 54 000 | - |
| - Branwell | - | R46 000 |
| General reserve | 30 000 | - |
| Provision for doubtful debts | 1 000 | 1 000 |
| Accumulated depreciation - |  |  |
| furniture and fittings | 6 000 | - |
| motor vehicles | 7 000 | 5 000 |
| Creditors | 28 000 | 22 000 |
| Mortgage bond | - | 16 000 |
|  | R206 000 | R90 000 |

The company took over the businesses on the following terms:

A.    All the assets and liabilities of the partnership Charlotte and Anne were taken over at book values except for the following which were valued at:

| Land and buildings | - | R80 000 |
|---|---|---|
| Furniture and fittings | - | 7 000 |
| Debtors | - | at book value subject to a provision for doubtful debts of R3 000 |
| Goodwill | - | 28 000 |

The purchase consideration was settled by the issue of 180 000 ordinary shares to the partners.

# C16 CONTINUED

B.    All the assets and liabilities of the sole trader Branwell were taken
      over at book values except for motor vehicles and goodwill which were
      valued at R14 000 and R7 000 respectively.

      The purchase consideration was settled by the issue of 40 000 ordinary
      shares to Branwell.

Charlotte, Anne and Branwell were appointed as the company's first directors
and it was decided that the company would continue to use the  same ledgers
and journals which had been used by the partnership.   The company incurred
the following expenses:

      Share issue expenses                R12 000
      Preliminary expenses                 15 000


<u>YOU ARE REQUIRED TO</u>:

prepare the journal entries to record the purchase in terms of the agreements
in the journal of Delvers Limited.

(Narrations are not required.)

# C17

Pearl, Ruby and Sapphire were in partnership sharing profits and losses in the
ratio 2 : 2 : 1   Their balance sheet at 31 March 19x3 was as follows:

```
CAPITAL EMPLOYED
Capital                                                        R120 000
  Pearl                                          R60 000
  Ruby                                            40 000
  Sapphire                                        20 000
Current accounts                                                 3 000
  Pearl                                          R4 200
  Ruby                                          (3 200)
  Sapphire                                        2 000
General reserve                                                 15 000
                                                              R138 000
                                                              =======

EMPLOYMENT OF CAPITAL
Fixed assets                                                   R77 000
  Goodwill at cost                               R5 000
  Land and buildings at cost                     60 000
  Furniture at cost              R18 000
  Accumulated depreciation        6 000          12 000

Net current assets                                             61 000
  Current assets
    Stock                                        R32 000
    Debtors                      R28 000
    Provision for bad debts       4 000          24 000
    Bank                                          48 000
                                                R104 000
                                                =======

  Current liabilities
    Creditors                                    R43 000
                                                ======

                                                              R138 000
                                                              =======
```

<u>ADDITIONAL INFORMATION</u>

Sapphire decided to retire on 1 April 19x3 before the partnership was taken
over by Jewellers Limited.

For the purpose of Sapphire's retirement from the partnership it was agreed
that goodwill was to be valued at  R8 000, but was to remain in the books at
R5 000.   All the other assets were considered to be fairly valued. Sapphire
was paid the amount owing to him on 1 April 19x3.

Pearl and Ruby agreed that the new profit sharing ratio between themselves was
to be 2 : 1.

# C17 CONTINUED

Jewellers Limited was formed early in 19x3 to take over the business of Pearl and Ruby as a going concern from 1 April 19x3 on the following terms:

Goodwill was valued at R20 000, land and buildings at R85 000, furniture at R8 000, stock at R30 000 and debtors at R23 000. The bank account was not taken over by the company.

The company was formed with an authorised share capital of 600 000 ordinary shares of 50c each. The purchase consideration was settled by the issue of 240 000 fully paid shares in the company. The shares were to be divided between Pearl and Ruby in their profit sharing ratio.

It was decided that the company would continued to use the same ledger and journals of the partnership.


<u>YOU ARE REQUIRED TO</u>:

give the journal entries to record the retirement of Sapphire and the conversion of the partnership of Pearl and Ruby into a company on 1 April 19x3.

NARRATIONS ARE NOT REQUIRED.  GIVE YOUR WORKINGS.

# SECTION D

# COMPANY ACCOUNTING – PROFITS PRIOR TO RATIFICATION

# D1

J J du Toit was incorporated on 15 March 19x5.

On 28 February 19x5 an agreement had been  signed  between  J.J. du Toit and
F. de Beer, the latter acting as trustee for a company to be formed, to the
effect that the company would take over, as a going concern, the business of
J J du Toit with effect  from  the  date  of the  last  balance  sheet, viz.
31 December 19x4.

The purchase consideration was to be R50 000, plus interest at the  rate of
6% per annum, from 31 December 19x4 to the date of payment.

The  directors  of J J  du  Toit  Limited  formally adopted the agreement  on
31 March 19x5.

On 15 April 19x5 J J du Toit Limited received its certificate to commence
business and on 30 April 19x5 the purchase price was paid.

Assume the profits of the business amounted to R600 per month and assume that,
at 31 December 19x4,  it was agreed that the tangible net assets of the
business were worth R42 000.


<u>YOU ARE REQUIRED TO</u>:

State what figure should be regarded as being the  cost of the goodwill of the
business.

# D2

Knight Co (Pty) Ltd was incorporated on 1 September 19x4 with a share capital of 400 000 ordinary shares of no par value. The company was formed to take over the business of J. Knight as a going concern with effect from 1 July 19x4. The purchase consideration which was to be settled in cash included R50 000 paid for goodwill and R25 000 for the estimated pre-acquisition profits. All the tangible assets were considered to be fairly valued except for land and buildings which were to be taken over for R110 000.

On 1 November 19x4 the company ratified the contract. The purchase price was paid and the amount debited to J. Knight's capital account. No other entries were put through in connection with the acquisition of the business.

Stock was not taken at that date and the company continued with the same set of books. The same staff were employed at the same salaries.

No fixed assets had been purchased since 1 July 19x4.

The following trial balance was extracted at 30 June 19x5:

| | | |
|---|---:|---:|
| Administration expenses | | R12 240 |
| Audit fees | | 2 400 |
| Bank | | 57 480 |
| Building in the course of construction | | 57 000 |
| Capital account - J. Knight | | 85 000 |
| Creditors | R36 000 | |
| Debtors | 52 000 | |
| Furniture and fittings at cost less depreciation-<br>  1 July 19x4 | 6 000 | |
| Land and buildings - at cost 1 July 19x4 | 100 000 | |
| Motor vehicles - at cost less depreciation -<br>  1 July 19x4 | 12 000 | |
| Provisional taxation paid | 20 000 | |
| Purchases | | 309 000 |
| Salaries - administration | 48 000 | |
|         - directors | 16 000 | |
| Sales | 480 000 | |
| Selling expenses | 16 000 | |
| Stated capital (300 000 shares) | | 327 120 |
| Stock at 1 July 19x4 | 50 000 | |
| | R843 120 | R843 120 |

The following additional information is available:

1. Stock at 30 June 19x5 had cost R71 000 using the most recent prices which are all lower than net realisable value.
2. Depreciation is to be provided as follows:
   Motor vehicles - 20% p.a. on balance at 1 July 19x4.
   Furniture and fittings - 10% p.a. on balance at 1 July 19x4.
   No depreciation is provided on the completed buildings or on the buildings in the course of construction.

# D2 CONTINUED

3.     Turnover for July, August, September and October amounted to R150 000.
4.     The two directors were appointed on the incorporation of the company and in terms of the articles each is entitled to a fee of R600 p.a. but nothing has been paid or provided for.
5.     All debtors outstanding at 1 November 19x4 had paid their accounts except for L. Woodhouse who still owes R2 000. The directors agreed to write off this account.
6.     Included in debtors is an amount of R4 000 owing by J. Knight, a director, in respect of goods sold to him on 15 December 19x4 for R5 000.
7.     A provision for bad debts amounting to R2 300  is to be made.
8.     Audit fees are to be split in the ratio of turnover.
9.     South African Normal Tax amounted to R23 000.
10.    Land and buildings consist of an office block and warehouse situated on Stand 1374 Highbury Township. The building, the construction of which commenced in January 19x5, is a new warehouse and showroom which is being built on a vacant section of Stand 1374. The contract price for the building is R350 000. The architects certified that at 30 June 19x5 work valued at R74 000 had been completed. The company has arranged overdraft facilities for the financing of the contract.
11.    Preliminary expenses amounting to R1 360 and share issue expenses amounting to R1 520 have been written off.

<u>YOU ARE REQUIRED</u>:

to prepare the managerial financial statements of Knight Co (Pty) Ltd for the period ended 30 June 19x5, together with notes to the financial statements.

A statement of source and application of funds is NOT required.

# D3

Alex Williams entered into a contract dated 1 September 19x3 with the trustee for a company to be formed and called Williams Trading Company (Proprietary) Limited, to acquire Williams's business as a going concern with effect from 1 August 19x3.

All assets and liabilities were to be taken over at balance sheet values with the exception of land which was to be valued at R30 000.
The purchase price was agreed at R200 000 to be settled by the issue to Williams of 160 000 fully paid shares of R1 each at par and R40 000 in cash. Williams received the cheque for R40 000 on 20 November 19x3, and on the same day 160 000 ordinary  shares of R1 each in Williams Trading Company (Proprietary) Limited were issued to him.

The  company  was incorporated on 1 October 19x3 with a  share  capital of R400 000 divided into ordinary shares  of R1 each.  The certificate to commence business was issued on the same day.

On 1 November it formally ratified the contract with the vendor.  On the same date Williams was appointed the managing director of the company at a salary of R24 000 per annum.

Williams' balance sheet at 31 July 19x3 was as follows:

| | | | | | |
|---|---|---|---|---|---|
| Capital | | R160 000 | Fixed assets | | |
| Current liabilities | | |   Land at cost | | R10 000 |
|   Creditors | R30 000 | |   Buildings at cost | | 50 000 |
|   Bills payable | 5 000 | | Fixtures and fittings | | |
| | | 35 000 |   at cost less | | |
| | | |   depreciation | | 20 000 |
| | | | Delivery vans at cost | | |
| | | |   less depreciation | | 120 000 |
| | | | | | 120 000 |
| | | | Current assets | | |
| | | |   Stock | | R40 000 |
| | | |   Debtors | R33 000 | |
| | | |   Provision | | |
| | | |     for bad | | |
| | | |     debts | 3 000 | |
| | | | | | 30 000 |
| | | |   Bank | | 5 000 |
| | | | | | 75 000 |
| | | R195 000 | | | R195 000 |
| | | ======= | | | ======= |

# D3 CONTINUED

The same set of books was used by the company and at 31 July 19x4 the following trial balance was extracted:

| | | |
|---|---:|---:|
| Share capital (270 000 shares of R1 each) | | R270 000 |
| Goodwill | | R20 000 |
| Stock at 1 August 19x3 | | 40 000 |
| Debtors | | 62 000 |
| Buildings at cost | | 50 000 |
| Provision for bad debts | | 3 000 |
| Preliminary and issue expenses | | 4 500 |
| Preliminary expenses | R3 000 | |
| Share issue expense | 1 500 | |
| Land at cost | | 30 000 |
| Delivery vans at cost | | 40 000 |
| Fixtures and fittings at cost | | 20 000 |
| Purchases (net) | | 316 000 |
| Bank | | 64 500 |
| Salaries - staff | | 20 000 |
|       - managing director | | 18 000 |
| Sales (net) | | 400 000 |
| Creditors | | 42 000 |
| Commission - 6% on sales | | 24 000 |
| Other administrative expenses | | 6 000 |
| | | R715 000    R715 000 |

Stock at 31 July 19x4 was 19x4 R56 000, being the lower of cost or net realisable value.

Depreciation  on fixed assets is to be provided as follows:

      buildings at 4% per annum on cost.
      delivery vans at 25% per annum on cost
      fixtures and fittings at 10% per annum on cost.

One-third of the preliminary expenses and one-third of the shares issue expenses are to be written off.

The net sales for the months of August, September and October 19x3 were R22 000, R28 000 and R30 000 respectively.

The provision for bad debts is to remain unaltered.

The land consists of freehold stand 354 Fairland.  A shop buildings has been erected on the stand.

Prepare the company's balance sheet at 31 July 19x4 and the income statement for the period then ended.

Notes to the financial statements are required.

# D4

Smith and Jones who were in partnership entered into a contract to sell their business as a going concern to a company to be formed and to be called Rockies Limited.

The balance sheet of the partnership at 31 December 19x8 was as follows:

| CAPITAL | | | LAND AND BUILDINGS - | | |
|---|---|---|---|---|---|
| Smith | R20 000 | | at cost | | R20 000 |
| Jones | 10 000 | R30 000 | FURNITURE AND FITTINGS - | | |
| | | | at cost | R6 000 | |
| GENERAL RESERVE | | 7 000 | Accumulated depreciation | 1 000 | 5 000 |
| | | | | | 25 000 |
| NET CURRENT ASSETS | | 12 000 | | | |
| | | R37 000 | | | R37 000 |
| | | ====== | | | ====== |

The company was incorporated on 1 February 19x9 with an authorised share capital of 15 000 R1 shares to acquire the partnership business with effect from 1 January 19x9.  On 1 March 19x9 the company received its certificate to commence business and on 1 April 19x9 the directors ratified the contract with Smith and Jones.

The terms of the agreement with the vendors were as follows:

1.    Land and buildings would be taken over  at  an  agreed valuation of R26 000.
2.    All the other assets except stock, which was to be taken over at R2 000 less than book value, were agreed to be fairly valued.
3.    The purchase price was agreed at R50 000.

The company continued to use the books of the partnership from which the following trial balance was extracted at 31 December 19x9:

| | | |
|---|---|---|
| Amount paid to Smith and Jones in excess of their capital accounts | R20 000 | |
| Share capital - ordinary shares of R1 | | R15 000 |
| Share premium | 2 000 | |
| Profit on sale of land and building | 7 000 | |
| Gross profit for the year | | 60 000 |
| Furniture and fittings at cost | | 6 000 |
| ed depreciation - furniture and fittings | | 1 000 |
| Selling expenses | | 22 950 |
| Rent | 4 000 | |
| Directors' salaries | | 15 000 |
| Preliminary expenses | 800 | |
| Administration expenses | 12 000 | |
| Stock at cost | 10 000 | |
| General reserve | | 7 000 |
| Loan raised on 1 April 19x9 | | 10 000 |
| Interest on loan - payment on 1 October 19x9 | 500 | |
| Debtors | 11 000 | |
| Bank | 5 750 | |
| Creditors | 6 000 | 6 000 |
| | R108 000 | R108 000 |
| | ======= | ======= |

# D4 CONTINUED

<u>ADDITIONAL INFORMATION</u>:

1.  Land and buildings were sold on 28 February 19x9 for R27 000 after which date premises were rented at a monthly rental of R400.

2.  Smith and Jones had always marked up the cost of goods sold by 50% in order to determine selling prices.   The company found that because of increased competition it was necessary as from 1 May 19x9 to reduce the marked prices of all goods on hand by 20% to determine new selling prices.   All new stock received was marked at the newly determined selling prices.

    Sales were made as follows:
    | | |
    |---|---|
    | January | R10 000 |
    | February | 12 000 |
    | March | 14 000 |
    | April | 18 000 |
    | May - December | 252 000 |

3.  Depreciation must be provided on furniture and fittings at the rate of 20% p.a. on the balance at 1 January 19x9.

4.  Administration expenses have been evenly incurred during the year.

5.  The stock turnover has been calculated at 1,5 months. Stock is valued at the most recent prices per the suppliers' invoices. All stock on hand at 31 December 19x9 had a realisable value in excess of cost.

6.  Interest on the loan is payable 6 monthly in arrear on 1 October and 1 April each year.  The loan is repayable on 1 April 19y1.

<u>YOU ARE REQUIRED TO PREPARE FOR THE PERIOD ENDED 31 DECEMBER 19X9:</u>

(a)    Detailed income statement
(b)    Balance sheet
(c)    Accounting policies

The disclosure in the above must comply with the requirements of Schedule Four.

# D5

A trustee on behalf of a company to be formed, entered into a pre-incorporation contract with a sole proprietor in terms of which:

(1) The business was to be taken over with effect from 1 October 19x2 as a going concern.
(2) The purchase price was to be settled in cash on the date of ratification of the contract. Interest was to be charged at 20% per annum from 1 October.
(3) The purchase price of R49 500 was based on the interest of the proprietor with pro forma adjustments.

|  |  |
|---|---:|
| Capital - sole proprietor | R10 000 |
| Loan account - sole proprietor | 15 000 |
|  | 25 000 |
|  |  |
| Pro forma adjustments |  |
| Surplus of replacement cost of stock over original FIFO cost | 5 000 |
| Goodwill | 12 000 |
| Profit (estimated) for the period prior to ratification | 7 000 |
|  | R49 500 |

ADDITIONAL INFORMATION:

1. The company paid the purchase price (with interest) of R53 625 on the date of ratification.
2. In the period prior to ratification all the stock on hand at 1 October 19x2 was sold.
3. The book profit made in the period prior to ratification amounted to R13 000.
4. The trustee took over the existing books of the sole proprietor.
5. At 30 September 19x3 the trial balance of the company showed (inter alia) the following balances:

|  | Dr | Cr |
|---|---:|---:|
| Amount paid to sole proprietor | R53 625 |  |
| Capital - sole proprietor |  | R10 000 |
| Loan - sole proprietor |  | 15 000 |
| Stock at 1 October 19x2 | 20 000 |  |

<u>YOU ARE REQUIRED TO</u>:

1. Determine the period which elapsed between 1 October and the date of ratification.
2. Prepare the journal entry (entries) necessary to correct the above trial balance. Show how the profit/loss made prior to incorporation would appear in the first set of annual financial statements for the period ended 30 September 19x3.

IGNORE TAXATION.

# D6

Cohen and Moss, who were in partnership sharing profits and losses equally entered into a contract to sell their business as a going concern to Ruskies (Proprietary) Limited, a company to be formed.

The purchase consideration was fixed at R86 000 and Ruskies (Proprietary) Limited was to issue 86 000 shares at par to the partners equally.

The balance sheet of the partnership at 30 June 19x9 was as follows:

| | | | |
|---|---|---|---|
| CAPITAL - COHEN | R40 000 | LAND AND BUILDINGS AT COST | R35 000 |
| - MOSS | 20 000 | FURNITURE AT COST | R16 000 |
| | 60 000 | ACCUMULATED DEPRECIATION 6 000 | 10 000 |
| GENERAL RESERVE | 10 000 | NET CURRENT ASSETS | 25 000 |
| | R70 000 | | R70 000 |

The purchase agreement stated:

1. Land and buildings would be taken over at an agreed valuation of R40 000.
2. All the other tangible assets except for stock, which was to be taken over at R3 000 more than book value, were agreed to be fairly valued.
3. The partnership was to be taken over with effect form 1 July 19x9.

Ruskies (Proprietary) Limited was incorporated on 1 October 19x9 and when it received its certificate to commence business on 1 November 19x9, the directors formally ratified the contract with Cohen and Moss.

Ruskies (Proprietary) Limited continued to use the books of the partnership from which the following trial balance was extracted at 30 June 19x0.

| | | |
|---|---|---|
| Capital - Cohen | R 3 000 | |
| Capital - Moss | 23 000 | |
| Share capital (R1 shares) | | R86 000 |
| Profit on sale of land and buildings | | 11 000 |
| Gross profit for the year | | 154 000 |
| Furniture at cost | 16 000 | |
| Accumulated depreciation | | 6 000 |
| Selling expenses | 42 000 | |
| Rent | 5 600 | |
| Directors' salaries | 30 000 | |
| Preliminary and share issue expenses (R1 000 each) | 2 000 | |
| Administration expenses | 18 000 | |
| Stock at cost | 24 000 | |
| General reserve | | 10 000 |
| Debtors | 40 000 | |
| Cash at bank | 69 900 | |
| Creditors | | 6 500 |
| | 273 500 | R273 500 |

# D6 CONTINUED



<u>ADDITIONAL INFORMATION</u>:

1.  The land and buildings were sold on 31 December 19x9 for R46 000 after which date premises were rented at a monthly rental of R800 payable on the first day of each month.

2.  Cohen and Moss had always marked goods up to achieve a 50% gross profit on sales.  The company continued this policy without adjustment to existing stock until 1 November 19x9 when, because of increased competition, it was necessary to reduce the marked prices of all goods on hand by 25% to determine new selling prices.  All new stock received was marked according to the new sales policy.  All stock taken over from the partnership had been sold by 31 October 19x9.

    Sales were made as follows:

    | | |
    |---|---|
    | July | R15 000 |
    | August | 18 000 |
    | September | 24 000 |
    | October | 27 000 |
    | November - June | 336 000 |

3.  Depreciation must be provided at the rate of 15% p.a. on the value placed on furniture on 1 July 19x9.
4.  Administration expenses have been evenly incurred during the year.
5.  Selling expenses vary according to the value of sales.
6.  Stock is valued at the most recent prices per the suppliers' invoices. All stock on hand at 30 June 19x0 had a realisable value in excess of cost.
7.  As the directors of Ruskies (Proprietary) Limited wish to retain R15 000 in a general reserve and R5 000 in retained income, the balance must be declared as a dividend.  The articles of association contain no restrictions on the distribution of capital profits. The dividend will be paid on 31 July 19x0.
8.  Provide for company taxation amounting to R12 600.


<u>YOU ARE REQUIRED TO</u>:

(a)  Prepare the journal entries in Ruskies (Pty) Ltd's journal on 30 June 19x0 to correct the balances appearing in the trial balance, prior to the preparation of the financial statements.

(b)  Prepare the detailed income statement of Ruskies (Pty) Ltd for the period to 30 June 19x0.

(c)  Prepare the detailed balance sheet of Ruskies (Pty) Ltd at 30 June 19x0.  <u>Notes are not required</u>.

# D7

Specious (Proprietary) Limited was formed to take over, as a going concern from 1 July 19x3, the business of the A.B. Syndicate, a partnership which speculated in stocks and shares on the Johannesburg Stock Exchange. The summarised balance sheet of the A.B. Syndicate at 30 June 19x3 was:

| | | | |
|---|---:|---|---:|
| Capital A | R5 000 | Investments | R8 000 |
| Capital B | 4 000 | Bank | 1 200 |
| | 9 000 | | |
| Creditors | 200 | | |
| | R9 200 | | R9 200 |
| | ===== | | ===== |

The purchase consideration was R10 000 which was to include all profits or losses incurred after 1 July 19x3. The company was incorporated on 1 September 19x3 with an authorised capital of R100 and on that date A and B each took 50 shares and paid for them in cash.

On 1 October 19x3 the vendor's agreement was ratified and the purchase consideration was settled in cash out of money borrowed from A and B.

The company used the same set of books as the partnership.

At 30 June 19x4 the following trial balance was extracted from the books:

| | | |
|---|---:|---:|
| Amount paid to A and B in excess of their capital accounts | R1 000 | |
| Brokers for shares purchased but not delivered | | R1 000 |
| Bank | 8 400 | |
| Dividends received | | 600 |
| Expenses (R100 per month) | 1 200 | |
| Furniture at cost (purchased 1 October 19x3) | 2 000 | |
| Investments at cost (market value R13 000) | 12 050 | |
| Loan "A" | | 5 500 |
| Loan "B" | | 4 500 |
| Preliminary and share issue expenses | 50 | |
| Profits on share dealings | | 13 000 |
| Share capital in R1 shares | | 100 |
| | R24 700 | R24 700 |
| | ====== | ====== |

(1) No investments were purchased before 1 October 19x3 but all the investments on hand at 30 June 19x3 were sold on 2 September 19x3 and realised R10 000. The profit on this transaction is included in the figure for the profits on share dealings (net).
(2) Furniture must be depreciated by R80.
(3) No dividends were received or declared before 1 October 19x3.
(4) A dividend of R3 000 has been proposed.
(5) Write off preliminary and share issue expenses.
(6) The loan accounts are free of interest, but must be repaid on or before 31 October 19x4.

<u>YOU ARE REQUIRED</u>:

To prepare the managerial financial statements of Specious (Proprietary) Limited at 30 June 19x4.
There were no director's emoluments. Ignore taxation.

## D8

On 1 February 19x4 a trustee on behalf of a company to be formed, signed a contract with  A Ires for the acquisition of his business as a going concern from 1 January 19x4.   The company, Xerxes Ltd was incorporated on 1 March 19x4 and was granted a certificate to commence business on 15 March 19x4. On 1 April 19x4 the company ratified the contract.

The balance sheet of A Ires at 31 December 19x3 was as follows:

```
Capital - A Ires                R36 000
                                ======
Furniture and fittings           R6 000
Stock                            27 000
Cash                              3 000
                                R36 000
                                ======
```

The tangible assets were considered to be fairly valued in the books and the purchase price of R54 000 was settled in cash.

The same set of books was used, and  the  net  profit  for  the  year ended 31 December 19x4 was R43 200.

Profits were earned evenly throughout the year.

At 31 December 19x4 the only reserve in the company's balance sheet was a distributable reserve (retained income).

Calculate the cost at which goodwill should be reflected in the company's books.

# D9

Smile entered into a contract dated 28 February 19x4 with a trustee of a company to be formed called Smiley Grin Ltd.  The terms of the contract were that the company would acquire all of the assets and liabilities of Smile's business with effect from 1 January 19x4 for R25 000.   The company was incorporated on  1 March 19x4 and formally ratified the contract on 15 March. It only received its certificate to commence business on 31 March 19x4.

Smile's balance sheet at 31 December 19x3 was as follows:

<u>Capital employed</u>

| | |
|---|---:|
| Smile - capital | R20 000 |

<u>Employment of capital</u>

| | | |
|---|---:|---:|
| Fixed assets | | R5 000 |
|   Motor vehicle at cost | R10 000 | |
|   Accumulated depreciation | 5 000 | |
| Net current assets | | 15 000 |
| Current assets | | |
|   Stock | R6 000 | |
|   Debtors | 4 000 | |
|   Bank | 8 000 | |
| | R18 000 | |
| Current liabilities | | |
|   Creditors | | R3 000 |
| | | R20 000 |

The company continued to use the books of Smile.   The books had not been ruled off during the year and the trial balance at 31 December 19x4  is as follows:

| | | |
|---|---:|---:|
| Share capital | | R10 000 |
| Share premium | | 10 000 |
| Preliminary and share issue expenses | R2 000 | |
| Motor vehicle | 12 000 | |
| Accumulated depreciation | 5 000 | |
| Stock (31 December 19x3) | 6 000 | |
| Purchases | 92 000 | |
| Debtors | 3 000 | |
| Bank | 3 000 | |
| Sales (earned evenly throughout the year) | 120 000 | |
| Directors' emoluments | 12 000 | |
| Other expenses | 12 000 | |
| Goodwill | 3 000 | |
| | R145 000 | R145 000 |

# D9 CONTINUED

Additional information:

1. The purchase consideration was paid in cash.
2. In determining the purchase price the motor vehicle was considered to be worth R7 000.   Its estimated life was not changed.
   All other tangible assets were fairly valued.
3. Depreciation on motor vehicles has always been 20% on cost.
4. A gross profit percentage of 25% was consistently earned throughout the year.
5. The average monthly expenditure (excluding depreciation and directors' emoluments) for the last 3 months was twice the average monthly expenditure for the previous 9 months.
6. No fixed assets have been acquired or sold during the year.


<u>YOU ARE REQUIRED TO</u>:

Basing your answer on the above information you are required to:

(a) Give the entries that were made in the books when the company was formed and the purchase consideration paid.
(b) Give any further entry/ies to close the books at 31 December 19x4 so that they reveal the true facts at that date.

# D10

A Robick and B Oddy were in partnership sharing profits and losses equally.
At 31 December 19x4, their balance sheet was as follows:

CAPITAL EMPLOYED

```
Capital  -  A Robick                              R150 000
         -  B Oddy                                 180 000    R330 000
General reserve                                                120 000
                                                              R450 000
                                                              =======
```

EMPLOYMENT OF CAPITAL

```
Fixed assets                                                  R210 000
   Land and buildings at cost                     R150 000
   Furniture at cost                     R75 000
   Accumulated depreciation              15 000     60 000

Net current assets                                            240 000
   Current assets
      Stock                                       R114 000
      Debtors                                      141 000
      Bank                                          30 000
                                                  R285 000
                                                  =======

   Current liabilities
      Creditors                                    R45 000
                                                   ======
                                                              R450 000
                                                              =======
```

On 15 January 19x5, A Robick, acting as agent for a company to be formed,
entered into an agreement for the purchase of the business of the partnership.
The agreement provided, inter alia, that:

- The purchase price was to be R600 000.
- The effective date of purchase was to be 1 January 19x5.
- Interest at the rate of 18% p.a. was to be paid on the purchase price
  from 1 January 19x5 to the date of payment. Payment was made on 1 April
  19x5.
- All tangible assets were agreed to be worth their book values with the
  exception of land and buildings which were agreed to be worth R225 000.

The company, Health Kicklet (Pty) Ltd, was incorporated on 1 March 19x5.   On
1 April 19x5 the company ratified the contract for the purchase of the
business A Robick and B Oddy and obtained a certificate to commence business.

The stock was not taken on 31 March 19x5, nor was a new set of books opened
for the company.   The following trial balance was extracted at 31 December
19x5:

# D10 CONTINUED

<u>HEALTH KICKLET (PTY) LTD - TRIAL BALANCE AT 31 DECEMBER 19X5</u>

| | | |
|---|---:|---:|
| Accounts payable | | R72 600 |
| Accounts receivable | R86 950 | |
| Advertising | 4 800 | |
| Audit fees | 2 400 | |
| Bank overdraft | | 10 200 |
| Capital - A Robick | | 150 000 |
|     - B Oddy | | 180 000 |
| Directors' fees | 6 300 | |
| Furniture, at cost | 75 000 | |
| General expenses | 12 600 | |
| General reserve | | 120 000 |
| Insurance | 12 000 | |
| Land and buildings, at cost | 200 000 | |
| Payment to partnership | 627 000 | |
| Preliminary expenses | 8 000 | |
| Provisional tax payment | 750 | |
| Provision for depreciation - furniture | | 15 000 |
| Purchases | 675 000 | |
| Receiver of Revenue - taxation owing | | 1 000 |
| Sales | | 900 000 |
| Salaries - managing director | 30 000 | |
|     - staff | 48 000 | |
| Salesmen's commission | 45 000 | |
| Share capital (R1 shares - authorised and issued) | | 500 000 |
| Stock | 114 000 | |
| Taxation | 1 000 | |
| | R1 948 800 | R1 948 800 |

You are provided with the following information:-

1)    Sales for the first four months of the year were:

      January R54 000, February R57 000, March R69 000, April R75 000
      A constant rate of mark-up has been maintained throughout the year.
      Sales comprise gross sales to customers, less returns.
2)    Expenses were incurred as follows:
      .    All the advertising expenses were incurred in a campaign which
           started in July 19x5
      .    The partnership did not have an auditor
      .    There were no changes in staff or salaries since 1 January 19x5.
      .    Depreciation of furniture was to be maintained at the rate of 20%
           per annum on the cost to the partnership.
      .    General expenses were incurred evenly throughout the year
      .    The amount debited to insurance relates to a policy taken out by
           the company covering the period 1 July 19x5 to 30 June 19x6.
      .    There was no change in the rate of commission paid to salesmen.

3)    The cost of stock at 31 December 19x5, using the first in, first out
      method, was calculated at R69 000.  The stock was all merchandise.
4)    Included in preliminary expenses, which are not to be written off, are
      share issue expenses of R3 000.
5)    On 1 September 19x5 the company advanced R150 000 to a director,
       X R Cise enable him to purchase a house.  This amount was repaid by
      Cise  on 28 December 19x5.
6)    Land and buildings consist of office buildings on Erf 5, Eastgate.
      This asset has been mortgaged as security for the company's bank
      overdraft.

<u>YOU ARE REQUIRED TO</u>:

(a)   Calculate the profits to be reported by the company - a detailed income
      statement is <u>NOT</u> required.
(b)   Prepare the balance sheet of Health Kicklet (Pty) Ltd at 31 December
      19x5, together with the accounting policy notes and any other notes you
      consider necessary.

      Show all workings.

# D11

The following set of accounts prepared by an inexperienced bookkeeper are presented to you:

<u>CONCRETE COMPANY LIMITED</u>

<u>INCOME STATEMENT FOR THE YEAR ENDED 28 FEBRUARY 19x2</u>

| | | | |
|---|---|---|---|
| Stock, 1 March 19x1 | R42 000 | Sales | R450 000 |
| Purchases | 162 000 | Stock 28 February 19x2 | 54 000 |
| Depreciation - office equipment | 720 | | |
| Depreciation - motor vehicles | 16 200 | | |
| Directors' fees | 1 800 | | |
| Dividend paid | 30 000 | | |
| General expenses | 14 400 | | |
| Provisional tax payments | 16 380 | | |
| Rent | 25 200 | | |
| Preliminary expenses | 1 000 | | |
| Share issue capital | 2 000 | | |
| Bad debts | 1 800 | | |
| Salaries - staff | 138 000 | | |
| Salary - managing director | 18 000 | | |
| Balance | 34 000 | | |
| | R504 000 | | R504 000 |
| | ======= | | ======= |

<u>BALANCE SHEET AT 28 FEBRUARY 19x2</u>

| | | | Cost | Depre-<br>ciation | |
|---|---|---|---|---|---|
| Share capital | R180 000 | Office equipment | R14 400 | R720 | R13 680 |
| Retained income | 34 500 | Motor vehicles | 90 000 | 16 200 | 73 800 |
| Reserve for bad debts | 1 800 | | R104 400 | R16 920 | 87 480 |
| Creditors | 34 800 | Goodwill | ================= | | 18 000 |
| | | Stock | | | 54 000 |
| | | Debtors | | | 75 540 |
| | | Bank | | | 16 080 |
| | R251 100 | | | | R251 100 |
| | ======= | | | | ======= |

Upon investigation you find the following additional information:

1. The company was incorporated on 1 April 19x1 with an authorised share capital of R180 000 in R1 shares.
   48 000 shares were issued to the public at a premium of 25 cents per share on 1 June 19x1.

2. The company received its certificate to commence business on 15 May 19x1 and on 1 June ratified a contract which had been entered into by an agent on behalf of the company.

# D11 CONTINUED

In terms of this contract the business of J Smith was acquired as a going concern on 1 March 19x1 for R120 000.  The tangible assets were agreed to be fairly valued.  The purchase consideration was settled by the issue of 108 000 R1 shares.

The same set of books (as used by J Smith) was used by the company and the entry by the bookkeeper to record the acquisition of the business and allotments of shares in satisfaction of the purchase consideration was:

```
GOODWILL                        18 000
CAPITAL - J SMITH              102 000
        SHARE CAPITAL                      120 000
```

3.　　The company retained all Smith's employees at the same salaries and appointed a managing director at a salary of R3 000 per month.  At 28 February 19x2 no directors' fees were outstanding.

4.　　All fixed assets, except one delivery truck purchased on 1 June 19x1 for R36 000, were acquired from Mr Smith.

5.　　General expenses were incurred evenly throughout the year and rent has remained constant.  Depreciation has been provided for as follows:

Office furniture at the rate of 5% per annum
Motor vehicles  at the rate of 20% per annum.

6.　　The bad debt provided for was incurred during May 19x1 and the amount involved of R1 800 was placed in a reserve.

7.　　South African normal company taxation payable by the company for he period ended 28 February  19x2 has been accurately estimated at R17 400.

8.　　The preliminary and share issue expenses must be written off.  These are not tax deductible expenses.

9.　　The company paid a dividend of R30 000 on 15 February 19x2.

10.　　Turnover was as follows:

```
March   19x1                    R21 000
April   19x1                     27 000
May     19x1                     24 000
June    19x1 - February 19x2    378 000    R450 000
```

The pricing policy has remained constant throughout the year.


<u>YOU ARE REQUIRED TO</u> :

Redraft the above income statement and the balance sheet, with supporting notes,  to comply with the Companies Act 1973 and generally accepted accounting practice, for presentation to shareholders.

A STATEMENT OF ACCOUNTING POLICIES IS NOT REQUIRED.

# D12

R.E.D. Dust entered into a contract dated 1 August 19x3 with a trustee for a company to be formed entitled Dustbowl Trading Co. Ltd.

In terms of the contract, the company was to acquired Dust's business as a going concern with effect from 1 July 19x3, subject to the adjustment of the values of certain assets appearing in Dust's balance sheet at that date, as follows:

> Stock was to be taken over at R20 000.
> An amount of R1 000 owing by G. Green and included in the debtors' balances was to be written off as bad.

The company was incorporated on 1 September 19x3 with a share capital of 300 000 ordinary shares of R1 each.

On 1 October 19x3 it formally ratified the contract with the vendor and appointed Dust as managing director at a salary of R16 000 per annum.

R.E.D. Dust's balance sheet at 30 June 19x3 was as follows:

### BALANCE SHEET AT 30 JUNE 19x3

| | | | |
|---|---|---|---|
| Capital | R130 000 | Land and buildings | R25 000 |
| Creditors | 15 000 | Motor vehicles | 70 000 |
| Bank | 5 000 | Furniture | 10 000 |
| | | Stock | 30 000 |
| | | Debtors | 15 000 |
| | R150 000 | | R150 000 |

The purchase price was agreed at R129 000 to be settled by the issue as fully paid of 100 000 shares of R1 each and R29 000 in cash. Dust was paid on 15 October 19x3.

The same set of books was used by the company and at 30 June 19x4 the following trial balance was extracted:

### TRIAL BALANCE AT 30 JUNE 19x4

| | | |
|---|---|---|
| Share capital | | R250 000 |
| Goodwill | R10 000 | |
| Stock at 1 July 19x3 | 20 000 | |
| Debtors | 53 550 | |
| Preliminary expenses | 3 250 | |
| Land and buildings at cost | 60 000 | |
| Motor vehicles at cost | 70 000 | |
| Furniture at cost | 10 000 | |
| Purchases | 197 500 | |
| Bank | 55 000 | |
| Salaries - staff | 14 000 | |
| Managing director | 12 000 | |
| Sales | | 250 000 |
| Creditors | | 25 000 |
| Commission - 5% on sales | 12 500 | |
| Other administrative expenses | 7 200 | |
| | R525 000 | R525 000 |

# D12 CONTINUED

(1)   Stock at 30 June 19x4 had cost R47 500.

(2)   The land and buildings consist  of Stand 821 Inisville and the shop
      buildings thereon    taken over from Dust and the adjoining Stand 822
      and the shop buildings thereon  purchased by the Company for R35 000 on
      1 January 19x4.

      Neither property has as yet been transferred.  Transfer duty and costs
      relating to Stand 822 are estimated at R3 750.

(3)   Depreciation on assets is to be provided as follows:

              Land and buildings          2% per annum.
              Motor vehicles             20% per annum.
              Furniture                   5% per annum.

(4)   The preliminary expenses of R3 250, in which are included share issue
      expenses of R2 000, must be written off.

(5)   Turnover during July, August and September 19x3 was R12 000, R14 000
      and R14 000 respectively.

Prepare the company's balance sheet at 30 June 19x4 and the supporting
statements.

# D13

A Archer and B Bower were in partnership sharing profits and losses in the ratio 3 : 2.  At 31 March 19x8 their balance sheet was as follows:

CAPITAL EMPLOYED

```
CAPITAL                                                    R110 000
  Archer                                    R50 000
  Bower                                       60 000
GENERAL RESERVE                                              40 000
                                                           R150 000
                                                           =======

EMPLOYMENT OF CAPITAL
FIXED ASSETS                                                70 000
  Land and buildings at cost                  50 000
  Furniture at cost             R25 000
  Accumulated depreciation        5 000       20 000
NET CURRENT ASSETS                                          80 000
  CURRENT ASSETS
    Stock                                     38 000
    Debtors                                   47 000
    Bank                                      10 000
                                             R95 000
                                             ======

  CURRENT LIABILITIES
    Creditors                                R15 000
                                             ======

                                                           R150 000
                                                           =======
```

On 30 April 19x8 Archer acting as agent for a company to be formed entered into an agreement for the purchase of the business of the partnership from the last balance sheet dated 31 March 19x8.  The agreement provided that:

(i)    The purchase consideration was R 200 000 payable in cash.

(ii)   The purchase price was to be paid one month after the company was incorporated.

(iii)  Interest at the rate of 6% p.a. was to be paid on the purchase price from 1 April 19x8 to the date of payment.

(iv)   All the tangible assets were agreed to be worth their book values with the exception of the land and buildings which were agreed to be worth R85 000.

The company Archbow (Proprietary) Limited was incorporated on 31 May 19x8 with an authorised share capital of 300 000 shares of R1 each.  On 15 June 19x8 the company obtained a certificate to commence business and ratified the contract on 30 June 19x8.

The amount owing to the vendors was paid on due date.

# D13 CONTINUED

The same set of books was used by the company and the following trial balance
was extracted at 31 March 19x9.

| | | |
|---|---:|---:|
| Advertising | R1 800 | |
| Audit fees | 900 | |
| Bank | 35 300 | |
| Capital - Archer | | R50 000 |
|        - Bower | | 60 000 |
| Creditors | | 23 200 |
| Debtors | 116 400 | |
| Delivery expenses on sales | 3 600 | |
| Directors' fees | 2 100 | |
| Furniture at cost | 25 000 | |
| General expenses | 4 200 | |
| General reserve | | 40 000 |
| Insurance | 600 | |
| Land and buildings at cost | 50 000 | |
| Payment to Archer and Bower | 203 000 | |
| Preliminary expenses | 2 000 | |
| Provision for depreciation - furniture | | 5 000 |
| Purchases | 225 000 | |
| Rates | 10 050 | |
| Salaries - managing director | 2 250 | |
|        - staff | 12 000 | |
| Sales | | 320 000 |
| Share capital | | 250 000 |
| Stock 31 March 19x8 | 38 000 | |
| Salesmens' commission | 16 000 | |
| | R748 200 | R748 200 |

<u>NOTES</u>:

1. Stock on hand at 31 March 19x9 amounted to R23 000. Stock is valued using the average cost method.
2. Sales for the first six months of the year were as follows:

   | | | |
   |---|---|---|
   | April R18 000 | June R23 000 | August R35 000 |
   | May R19 000 | July R25 000 | September R40 000 |

3. The partnership never advertised.
4. The books of the partnership had never been audited.
5. There were no changes in staff or salaries since 1 April 19x8.
6. There were no changes in insurance during the year and no insurance had been paid in advance.
7. The monthly rates which had been unaltered for many years were increased by 20% from 1 September 19x8.
8. Depreciation of furniture must be written off at 10% p.a. on the book value at 31 March 19x8.
9. Included in preliminary expenses are share issue expenses of R500.
10. Land and buildings consist of an office block and showroom situated on stand 134 Target Township.

<u>YOU ARE REQUIRED TO</u>:

prepare management accounts of Archbow (Proprietary) Limited at 31 March 19x9.

NOTES TO THE FINANCIAL STATEMENTS ARE NOT REQUIRED.

# D14

On 1 September 19x2 A Spiros sold his business as a going concern to the Balfour Implement Company (Proprietary) Limited, the sale to be retrospective to 1 July 19x2. Spiros did not keep proper books and the following information was all that could be obtained:

1.  Assets and liabilities at 1 September 19x2:

    | | | |
    |---|---|---:|
    | Cash | R | 741 |
    | Debtors | | 3 047 |
    | Vehicles | | 2 400 |
    | Stock | | 2 243 |
    | Prepaid expenses | | 433 |
    | Creditors | | 3 973 |

2.  The capital invested in the business at 1 July 19x2 was R3 990, and Spiros had drawn R300 since that date. No fresh capital had been introduced.

3.  Purchases during the period are stated at R10 855 but it is found that R50 of this was actually a loan to an employee. (This amount had not been included in the assets and liabilities at 1 September 19x2).

4.  Vehicles were valued at R2 460 at 1 July 19x2. No vehicles had been purchased or sold during the period.

5.  Administration expenses paid in cash during the period amounted to R3 233. No amounts were owing to sundry creditors in respect of administration expenses and the sum of R276 had been prepaid on 1 July 19x2.

6.  Stock on hand at 1 July 19x2 was R1 813.

7.  Bad debts amounting to R175 had been written off during the two months.

<u>YOU ARE REQUIRED TO</u>:

1.  Determine a fair purchase price of the business from the above and the following information:-

    (a) The parties agree that the company will take over all assets and liabilities and accept the figures at 1 September 19x2 as being fair.
    (b) Goodwill is valued at R5 000.
    (c) Spiros has agreed to accept R1 000 in lieu of the net profits earned for the two months, and difference between this figure and actual profits to be at the company's risk.

2.  Set out the income statement for the two months.

3.  Set out the journal entry in the company's books giving effect to the acquisition. (Narrations are not required).

The Certificate of Incorporation of the Balfour Implement Company (Proprietary) Limited was dated 1 September 19x2.

# D15

From the following information prepare the balance sheet of Drake Limited at 30 September 19x5 and the supporting accounts.

Fowler Brothers entered into a contract dated 1 November 19x4 with a trustee for a company to be formed and to be called Drake Limited.  In terms of the contract  the company acquired Fowler Brother's business as a going concern as  from  1 October 19x4, at the book value as shown by the balance sheet of the latter, plus goodwill of R6 000.

The company was formed on 1 December 19x4 with a share capital of  R20 000 in shares of R1 each.  On 30 December 19x4 it ratified the contract with Fowler Brothers and on 31 January 19x5 it received its certificate to commence business.

The purchase price was settled in cash by Drake Limited on 22 February 19x5.

Fowlers Brothers' balance sheet at 30 September 19x4 was as follows:

| Capital - A Fowler | R10 000 | | Land and buildings | R5 000 |
|---|---|---|---|---|
| - B Fowler | 6 000 | R16 000 | Furniture | 1 000 |
| Creditors | | 2 000 | Motor lorries | 6 000 |
| Bank | | 1 000 | Stock | 4 000 |
| | | | Debtors | 3 000 |
| | | R19 000 | | R19 000 |
| | | ====== | | ====== |

The same set of books was used and at 30 September 19x5 the following trial balance was extracted:

| | | |
|---|---|---|
| Bank | R6 100 | |
| Commission paid | 1 800 | |
| Creditors | | R2 900 |
| Debtors | 4 500 | |
| Furniture | 1 000 | |
| General expenses | 1 500 | |
| Goodwill | 6 000 | |
| Land and buildings | | 2 000 |
| Motor lorries | 6 000 | |
| Preliminary (R200) and issue (R300) expenses | 500 | |
| Purchases | 24 500 | |
| Rent | 1 800 | |
| Salaries | 7 200 | |
| Sales | | 40 000 |
| Share capital | | 20 000 |
| Stock | 4 000 | |
| | R64 900 | R64 900 |
| | ====== | ====== |

# D15 CONTINUED

<u>NOTES</u>:

1.  Stock at 30 September 19x5 was R4 500.  The land and buildings were sold at 31 March 19x5 and from that date rent was paid.

2.  The credit balance on land and buildings represents the difference between their sale price R7 000 and the price at which they are acquired R5 000.  The articles of Drake Limited provide that any profit on the sale of a fixed asset shall not be available for dividend.

3.  Depreciation is to be provided as follows:

    | | | |
    |---|---|---|
    | Land and buildings | – | 3% per annum |
    | Motor lorries | – | 20% per annum |
    | Furniture | – | 6% per annum |

    On the balances at 30 September 19x4.

4.  Turnover for October 19x4 to January 19x5 was as follows:

    | | |
    |---|---|
    | October | R2 200 |
    | November | 2 200 |
    | December | 2 600 |
    | January | 2 000 |

5.  One half of the preliminary and share issue expenses is to be written off.

6.  Included in salaries is the sum of R3 000 for the salary of the managing director from 1 March 19x5 to 30 September 19x5.

7.  Commission is payable on all sales at 5%.

# D16



Strange and Company Limited was incorporated on 29 August 19x3 with a share capital of R400 000 in ordinary shares of R1 each. On 1 September it ratified a contract to take over, as a going concern, the business of Friend and Foe with effect from 1 July 19x3. Stock was not taken at 1 September 19x3 and the company used the same set of books.

75 000 shares were issued to the vendors in full settlement of the purchase price of the business taken over and 125 000 shares were issued to the public.

From the above information and the following balances extracted from the books of Strange and Company Limited at 30 June 19x4, you are required to prepare the financial statements at 30 June 19x4 in accordance with generally accepted practice and Schedule Four of the Companies Act.

| | | |
|---|---:|---:|
| Advertising | | R5 100 |
| Bank (debit balance) | | 38 700 |
| Customs duty | | 10 000 |
| Delivery outwards | | 6 800 |
| Directors' fees | | 14 000 |
| 10% debentures | | 60 000 |
| Furniture and fixtures at cost | | 13 200 |
| Goodwill at cost | | 15 000 |
| General expenses | | 3 000 |
| Importing charges | | 2 500 |
| Interest on debentures | | 1 500 |
| Land and buildings at cost | | 140 000 |
| Motor vehicles at cost | | 3 000 |
| Purchases | | 200 000 |
| Preliminary expenses (including share issue expenses R1 200) | | 2 000 |
| Railage inwards | | 7 500 |
| Sales | | 340 000 |
| Stock at 1 July 19x3 | | 35 000 |
| Salaries - staff | R36 000 | |
|     managing director | 10 000 | 46 000 |
| Debtors | | 86 500 |
| Creditors | | 29 800 |

# D16 CONTINUED

The following information is provided:

(a)     Stock at 30 June 19x4 had cost R51 000 and is valued using the average
        cost method.
(b)     Preliminary expenses (including share issue expenses) are to be written
        off so a to maintain distributable reserves at the maximum amount.
(c)     Depreciation is to be provided as follows:
                Furniture and fixtures at 5% per annum.
                Motor vehicles at 10% per annum.
(d)     60 unsecured 10% debentures of R1 000 each were issued on 31 December
        19x3 and are repayable on 31 December 19x9.  Interest is due during  on
        31 March and 30 September each year.
(e)     Turnover during July  and August 19x3 was R18 000 and R22 000
        respectively.
(f)     The increase in turnover for the last ten months was due to an
        intensive advertising campaign carried out by the company.  Friend and
        Foe had never advertised.
(g)     The land and buildings consists of a shop on freehold Stand 17 Lakeside
        bought by Friend and Foe for R130 000.
(h)     The taxation charge for the period amounted to R19 600.  No provisional
        payments have been made to the Receiver of Revenue.

# D17

On 1 February 19x9 a trustee, on behalf of a company about to be formed, signed a contract with A for the acquisition of his business as a going concern from 1 January 19x9.   The company X Limited, was incorporated on 1 March 19x9 and was granted a certificate to commence business on 15 March 19x9.   On 1 April 19x9 the company ratified the contract.

A's balance sheet at 31 December 19x8 was as follows:

| Capital | R36 000 | Furniture and fittings | R6 000 |
|---|---|---|---|
| | | Stock | 27 000 |
| | | Cash | 3 000 |
| | R36 000 | | R36 000 |
| | ====== | | ====== |

The tangible assets were considered to be fairly valued in the books and the purchase price of R50 000 was settled in cash.

The company did not open a new set of books and an analysis of the results of operations shows:

1.    The business of the company is seasonal and the turnover in January, November and December was double that achieved in the other months.
2.    A standard gross profit percentage on sale of 33 1/3% was achieved throughout the period.
3.    Selling expenses amounted to 10% of sales.
4.    Administration expenses amounted to R7 500 per month.
5.    Expenses incurred by the company only, R12 500.
6.    Net income for the year R10 900.


<u>YOU ARE REQUIRED TO</u>:

Calculate the value to be placed on GOODWILL in the company's balance sheetat 31 December 19x9.

# D18

P. Pink and B. Blue were in partnership sharing profits and losses in the ratio 3:1.  At 31 December 19x5, their balance sheet was as follows:

| Capital | | | Land and building, at | | |
|---|---|---|---|---|---|
| Pink | R100 000 | | cost | | R100 000 |
| Blue | 120 000 | R220 000 | Furniture, at cost | R50 000 | |
| General reserve | | 80 000 | Accumulated depn. | 10 000 | 40 000 |
| Creditors | | 30 000 | Stock | | 76 000 |
| | | | Debtors | | 94 000 |
| | | | Bank | | 20 000 |
| | | R330 000 | | | R330 000 |
| | | ======= | | | ======= |

On 31 January 19x6, Pink, acting as agent for the company to be formed, entered into an agreement for the purchase of the business of the partnership.

The agreement provided, inter alia, that:

(a)   The purchase price of the business was to be R400 000.
(b)   The effective date of purchase was to be 1 January 19x6 and that any profits earned after that date would accrue to the company.
(c)   The purchase price was to be paid one month after the company was incorporated.
(d)   Interest at the rate of 6% per annum was to be paid on the purchase price from 1 January 19x6 to the date of payment.
(e)   All tangible assets were agreed to be worth their book values with the exception of the land and buildings consisting of a shop on Erf 2900 Benoni, which were agreed to be worth R150 000.

The company, Colours (Proprietary) Limited, was incorporated on 1 April 19x6 with an authorised share capital of R500 000 divided into shares of R1 each. On the same day all the shares were issued at par and for cash.  On 1 April 19x6 the company  also ratified the contract for the purchase of the business of Pink and Blue and obtained a certificate to commence business.

The amount due to the vendors was paid on 30 April 19x6.

Stock was not taken on 31 March 19x6, nor was a new set of books opened for the company.  From the same set of books as used by the partnership, the following trial balance was extracted at 31 December 19x6.

# D18 CONTINUED

<u>COLOURS (PROPRIETARY) LIMITED TRIAL BALANCE AT 31 DECEMBER 19X6</u>

| | | |
|---|---:|---:|
| Advertising | R3 600 | |
| Audit fees | 1 800 | |
| Bank | 70 600 | |
| Bills receivable | 49 400 | |
| Creditors | | R48 400 |
| Capital - Pink | | 100 000 |
| - Blue | | 120 000 |
| Debtors | 138 400 | |
| Delivery expenses | 7 200 | |
| Directors' fees | 4 200 | |
| Furniture, at cost | 50 000 | |
| General expenses | 8 400 | |
| General reserve | | 80 000 |
| Insurance | 1 200 | |
| Land and buildings, at cost | 105 000 | |
| Payment to Pink  and Blue | 408 000 | |
| Share capital | | 500 000 |
| Purchases | 450 000 | |
| Accumulated depreciation - furniture | | 10 000 |
| South African normal taxation | 3 264 | |
| Preliminary expenses | 4 000 | |
| Rent | 20 100 | |
| Sales | | 600 000 |
| Salaries - managing director | 4 500 | |
| - staff | 24 000 | |
| Stock | 76 000 | |
| Taxation owing at 31 December 19x6 | | 1 264 |
| Travellers' commission | 30 000 | |
| | R1 459 664 | R1 459 664 |

<u>NOTES</u>:

(1)   The cost of stock at 31 December 19x6, using the first in, first out method, was calculated at R46 000.  The stock was all finished goods and for every item the net realisable value was more than the cost.

A constant rate of mark-up has been maintained throughout the year

(2)   Sales for the first six month of the year were analysed as follows:

| | | | | | |
|---|---|---|---|---|---|
| January | R36 000 | March | R46 000 | May | R70 000 |
| February | R38 000 | April | R50 000 | June | R80 000 |

(3)   All the advertising expenses were incurred in a campaign which was started in May 19x6.

(4)   There were no changes in staff or salaries since 1 January 19x6.

(5)   The partnership did not have an auditor.

# D18 CONTINUED

(6)   General expenses incurred evenly throughout the year.

(7)   There were no changes in insurance during the year and no insurance has been paid in advance.

(8)   Rent is all in respect of premises in Johannesburg. The monthly rental which has been unaltered for many years was increased by 20% from 1 June 19x6.

(9)   There was no  change in the rate of commission payable to travellers.

(10)  Delivery expenses vary in direct proportion to the money value of sales.

(11)  Depreciation of furniture must still be written off at the rate of 10% per annum on its cost to the partnership.

(12)  Included in preliminary expenses, which are not to be written off, are share issue expenses of R1 500.

(13)  The taxation estimate of R3 264 may be assumed to be correct.

(14)  Sales comprise gross sales to customers, less returns.


<u>YOU ARE REQUIRED</u>:

to prepare the balance sheet of Colours (Proprietary) Limited at 31 December 19x6, together with an income statement for the period ended on that date to comply with Schedule 4 and generally accepted accounting practice.

# D19

E Dundas and A  Banbury were in partnership as Ernest Dundas and Company sharing profits and losses: 20 to 17.

Accounts were prepared and the books closed off at 31 December.  On the following 1 April, Dundas and  Banbury Limited was registered to acquire the business of Ernest Dundas and Company as from 1 January.  Ratification date was 1 May.

The sale and purchase agreement provides:

(a)    Purchase consideration 6 000 preference shares R1 each fully paid.
                              600 ordinary shares R1 each fully paid.

(b)    Vendors to retain cash and debtors and to pay off liabilities.  All tangible assets considered to be fairly valued.

(c)    Each of the partners to subscribe in cash for one-half of the balance of authorised capital, 850 preference shares and 50 ordinary shares.

       The Articles of Association appoint E Dundas and A  Banbury directors with fees of R100 per month each from the date of incorporation.

<u>YOU ARE REQUIRED TO</u>:

assist the directors in the preparation of accounts to 30 September.  You find that the books have been carried on without a break since 1 January, and that no entries arising from the formation of the company or its acquisition of the business have been made.

The trial balance at 30 September was as follows:

| | | |
|---|---:|---:|
| A Banbury - capital at 1 January | | R2 860 |
|        drawings during period | R250 | |
| E Dundas  - capital at 1 January | | 3 000 |
|        drawings during period | 300 | |
| E Dundas and A Banbury for shares | | 900 |
| Buildings | 3 800 | |
| Creditors (R1 500 owing at 1 January having been paid) | 700 | |
| Debtors (R1 000 due at 1 January having been received) | | 950 |
| Formation of company expenses | 150 | |
| Furniture and fittings (balance at 1 January R360) | 460 | |
| Office expenses | 350 | |
| Plant and machinery (balance 1 January R1 200) | 1 500 | |
| Purchases | 2 000 | |
| Sales | 8 200 | |
| Salaries | 400 | |
| Selling expenses | 600 | |
| Stock - 1 January | 500 | |
| Wages | 800 | |
| Bank (balance at bank at 1 January R500) | 3 600 | |
| | R15 660 | R15 660 |

# D19 CONTINUED

The following is additional information:

E Dundas and A  Banbury have agreed between themselves to take preference shares for the amount of their capital at 1 January.

The average of the monthly sales (which are of one commodity at a fixed price) for the first four months was one-half that of the average monthly sales for the  remainder of the period.

The running expenditure each month was constant.

The stock at 30 September is valued at R700.

Plant and machinery is to be depreciated at 5 percent per annum, and furniture and fittings at 10 percent per annum, in  both  cases  on  the  balances  at 1 January.

Preliminary expenses are to be written off.


<u>YOU ARE REQUIRED</u>:

(i)   To prepare the journal entries to put the books in order.

(ii)  To show the shareholdings acquired by the partners.

(iii) To  prepare  the company's  income  statement  and  balance  sheet  at 30 September.


<u>NOTES</u>

1)    Ignore taxation

2)    Work to nearest rand where applicable.

# D20

Mr B Kirk trading as Deal Sales sells specialised cameras to the public.  The
balance sheet of Deal Sales at 1 January 19x9, was as follows:

| | | | | |
|---|---|---|---|---|
| Capital | R23 725 | Land and buildings | | R36 000 |
| 8% Loan | 45 000 | Furniture and fittings | R25 000 | |
| | | Accumulated depreciation | 7 450 | 17 550 |
| Bank overdraft | 11 880 | Stock | | 22 870 |
| Debtors | 4 185 | | | |
| | R80 605 | | | R80 605 |
| | ====== | | | ====== |

1.  On 1 January 19x9 Kirk entered into an agreement with the trustee of a
    company to be formed.    The agreement included the following
    stipulations:

    (a)   The business of B Kirk would be acquired as a going concern with
          effect from 1 January 19x9, subject to the agreement being
          ratified by the company.
    (b)   The tangible assets and liabilities would be acquired at book
          values with the exception of land and buildings which were
          revalued for the purpose of the agreement by a sworn appraiser at
          replacement cost of R47 500.
    (c)   The purchase price was to be settled by the issue of 20 000 R1
          ordinary shares.

2.  The company Deal Sales (Proprietary) Limited was incorporated on 31
    March 19x9 with an authorised share capital of 60 000 R1 ordinary
    shares and 20 000 10% cumulative preference shares of R2 each.   On 31
    March 19x9 the company issued 200 ordinary shares at par to the
    subscribers to the memorandum.

    On 30 April 19x9 the company ratified the agreement, issued the shares
    to B Kirk in terms of the agreement and appointed him as managing
    director at a monthly salary of R1 000 per month, plus travelling
    allowance of R350 per month.

    On 30 June 19x9 the company redeemed the 8% loan by the issue of 20 000
    preference shares to the lender.

3.  The company continued to record its transactions in the journals and
    the ledger previously used by Mr B Kirk.

    A trial balance at 31 December 19x9 was extracted at 31 December 19x9
    and was as follows:

# D20 CONTINUED

<u>TRIAL BALANCE AT 31.12.x9</u>

| | | |
|---|---:|---:|
| Creditors | | R16 000 |
| Debtors | R6 400 | |
| Bank | 2 125 | |
| Furniture and fittings | 25 000 | |
| Land and buildings | 36 000 | |
| Capital - Kirk | 23 725 | |
| Purchases | 59 130 | |
| Stock | 22 870 | |
| Sales | 74 400 | |
| Subscribers to the memo | 200 | |
| cumulated depreciation: | | |
| Furniture and fittings | 7 450 | |
| Loan | 5 000 | |
| Interest | 1 800 | |
| Travelling | 3 800 | |
| Fees - director | 3 800 | |
| Fees - auditor | 350 | |
| Drawings | 100 | |
| Moving expenses | 800 | |
| Investments | 1 300 | |
| Salaries and wages (excluding director) | 3 300 | |
| | R166 775 | R166 775 |
| | ======= | ======= |

No adjustments had been made to record the change of ownership or the issue of the shares, both ordinary and preference.  The cash received from subscribers to the memorandum was credited to "subscribers to the memorandum account".

On 1 March B Kirk withdrew R100 cash for his own private use.

During August 19x9 the company bought 500 shares in Scuppa Limited for R1 200 and 900 shares in Duppa (Proprietary) Limited for R800.  The shares in Scuppa Limited were bought for speculation and half of the shares were sold for R700 on 1 December 19x9.  The directors resolved that the full selling price be credited to the share investment account and that the profit be treated as income only when the balance of the shares were sold.  On 31 December 19x9 Scuppa's shares were quoted on the Johannesburg Stock Exchange at R1,50 each, whilst those of Duppa were valued by the directors at R1,00 each.

5.      On 1 February 19x9 Kirk leased two delivery vans for the business at a total monthly charge of R60 which was debited to travelling expenses. The company continued this leasing arrangement and the following is a summary of the travelling expenses account:

| | |
|---|---:|
| Lease expense for delivery vans | R720 |
| Allowance for travelling paid to Mr Kirk | 2 800 |
| Hotel expenses incurred in August refunded to Mr Kirk | 280 |
| | R3 800 |
| | ===== |

# D20 CONTINUED

6.    The company continued with Kirk's original policy for depreciation of fixed assets which was not to depreciate land and buildings and to depreciate furniture and fittings by 20% per annum using the reducing balance method.

7.    Stock was sold evenly through the year and a consistent mark up was applied throughout except for a few weeks during September and October when a promotion was held.  During the promotion period selling prices were dropped by 10% and sales amounting to R5 400 were earned.

    Stock valued at first-in-first-out cost of R22 000 was on hand at 31 December 19x9.  Stock comprises cameras which the company is certain to sell as there is a great demand for the particular models.

8.    The company incurred an assessed loss for tax purposes for the period ended 31 December 19x9.

9.    On 31 December 19x9 the company finalised the sale of the land and buildings for R50 000.  The company will move to rented premises from 1 January 19y0.  No entry had been made to record this transaction and a cheque for the selling price was only received on 2 January 19y0. The amount paid for expenses represents a deposit of R890 paid to Long Distance Limited who are contracted to transport the furniture, equipment and stock to the new rented premises on 1 January 19y0.  In terms of the company's articles of association profits on the sale of fixed assets are not available for distribution.

10.    Apart from any inferences to the contrary from the above information the revenue and expenses of the business were earned or incurred evenly throughout the year.

11.    The directors decided not to declare any dividends for the period ended 31 December 19x9.


<u>YOU ARE REQUIRED TO</u>:

(a)    Record the necessary journal entries to adjust the ledger account balances as per the trial balance.

(b)    Prepare a detailed income statement for the period ended 31 December 19x9, and a detailed balance sheet at that date for Deal Sales (Proprietary) Limited.

    NOTES TO THE FINANCIAL STATEMENTS ARE NOT REQUIRED.

# D21

A Bernstein (Proprietary) Limited was incorporated on 1 April 19x4 to take over the business of A Bernstein as a going concern with effect from 1 January 19x4.   The purchase consideration was settled in cash.   Stock was not taken at 31 March 19x4 and the same set of books was used.   The same staff were employed at the same salaries as they had been paid before, and the same premises were occupied at the same rent.   Mr Bernstein was employed as managing director by the company at a salary of R1 000 per month.   The turnover for the first three months of the year was R20 000.   The increase in turnover for the last nine months was due to an intensive advertising campaign carried out by the company.   (Mr Bernstein had never advertised.) All sales were made through agents who received 10% commission.

The vendor's agreement was adopted on the date of incorporation.

The following trial balance was extracted at 31 December 19x4:

| | | |
|---|---:|---:|
| Authorised capital in R1 shares | | R100 000 |
| Unissued capital | R51 000 | |
| Stock on hand at 31 December 19x3 | 20 000 | |
| Debtors | | 10 000 |
| Trade creditors | 25 000 | |
| Sales | | 120 000 |
| Goodwill at cost | 15 000 | |
| Purchases | 100 000 | |
| Preliminary expenses | 5 000 | |
| Bank | 9 000 | |
| Advertising | | 6 000 |
| Rent | | 6 000 |
| Agents' commission | 12 000 | |
| Salaries - managing director | | 9 000 |
|        - staff | 16 000 | |
| General expenses | 4 000 | |
| | R254 000 | R254 000 |

Stock at 31 December 19x4 had cost R30 000.

Included in preliminary expenses are share issue expenses of R2 000.

There were three directors, and, according to the articles, each was entitled to fees of R100 per month, but nothing had been paid or provided.

Prepare the company's balance sheet at 31 December 19x4 and supporting statements.

# SECTION E

# COMPANY ACCOUNTING – FINANCIAL STATEMENTS AND DISCLOSURE REQUIREMENTS

# E1

Where should the following items be shown in the financial statements of a limited company:

(a)    preference dividends in arrear?
(b)    discount on debentures issued?
(c)    provision for doubtful debts?
(d)    liability on bills discounted but not matured?
(e)    provision for depreciation of furniture?
(f)    a provision against bills discounted when it is known that the acceptor is insolvent?

# E2

The directors of X (Pty) Ltd are entitled to the following remuneration:

(a)    Fees of R105 per annum per director.
(b)    A commission of 2 1/2% of all dividends paid during any financial year.
(c)    A commission of 4% of the net profit of the company after providing for
       taxation.

You are supplied with the following information:

(1)    There are four directors of the company.
(2)    The issued capital of X (Pty) Ltd is 200 000 shares of 50c each fully
       paid.
(3)    A dividend of 20% was paid during the financial year.
(4)    The net profit of the company before taxation and before providing for
       any directors' remuneration was R60 000.
(5)    Taxation is to be provided at the rate of 40c in the R.

Calculate the total remuneration payable to the directors of X (Pty) Ltd.

## E3

Snow, Tucker, Urwin and Venn are the directors of The Glorious Marmalade Co. Ltd.   They have been on the board for the whole year ended 30 June 19x2. Tucker is the managing director.   The articles of that company provide inter alia:

(1)   Each director is to receive fees of R1 050 per annum.
(2)   The directors are to receive additional remuneration of 2 1/2% of all dividends declared, which remuneration is to be divided equally among the directors.
(3)   The managing director is to receive a commission of 3% of the net profit after charging taxation and the fees mentioned in (1) and (2) above and after charging the commission.

All the authorised capital of the company has been issued.

The capital of the company is as follows:

| | |
|---|---|
| 6% preference share capital | R100 000 |
| Ordinary share capital | R1 000 000 |

The preference share capital is divided into fully paid shares of R1 each.

The ordinary share capital is divided into shares of R1 each.

During the year the preference dividend and ordinary dividends of 10% and 25% were declared.

The net profit for the year ended 30 June 19x2 before charging taxation and before charging any directors' remuneration is R738 560.

The taxation amounts to R284 620.

Draw up a statement showing what amount Tucker will receive.

# E4

On 1 January 19x1 Gamma Limited purchased plant for R200 000.    The company used the reducing balance method of calculating depreciation, the rate of depreciation being 20% per annum.

On 31 December 19x4 the directors decided to change to the straight line method of calculating depreciation in respect of plant retrospectively to 1 January 19x1.  It was agreed that the estimated life of the plant was 8 years and the estimated residual value R20 000.

The following draft income statements had been prepared for the years ended 31 December by the bookkeeper who had not been told of the directors' decision.

|                                              | 19x4      | 19x3      |
|----------------------------------------------|-----------|-----------|
| Turnover                                     | R600 000  | R550 000  |
| Net operating income before depreciation     | 240 000   | 220 000   |
| Depreciation - plant                         | 20 480    | 25 600    |
| Depreciation - other assets                  | 15 000    | 12 000    |
| Net operating income                         | 204 520   | 182 400   |
| Dividend declared                            | 180 000   | 150 000   |
| Retained income for the year                 | 24 520    | 32 400    |
| Retained income at beginning of year         | 48 500    | 16 100    |
| Retained income per balance sheet            | R 73 020  | R 48 500  |

<u>YOU ARE REQUIRED TO</u>:

 (i)   redraft the income statements for publication, AND
(ii)   prepare the relevant notes to the financial statements.

IGNORE TAXATION.

# E5

The directors of a holding company are Archer, Brits, Cross and Denis.
Archer is chairman and Brits is managing director. The directors of its only
subsidiary company are Archer, Cross and Elliott. Cross is chairman and
Elliott is managing director. Farran is secretary of the holding company and
Denis is secretary of the subsidiary.

The following are the fees and other emoluments payable by each company per
annum:

|  | Holding Company | Subsidiary Company |
|---|---|---|
| Each director, except managing director | R500 | R200 |
| Chairman, additional fees | 300 | 200 |
| Chairman, entertainment allowance | 200 | 200 |
| Managing director, salary | 4 000 | 3 000 |
| Secretary, salary | 3 000 | 2 400 |

What notes would you expect would be disclosed in the financial statements of
the holding company to comply with Section 297 of the Companies Act? Prepare
a statement showing how you have arrived at the amounts.

# E6

The executives of Springbok Limited during the financial year ended 30 June 19x5 were:

| | |
|---|---|
| Directors: | A - Chairman |
| | B - Managing director |
| | C |
| | D - Alternate M |
| | |
| Secretary: | M - Alternate to D |
| Sales manager: | E - was appointed alternate director to C on 2 January 19x5 |
| | |
| Production manager: | D |

Alternate directors do not received directors fees.

In 19x1 the company purchased 80% of the shares in Aussie Limited. The executives of this company during the financial year ended 30 June 19x5 were:

| | |
|---|---|
| Directors: | B - Chairman |
| | C - Managing director |
| | D - appointed 1 October 19x4 |
| Secretary: | V |

The fees, allowances, salaries and other payments to which they were entitled for the year ended 30 June 19x5 were as follows:

| | Springbok Limited | Aussie Limited |
|---|---|---|
| Chairman - fees per annum | R1 500 | R1 300 |
| Directors other than the chairman (excluding alternates) fees per annum | 1 200 | 600 |
| Managing director - salary per annum | 12 000 | 10 000 |
| Managing director - entertainment allowance per annum | 1 200 | 600 |
| Secretary - salary per annum | 10 000 | 8 000 |
| Sales manager - salary per annum | 7 000 | - |
| Production manager - salary per annum | 9 000 | - |

Sales manager - non-pensionable commission of 1% of the annual profits after allowing for his commission. This commission is paid in a lump sum at the end of the financial year.

The managing directors, the secretaries and the sales manager each have the free use of a motor car. This privilege is considered to be worth R300 per annum.

The managing directors and all employees of both companies are members of the Lions Pension Fund. They contribute 5% of their salaries and the companies contribute on a R for R basis.

# E6 CONTINUED

S, a former managing director of Springbok Limited, drew a pension of R300 per month from the pension fund during the year ended 30 June 19x5. As a result of inflation, this had become inadequate and was supplemented by payments made by Springbok Limited amounting to R3 000.

The profit of Springbok Limited for the year, before allowing for the commission was R333 300.  Profits are earned evenly throughout the year.

<u>YOU ARE REQUIRED:</u>

To give the information regarding directors' remuneration required to be disclosed in terms of the Companies Act in the financial statements of Springbok Limited for the year ended 30 June 19x5.

On 1 January 19x7 the directors of Phoenix Manufacturers Ltd were O,P,Q and X.
O,P and Q held office throughout the year ended 31 December 19x7.  X who had been managing director of the company retired on 30 June 19x7 and R was elected to the board and appointed managing director in his place on 1 July 19x7.

O is the chairman and A,B and C were alternates to O,P and Q throughout the year.  R until his appointment as managing director had been an alternate to X.

The following fees and emoluments are paid by the company:

| | |
|---|---|
| Each director (except alternates who do not receive fees) | R4 000 per annum |
| Chairman - additional fee | 1 500 " |
| Managing director - salary | 16 000 " |
| Managing director - entertainment allowance | 1 200 " |

In addition the managing director has the free use of a company car (see note (4) below).

Details of emoluments paid to alternate directors are as follows:

| | | |
|---|---|---|
| A | Data processing manager - salary | R12 000 per annum |
| B | Production manager - salary | 11 000 " |
| C | Marketing manager - salary | 10 000 " |
| R | Financial manager prior to his appointment as managing director - salary | 14 000 " |

In addition all the above had the free use of a company car (see note (4) below).

<u>Additional information:</u>

1.  X who had been managing director until his retirement on 30 June 19x7 at a salary of R16 000 per annum, receives a pension of R5 000 per annum from the company's pension fund which is supplemented at the rate of R3 000 per annum by the company.

2.  All employees including salaried directors contribute 2 1/2% of their basic salaries to a recognised pension fund and the company contributes 5% on their behalf.

3.  During May 19x7, O the chairman, went on an overseas business trip on behalf of the company and was advanced an amount of R2 500.  Upon his return on 30 May 19x7 he presented vouchers for R2 300 and repaid R200 to the company.

4.  The benefit  of the free use of a company car is estimated at R50 per month.

# E7 CONTINUED

5.      B, the production manager was granted a loan of R15 000 during 19x6 to enable him to purchase a house near the company's factory.  The balance of the loan on 1 January 19x7 was R12 000 on which interest totalling R600 was charged during the year.  B repaid an amount of R3 000 during the year ended 31 December 19x7.

6.      Upon examination of the financial statements for the year ended 31 December 19x7 you find that directors emoluments have not been separately disclosed in the income statement and that the amount owing by B on loan account had been added to the debtors balance shown in the balance sheet.

<u>YOU ARE REQUIRED TO</u>:


To show how the above items should be disclosed by way of note to the financial statements of Phoenix Manufacturers Ltd for the year ended 31 December 19x7.

**E8**

(a)  The directors of X (Pty) Limited are entitled to the following
     remuneration:-

     (a)   Fees of R105 per annum director

     (b)   A commission of 2 1/2% of all dividends paid during any financial
           year.

     (c)   A commission of 4% of the net profit after commission of the
           company and after providing for taxation.

     Commission are shared equally between the directors.

     You are supplied with the following information :-

     (1)   The are four directors of the company.
     (2)   The issued capital of X (Pty) Limited is 200 000 shares of 50c
           each fully paid.
     (3)   A dividend of 20 cents per share was paid during the financial
           year.
     (4)   The profit of the company before taxation and before providing
           for any directors' remuneration was R60 000.
     (5)   Taxation is to be provided at the rate of 40c in the R.

     SHOW HOW DIRECTORS' REMUNERATION WOULD BE SHOWN IN THE NOTES TO THE
     FINANCIAL STATEMENTS.

(b)  The directors of ABC Limited throughout the year ended 30 June 19x8
     were:

     P managing director, Q chairman, R financial director, S production
     manager.

     T the company secretary was appointed director on 1 January 19x8, and
     U the factory manager was appointed alternate to S during the latter's
     absence on company business during the last quarter of the financial
     year.

     The following salaries were paid during the year ended 30 June 19x8:
     P R15 000; R R12 000; S R12 000; T R12 000;  U R11 000.

     The company deducts pension fund contributions at the rate of 5% of
     basic pay and contributes on a rand for rand basis when paying over the
     deductions to the pension fund.

     The chairman and managing director each received an entertainment
     allowance of R1 200 during the year.  Each senior employee had the use
     of a company car, the benefit of which is assessed at R400 per annum.
     During the absence of S his car was used on company business.

     SHOW HOW THE DIRECTORS' REMUNERATION WOULD BE DISCLOSED BY WAY OF NOTE
     TO THE FINANCIAL STATEMENTS FOR THE YEAR ENDED 30 JUNE 19x8.

**E9**

Throughout the year ended 31 December 19x1 the directors of a company were,
A, B, C and D.  A was chairman and B was managing director.  E was secretary.
On 1 October 19x1 E was appointed as C's alternate.

At the begining of 19x1 the directors of a second company were Y, Z, B and C.
Y was chairman and Z managing director.  X was secretary.  On 1 July 19x1 the
second company became the first company's subsidiary.  Y resigned from the
board and E was appointed to take his place as chairman.

The fees (payable quarterly) and salaries (payable monthly) during 19x1 were
as follows:-

|  | First company | Second company |
|---|---|---|
| Every director, except alternates, fees | R    500 per annum | R 400 per annum |
| Chairman, additional fees | 500  "    " | 400  "    " |
| Managing director, salary | 20 000  "    " | 15 000  "    " |
| Secretary, salary | 8 000  "    " | 7 500  "    " |

Both managing directors were entitled to use a company car for private
purposes, a privilege considered to be worth R1 000 per annum.

<u>YOU ARE REQUIRED TO GIVE:</u>

The information regarding directors' remuneration which would appear in the
first company's annual financial statements for the year ended 31 December
19x1.

# E10

H Limited has an 80% interest in S Limited and during the year subscribed for and was allotted R100 000 debentures in X Limited on condition that it would have the right to nominate one person to the board of X Limited.

<u>H Limited</u>  Directors and managers during the year ended 31 December 19x8:-

- A -  director for whole year, appointed chairman in place of F on 1 July 19x8
- B -  director for whole year, appointed managing director in place of F on 1 July 19x8
- C -  director throughout year
- D -  director throughout year
- E -  appointed alternate to A from 1 July 19x8
- F -  chairman and managing director until his retirement on 30 June 19x8
- G -  secretary for whole year

Emoluments -
- Fees  - each director receives fees of R500 per quarter
- Additional fee - chairman receives R200 additional fee per quarter
- Entertainment allowance - each director receives R100 per quarter
- Salaries - managing director R30 000 per annum; secretary R15 000 per annum
- Honorarium - E was voted an honorarium of R100 for his services as alternate to A
- Pension contributions - 10% is deducted from basic salaries and the company contributes on a rand for rand basis

When F retired he drew a lump sum of R25 000 from the pension fund and receives from that fund a pension of R200 per month.  The company has augmented his pension to the extent of R150 per month since 1 July 19x8 as it was considered that R200 per month was inadequate.

F also received from Z Limited, which bought his entire shareholding in H Limited and thereby gained control that company, a sum of R450 000.  It was a condition of the sale of shares that F would retire earlier than his contract of employment stipulated and that Z Limited would compensate him for doing so.

<u>S Limited</u>  Directors and managers during year ended 31 December 19x8:-

- A -  directors for whole year and managing director from 1 July 19x8
- B -  director and secretary for whole year
- C -  director for whole year and chairman from 1 July 19x8
- D -  director for whole year
- F -  chairman and managing director until his retirement on 30 June 19x9

Emoluments -
- Fees - each director receives R100 per quarter
- Additional fee - chairman receives  R500 per annum
- Salaries - managing director R20 000 per annum; secretary R10 000 per annum
- Pension - there is no pension fund

<u>YOU ARE REQUIRED TO</u>:

To show how directors' remuneration would be disclosed in the following annual financial statements for the year ended 31 December 19x8.

(1)    S LIMITED                          161

(2)    H LIMITED

(3)    H LIMITED and its subsidiary company.

# E11

The directors of Unsure Limited at 1 July 19x5 were A, B, C and D.  A was chairman of the board, B was managing director, C was sales manager in Johannesburg, D was manager in Cape Town, E was sales manager in Cape Town.

Each director is entitled to a fee of R100 per quarter.

The chairman received an additional fee of R500 per annum and an entertainment allowance of R300 per annum.

Amounts paid to executives are as follows

| | |
|---|---|
| Managing director's salary | R10 000 per annum |
| Manager Cape Town's salary | 9 000 per annum |
| Sales manager Johannesburg's salary | 8 000 per annum |
| Sales manager Cape Town's salary | 5 000 per annum |

The sales manager Cape Town is also entitled to a commission of 2% of the profits of the Cape Town branch after allowing for his commission.

The chairman contributes R300 per annum and the executives contributes 5% of their salaries to a pension fund.  The company contributes to the pension fund on a R for R basis.

D and E are each allowed R125 per meeting to attend board meetings.  Five meetings were held during the financial year ended 30 June 19x6.

C was asked, on the termination of his contract with the company on 31 March 19x6 to retire but nevertheless was paid R10 000 in respect of compensation for loss of office.

In addition, in terms of the constitution of the pension fund, C drew a lump sum of R3 000 and became entitled to R200 per month pension.

Profits for the year before allowing for commission were:

Johannesburg        R127 500            Cape Town R76 500


<u>YOU ARE REQUIRED TO</u>:

To show how the above would be shown in the financial statements of Unsure Limited for the year ended 30 June 19x6.

# E12

The directors of a holding company are Connors, McEnroe, Lendl and Borg. Connors is chairman and McEnroe is managing director. The directors of its only subsidiary are Connors, Lendl and Vilas. Lendl is chairman and Vilas is managing director. Kriek is secretary of the holding company and Borg is secretary of the subsidiary.

The following are the fees and other emoluments payable by each company per annum:

|  | Holding Company | Subsidiary Company |
|---|---|---|
| Each director, fees | R1 000 | R400 |
| Chairman, additional fees | 600 | 400 |
| Chairman, entertainment allowance | 400 | 400 |
| Managing director, salary | 8 000 | 6 000 |
| Secretary, salary | 6 000 | 4 800 |

The managing directors of each company had the free use of a motor car. This privilege is considered to be worth R700 per annum.

The holding company also pays a pension of R200 per month to an ex-director Mr Laver, since the amount he receives from the pension fund (R100 per month) was felt to be insufficient. Mr Laver had been the managing director when he was employed by the company.

All the above persons have held their positions during the whole of the financial year.


<u>REQUIRED</u>:

What notes would you expect would be disclosed in the financial statements of the holding company to comply with Section 297 of the Companies Act (i.e. directors' remuneration)? Prepare a statement showing how you have arrived at the amounts.

# E13

The Happy-Go-Lucky Company Limited had the following share capital for the full year ended 31 December 19x0:

```
SHARE CAPITAL
   AUTHORISED AND ISSUED
      200 000 ordinary shares of R2 each                          R400 000
      100 000 10% non-cumulative preference shares of R1 each       100 000
       10 000 6% cumulative preference shares of R10 each           100 000
                                                                    R600 000
                                                                    =======
```

(1)   At 30 June 19x0 the directors were of the opinion that the company was going to achieve budgeted profits for the year, therefore they declared an interim dividend of 5% on the non- cumulative preference shares and 3% on the cumulative preference shares.

(2)   However, at year end the expected profits did not materialise and the directors resolved not to declare any final dividends.

(3)   The net income for the year after tax and outside shareholders' interests (but before taking account of an extraordinary loss of R40 000) was R50 000.


<u>YOU ARE REQUIRED TO</u>:

Calculate the earnings per share for the year.

# E14

<u>PART A</u>

Statement AC103 "Extraordinary items and prior year adjustments" and statement AC104 "Earnings per share" were published on the same date.


<u>YOU ARE REQUIRED TO</u>:

(a)   List the objectives behind each statement

(b)   Comment on the inter-relationship of the two statements.

<u>PART B</u>

The following information was extracted from the income statement and notes to the financial statements of a listed company whose financial year ended on 30 June 19x3:

|  | <u>R000's</u> |
|---|---:|
| Operating profit | R10 368 |
| Taxation | <u>3 670</u> |
|   SA Normal tax - current charge | 3 739 |
|                 - overprovision in prior year | <u>(69)</u> |
| Non trading losses and provisions | 1 592 |
|   Provision for losses in subsidiaries | 104 |
|   Loss on disposal of subsidiaries | 1 548 |
|   Net profit on disposal of properties | <u>(60)</u> |
| Outside shareholders' interest | 1 019 |
| Extraordinary items | |
|   Provision for loss on nationalisation | |
|   and confiscation of group assets | 447 |
| Preference dividends | <u>200</u> |
|   Payment of arrear dividends for 19x1, 19x2 | 160 |
|   Payment of portion of dividend for | <u>40</u> |

| Share capital | <u>R000's</u> |
|---|---:|
|   Issued | |
|     800 000 5% cumulative preference shares of R2 each | 1 600 |
|     22 500 000 ordinary shares of 50c each | 11 250 |

There were no changes in the issued share capital during the year.


<u>YOU ARE REQUIRED TO</u>:

(a)   Calculate earnings per share for the year ended 30 June 19x3.

(b)   Justify (give reasons for) your treatment in the above calculations of

        (i)    Taxation
        (ii)   Outside shareholders
        (iii)  Preference dividends
        (iv)   Non trading losses
        (v)    Extraordinary items

# E15

<u>COMPANY'S AUTHORISED SHARE CAPITAL</u>

| | |
|---|---:|
| 500 000 ordinary shares of no par value | - |
| 10 000 preference share of R10 each | R100 000 |
| | ======= |

<u>ISSUED SHARE CAPITAL</u>     <u>31/12/x8</u>

| | |
|---|---:|
| 300 000 ordinary shares of no par value - stated capital account | R405 000 |
| 5 400 preference shares of R10 each | 54 000 |

The preference shares are redeemable at par on 1 July 19x9.

| <u>EXTRACT FROM INCOME STATEMENT</u> | <u>31/12/x9</u> | <u>31/12/x8</u> |
|---|---:|---:|
| Net income before tax | 105 500 | 80 000 |
| Taxation | 40 200 | 32 000 |
| Preference dividends paid | ? | 5 400 |
| Ordinary dividend paid - 31 December | 20 000 | 15 000 |

<u>NOTES</u>

During the year the company redeemed the preference shares out of the proceeds of a fresh issue of shares of no par value to the public at the lowest price possible without the legal requirement of a special resolution.

The issue was fully subscribed and allotment took place on 1 July 19x9.

CALCULATE EARNINGS AND DIVIDENDS PER SHARE FOR 19x8
                                      FOR 19x9

# E16

The following information was extracted from the books of A Company Limited.

| | |
|---|---:|
| Net income per the income statement (before tax and dividends) for the year ended 28 February 19x5 | R1 202 500 |
| S A normal tax payable for the year to 28 February 19x5 | 400 000 |
| Preference dividend paid 28 February 19x5 | 15 000 |
| Ordinary dividend proposed | 30 000 |
| 10% preference shares of R1 each in issue at 1 March 19x4 | 150 000 |
| Ordinary shares of R1 each in issue at 1 March 19x4 | 1 000 000 |
| Ordinary shares of R1 each issued on 30 November 19x4 | 200 000 |

<u>YOU ARE REQUIRED TO</u>:

calculate the earnings and dividends per share for the year ended 28 February 19x5.

# E17

A company's income statement for the year ended 31 December 19x9 was prepared
as follows:

```
NET OPERATING INCOME                                              R550 000
DEBENTURE INTEREST                                                  20 000
NET INCOME BEFORE TAXATION                                         530 000
TAXATION                                                           219 000
NET INCOME BEFORE EXTRAORDINARY ITEM                              311 000
EXTRAORDINARY ITEM                                                 54 000
NET INCOME                                                        365 000
TRANSFER TO NON-DISTRIBUTABLE RESERVE                              30 000
                                                                 335 000

DIVIDENDS
  Ordinary                                  R100 000
  Preference                                   6 000             106 000
RETAINED INCOME FOR THE YEAR                                     229 000
RETAINED INCOME AT 31 DECEMBER 19x8                              72 000
PRIOR YEAR ADJUSTMENT                                             2 000
RETAINED INCOME PER BALANCE SHEET                               R303 000
                                                               =======
```

The issued share capital on 1 January 19x9 was -

    300 000 ordinary shares of R1 each
     60 000 10% preference shares of R1 each

On 1 April 19x9 a further 120 000 ordinary shares of R1 each were issued for
cash at a premium of 50 cents per share.

On 1 October 19x9 there was a capitalisation issue of one new ordinary share
for every three ordinary shares held.

<u>CALCULATE</u>:

The earnings and dividends per share for the year ended 31 December 19x9.

# E18

An unqualified accountant has prepared the following calculation for earnings per share:

(1)    A company's shareholders' interest at December 31, was:

|  | 19x1<br>R'000 | 19x0<br>R'000 |
|---|---|---|
| Share capital ordinary shares of R1 each | 9 000 | 1 000 |
| Share premium | 14 000 | - |
| Reserves | 12 000 | 10 000 |
|  | 35 000 | 11 000 |

(2)    Earnings     4 500     2 000

(3)    Extraordinary item     (500)     -

(4)    Dividends - declared 31 December     2 000     1 000

(5)    On June 30, 19x1 the company issued 2 000 000 shares at a premium of R10 per share to acquire a business enterprise.

(6)    On September 30, 19x1 the company had a capitalisation issued of 6 000 000 shares out of the share premium.

The earnings per share was calculated as follows:

|  | 19x1<br>R'000 | 19x0<br>R'000 |
|---|---|---|
| Earnings | 4 500 | 2 000 |
| Original shares | 1 000 | 1 000 |
| New issue:  50% of 2 000 000 | 1 000 | - |
| Capitalisation issue | 6 000 | 3 000 |
|  | 8 000 | 4 000 |
| Earnings per share | 56,3 cents | 50,0 cents |

## YOU ARE REQUIRED TO:

1)    State whether the way in which earnings per share has been calculated is correct.

2)    Give reasons for your answer supported by calculations if you believe the workings were not justifiable.

3)    Give the disclosure of EARNINGS PER SHARE and DIVIDENDS PER SHARE in the published financial statements for the year ended 31 December 19x1 based on your assessment of the facts presented.

# E19

The following is the published income statement of X Limited for the year ended 28 February 19x3:

|                                                                              | 19x3     | 19x2     |
|------------------------------------------------------------------------------|---------:|---------:|
| Trading profit for the year before allowing for the items disclosed separately below | R250 000 | R100 000 |
| Depreciation                                                                 | 20 000   | 10 000   |
| Directors' emoluments                                                        | 10 000   | 10 000   |
|                                                                              | 220 000  | 80 000   |
| Commission received                                                          | 30 000   | -        |
|                                                                              | 250 000  | 80 000   |
| Taxation                                                                     | 120 000  | 35 000   |
|                                                                              | 130 000  | 45 000   |
| Retained income at beginning of year                                         | 55 000   | 35 000   |
|                                                                              | 185 000  | 80 000   |
| Transfer to general reserve                                                  | 50 000   | -        |
| Preference dividend                                                          | 25 000   | 25 000   |
| Ordinary dividend                                                            | 50 000   | -        |
| Retained income per balance sheet                                            | R60 000  | R55 000  |

At 1 March 19x1 the capital of the company was 500 000 five per cent preference shares of R1 each and 1 000 000 ordinary shares of R1 each. On 1 December 19x2 the company issued a further 1 000 000 ordinary shares to existing ordinary shareholders at par for cash. In December 19x2 the rate of commission received from an overseas principal was increased from 10% to 15% retrospectively from 1 October 19x0. Of the R30 000 shown in the income statement, R24 000 is calculated on the relevant turnover for the year ended 29 February 19x2 and R6 000 on that for the previous financial year.

Tax rates were 40c in 19x2 and 41c in 19x3.

The ordinary dividend was declated on 31 December 19x3.

<u>YOU ARE REQUIRED TO:</u>

to calculate the earnings and dividends per ordinary share, correct to one decimal place of a cent, for the years ended 28 February 19x3 and 29 February 19x2 as they would be shown in the accounts for the year ended 28 February 19x3.

# E20

1.   A Limited's income statement at 31 March 19x9 was as follows:

| | |
|---|---:|
| Net operating income | R279 810 |
| Taxation | 155 644 |
| | 124 166 |
| Attributable to outside shareholders | 13 746 |
| Net income before extraordinary item | 110 420 |
| Extraordinary item | 40 000 |
| Net income after extraordinary item | 150 420 |
| Preference dividend | 15 000 |
| | 135 420 |
| Ordinary dividend | 72 000 |
| Retained income for the year | 63 420 |
| Retained income at 31 March 19x8 | 84 716 |
| Retained income per balance sheet | 148 136 |

The issued share capital of A Limited at 1 April 19x8 was as follows:

600 000 ordinary shares of 50c each
150 000 10% preference shares of R1 each.

(a)   The issued share capital had not changed during the year.

(b)   On 1 October 19x8  a capitalisation issue of 1 share for every 5 shares
held was made.

(c)   On 30 June 19x8 a fresh issue was made to the public to take up 120 000
shares at R1,00 each.   The issue was underwritten and the shares were
allotted on 31 August 19x8.

(d)   The ordinary dividend was paid on 31 March 19x9.


<u>YOU ARE REQUIRED TO CALCULATE IN RESPECT OF EACH OF THE ABOVE</u>

the earnings and dividends per share for the year ended 31 March 19x9

    (a)   .................... cents

    (b)   ................... cents

    (c)   ................... cents

Give the basis of calculation in each instance.

# E21

WAS Limited, a company listed on the JSE, is about to finalise its annual financial statements for the year ended 30 June 19x5.   The company wishes to maximise its earnings per share figure within the framework of codified GAAP.

Net income after tax had provisionally been computed at R1 435 000.   Tax had been calculated at 50 cents in the rand.   On investigation you determine the following:

(1)     Included in net income is a surplus of R100 000 on the sale of the company's only building.   This building was disposed of as a result of the expropriation of the land by the government.   This profit is not taxable.

(2)     The value of closing stock includes insurance costs on goods-in-transit, covering the period from the date of shipment of the stock to the date of receipt, of R4 200.

(3)     The company had an approved claim of R100 000 on YMK (Proprietary) Limited, a trade debtor in liquidation.   Three weeks subsequent to the year end notification was received from the liquidator that a declaration of 30 cents in the Rand would be made.   Previously it had been thought that a declaration of 50 cents in the Rand was likely and accordingly only R50 000 of the claim had been written off as bad.

Issued share capital at 30 June 19x4 was 1 000 000 ordinary shares of R1 each. On 2 January 19x5 the company issued a further 200 000 shares at R1,20 each. On 31 March 19x5 a capitalisation issue of 1 share for every 2 held was made.

Net income after tax for 19x4 was R1 250 000.


<u>YOU ARE REQUIRED TO</u>:

Compute the earnings per share for disclosure in the 19x5 financial statements in accordance with AC104 for the years ended 30 June 19x4 and 19x5.

The note to be included in the financial statements must also be given.

SHOW YOUR WORKINGS IN DETAIL.

## E22

Chipp Company Ltd had an authorised and issued share capital of 500 000 ordinary shares on 1 January 19x1.

On 1 March 19x1 it increased its authorised share capital to 2 500 000 ordinary shares by a special resolution at the annual general meeting. By a second special resolution 20 000 shares were set aside for the executive share option plan.

On 1 May 19x1 the executives exercised their options to acquire the 20 000 shares at R2 per share. The shares were duly issued. One executive immediately disposed of 1 500 shares.

On 1 October 19x1 Chipp Company Ltd declared a 4 for 1 share split. All the old share certificates were submitted to the transfer secretaries and new certificates were issued.

You are required to determine the number of shares in issue for purposes of the earnings per share calculation for :

1.      The year ended 31 December 19x1

2.      The adjusted EPS calculation for the year ended 31 December 19x0, assuming that 500 000 ordinary shares had been in issue for the whole of 19x0.

# E23

Throughout the year ended 31 December 19x1 the issued and fully paid capital of a company consisted of 400 000 ordinary shares and 200 000 eight percent preference shares, all of R1 each.   Dividends on both classes are paid in July and January to shareholders registered on 30 June and 31 December respectively.   On 31 January 19x2 the company utilised its distributable reserves to make a capitalisation issue of one fully paid ordinary share for every four ordinary shares held.   On 1 July 19x2 it acquired the whole share capital of a company and, in settlement of the purchase price, it issued as fully paid 100 000 ordinary shares and 50 000 eight percent preference shares. As the negotiations to acquire the shares had been completed by 31 March 19x2, the income of the new subsidiary company after this date was brought into the consolidated income statement for the year ended 31 December 19x2.

The following is an extract from the consolidated income statements which were issued to shareholders for the years ended 31 December:

|  | 19x1 | | 19x2 | |
|---|---|---|---|---|
| Net income, before taking into account the items shown separately below | R150 000 | | R177 700 | |
| Interest on overdraft | R1 000 | | R1 200 | |
| Depreciation of fixed assets | 23 000 | 24 000 | 26 500 | 27 700 |
| Net income before tax | | 126 000 | | 150 000 |
| SA normal tax | | 52 500 | | 62 000 |
| Net income after tax | | 73 500 | | 88 000 |
| Dividends declared to shareholders | | | | |
| registered on 30 June | | | | |
| preference | 8 000 | | 8 000 | |
| ordinary | 8 000 | | 10 000 | |
| registered on 31 December | | | | |
| preference | 8 000 | | 10 000 | |
| ordinary | 8 000 | 32 000 | 15 000 | 43 000 |
| Retained income for the year | | R41 500 | | R45 000 |

<u>YOU ARE REQUIRED TO</u>:

prepare a statement of earnings and dividends per ordinary share as it should appear in the financial statements for the year ended 31 December 19x2 in terms of statement AC104.   Comparative figures must be included.

**E24**

The following information relates to PET Limited, a manufacturing company, for
the years ended 31 December 19x9 and 19x8.

|                                              | 19x9      | 19x8      |
|----------------------------------------------|-----------|-----------|
|                                              | (R'000s)  | (R'000s)  |
| Ordinary share capital (R1 shares)           | 500       | 400       |
| Preference share capital (R1 shares)         | 100       | 100       |
| Net income before interest and taxation      | 190       | 125       |
| Interest paid on long-term borrowings        | 20        | 20        |
| Preference dividends paid                    | 10        | 10        |
| Ordinary dividends paid 31 December          | 40        | 30        |
| Rate of taxation                             | 50%       | 40%       |

<u>NOTES</u>:

1. There are no arrears on interest paid or preference dividends.
2. The share issue took place on 1 July 19x9.   There had been no other
   share issue since incorporation.
3. The net income of the company corresponds with its taxable income.

<u>YOU ARE REQUIRED TO</u>:

calculate the earnings and dividends per share for 19x9 and 19x8, and show how
this information should be presented in the financial statements of PET
Limited.

BAT Limited was formed during 19x7 with an authorised share capital of R2 500 000 as follows:

| | |
|---|---|
| Ordinary shares of 50c each | R2 000 000 |
| 10% preference shares of R1 each | 500 000 |
| | R2 500 000 |
| | ========= |

The issued share capital of BAT Limited was:

| | |
|---|---|
| Ordinary shares of 50c each | R1 000 000 |
| 10% preference shares of R1 each | 500 000 |
| | R1 500 000 |
| | ========= |

During the financial year ended 31 December 19x9 the company carried out the following:

(a)   On 31 March 19x9 it made a rights issue of one ordinary share of 50c each for each two ordinary shares previously held;  and
(b)   On 30 June 19x9 it made a capitalisation issue from its distributable reserves of one ordinary share of 50c each for every three ordinary shares previously held.

<u>NOTE</u>:

All shares were taken up.

The after taxation net income of the company amounted to R261 250 for 19x9 and R200 000 for 19x8.

Preference dividends are paid on 30 June and 31 December in each year.   The dividends paid on the ordinary shares in both 19x9 and 19x8 were as follows:

1.   An interim dividend of 5% paid in May;  and
2.   A final dividend of 10% paid in December.

<u>YOU ARE REQUIRED TO</u>:

calculate the earnings and dividends per share and give the presentation of this item in the income statement of BAT Limited for 19x9, giving the comparative figures for 19x8.

Mac Stores Limited is a company whose main business is that of retailing appliances.

The following information was extracted from its balance sheet at 28 February 19x1 and its draft balance sheet at 28 February 19x2:

|                                              | 19x1    |          | 19x2    |          |
|----------------------------------------------|---------|----------|---------|----------|
| Bank                                         | R15 000 |          | R32 000 |          |
| Furniture and equipment, at cost             |         |          |         |          |
|   less depreciation                | 8 000   |          | 8 200   |          |
| Land and buildings, at cost                  | 112 609 |          | 112 609 |          |
| Listed investments, at cost                  | 8 000   |          | -       |          |
| Loan portion of taxation                     | 1 609   |          | 2 009   |          |
| Long term loans                              |         | R75 000  |         | R90 000  |
| Retained income                              |         | 32 115   |         | 32 915   |
| Share capital in R1 shares                   |         | 100 000  |         | 135 000  |
| Share premium                                |         |          |         | 25 000   |
| Six percent convertible debentures           |         | 50 000   |         |          |
| Net current assets (other)                   | 111 897 |          | 128 097 |          |
|                                              | R257 115 | R257 115 | R282 915 | R282 915 |

The following information appeared on the draft income statement for the year ended 28 February 19x2.

| | |
|---|---:|
| Net income after allowing for interest paid (R10 000), depreciation, loss on sale of furniture and equipment and normal tax | R5 626 |
| Profit on sale of listed investments, net of normal tax | 174 |
| | 5 800 |
| Retained income at 28 February 19x1 | 32 115 |
| | 37 915 |
| Capitalisation issue of 5 shares for every 100 shares held | 5 000 |
| Retained income at 28 February 19x2 | R32 915 |

The following are summaries of the furniture and equipment and accumulated depreciation accounts:

<u>FURNITURE AND EQUIPMENT</u>

| | | | |
|---|---:|---|---:|
| Balance at 28 February 19x1 | R10 610 | Debtors | R2 000 |
| Creditors | 4 020 | Accumulated depreciation | 409 |
| | | Loss on sale | 315 |
| | | Balance at 28 February 19x2 | 11 960 |
| | R14 630 | | R14 630 |

# E26 CONTINUED

<u>ACCUMULATED DEPRECIATION</u>

| | | | |
|---|---|---|---|
| Furniture and equipment | R409 | Balance at 28 February 19x1 | R2 610 |
| Balance at 28 February 19x2 | 3 706 | Depreciation | 1 505 |
| | R4 115 | | R4 115 |
| | ===== | | ===== |

<u>REQUIRED</u>:

1.    The profit on the sale of listed investments has been treated in the draft accounts as an extraordinary item.

      Do you agree with this treatment?

      Give reasons for your argument.

2.    Show how taxation would appear in the notes to the annual financial statements for the year ended 28 February 19x2 in support of the extract of the income statement.

3.    Prepare a cash flow statement for the year ended 28 February 19x2.

Assume a tax rate of 42%.

# E27

The following draft accounting policy notes have been prepared for inclusion in your client's annual financial statements.

ACCOUNTING POLICIES

1.    Stock is valued at the lower of cost and net realisable value.

2.    Fixed assets are depreciated on bases appropriate to reduce costs to estimated residual values over their useful lives.

3.    Turnover comprises sales to customers and other revenue.

The following matters came to your notice.

1.    The company is a manufacturing concern which employs  a computerised perpetual inventory costing system based on a program which charges out the oldest stock first.  This program was introduced 4 years ago and is running smoothly.  For costing and control purposes the variable costing system is used but, for financial reporting, to achieve matching, manufacturing overheads are absorbed on the basis of actual production for the year.

2.    Fixed assets comprise goodwill, land, buildings, plant, motor vehicles and furniture.  The directors are of the opinion that due to the profitability of the company there is no need to write off goodwill. They also consider it ridiculous, in times of inflation, to reflect the buildings at a figure lower than cost.  As far as the other assets are concerned, they agree that by writing off a constant amount in respect of each asset each year, comparability, as far as depreciation is concerned, will be best achieved.

3.    The company's main business is the sale of its finished products. However, it derives other income from commission for introducing customers to a company servicing its products, rental income from sub-letting portion of its warehouse, and sales from a non-profit-making canteen run for the benefit of the staff.

<u>YOU ARE REQUIRED TO:</u>

1.    REDRAFT the statement of accounting policies to comply with good disclosure and reporting practice.

2.    STATE what further information would be disclosed in the notes to the financial statements in respect of items dealt with in the statement of accounting policies.

# E28

The following notes form part of the draft annual financial statements of
Excell Limited at 30 June 19x3.

1.    ACCOUNTING POLICIES

1.1   Depreciation of fixed assets

      Buildings and plant are depreciated on a straight line basis at the
      rate of 2 1/2% and 10% per annum respectively.

      Land is not depreciated.

1.2   Stock

      Stocks are stated at the lower of cost and net realisable value using
      the first-in-first-out method.  The cost of finished goods includes an
      appropriate allocation of overheads.  During the current year an amount
      of R50 000 was set aside to meet expected future increases in the cost
      of raw materials.

2.    SHARE CAPITAL

      Authorised and issued

      100 000 ordinary shares of no par value                    R105 000
       45 000 8% preference shares of R1 each                      45 000
                                                                  R150 000
                                                                  =======

3.    LONG TERM LIABILITIES

      10% R100 debentures - R100 000

      The debentures which were raised in 19x1 are secured by mortgage over
      land and buildings and are repayable on 30 June 19y2.  Interest which
      is likewise secured has been paid to date.

4.    FIXED ASSETS

|          | COST     | ACCUMULATED DEPRECIATION | NET VALUE VALUE |
|----------|----------|--------------------------|-----------------|
| Land     | R20 000  | -                        | R20 000         |
| Buildings| 150 000  | R 7 500                  | 142 500         |
| Plant    | 81 640   | 16 328                   | 65 313          |
|          | R251 640 | R23 828                  | R227 812        |
|          | =======  | ======                   | =======         |

The land is Stand 456 Benrose on which are factory buildings.
The land and buildings were purchased on 1 July 19x1.

During  the year a vacant piece of land which had cost R20 000 was sold
for R40 000.  In terms of the Articles of Association such surpluses
are not available for distribution as dividends.
During the  year a vacant piece of land which had cost R20 000 was sold
for R40 000.  In terms of the Articles of Association such surpluses
are not available for distribution as dividends.

# E28 CONTINUED

5.    INVESTMENTS

The company acquired 20 000 shares in Peerless (Proprietary) Limited at a cost of R24 500 to ensure a constant supply of raw materials. The directors valued this investment at R24 500. A dividend of R2 000 was received on this investment during the year.

6.    STOCKS

| | |
|---|---:|
| Raw materials | R42 618 |
| Finished goods | 40 070 |
| | R82 688 |
| | ====== |

7.    DEBTORS - R71 500

Included in the above amount is a housing loan to Mr B, managing director:

| | |
|---|---:|
| Balance outstanding at 30 June 19x2 | R9 000 |
| Repaid during year | 4 000 |
| Balance outstanding at 30 June 19x3 | R5 000 |
| | ===== |

8.    CREDITORS - R21 716

| | |
|---|---:|
| Trade creditors | R5 116 |
| Shareholders for dividends | 13 600 |
| Taxation | 1 000 |
| Audit fees | 2 000 |
| | R21 716 |
| | ====== |

9.    BANK OVERDRAFT - R14 784

Secured by pledge of debtors balances amounting to R66 500. During the year interest amounting to R1 286 was paid.

10.    TAXATION

An amount of R51 400 has been provided in respect of South African normal taxation for the year.

ADDITIONAL INFORMATION

(i)    Preliminary expenses amounting to R5 000 were incurred when the company was incorporated and have not yet been written off. The directors wish to write off the full amount in the current year without using distributable reserves for this purpose. No entries have yet been made in the books in this respect.

(ii)    Cost of sales for the year amounted to R1 081 430 on which a mark- up of 20% was achieved. The cost of sales figure includes all depreciation charged for the year in respect of buildings and plant.

# E28 CONTINUED

Administration and selling expenses (excluding directors'remuneration and interest paid but including audit fees of R2 000) amounted to R60 000.

(iii) The directors of the company throughout the year were A, B, C and D who were paid fees of R250 each per quarter.  The chairman, A, was paid an additional fee of R1 000.

The managing director, B, was paid a salary of R20 000 and contributed 5% to the company's pension fund to which the company contributes on a Rand for Rand basis.

In addition the company paid an amount of R1 000 to Mr X, a past director, to supplement the pension of R10 000 which he receives from the pension fund.

(iv)  During the year the company made two provisional tax payments totalling R50 400.

(v)  The dividend on the preference shares was declared on 25 June 19x3 and on the same date a dividend totalling R10 000 was declared on the ordinary share capital.

(vi)  The balance of retained income at 30 June 19x2 was R50 000 (credit).


<u>YOU ARE REQUIRED TO</u>:

Prepare the income statement for the year ended 30 June 19x3 and the balance sheet at 30 June 19x3 for Excell Limited with all relevant notes and accounting policies for this period in a format suitable for publication in compliance with the Companies Act (1973) and generally accepted accounting practice.

# E29

The following balances were extracted from the books of ABC Manufacturers
Limited at 30 June 19x5.  Most of the closing entries had been passed but the
bank balance had been omitted.

| | |
|---|---:|
| Retained income | R41 000 |
| Buildings, cost | 60 000 |
| Creditors | 43 900 |
| General reserve | 75 000 |
| Debtors | 60 000 |
| Five percent debentures | 100 000 |
| Furniture, cost | 8 000 |
| Goodwill, cost | 10 000 |
| Investments in listed companies (market value R125 000) | 90 000 |
| Land, cost | 20 000 |
| Loan to subsidiary company | 120 000 |
| Plant, cost | 80 000 |
| Accumulated depreciation - buildings | 5 000 |
| Accumulated depreciation - furniture | 2 000 |
| Accumulated depreciation - plant | 30 000 |
| Provision for taxation, overprovision to 30 June 19x4 | 1 000 |
| Provisional taxation paid | 13 900 |
| Share capital, authorised and issued (in 50c shares) | 500 000 |
| Shares in subsidiary company, cost | 200 000 |
| Stock | 120 000 |

You are in possession of the following additional information:

(a)   The original issue of debentures was R200 000.   They were redeemable
      by annual drawings of R25 000, the first drawings taking place on 30
      June 19x2.   Interest is payable on 30 June each year.
(b)   The net income for the year ended 30 June 19x5, before allowing for
      taxation, was R86 000, which included
      (i)   a dividend from the subsidiary company R20 000
      (ii)   interest on the loan to the subsidiary company R6 000
      (iii) dividends on investments in quoted securities R12 000.
(c)   Depreciation has been provided for the year as follows:
      (i)   Buildings           R1 000
      (ii)   Furniture           R500
      (iii) Plant               R7 000.
(d)   The balance on provision for taxation account is the amount
      overprovided for the previous year.   South African normal taxation for
      the year to 30 June 19x5 will amount to R14 000.
(e)   The directors of the company are Paton, Quincy, Ross and Stocks, each
      of whom was paid director's fees of R200 on the last day of each
      quarter.   Paton is managing director and received a salary of R6 000
      per annum.
(f)   During the year an interim dividend of 4% and a final dividend of 6%
      were paid.
(g)   At 30 June 19x5 R25 000 must be transferred to the general reserve.

Prepare the financial statements for submission to shareholders.
Any essential information not given may be assumed.

# E30

1. The following items appear, inter alia, in the balance sheet of XY Manufacturers Limited.

<u>Investments</u> - Listed - cost     R12 000
                  Unlisted - cost     15 000

<u>Current assets</u>
    Stock     8 000
    Loan to director     5 000

You ascertain:

(1) Listed investments consist of shares in five different companies and the directors refuse to disclose the number of shares held in each company.

Unlisted investments consist of shares in one company only and the directors are of the opinion that they are worth 50% more than the cost.

(2) The company has stocks of raw materials and finished goods on hand and also the usual maintenance stores carried by a manufacturing company. There is no work in progress.

(3) The loan was made to the director in a previous financial period (while he was a director) and he has made regular repayments of R100 per month throughout the year. All interest on the loan has also been paid up to date.

Using your imagination where insufficient information has been supplied you are required to give all the notes which would appear in the published notes to the financial statements.

**E31**

From the following list of balances of Enigra Limited and the additional information supplied, prepare the balance sheet at 30 June 19x2 and the income statement for the year ended on that date for submission to the annual general meeting.  Comparative figures and auditors' report are not required.  While consolidated accounts will be prepared, you are not required to do so.

<u>DEBIT BALANCES</u>

| | |
|---|---:|
| Freehold property, at cost | R75 000 |
| Plant, equipment and furniture, at cost | 140 000 |
| Stock and stores | 95 000 |
| General, selling and administrative expenses | 69 500 |
| Debtors - trade | 60 000 |
| Fixed investments (listed), at cost | 10 000 |
| Interest paid:  bank overdraft | 500 |
| loan (to 31 December 19x1) | 1 000 |
| Directors' fees for services as directors | 3 000 |
| Directors' managerial remuneration | 10 000 |
| Provision for taxation (underprovision) | 300 |
| Loan portion of taxation | 300 |
| Shares in subsidiary company - at cost | 5 000 |
| Loan to subsidiary company | 1 000 |
| Provisional tax paid | <u>20 000</u> |
| | R490 600 |
| | ======= |

<u>CREDIT BALANCES</u>

| | | |
|---|---:|---:|
| Issued share capital - 100 000 shares | | R100 000 |
| Ten per cent loan secured (including interest) | | |
|   by mortgage of freehold property | | 20 000 |
| Bank overdraft | | 6 000 |
| Non-distributable reserve | | 15 000 |
| General reserve | | 60 000 |
| Dividends received | | 500 |
| Fixed assets replacement reserve | | 20 000 |
| Provision for doubtful debts | | 5 000 |
| Employees for leave pay due (estimate) | | 6 000 |
| Creditors | | 50 500 |
| Trading profit | | 153 600 |
| Retained income - 30 June 19x1 | | 4 000 |
| Accumulated depreciation - plant, equipment | | |
|   and furniture - balance 30 June 19x1 | R37 000 | |
|   depreciation 19x2 | <u>13 000</u> | <u>50 000</u> |
| | | R490 600 |
| | | ======= |

Additional information:

1.  During the year an item of plant costing R1 600 and having a book value of R200 was sold for R600.  No entries were made in the books of the company other than the crediting of the proceeds of the sale to general selling and administrative expenses.

# E31 CONTINUED

2.    The market value of the fixed investments at 30 June 19x2 was R9 000. The directors will not write down the investment to its market value.

3.    The company values the stock using the first-in-first out method. All stocks have a value in excess of cost and are made up as follows:

| | |
|---|---|
| Raw materials | R35 000 |
| Consumable stores | 5 000 |
| Finished goods | 55 000 |
| | R95 000 |

4.    General, selling and administrative expenses include:

    (a)   Contributions amounting to R1 000 to a medical aid society.  Of this R100 was in respect of a director.
    (b)   Auditors' fees of R5 000.
    (c)   Auditors' expenses amounting to R500.

5.    The fixed investments consist of 2 000 shares in Y Limited which has a total issued capital of 10 000 shares.

6.    The directors recommend that, at the annual general meeting, a dividend of 10c per share on the issued share capital be declared.

7.    The directors resolved to transfer R10 000 to general reserve and R20 000 to fixed assets replacement reserve.

8.    On 15 June 19x2 the company entered into a contract for the construction of a new store room at a cost of R10 000.  Overdraft facilities are available to finance this contract.

9.    The authorised capital of the company is R150 000 divided into 150 000 shares of R1 each.  By a special resolution of shareholders passed on 10 September 19x1, the unissued shares were placed under the control of the directors with power to issue the shares at any time on such terms and conditions as they think fit.

10.    The investment in the subsidiary company represents the total share capital of the X Company Limited, acquired on 1 July 19x1.  This was the only transaction involving investments which was made during the year.  No dividend was received during the year from the subsidiary company, which made a loss of R700 for the year.

11.    The amount shown as due to employees for leave pay was calculated several years previously and has not been amended since.

12.    SA normal tax amounting to R21 250 must be provided for.

# E32

At 31 December 19x7 a company owned two properties:

(a)  Stand 128 Emm Township, with a factory building thereon, purchased in 19x1 for R20 000.
     Extensions were made to the building in 19x3 at a cost of R20 000. This property was mortgaged in 19x4 to secure an issue of 1 000 10% debentures of R10 each which will be redeemed in 19x9.

(b)  Stand 129 Emm Township, with a derelict factory building thereon, purchased in October 19x7 for R40 000.
     The land is to be cleared and an office block erected.
     A contract for the clearing of the land at a cost of R15 000 has been entered into.  One third of the land has been cleared.

     The following payments have been made:

     Cost of land                                    R40 000
     Clearing of land                                  3 000
     Architects' fees - plans new building             6 000

     The company is negotiating a contract with a large construction company for the erection of the office block.  The approximate cost of the building will be R150 000.  A new share issue of at least R100 000 will be necessary to raise the funds.


<u>YOU ARE REQUIRED TO</u>:

give all the information which would be contained in the financial statements of Phoenix Manufacturers Ltd  for the year ended 31 December 19x7 with regard to the above information.

**E33**

<u>ZED LIMITED</u>

<u>BALANCE SHEET AT 31 DECEMBER</u>

| <u>CAPITAL EMPLOYED</u> | | <u>19X8</u> | | <u>19X7</u> |
|---|---|---|---|---|
| ORDINARY SHARE CAPITAL | | R100 000 | | R100 000 |
| NON DISTRIBUTABLE RESERVE | | 20 000 | | - |
| DISTRIBUTABLE RESERVE | | <u>48 000</u> | | <u>43 000</u> |
| | | R168 000 | | R143 400 |
| | | ======= | | ======= |

<u>EMPLOYMENT OF CAPITAL</u>

| | | | | 19X8 | | 19X7 |
|---|---|---|---|---|---|---|
| FIXED ASSETS | | | | R85 250 | | R74 500 |
| INVESTMENT IN SUBSIDIARY COMPANY | | | | 10 000 | | 10 000 |
| NET CURRENT ASSETS | | | | 72 750 | | 58 900 |
|   CURRENT ASSETS | | | | | | |
|     Stock | R42 000 | | R40 000 | | | |
|     Debtors | 38 000 | | 33 000 | | | |
|     Bank | <u>12 000</u> | | <u>8 000</u> | | | |
| | R92 000 | | R81 000 | | | |
| | ====== | | ====== | | | |
|   CURRENT LIABILITIES | | | | | | |
|     Creditors | R19 250 | | R22 100 | | | |
| | ====== | | ====== | | | |
| | | | | <u>R168 000</u> | | <u>R143 400</u> |
| | | | | ======= | | ======= |

<u>INCOME STATEMENT FOR THE YEAR ENDED 31 DECEMBER</u>

| | <u>19X8</u> | <u>19X7</u> |
|---|---|---|
| TURNOVER | R257 698 | R201 763 |
| | ======= | ======= |
| OPERATING INCOME | R23 950 | R17 632 |
| DIVIDENDS FROM SUBSIDIARY COMPANY | <u>1 000</u> | <u>1 000</u> |
| NET INCOME BEFORE TAXATION | 24 950 | 18 632 |
| TAXATION | <u>10 350</u> | <u>7 732</u> |
| NET INCOME | 14 600 | 10 900 |
| DIVIDEND | <u>10 000</u> | <u>8 000</u> |
| RETAINED INCOME FOR THE YEAR | 4 600 | 2 900 |
| RETAINED INCOME AT 1 JANUARY | <u>43 400</u> | <u>40 500</u> |
| RETAINED INCOME PER BALANCE SHEET | R48 000 | R43 400 |
| | ====== | ====== |

## E33 CONTINUED

1.   The following are the details of fixed assets:

|  | 19X7 | | | | 19X8 | | |
|---|---|---|---|---|---|---|---|
| COST | ACCUMULATED DEPRECIATION | NET | | VALUATION | COST | ACCUMULATED DEPRECIATION | NET |
| R30 000 | | R30 000 | Land and buildings | R50 000 | | | R50 000 |
| 50 000 | R25 000 | 25 000 | Plant | | R50 000 | R30 000 | 20 000 |
| 24 000 | 8 000 | 16 000 | Motor vehicles | | 24 000 | 12 000 | 12 000 |
| 5 000 | 1 500 | 3 500 | Furniture | | 5 000 | 1 750 | 3 250 |
| R109 000 | R34 500 | R74 500 | | R50 000 | R79 000 | R43 750 | R85 250 |
| ====== | ====== | ====== | | ====== | ====== | ====== | ====== |

2.   Included in debtors is the dividend of R1 000 declared by the subsidiary company on 15 December 19x8 and payable on 12 January 19x9.

<u>YOU ARE REQUIRED TO:</u>

Record all the notes which you would expect to be attached to the financial statements of Zed Limited at 31 December 19x8.

THE NOTES MUST BE DEALT WITHIN IN A LOGICAL SEQUENCE.
YOU MAY MAKE ANY ASSUMPTIONS WHICH YOU FEEL NECESSARY.
COMPARATIVE FIGURES NEED NOT BE GIVEN IN YOUR ANSWER.

# E34

Horseshoe Limited is a manufacturing company.

Its balance sheet at 30 June 19x2 and income statement for the year ended on that date are being prepared for presentation to shareholders.

What is the minimum information you consider acceptable in the above documents regarding the following?

(Assume any essential information not given).

(a)    The company has the following investments:

Johannesburg
      Stock Exchange

|  |  | Cost | value at 30 June 19x2 |
|---|---|---|---|
| 1. | 20 000 ordinary shares of R1 each in A.A. Limited | R80 000 | R98 000 |
| 2. | 80 000 ordinary shares of R1 each on B.B. Limited | R50 000 | R70 000 |
| 3. | R40 000 7% S.A. Republic stock redeemable 19x9 | R40 000 | R40 200 |
| 4. | 2 000 8% debentures of R10 each in C (Pty) Ltd | R20 000 | - |

NOTE: Investments (1) and (2) above were purchased as speculations, the stock in (3) above was purchased as part of a scheme for the eventual repayment of debentures issued by Horseshoe Limited and the debentures in (4) above were purchased so as to ensure a regular supply of raw materials to Horseshoe Limited's factory.

(b)    The directors of Horseshoe Limited at 30 June 19x1 were A, B, C and X. D was the general manager and E was the secretary.

On 31 July 19x1 X, the managing director, was forced by the board to retire.  The company agreed to pay him three years' salary in full setlement of the company's obligations under a service contract with him.  In addition X received a lump sum of R8 000 from the pension fund.

On 2 January 19x2 D was appointed managing director and relinquished his post as general manager.

A has been chairman of the board for the whole year.

# E34 CONTINUED

The following emoluments were paid by the company during the year:-

<pre>
    Each director R100 per month in arrear
    Chairman - additional fee                   R1 000 per annum
             - entertainment allowance           R100 per month
</pre>

General manager's salary at the rate of  R24 000 per annum payble monthly.
Managing director's salary at the rate of R36 000 per annum payable monthly.
Secretary's salary  at the rate of R18 000 per annum payable monthly.
Managing director's entertainment allowance R200 per month.

Each employee of the company and the managing director pays 5% of his salary to a pension fund and the company contributes a like amount.

The chairman, managing director and the secretary each have the use of a motor car, the use of which is agreed to be worth R50 per month to each of them.

(c)     On 1 March 19x2 E was granted a loan of R30 000 at 5% per annum to build a house near the company's premises.  He has paid his interest up to date, but has made no repayment of the capital sum.  This loan was made in terms of a scheme to enable employees to own their own houses.

(d)     The issued share capital  of the company at  30 June 19x2 consisted of 100 000 ordinary shares of R1 each, and 50 000 redeemable preference shares of R1 each.  The preference shares are redeemable at a premium on 30 June 19x3.

The following are the summarised balance sheets of Eastern Limited at 30 June.

|  | 19x3 | | 19x4 | |
|---|---|---|---|---|
| <u>Share capital</u> | | | | |
| Authorised - shares of R1 each | | R200 000 | | R200 000 |
| | | ======= | | ======= |
| Issued - shares of R1 each | R90 000 | | R140 000 | |
| Share premium | 20 000 | 110 000 | 15 000 | 155 000 |
| <u>Distributable reserves</u> | | | | |
| General reserve | 40 000 | | 54 000 | |
| Retained income | 60 000 | 100 000 | 62 000 | 166 000 |
| | | 210 000 | | 271 000 |
| <u>Long-term liabilities</u> | | 58 000 | | 70 000 |
| | | R268 000 | | R341 000 |
| | | ======= | | ======= |
| | | | | |
| <u>Fixed assets</u> | | | | |
| Cost | R250 000 | | R274 000 | |
| Accumulated depreciation | 90 000 | R160 000 | 114 000 | R160 000 |
| <u>Unlisted investments</u> - at cost | | 20 000 | | 20 000 |
| Net current assets | | 88 000 | | 161 000 |
| <u>Current assets</u> | | | | |
| Stock | R86 000 | | R110 000 | |
| Debtors | 90 000 | | 114 000 | |
| Bank | 24 000 | | 40 000 | |
| | R200 000 | | R264 000 | |
| | ======= | | ======= | |
| <u>Current liabilities</u> | | | | |
| Creditors | R100 000 | | R89 000 | |
| Proposed dividend | 12 000 | | 14 000 | |
| | R112 000 | | R103 000 | |
| | ======= | | ======= | |
| | | R268 000 | | R341 000 |
| | | ======= | | ======= |

The following additional information is available:

1. On 30 June 19x4 fixed assets costing R10 000 and in respect of which R6 000 had been provided for depreciation to the date of sale were sold for R2 000.

2. The investments held at 30 June 19x3 were sold in October 19x3 for R30 000. In January 19x4 investments were purchased at a cost of R20 000.

3. During the 19x4 financial year an amount of R30 000, being part of the balance of unappropriated profits, was capitalised by the issue of 30 000 fully paid shares to members at par.

4. During the 19x4 financial year the company made a capitalisation issue of 10 000 fully paid shares out of the share premium account.

# E35 CONTINUED

5.     In May 19x4 the company issued 10 000 shares to the public at a premium of 50 cents per share for cash.

6.     The dividend proposed for 19x3 was paid in October 19x3 and an interim dividend of R7 000 was paid in March 19x4.

<u>YOU ARE REQUIRED TO</u>:

1.     show the retained income account for the year ended 30 June 19x4.

2.     prepare a statement of retained income for publication for the year ended 30 June 19x4.

# E36

The following information refers to Surf Enterprises Limited at 30 June 19x9.

1.    The authorised share capital consists of:

        200 000 ordinary shares of R1 each
        100 000 6% redeemable preference shares of R1 each

2.    The company was incorporated ten years ago and immediately thereafter shares were alloted as follows:

        20 000 ordinary shares to the subscribers to the memorandum of association at par

        80 000 ordinary shares of R1 each at a premium of 10 cents per share.  The share premium on these shares had not been utilised at 30 June 19x8.

        100 000 6% redeemable preference shares of  R1 each at par redeemable at a premium of 30 cents per share at any date after 30 June 19x8.

3     On 2 January 19x9, 20 000 ordinary shares were issued at a premium of 50 cents per share for part redemption of the preference shares.  The first 40 000 preference shares were redeemed on 2 January 19x9 and no further redemption of preference shares was made after this date.

4.    At an annual general meeting held on 30 September 19x8 directors were given authority to issue  the unissued ordinary shares at any time to finance the business of the company.  This authority was granted for a period of one year.

5.    After all the adjustments at 30 June 19x9  were made, the balances on the following accounts were:-

| | |
|---|---:|
| General reserve | R10 000 |
| Reserve for increased replacement cost of fixed assets | 7 000 |
| Retained income at 1 July 19x8 | 12 000 |
| Retained income for the current year | 46 800 |

6.    On 2 January 19x4, 1 000 ten percent debentures of R100 each were allotted.  These debentures are redeemable in equal annual drawings of R10 000.  The first drawing fell due and was paid on 31 December 19x7, and all subsequent drawings have been paid on time. Interest is payable half yearly on 30 June and 31 December of each year.

7.    The 10% debentures are secured by first mortgage over land and buildings
situated on Stand 842 Jeffrey's Bay.  The land and buildings were acquired on 1 June 19x4 for R120 000.  During the 19x9 financial year, improvements on buildings estimated to amount to R50 000 when complete, were commenced.

Cost of improvements up to 30 June 19x9 amounted to R27 000.

## E36 CONTINUED

8.   Plant and machinery at cost less accumulated depreciation at 30 June
     19x9 is R90 000.  All plant and machinery was acquired on 1 July 19x7
     and depreciation is being written off at 20% per annum straight line.

9.   Furniture and fittings at cost at 30 June 19x9 was R14 000, and
     accumulated depreciation at that date amounted to R6 000.

10.  Investments at 30 June 19x9 were

     (a)   30 000 ordinary shares of R1 each in Tube-Rider Ltd at cost
           R40 000 - (market value R50 000).

           The total issued share capital of Tube-Rider is 40 000 ordinary
           shares of R1 each.

     (b)   1 000 10% debentures  of  R10  each in Tube-Rider Ltd at cost
           R10 000 - (market value R10 000).

     (c)   20 000 ordinary shares of R1 each in Wipe-out (Proprietary) Ltd
           at cost R20 000 - (directors valuation R30 000).  The total
           issued share capital is 100 000 ordinary shares of R1 each.

11.  Stock is valued at cost using the first in first out method and
     comprises merchandise only.  Total stock at 30 June 19x9 is R65 000.

12.  Debtors amounted to R79 000 and included in this amount are balances
     owing by directors of the company amounting to R7 000.  R3 000 of this
     amount is owed by Mr Tompson in respect of a loan of R6 000 granted in
     January 19x8  and reduced to R5 000 at 30 June.  The balance of R3 000
     still owing is due on 30 September 19x9.  The remaining R4 000 is a
     loan of R4 500 granted to Mr Pearman in March 19x9.

13.  A final dividend of 5% on all issued ordinary shares and the normal
     preference dividend were declared but unpaid at 30 June 19x9.  These
     amounts together with the provision for taxation amounting to  R18 700
     were included in creditors totalling R101 400.

14.  Bank overdraft at 30 June 19x9 amounted to R5 800.


<u>YOU ARE REQUIRED TO</u>:

prepare the balance sheet with the supporting notes of Surf Enterprises
Limited at 30 June 19x9 in compliance with the requirements of the Companies
Act of 1973 in a form suitable for publication.  (Assume that all adjustments
required have been done.)

NOTE:  Comparative figures are not required.

The following list of balances is extracted from the books of Alpha Manufacturing Company Limited at 30 June 19x4.

| | |
|---|---:|
| Retained income (credit balance at 30 June 19x3) | R5 000 |
| Bank  -  current account | 5 400 |
| Bank  -  fixed deposit account | 12 000 |
| Directors' fees | 1 500 |
| General reserve | 40 000 |
| Goodwill (cost) | 20 000 |
| Interest paid | 600 |
| Land and buildings (cost) | 30 000 |
| Loan secured by mortgage over immovable property | 15 000 |
| Loans to directors | 1 500 |
| Manufactured stock on hand (at 30 June 19x3) | 15 000 |
| Office furniture (cost) | 5 000 |
| Plant (cost) | 25 000 |
| Provision for amounts written off goodwill | 18 000 |
| Accumulated depreciation  -  furniture | 2 000 |
| Accumulated depreciation  -  plant | 10 000 |
| Provisional taxation paid | 2 000 |
| Raw materials on hand (at 30 June 19x4) | 17 000 |
| Raw materials sold (cost) | 3 000 |
| Raw materials used (cost) | 36 000 |
| Salaries and wages (factory) | 40 000 |
| Salaries and wages (office) | 5 000 |
| Sales of manufactured stocks | 96 000 |
| Sales of raw materials | 5 000 |
| Share capital (authorised - in shares of R1 each) | 100 000 |
| Share capital (unissued) | 40 000 |
| Sundry creditors | 6 000 |
| Sundry debtors | 26 000 |
| Sundry overhead charges (factory) | 8 000 |
| Sundry overhead charges (office) | 2 000 |
| Work in progress (30 June 19x3) | 2 000 |

The following additional information is supplied:

1. A provision for workmen's compensation insurance of 1% of the salaries and wages for the year, both factory and office, is to be made.

2. The directors recommend a dividend of 10%.

3. South African normal  taxation for the year is accurately estimated at R2 100.

4. The loan secured by the immovable property bears interest at the rate of 4% per annum and falls due to be repaid on 30 September 19x4. Interest has been paid to 31 March 19x4 but no provision for the interest accrued has yet been made.

5. Goodwill must be written off completely and provision made for depreciation of plant at 10% on cost and furniture at 5% on cost.

# E37 CONTINUED

6.    The cost of work-in-progress at 30 June 19x4 is R2 400.

7.    The cost of manufactured goods sold during the year is R80 000. There are no stock shortages.

8.    The sale of raw materials is an isolated transaction made possible by exceptional conditions unlikely to recur.

9.    The unissued capital is under option until 30 June 19x8 at R1,20 per share.

10.   On the last day of the financial year cheques totalling R1 500 were drawn in favour of the directors in respect of their fees due at that date. Another employee then drew a second lot of cheques in error and these were signed and dispatched. When the cash book was written up the second lot of cheques was debited to "loans to directors' account". These cheques were subsequently returned by the directors and cancelled but they were not written back in the cash book until July 19x4.

<u>YOU ARE REQUIRED TO PREPARE</u>:

(a)    financial statements of Alpha Manufacturing Company Limited at 30 June 19x4 for publication.

(b)    rough workings showing how your figures are arrived at.

Comparative figure may be omitted and any essential information may be assumed. A statement of source and application of funds is <u>not</u> required.

The following trial balance was extracted from the books of the Bicycle Manufacturing Company Limited at 30 June 19x5:

| | | |
|---|--:|--:|
| Retained income - at 30 June 19x4 | | R1 000 |
| Audit fee | R200 | |
| Bank | | 600 |
| Creditors | | 8 950 |
| Debtors | 22 000 | |
| Delivery wages | 1 800 | |
| Directors' fees | 500 | |
| Factory expenses | 300 | |
| Factory wages | 12 000 | |
| Goodwill, at cost | 5 000 | |
| Interest on loan to subsidiary company | | 1 000 |
| Interest on treasury bills | | 500 |
| Land and buildings, at cost | 10 000 | |
| Loan to subsidiary company | 15 000 | |
| Office general expenses | 400 | |
| Plant at cost less depreciation to 30 June 19x4 | | |
|   (cost R25 000) | 20 000 | |
| Power | 1 500 | |
| Preliminary expenses, amount expended | 3 000 | |
| Provision for taxation overprovided to | | |
|   30 June 19x4 | | 500 |
| Provisional taxation paid | 3 950 | |
| Purchase of raw materials | 20 000 | |
| Salaries | 3 000 | |
| Sales | | 60 500 |
| Share capital | | 100 000 |
| Share premium | | 5 000 |
| Shares in subsidiary company, at cost | 25 000 | |
| Stock at 30 June 19x4 | | |
|   Manufactured goods | 11 000 | |
|   Partly manufactured goods | 1 500 | |
|   Raw materials | 7 000 | |
| Telephone and postages | 500 | |
| Treasury bills | 10 000 | |
| Vehicles (delivery) at cost less depreciation | | |
|   to 30 June 19x4 (cost R3 000) | 2 000 | |
| Workmen's compensation insurance (all factory | | |
|   employees) | 1 200 | |
| | R177 450 | R177 450 |

The company owns 80% of the shares in the subsidiary company.

Stocks of raw materials on hand at 30 June 19x5 amounted to R3 000 and partly manufactured goods to R500.

The company adopts the F.I.F.O. system of charging out stocks.

# E38 CONTINUED

The company manufactures nothing but bicycles.   There were 2 600 bicycles on hand at 30 June 19x4 10 000 were manufactured during the year, and there were 2 500 on hand at 30 June 19x5.   All bicycles were accounted for.

Plant must be depreciated at the rate of 10% per annum and vehicles at 20% per annum, both on the reducing balances.

South African normal taxation is accurately estimated at R4 000 for the year. The amount of R500 in the trial balance is an over provision made in the previous year.

Half the preliminary expenses must be written off.

The directors of the Bicycle Manufacturing Company are Abel, Brown, Charlton, Davis and Eccles, each of whom received R100 per annum in fees.

The directors of the subsidiary company are Abel, Charlton, Eccles and George, each of whom is entitled to one per cent of its profits as director's remuneration.   The profit of the subsidiary company for the year ended 30 June 19x5 before allowing for directors' remuneration, was R5 000.

Included in the debtors balance is an amount of R1 000 lent to Brown in July 19x4.   Abel and George each owe R2 000 to the subsidiary company on loan account.   They borrowed these amounts during August 19x4.

The share capital of the Bicycle Manufacturing Company Limited is R250 000 divided into shares of R1 each.

The land and buildings are situated on Stand 1357 Humber Township in the Municipality of Raleigh and were acquired in 19x0.

Stock is always valued at the lower of cost or net realisable value.

Partly manufactured goods are always valued at cost of material, labour and direct overheads.

<u>YOU ARE REQUIRED TO</u>:

prepare the balance sheet, income statement and notes thereto of the holding company in compliance with the Companies Act 1973.   Comparative figures are not wanted.   Calculations to the nearest R.

# E39

The following is the balance sheet of Parker Limited at 31 December 19x4:-

<u>Authorised and issued</u>
100 000 ordinary shares of no par value -

| | | |
|---|---|---|
| stated capital account | | R175 000 |

<u>Distributable reserves</u>

| | | |
|---|---|---|
| | | 30 000 |
| General reserve | R25 000 | |
| Retained income | 5 000 | |
| | | 205 000 |

<u>Long term liabilities</u>

| | | |
|---|---|---|
| | | 40 000 |
| 10% Secured debentures of R10 each | | R245 000 |
| | | ======= |

| Fixed assets | Cost | Accumulated depreciation | |
|---|---|---|---|
| Land | R30 000 | | R30 000 |
| Plant | 100 000 | R40 000 | 60 000 |
| Delivery vehicles | 40 000 | 10 000 | 30 000 |
| Furniture | 5 000 | 1 000 | 4 000 |
| | R175 000 | R51 000 | 124 000 |
| | ========================= | | |

| | | |
|---|---|---|
| Leasehold property at cost | 50 000 | |
| Less: leasehold redemption fund | 25 000 | 25 000 |
| | | 149 000 |

| <u>Investments</u> - at cost | | |
|---|---|---|
| | | 75 000 |
| Listed | 50 000 | |
| Unlisted | 25 000 | |

| <u>Net current assets</u> | | |
|---|---|---|
| | | 19 500 |
|   <u>Current assets</u> | | |
| Stock | 40 000 | |
| Debtors | 30 000 | |
| Bank | 10 000 | |
| | 80 000 | |
| | ====== | |
|   <u>Current liabilities</u> | | |
| Trade creditors | 15 500 | |
| Shareholders for dividend | 25 000 | |
| Debentures | 20 000 | |
| | R60 500 | |
| | ====== | |

| <u>Preliminary and issue expenses</u> | | |
|---|---|---|
| | | 1 500 |
| Preliminary expenses | 1 000 | |
| Share issue expenses | 500 | |
| | | R245 000 |
| | | ======= |

(The notes to the above balance sheet have been <u>omitted</u>)

# E39 CONTINUED

The following is a summarised statement of source and application of  funds
or the year ended 31 December 19x5:-

| Source | | Application | |
|---|---|---|---|
| Net profit before taxation | R29 000 | Purchase of plant | R16 000 |
| Profit on sale of | | Purchase of delivery | |
|   investments | (1 000) |   vehicle | 5 000 |
| | 28 000 | Redemption of 2 000 | |
| | |    debentures of R10 each | 20 000 |
| Loss on sale of plant | 2 000 | Interim dividend paid | 8 000 |
| Depreciation : | | Final dividend declared | 20 000 |
| Leasehold redemption fund | 5 000 | South African normal tax | 9 000 |
| Plant | 15 000 | Investments | 5 000 |
| Delivery vehicles | 12 000 | | |
| Furniture | 150 | | |
| | 62 250 | | |
| Proceeds from sale of listed | | | |
|   investments | 3 000 | | |
| Proceeds from sale of plant | 5 000 | | |
| 5% loan raised - secured by second | | | |
|   mortgage of land | 10 000 | | |
| Decrease in working capital | 2 750 | | |
| | R83 000 | | R83 000 |

## Schedule of changes in working capital

| | | | |
|---|---|---|---|
| Cash withdrawn | R11 900 | Increase in debtors | R 7 650 |
| Increase in trade creditors | 2 000 | Decrease in shareholders | |
| Increase in creditors for | |   for dividends | 5 000 |
|   interest on loan | 250 | Decrease in working capital | 2 750 |
| Decrease in stock | 1 250 | | |
| | R15 400 | | R15 400 |

Notes:-

(1)    Plant which had cost R11 000 was sold on 1 January 19x5.

(2)    It was decided that half of the preliminary and share issue expenses
were to be written off.  The directors decided not to use distributable
reserves for this purpose.

(3)    An amount of R10 000 was transferred out of general reserve during the
year to meet various appropriations.

(4)    The debentures  are being redeemed by equal annual drawings on 31
December each year and are secured by a first mortgage over the land
owned by the company.

(5)    The 5% loan of R10 000 raised during the year is repayable on 30  June
19x9.

(6)    The land owned by the company is an industrial site, Stand No. 111 in
Industron Township and was purchased in 19x1.  No other property has
since been purchased.

(7)   The leasehold property, acquired under a ten year lease which expires on 31 December 19x9, consists of a warehouse and office block on Stand 112 in Industron Township.

(8)   At 31 December 19x4 the investments consisted of the following:

|  |  |
|---|---|
| 25 000 S.A. Government 19x9 10% stock | R25 000 |
| 12 500 shares in Anglo American Limited | 25 000 |
| 25 000 shares of R1 each in Parkson (Pty) Limited | <u>25 000</u> |
|  | R75 000 |

The only investment during the year was R5 000 SA Government 19x9 10% stock which was purchased at par.

During the year 1 000 shares in Anglo American Limited were sold.  The market values at 31 December 19x5 were as follows:

|  |  |
|---|---|
| S.A. Government 19x9 10% stock | R102% |
| Anglo American Limited | R3 per share |

The directors valued the investment in Parkson (Pty) Limited at cost.

(9)   Stock consists of merchandise only and was valued by the F.I.F.O. method as in previous years at the lower of cost or net realisable value.

<u>YOU ARE REQUIRED TO</u>:

prepare a balance sheet with appropriate notes at 31 December 19x5.

**E40**

The following trial balance was extracted from the books of New Act Limited, at 30 June 19x4:

| | | |
|---|---:|---:|
| Administration expenses | R16 000 | |
| Advertising | 2 000 | |
| Audit fee | 6 200 | |
| Bank | 76 000 | |
| Creditors | | R248 000 |
| Debentures | | 100 000 |
| Debtors | 144 000 | |
| Depreciation of fixtures and fittings | 7 400 | |
| Directors' fees | 12 000 | |
| Dividends received | | 14 000 |
| Fixtures  and fittings, at cost | 86 000 | |
| General reserve | | 70 000 |
| Goodwill, at cost | 75 000 | |
| Interest | 12 500 | |
| Investments | 120 000 | |
| Land and buildings | 250 000 | |
| Overprovision  for taxation - 19x3 | | 500 |
| Preference dividend paid to 30 June 19x4 | 1 600 | |
| Proceeds of issue of shares | | 17 500 |
| Provision for depreciation - fixtures and fittings | | 27 000 |
| Purchases | 642 000 | |
| Rent | 18 200 | |
| Salaries | 39 800 | |
| Sales | | 820 000 |
| Share capital - ordinary (330 000 shares) | | 330 000 |
|              - preference (20 000 shares) | | 20 000 |
| Share issue expenses | 2 000 | |
| Share premium account | | 1 000 |
| Stock at 30 June 19x3 | 240 000 | |
| Surplus on revaluation of land buildings | | 4 000 |
| Retained income at 30 June 19x3 | | |
| | R1 750 700 | R1 750 700 |
| | ========= | ========= |

<u>NOTES</u>

1.    The authorised share capital of the company at 30 June 19x3 was:
         20 000 eight per cent preference shares of R1 each
         500 000 ordinary shares of no par value

2.    The amount of R17 500  was received on the issue of 10 000 ordinary shares in May 19x4.  The amount  of R2 000 of share issue expenses was incurred in respect of this issue.  The directors wish the share issue expenses to be written off and, if it is possible, would like this to be done in such a way as to leave the maximum possible balance  of retained income available for dividends.

3.    10 000 Debentures of R10 each were issued for a period of 10 years on 1 April, six years previously.  The debentures and any outstanding interest are secured by a first mortgage over land and buildings.

# E40 CONTINUED

Interest at the rate  of 10% is payable on 31 March each year.   Other than for the payment of the interest in March 19x4 no entries  have been made in the books in respect of interest  on the debentures during the year to 30 June 19x4.

4.   Land and buildings consist of a warehouse complex.  The property was acquired shortly after the formation of the company in 19w2 for a purchase consideration of R120 000.  Between  19w2 and the end of 19x3 additions to the property were made at various times at a total cost of R80 000.  Despite attempts to do so, it has not been possible  to establish the cost of each addition.  It is the company policy to revalue land and buildings every ten years and early in 19x4, the property was valued, and the following is a copy of a letter from the valuer:

B Fair - Sworn Appraiser  
P O Box 123  
<u>JOHANNESBURG</u>  
10 January 19x4

The Directors,  
New Act Limited.


Dear Sirs

Re:   <u>VALUATION OF WAREHOUSE ON STAND 01 NIX TOWNSHIP</u>

I hereby certify that on 2 January 19x4, I valued the above mentioned property at a valuation of R240 000 (Two hundred and forty thousand rand).  As the property is not let to an outside tenant, the valuation is based on sales of similar properties in the same township.

Yours faithfully


<u>B FAIR</u>


As the valuation exceeds the book value of the asset, the value of land and buildings was  increased in the books.  In March 19x4, a further addition was made to the property at a cost of R10 000.

5.   The following analysis of the investments was made for audit purposes:

| Name of share | Cost per share | Total cost | Market value per share | Directors valuation per share | Dividends received |
|---|---|---|---|---|---|
| A Ltd | 450 cents | R45 000 | 500 cents | 500 cents | R4 000 |
| B (Pty) Ltd | 75 cents | 15 000 | Not listed | 100 cents | Nil |
| C (Pty) Ltd | 200 cents | 10 000 | Not listed | 250 cents | 2 000 |
| D Ltd | 50 cents | 40 000 | 60 cents | 60 cents | 3 000 |
| E Ltd | 100 cents | 10 000 | 100 cents | 100 cents | 1 000 |
| | | R120 000 | | | R10 000 |

# E40 CONTINUED

During the year 20 000  shares in F (Pty) Limited were  sold at book value.
A dividend of R4 000 had been received before the shares were sold.  None of
the companies  in which the investments were held are subsidiary companies.

6.      Stock on hand at 30 June 19x4, was calculated at R280 000.  This value
        was arrived at using the same method as  has always been used by the
        company.   In calculating the cost of an article, where the actual cost
        cannot be  identified because  of other similar items, it is assumed
        that the article on hand  remains from the most recent acquisition  of
        that type of item.  The only exception to this procedure is where it is
        felt that a loss  will be incurred in disposing  of an article in which
        case the expected loss is deducted  from the cost of the article.  The
        company does not conduct any manufacturing activities.

7.      Included in salaries are amounts totalling R8 400, being the salary
        payable to the accountant of the  company who has since May 19x2 also
        been a director of the company.

8.      Taxation for the year ended 30 June 19x4, has been calculated as
        follows:

              S.A. normal tax              R41 000
              Recoverable loan levy          1 000
                                           R42 000
                                           ======

        Provisional  tax payments were made as follows and have been included
        in debtors:

              31 December 19x3             R20 000
              30 June 19x4                  14 000
                                           R34 000
                                           ======

        The recoverable  loan  levy paid in  previous  years  is  included in
        debtors.

        Other than for the payments of provisional tax, no entries in respect
        of taxation have been made in the books for the year ended 30 June
        19x4.

9.      The directors have agreed that a recommendation should be made, at the
        annual general meeting to be held in about September 19x4, that a
        dividend of 10 cents per share should be paid to all shareholders
        registered on 30 June 19x4.

10.     The directors have decided that a further R10 000 should be transferred
        to the general reserve.

<u>YOU ARE REQUIRED TO</u>:

prepare a balance sheet for New Act Limited, as at 30 June 19x4, together with an income statement for the year then ended.    The requirements of the Companies Act, 1973, must be complied with and the information should be set out in a manner that you consider most  desirable.

Comparative figures are to be omitted and a cash flow statement is not required.

**E41**

The following list of balances has been extracted from the books of Banlon
Limited at 31 December 19x0:

| | | |
|---|---|---:|
| Share capital | | |
| Ordinary shares | | R200 000 |
| 7% redeemable preference shares | | 60 000 |
| Provision for depreciation of plant and equipment, | | |
| 31 December 19x0 | | 42 000 |
| Plant and equipment at cost | | 198 000 |
| Land and buildings at cost | | 151 500 |
| Patents and trade marks at cost | | 30 000 |
| Investments at cost: | | |
| 30 000 ordinary shares in Delta Limited | | 36 000 |
| 22 500 ordinary shares in Gamma Limited | | 30 000 |
| Trading profit | | 129 000 |
| Work-in-progress, at 31 December 19x0 | | 12 000 |
| Finished goods on hand, 31 December 19x0 | | 45 000 |
| Raw materials on hand, 31 December 19x0 | | 6 000 |
| Selling and distribution expenses | | 18 000 |
| Administration expenses | | 28 800 |
| Profit on sale of plant and equipment | | 3 000 |
| Retained income at beginning of year | Cr. | 15 000 |
| Dividends - Delta Limited | | 1 800 |
|      - Gamma Limited | | 9 000 |
| Cash paid to preference shareholders on | | |
| redemption of 20 000 shares at a premium | | |
| of 5% on 30 June 19x0 | | 21 700 |
| Bank overdraft | | 18 000 |
| Creditors, including accrued debenture interest | | 24 700 |
| 7% first mortgage debentures | | 60 000 |
| Debtors | | 75 500 |
| General reserve | | 90 000 |

<u>Additional information available:</u>

1.    "Debtors" include:
    R30 000 provisional payments in respect of South African income tax.
    R5 000 owing by Gamma Limited.
    R900 dividend receivable from Delta Limited.

2.    "Administration expenses" include:

| | |
|---|---:|
| Interest on debentures and bank overdraft | R5 800 |
| Secretary's salary | 4 000 |
| Managing director's salary | 6 000 |
| Directors' fees | 1 200 |
| Auditors' remuneration - voted for at annual general meeting | 2 500 |

3.    During the year plant which had cost R24 000 and on which R9 000
depreciation had been provided was sold for R18 000. There were no
other sales of plant and equipment and none was purchased during the
year.

# E41 CONTINUED

4. The accumulated depreciation of plant and equipment at the beginning of the year was R33 000.

5. The debentures are secured by a mortgage over land and buildings. Interest is payable half yearly in arrear on 1 January and 1 July.

6. The authorised share capital consists of:

   240 000 ordinary shares of R1 each.
    60 000 7% redeemable preference shares of R1 each.
   The redeemable preference shares are redeemable on, or at company's option before 1 July 19x3 at a premium of 5%.

7. No new shares were issued during the year.

8. The issued share capital of Delta Limited is R120 000 and the relevant shares were acquired during the year as a speculation. These shares were quoted on the Johannesburg Stock Exchange at R1,30 "ex-div." per share of R1 each on 31 December 19x0.

9. The issued share capital of Gamma Limited is R30 000 in shares of R1 each. The shares in Gamma Limited were acquired on 1 January 19x0, and all the directors of Gamma Limited are also directors of Banlon Limited, but the manager of Gamma Limited is not on the board.

   The following is the retained income account of Gamma Limited for the year to 31 December 19x0:

   | | | | |
   |---|---|---|---|
   | Taxation for the year | R5 100 | Balance at beginning | |
   | Directors' fees | 900 | of year | R6 000 |
   | Dividends paid 31.12.19x0 | 12 000 | Income for the year | 24 000 |
   | Balance 31.12.19x0 | 12 000 | | |
   | | R30 000 | | R30 000 |

10. Provision must be made for the following:

    (a) South African normal income tax at 40% of the net profit for the year. Ignore loan portion of taxation.
    (b) Annual preference dividend.
    (c) Proposed 15% dividend to ordinary shareholders.

11. No group accounts must be prepared since Banlon Limited is the wholly-owned subsidiary of another company registered in the Republic.

12. It may be assumed that "selling and distribution expenses" and "administration expenses" do not include any disallowable expenditure for income tax purposes. Tax and book values of fixed assets are equal.

<u>YOU ARE REQUIRED TO</u>:

prepare the annual financial statements for the year ended 31 December 19x0 for submission to the annual general meeting.

# E42

The attached financial statements have been prepared by the inexperienced accountant of X Limited for the year ended 31 March 1980.

You have reviewed these statements and have established that:

(a)  the figures have been correctly extracted from the final trial balance.
(b)  there are no casting errors.
(c)  the notes are all properly cross referenced and the figures in the statements agree with the figures in the notes.
(d)  there are certain disclosure omissions and errors in presentation or generally accepted accounting practice purposes.


<u>YOU ARE REQUIRED TO</u>:

Examine these financial statements and list in point form under the following broad headings those items which have not been properly dealt with in terms of the Companies Act, 1973 and GAAP, detailing the omissions.

DO NOT MAKE <u>UNNECESSARY</u> ASSUMPTIONS

(i)    Share capital
(ii)   Long term liabilities
(iii)  Fixed assets
(iv)   Investments
 (v)   Income statement.

<u>BALANCE SHEET</u>

| | Notes | 19x0 | | 19x9 | |
|---|---|---|---|---|---|
| SHARE CAPITAL | 1 | | R900 000 | | R900 000 |
| NON-DISTRIBUTABLE RESERVES | 2 | | 32 500 | | 20 000 |
| DISTRIBUTABLE RESERVES | 3 | | 932 331 | | 634 518 |
| SHAREHOLDERS' FUNDS | | | 1 864 831 | | 554 518 |
| DEFERRED TAX | | | 103 000 | | 68 000 |
| LONG TERM LIABILITIES | 4 | | 328 755 | | 129 800 |
| | | | 2 296 586 | | 1 753 318 |
| | | | ========= | | ========= |
| EMPLOYMENT CAPITAL | | | | | |
| FIXED ASSETS | 5 | | R1 970 697 | | R1 339 191 |
| INVESTMENTS | 6 | | 265 807 | | 240 670 |
| LOAN PORTION OF TAX | | | 43 715 | | 71 856 |
| CURRENT ASSETS | | | 1 413 182 | | 911 728 |
|   Stock | 7 | R1 042 113 | | R673 728 | |
|   Debtors | | 368 629 | | 268 500 | |
|   Cash | | 204 000 | | 5 000 | |
| | | | 3 693 401 | | 2 653 445 |
| CURRENT LIABILITIES | | | 1 396 815 | | 810 127 |
|   Creditors | | 1 018 190 | | 592 477 | |
|   Taxation | | 45 703 | | 27 850 | |
|   Shareholders for dividend | | 80 000 | | 140 000 | |
|   Bank overdraft | | 252 922 | | 49 800 | |
| | | | R2 296 586 | | R1 753 318 |
| | | | ========= | | ========= |

## E42 CONTINUED

| INCOME STATEMENT | | 19x0 | 19x9 |
|---|---|---|---|
| PROFIT FOR THE YEAR | | R182 527 | R283 061 |
| Including: | | | |
| Interest from loan portion of tax | | 2 177 | 1 462 |
| Surplus on the disposal of fixed assets | | 722 | - |
| Surplus on the revaluation of land | | 12 500 | - |
| Dividends received | | 100 000 | 65 000 |
| Recovery of legal expenses and damages | | 50 000 | - |
| and after charging: | | | |
| Loss on the disposal of fixed assets | | 400 | 363 |
| Loss on fire claim | | 200 000 | - |
| Depreciation | | 271 178 | 178 982 |
| Interest paid | | 111 677 | 132 561 |
| Provision for legal expenses in pendinw suit | | - | 30 000 |
| Administrative fees | | 21 324 | 16 080 |
| Auditors remuneration: | | | |
| Audit fees | | 13 640 | 8 050 |
| Expenses | | 865 | 600 |
| Dividend paid | | 80 000 | 140 000 |
| Tax | 10 | 72 214 | 128 032 |
| NET INCOME | | 310 313 | 55 029 |
| TRANSFER TO NON-DISTRIBUTABLE RESERVE | | 12 500 | - |
| RETAINED INCOME FOR THE YEAR | | 297 813 | 55 029 |
| RETAINED INCOME AT BEGINNING OF THE YEAR | | 484 518 | 492 489 |
| RETAINED INCOME AT END OF THE YEAR | | R782 331 | R484 518 |

NOTES TO THE FINANCIAL STATEMENTS

1.   SHARE CAPITAL
     ISSUED

| | |
|---|---|
| 1 000 000 ordinary shares of 50c each | R500 000 |
| 200 000 preference shares of R2 each | 400 000 |
| | R900 000 |

2.   NON-DISTRIBUTABLE RESERVES

| | |
|---|---|
| Reserve arising from the revaluation of land brought forward | R20 000 |
| Increase arising from the revaluation on 2 January 19x0 | 12 500 |
| | R32 500 |

3.   DISTRIBUTABLE RESERVES

| | |
|---|---|
| Retained income | R782 331 |
| General | 150 000 |
| | R932 331 |

# E42 CONTINUED

4.    <u>LONG TERM LIABILITIES</u>
SECURED
Loan secured by first mortgage over erf 17760 with
buildings thereon.  Rate of interest is 11% per annum.
Repayable in monthly instalments of R140 to 19y7        R28 755

UNSECURED
Bank loan at interest rate of 13% per annum.  Repayable
in equal annual instalments of R75 000 commencing on
1  April 19x1        <u>300 000</u>
R328 755
=======

5.    <u>FIXED ASSETS</u>

|                                               | <u>Cost/valuation</u> | <u>Accumulated depreciation</u> |           |
| --------------------------------------------- | ---------------------: | ------------------------------: | --------: |
| Valuation at 1 January 19x0 plus subsequent addition at cost: |        |                                 |           |
| Land                                          | R415 219              | -                               | R415 219  |
| Buildings                                     | 870 547               | R35 756                         | 834 791   |
| At cost:                                      |                       |                                 |           |
| Plant and equipment                           | 707 164               | 154 983                         | 552 181   |
| Transport and earthmoving equipment           | 349 499               | 181 093                         | 168 506   |
|                                               | R2 342 529            | R371 832                        | R1 970 697 |
|                                               | =========             | =======                         | ========= |

Details  of land and buildings are contained in a register.

6.    <u>INVESTMENTS</u>

| LISTED        | Number of <u>shares held</u> | Effective <u>holding</u> | Cost      |
| ------------- | ---------------------------: | -----------------------: | --------: |
| A Company Ltd | 20 700 250                   | 32%                      | R216 800  |
| B Company Ltd | 2 453 123                    | 5%                       | 14 557    |
| Other         | -                            | 1%                       | 8 450     |
|               |                              |                          | 239 807   |
| UNLISTED      |                              |                          |           |
| Z Company Ltd | 103 300                      | 25%                      | 26 000    |
| TOTAL INVESTMENTS |                          |                          | R265 807  |
|               |                              |                          | =======   |

7.    <u>STOCKS</u>
Stocks are valued on a basis consistent with that of prior years with
the exception of the company's work in progress, previously valued at
direct material and labour content, now valued at cost which includes
manufacturing overheads directly attributable to the process.  This has
had the effect of increasing the profit for the year and the company
and the group by R24 020.

# E42 CONTINUED

|  |  |
|---|---:|
| Raw materials - cost | R117 265 |
| Finished goods - factory cost | 479 779 |
| Consumable stores - cost | 358 285 |
| Work in progress - cost | 38 070 |
| Merchandise - cost | 48 723 |
|  | R1 042 113 |
|  | ========= |

8.    <u>CAPITAL COMMITMENTS</u>

|  |  |
|---|---:|
| Contracted for but not provided | R17 600 |
| Approved but not contracted | 57 258 |
|  | R74 858 |
|  | ====== |

9.    <u>TURNOVER</u>

Percentage increase in turnover compared with previous year    10,1%

10.    <u>TAX</u>

|  |  |
|---|---:|
| Normal tax | R70 931 |
| Adjustments - prior year - normal | 1 283 |
|  | R72 214 |
|  | ====== |

# E43

The following balance sheet is presented to you:

<u>XYZ LIMITED</u>

<u>SHARE CAPITAL</u>

| | | | | |
|---|---|---|---|---|
| R200 000  Shares of 50 cents each | | R250 000 | | |

<u>NON-DISTRIBUTABLE RESERVES</u>

| | | | | |
|---|---|---|---|---|
| Share premium | | R5 000 | | |
| Unrealised appreciation of land arising on revaluation | | 30 000 | <u>35 000</u> | |

<u>DISTRIBUTABLE RESERVES</u>

| | | | | |
|---|---|---|---|---|
| 70 000 | General | 70 000 | | |
| 10 000 | Retained income | <u>15 700</u> | 85 700 | |
| | | | | |
| 80 000 | MORTGAGE DEBENT | <u>85 000</u> | | |
| | | R390 000 | R450 700 | |
| | | ======= | ======= | |

<u>FIXED ASSETS</u>

| | | | | |
|---|---|---|---|---|
| 150 000 | Land and buildings | 150 000 | | |
| | Plant at cost | <u>160 000</u> | | |
| <u>126 000</u> | Less depreciation | 46 000 | <u>114 000</u> | R264 000 |

<u>INVESTMENTS</u>

| | | | | |
|---|---|---|---|---|
| 3 800 | Listed investments | 13 800 | | |
| <u>6 000</u> | Unlisted investments | <u>4 500</u> | 18 300 | |

<u>CURRENT ASSETS</u>

| | | | | |
|---|---|---|---|---|
| 128 000 | Stock | 136 000 | | |
| 84 000 | Debtors and bills | <u>118 400</u> | | |
| | | 254 400 | | |

<u>LESS CURRENT LIABILITIES</u>

| | | | | |
|---|---|---|---|---|
| 57 800 | Creditors | 36 000 | | |
| | Bank overdraft secured | | | |
| 50 000 | by pledge of bills receivable | 40 000 | | |
| 10 000 | Shareholders for dividend | <u>10 000</u> | 86 000 | <u>168 400</u> |
| | | R390 000 | | R450 700 |
| | | ======= | | ======= |

Notes:

(1)  There is a contingent liability for bills discounted but not yet matured.
(2)  There is an option over 250 000 shares at present unissued.

## E43 CONTINUED

<u>YOU ARE REQUIRED TO</u>:

(a)  list the ways in which the following balance sheet falls short of the requirements of the Companies Act and
(b)  list the items, which from a study of the balance sheet are likely to exist, which must  be shown separately in the income statement of XYZ Limited or in the notes to the financial statements.

**E44**

Big Reel Manufacturing Company Limited manufacturers a specific type of fishing reel and supplies retail shops throughout the country.  The following trial balance was extracted from the company's general ledger at the end of its third financial year.

<u>TRIAL BALANCE AT 31 DECEMBER 19x6</u>

|  | <u>DR.</u> | <u>CR.</u> |
|---|---:|---:|
| Accounts receivable | R26 510 | |
| Bad debts | 1 800 | |
| Bank overdraft | | R7 940 |
| Debentures - 8% | | 20 000 |
| Discount allowed | 600 | |
| Interest - on overdraft | 1 100 | |
|         - on bills payable | 400 | |
| Lease of plant and machinery | 1 000 | |
| Maintenance of factory plant | 410 | |
| Motor vehicles - at cost | 12 000 | |
| Office furniture - at cost | 4 000 | |
| Plant and machinery (factory) - see Note 1.2 | 49 200 | |
| Profit on sale of land and buildings | | 30 000 |
| Accumulated depreciation at 1.1.19x6 | | |
|     -    plant and machinery | | 8 200 |
|     -    motor vehicles | | 4 800 |
|     -    office furniture | | 600 |
| Purchases of raw materials | 32 000 | |
| Rent of land and buildings | 2 000 | |
| Retained income 1.1.19x6 | | 5 000 |
| Salaries - salesmen | 10 000 | |
| Salaries - administrative staff | 5 600 | |
| Sales | | 75 000 |
| Share capital - 80 000 ordinary shares | | 20 000 |
|             -  5 000 6% preference shares | | 5 000 |
| Stock 1.1.x6   - raw materials | 6 000 | |
|              - work-in-progress | - | |
|              - finished goods | 3 000 | |
| Wages - factory staff including production | | |
|        manager's remuneration | 17 220 | |
| Power | 2 100 | |
| Assessment rates | 1 600 | |
| | R176 540 | R176 540 |

# E44 CONTINUED

1.1.  Land and buildings originally costing R120 000 were sold for R150 000 on 1 August 19x6 from which date the company rented a different property a a yearly rental of R4 800.  Three-quarters of the building is used as the factory while the remainder is used for administration and selling functions.

1.2  Plant and machinery originality costing R2 000 on 1 January  19x5 was sold on 1 July 19x6 for R800.  The only entry passed to record the transaction was to debit bank with R800 and credit plant and machinery. The company then leased similar plant and machinery from 1 July 19x6 at a rate of R2 400 p.a.

1.3.  Motor vehicles compromise three motor cars used by the salesmen and one delivery van each bought for R3 000 on 1 January 19x4.

1.4  No office furniture was purchased or sold during 19x6.

1.5  Fixed assets are to be depreciated for 19x6, as in the past, as follows:

-       motor vehicles at 20% per annum using the straight line method
-       plant  and machinery  and office furniture at  10% per annum using
        the reducing balance method
-       land and building are not depreciated.

1.6  According to the company's articles of association profit made on the sale of fixed assets are available for dividend.

2.1  The company sold 5 400 fishing reels during 19x6.

2.2  All stock is accounted for using the first-in-first-out method.  The following details relate to stock at the respective dates.

|  | 31 December 19x5 | 31 December 19x6 |
|---|---|---|
| Raw materials | R6 000 | R8 000 |
| Partly finished items | - | 2 000 |
| units |  |  |
| - % complete materials | - | 75% |
| - % complete labour and overheads | - | 30% |
| Finished goods | 600 units | 1 200 |
| units |  |  |

2.3  The company pays a royalty of 20 cents for each completed unit.  The amount due for each year is paid in January of the following year.

2.4.  Finished units are transferred, immediately upon completion, from the factory to the storeroom at factory price.

# E44 CONTINUED

3. In addition to the items mentioned above the directors wish to provide for the following for the year ended 31 December 19x6:

|   |   |   |   |
|---|---|---|---|
| (1) | Audit expenses | - fee | R2 000 |
|   |   | - travelling expenses | 500 |
| (2) | Directors' fees | - Mr Able | 3 000 |
|   |   | - Mr Bain | 1 500 |
|   |   | - Mr Cain | 1 500 |

Mr Cain is the only director who is employed by the company in a capacity other than as a director. He is employed as a production manager and was paid a salary of R6 000 during 19x6. The firm is to supplement Mr Ding's (a past director) pension of R4 000 (from a recognised pension fund) with an additional R1 000 per annum.

(3) First and final dividends
- 6 cents per share for preference shareholders
- 10 cents per share for ordinary shareholders
(4) Interest on debentures for the full year.

4. Ignore taxation.

<u>YOU ARE REQUIRED TO</u>:

(a) prepare the company's statement of cost of goods manufactured for the year ended 31 December 19x6.

(b) Prepare the detailed income statement of the company for the year ended 31 December 19x6 in accordance with generally accepted accounting practice.

(Notes to the income statements are required. Do not calculate the earnings per share).

A balance sheet is <u>not</u> required.

ALL WORKINGS MUST BE GIVEN.

# E45

Extract from the trial balance of ABC (Pty) Limited for the year ended 30 June 19x4:

| | |
|---|---|
| Land (Plot 81 Sunninghill) acquired 1/1/19x2 at cost | R80 000 |
| Office buildings erected 30/6/19x4 | 50 000 |
| Fixtures and fittings at cost | 60 000 |
| Accumulated depreciation of fixtures and fittings at 1/7/19x3 | 10 000 |

## DEPRECIATION

Depreciation is calculated at 10% per annum reducing balance on fixtures and fittings.
No depreciation is calculated on land and buildings.

## REQUIRED:

(1)  If the balance sheet is only to reflect the book value of the above assets give the notes to the financial statements.

(2)  Distinguish between an accounting policy and an accounting basis.

# E46

Listed below are extracts of the unfinalised financial statements of X
Limited, a manufacturing company listed on the Johannesburg Stock Exchange.

| BALANCE SHEETS AT 31 DECEMBER | 19x4 | 19x3 |
|---|---|---|
| CAPITAL EMPLOYED | | |
| Ordinary share capital - R1 shares | R250 000 | R100 000 |
| Share premium | 50 000 | - |
| | 300 000 | 100 000 |
| General reserve | 25 000 | 75 000 |
| Retained income | 45 000 | 50 000 |
| Ordinary shareholders' funds | 370 000 | 225 000 |
| 12% cumulative preference shares | 100 000 | 100 000 |
| Total capital and reserves | 470 000 | 325 000 |
| Long-term liabilities | 250 000 | 690 000 |
| | R720 000 | R1015 000 |
| EMPLOYMENT OF CAPITAL | | |
| Fixed assets | R565 000 | R895 000 |
| Current assets | 185 000 | 180 000 |
|   Stock | 100 000 | 75 000 |
|   Debtors | 75 000 | 80 000 |
|   Bank | 10 000 | 25 000 |
| Current liabilities | 30 000 | 60 000 |
|   Creditors | 20 000 | 35 000 |
|   Accrued expenses | 10 000 | 25 000 |
| Net current assets | 155 000 | 120 000 |
| | R720 000 | R1015 000 |

| INCOME STATEMENTS FOR THE YEARS ENDED 31 DECEMBER | 19x4 | 19x3 |
|---|---|---|
| Turnover | R400 000 | R500 000 |
| Net income before tax | 120 000 | 194 000 |
| Taxation - S.A. normal current | (80 000) | (92 000) |
| Net income before extraordinary item | 40 000 | 102 000 |
| Extraordinary item (net of tax) | | |
| - loss of stock destroyed by flood | (45 000) | - |
| | (5 000) | 102 000 |
| Preference dividend | - | (12 000) |
| Net income attributable to ordinary shareholders | (5 000) | 90 000 |
| Ordinary dividend | - | (20 000) |
| | (5 000) | 70 000 |
| Transfer to general reserve | - | (50 000) |
| Retained income for the year | (5 000) | 20 000 |
| Retained income at beginning of year | 50 000 | 30 000 |
| Retained income per balance sheet | R45 000 | R50 000 |

# E46 CONTINUED

<u>NOTES</u>

1.  Before the finalisation of the financial statements at 31 December
    19X4, the directors of the company decided to depreciate the plant and
    machinery at the rate of 20% per annum on the reducing balance method.
    To date the plant and machinery has been depreciated at 20% per annum
    straight line.

    Analysis of the fixed asset accounts at 31 December 19x4 shows the
    following:

    | | | |
    |---|---|---:|
    | Furniture and fittings | - net book value | R50 000 |
    | Office machines | - net book value | 65 000 |
    | Plant and machinery | - net book value | 450 000 |
    | Per balance sheet | | R565 000 |

    The fixed assets registers show that all the plant and machinery was
    purchased on 30 June 19x1.

    No fixed assets were purchased or sold during 19x3 or 19x4.

    The change in the basis of calculating depreciation does not affect the
    taxation charge per the income statements.

2.  On 30 June 19x4 the company made a capitalisation issue out of
    distributable reserves to the existing shareholders on a 1 share for
    every 2 held basis.

3.  For the purposes of further expansion the company issued 100 000 R1
    shares to outsiders on 30 September 19x4 at R1,50 per share.

<u>YOU ARE REQUIRED TO</u>:

to prepare the income statement and supporting notes for the year
ended 31 December 19x4 in conformity with Schedule Four and generally accepted
accounting practice.

(Taxation at 50c in the Rand on the extraordinary item.)

# E47

The following is the trial balance of Air Supply (Pty) Limited at 30 September
19x4:

|  | Dr | Cr |
|---|---|---|
| Stated capital account (800 000 shares) |  | R920 000 |
| Retained income 30 September 19x3 |  | 269 000 |
| Profit before taxation for the year ended |  |  |
|   30 September 19x4 |  | 147 000 |
| Taxation | R70 000 |  |
| Preliminary and share issue expenses | 12 500 |  |
| Land and buildings, at cost | 300 000 |  |
| Plant, at cost | 660 000 |  |
| Accumulated depreciation - plant |  |  |
|   30 September 19x3 |  | 220 000 |
| Furniture, at cost | 12 400 |  |
| Accumulated depreciation - furniture |  |  |
|   30 September 19x3 |  | 4 800 |
| Listed investments, at cost | 90 000 |  |
| Stock | 442 300 |  |
| Debtors | 473 200 |  |
| Loan levy | 52 000 |  |
| Bank overdraft |  | 299 000 |
| Creditors |  | 140 600 |
| Receiver of Revenue |  | 12 000 |
| 10% Debentures |  | 100 000 |
|  | R2 112 400 | R2 112 400 |

## Additional information

1.  The authorised share capital is 2 000 000 ordinary shares of no par
    value.

2.  The directors wish to write off preliminary and share issue expenses in
    such a manner that the maximum amount is retained in distributable
    reserves.

3.  No depreciation has been provided on plant, and depreciation must be
    provided at 10% p.a. on cost.   Plant costing R6 000 was acquired on
    31 May 19x4.   There were no sales of plant, but an item which had cost
    R35 000 was scrapped on 1 February 19x4.   This item of plant was the
    only item fully depreciated at 30 September 19x3, and no journal entry
    was made to reflect the scrapping.

4.  Depreciation on furniture must be provided at 15% p.a. using the
    reducing balance method.  Furniture costing R3 000 was bought on 31
    March 19x4.  There were no disposals during the year.

5.	The net profit was arrived at after charging:

| | |
|---|---:|
| Administration expenses | R10 000 |
| Audit fee | 15 000 |
| Bad debts (normally R3 000) | 28 000 |
| Directors' fees | 5 000 |
| Interest on debentures and bank overdraft | 12 000 |
| Leasing charges - motor vehicles | 12 900 |
| Loss arising due to flooding of warehouse | 60 000 |
| Managing director's salary | 18 000 |
| Travelling and entertainment expenses | 16 000 |

All of the items listed above are allowable as deductions for tax purposes. The tax rate is 42%.

6.	Taxation at current rates has been provided, and the balance of R12 000 owed to the Receiver of Revenue represents the difference between the provision for taxation and provisional tax payments made during the year. No adjustments must be made to the taxation charge.

7.	Mr Springsteen and Mr Collins are the only two directors of the company. Each director receives fees of R2 500 p.a. Mr Springsteen is the chairman. Mr Collins is the managing director.

The travelling and entertainment expenses included in point 5. above, include and amount of R100 per month paid to the chairman, also R100 per month paid to the managing director, as an entertainment allowance.

All salaried employees contribute 10% of their salaries to a pension fund. The company contributes on a rand for rand basis.

Mr Springsteen has the use of a company car - this benefit is estimated to be worth R1 500 p.a.

The company also pays a pension of R4 000 p.a. to an ex-director, Mr Stewart since it was felt that the amount of R200 per month received by Mr Stewart from the pension fund was inadequate. Mr Stewart had also been sales manager during his term of employment with the company.

8.	The audit fee of R15 000 consists of:

| | | |
|---|---|---:|
| - | fee for the audit | R12 000 |
| - | expenses | 500 |
| - | management advisory services | 2 500 |

9.	Land and buildings comprise a factory and offices at 15 East Street, Band River, acquired in 19x8 at a cost of R240 000. Additions amounted to R37 000 in 19x3 and R23 000 in 19x6. On 1 October 19x3, Mr Seger (a sworn appraiser) valued the land and buildings in accordance with the latest municipal valuation, which was R350 000 in 19x3. Land and buildings are not depreciated. No entries have been made to record the revaluation.

**E47 CONTINUED**

10.    The company's listed investments comprise:

| Company | No. of shares | Cost | Market value | |
|---|---|---|---|---|
| | | | 1/10/x3 | 30/9/x4 |
| Queen Limited | 75 000 | R37 500 | R44 000 | R42 500 |
| Supertramp Limited | 40 000 | 52 500 | 55 000 | 41 000 |
| | | R90 000 | R99 000 | R83 500 |

No dividends were received from either of these companies.

11.    The 10% debentures are repayable in 5 equal instalments commencing on 31 March 19x5.

Interest is payable on 30 September each year, and the interest for the year ended 30 September 19x4 has been paid and included in the calculation of the profit for the year. The debentures are secured by a first mortgage bond over land and buildings.

12.    Included in debtors is an amount owing by one of the directors (Mr Collins) amounting to R7 000. The balance outstanding at the beginning of the year amounted to R20 000, but Mr Collins repaid R13 000 during the current year.

The company also advanced a sum of R6 000 to the other director, (Mr Springsteen) during the year. This amount was repaid by him on 20 September 19x4.

13.    Stock has been valued on a FIFO basis, which has been the company's policy for several years. Stock is reflected at the lower of cost or net realisable value, and consists of:

| | |
|---|---|
| Raw materials | R176 000 |
| Work in progress (including proportion of fixed overheads) | 29 800 |
| Consumable stores | 4 200 |
| Finished goods | 232 300 |

14.    Turnover for the year amounted to R1 925 000.

15.  The following information, inter alia, appeared in the minutes of the directors' meeting:

(i)  Legal action had been taken against the company in respect of allegedly defective products.  Compensation of R50 000 had been demanded, and the company's attorneys had been instructed to defend the action and it is  expected that they will be able to do so.

(ii)  The company had contracted to acquire plant costing R400 000 from West Germany.  Delivery  costs would amount  to  R25 000.  Detailed arrangements  have still to be made.  A three year loan had been arranged to finance this.

(iii) A major marketing drive was to be made in October, November and December 19x4 in order to launch a new product.  Advertising costs were expected to amount  to R49 000.

(iv)  A dividend of 4 cents per share was declared on 15 September 19x4,  payable on 1 November 19x4.   (No entry has been made for this dividend.)

<u>YOU ARE REQUIRED TO</u>:

prepare a balance sheet for Air Supply (Pty) Limited, at 30 September 19x4, together with an income statement for the year ended on that date.  The requirements of the Companies Act 1973 and GAAP must be complied with.

Note: (1)  Notes  to the financial  statements (OTHER THAN the accounting policy notes) MUST be supplied.
      (2)  Comparative figures are to be omitted.
      (3)  A cash flow statement is NOT required.
      (4)  Show all workings.

# E48

You are given the following extract from the financial statements of A B Limited at 31 December 19x5:

Earnings per share before extraordinary items    250,0 cents

On examination of the records of the company the following was noted:

1.  <u>CAPITAL STRUCTURE</u>

    Issued ordinary shares of R1,00 each at 31 December 19x5       R350 000

    The following movements took place during the year:

    a.  On 1 March 19x5 a capitalisation issue was made to the existing shareholders.  Each shareholder received 1 share for every 2 held.  A quarter of this issue was provided out of the share premium account, with the remainder provided from retained income.

    b.  On 30 June 19x5 the company issued 50 000 shares to the public at par.

    Issued preference share capital -
      100 000 12% cumulative preference shares of R1,00 each.

2.  <u>DIVIDENDS PAID DURING THE YEAR</u>

    On 31 December 19x5 the company declared and paid the annual preference dividend and a dividend of 15 cents per share to the ordinary shareholders registered on that date.

3.  During the year the company lost all of its stock during the drought period.  The cost of the loss was R50 000.  (Allowable for tax.)

4.  The directors of the company decided that for the purposes of providing for the replacement of plant and machinery, R50 000 should be transferred to the asset replacement reserve.

5.  Land and buildings were revalued from R200 000 to R425 000.

6.  R225 000 was transferred to the general reserve.

7.  Retained income as at 1 January 19x5 was R20 000.

8.  Tax is at 50 cents in the rand.

# E48 CONTINUED

<u>YOU ARE REQUIRED TO</u>:

a.   reconstruct the income statement of A B Limited for the year ended
     31 December 19x5 in accordance with Schedule 4 of the Companies Act and
     the generally accepted accounting practice statements.
b.   give the disclosure for earnings and dividends per share as required by
     AC104.

# E49

Critically examine the following extracts from various different (adapted) companies' annual financial statements.

<u>YOU ARE REQUIRED FOR EACH EXTRACT TO:</u>

1.  List any omissions (non-compliance) with the minimum disclosure requirements of Schedule 4 of the Companies Act relating to the extract.

2.  List any additional information given which is not required by the Act relating to the extract.

3.  Comment on the effect of any omission and/or additional disclosure and/or general set out within the context of the objective of the financial statements which is to "provide useful information for economic decision to present and potential investors and creditors".

    Your answer should be set out in columnar form (over a double page if necessary).  If any aspect is not applicable to an extract, record N/A.

Columns required:

| <u>Ref.</u> | <u>Omissions</u> | <u>Additional Disclosure</u> | <u>Comment</u> |
|---|---|---|---|
| 1. | | | |
| 2. | | | |
| 3. | | | |

etc.


1.  ACCOUNTING POLICIES

    1.1  Depreciation

        Depreciation is determined on various bases appropriate to the use of the different classes of assets, so as to write the assets off over their respective useful lives.  Land is not depreciated and it is a company policy not to depreciate buildings.

        Stock

        Details under this heading are reflected in Note 9 to the financial statements.

|  |  | <u>19x3</u> | <u>19x2</u> |
|---|---|---|---|
| 9. | STOCKS | | |
| | Raw materials | R253 000 | R209 000 |
| | Merchandise | 11 323 000 | 9 930 000 |
| | | R11 576 000 | R10 139 000 |
| | | ========== | ========== |

# E49 CONTINUED

Stock of merchandise have  been valued at the lower of cost or net realisable value.  Raw materials have been valued at the lower of average purchase price or net realisable value.  Cost has been determined on the first-in-first- out basis.  Due allowance has been made for obsolete, redundant and slow-moving stocks.

2.  TURNOVER

Turnover comprises sales to customers less returns and allowances.  For comparison purposes sales relative to the Owen Jones division which was sold during the 19x2 year and the Joubert  Mills division  which was sold during the 19x3 year have been taken into account in arriving at the following:

|  | 19x3 | 19x2 |
|---|---|---|
| Total sales | R11 910 967 | R16 590 923 |
| Less - |  |  |
|  Applicable to Owen Jones division | - | 7 371 585 |
|  Applicable to Joubert Mills division | 639 324 | 812 911 |
| Sales for the company as now constituted |  |  |
|  | ========== | ========= |

3.  INTEREST PAID

|  | 19x3 | 19x2 |
|---|---|---|
| Interest paid |  |  |
| -    revolving credit facilities (19x2 - |  |  |
|      net of rebate of R440 000) | 133 514 | R257 865 |
| - Long term loans and extended credit | 202 310 | 201 563 |
| -    Other | 406 019 | 398 873 |
|  | 741 843 | 858 301 |
| Less: interest received | 256 823 | 14 829 |
|  | R485 020 | R843 472 |
|  | ======= | ======= |

4.  CAPITAL COMMENT

|  | 19x3<br>R'000 | 19x2<br>R'000 |
|---|---|---|
| An agreement has been entered into for the erection of factory building amounting to | 155 | - |

5.  DIRECTORS' EMOLUMENTS

|  | 19x3 | 19x2 |
|---|---|---|
| Management fees | R33 000 | R33 000 |
| Fees | 11 000 | 10 000 |
| Other emoluments | 52 550 | 62 200 |
| From other companies | 30 070 | 33 571 |
|  | R126 620 | R138 771 |
|  | ======= | ======= |

# E50

The following balances appeared, amongst others in the trial balance of
Westerns Limited at 30 June 19x7:

| | |
|---|---:|
| Stated capital account - 30 000 ordinary no par value shares | R60 000 |
| Retained income 1 July 19x6 | 7 600 |
| Sales | 763 100 |
| Pre-incorporation profits | 12 600 |
| General reserve | 8 000 |
| Machinery replacement reserve | 28 000 |
| 10% - R10 debentures (R9 000 redeemed at 28.2.19x7) | 36 000 |
| Plant and equipment - at cost | 236 000 |
|        - accumulated depreciation 30.6.19x6 | 90 000 |
| Dividends received  - Primrose Limited | 640 |
|        - Shermas Limited | 1 360 |
| Interest received on loan to Shermas Limited | 2 360 |
| Payments to Receiver of Revenue (including taxation of R1 100 underprovided in respect of 19x6 year of assessment) | 37 640 |
| Cost of sales | 460 320 |
| 2 000 shares of R1 each in Primrose Limited at cost (Issued capital 260 000 shares) | 5 000 |
| 2 000 shares of 50c each in Diesel Limited at cost (Issued capital 100 000 shares) | 1 000 |
| 20 shares of R1 each in Shermas Limited at cost (Issued capital 20 shares) | 20 |
| Administration and selling expenses | 177 480 |
| Payment received for breach of contract by supplier of raw material | 6 000 |
| Debenture interest accrued 30.6.19x6 | 1 500 |
| Land and buildings at cost | 15 000 |

Further information:

1. On 31 March 19x7 a machine had been sold for R13 100 which amount was credited to sales.  The machine had originally cost R16 000 and total depreciation at 30 June 19x6 amounted to R4 000.  No entry other than the above had been made in the books in this respect.

2. Depreciation of plant and equipment must be provided for at 10% per annum on cost.

3. Administration and selling expenses consisted of the following:

| | |
|---|---:|
| Interest on bank overdraft | R5 720 |
| Interest paid on debentures (interest payable on 28.2 and 31.8) | 4 500 |
| Managing director's salary | 32 000 |
| Fees for services as directors | 16 000 |
| Fees paid to transfer secretaries | 7 500 |
| Salaries and wages | 88 000 |
| Office expenses | 16 400 |
| Sundry expenses | 2 068 |
| | R172 980 |

# E50 CONTINUED

4.  Provision must be made for normal South African company taxation
    R37 660, (on trading profits) audit fees R7 000 and travelling expenses
    of auditors R1 700.

5.  The directors recommended the following at 30 June 19x7:

    (i)   a dividend of R9 600
    (ii)  transfer to general reserve R20 000.

6.  The shares of Primrose Limited are traded at R2,80 each on the
    Johannesburg Stock Exchange. The shares in Diesel Limited and Shermas
    Limited are not quoted and are valued by the directors at R800 and
    R1 200 respectively.

7.  Tax rate 40%.


<u>YOU ARE REQUIRED TO</u>:

prepare the income statement for the year ended 30 June 19x7 in accordance
with the Companies Act 1973, as amended, showing only the items required to
be separately disclosed but taking cognisance of good accounting practice.

# E51

The following income statement for the 19x7 financial year was prepared by the bookkeeper of Quail Limited and presented to the company's auditor.

<u>INCOME STATEMENT 31 DECEMBER 19x7</u>

| | | | | |
|---|---|---|---|---|
| Audit fee | R1 300 | Sales | | R140 000 |
| Dividends paid | 2 000 | Less cost of sales | | 90 000 |
| Debenture redemption | | Gross profit | | 50 000 |
|   and interest | 5 200 | Profit on sale of land | | 24 000 |
| Motor and travelling | | Dividends received - | | |
|   expenses | 7 300 |   shares in Snipe (Pty) Ltd | | 1 000 |
| Rates | 400 | | | |
| Salaries and wages - | | | | |
|   managing director | 8 000 | | | |
|   secretarial | 4 000 | | | |
|   other | 9 000 | | | |
| Selling and administrative | | | | |
|   expenses | 4 500 | | | |
| Tax payments | 3 000 | | | |
| Net profit | 30 300 | | | |
| | R75 000 | | | R75 000 |

During the course of the audit it was discovered that the above statement had been prepared on a CASH BASIS and was in fact an accurate summary of the company's cash and bank transactions for 19x7. All the business documents for the period had been systematically filed and from these and the minutes of directors' meetings the auditor obtained the following information:

1.    Certain relevant balances and amounts outstanding at 31 December

| | 19x6 | 19x7 |
|---|---|---|
| Accounts payable - trade creditors<br>  (see note 2) | R6 000 | R9 000 |
| Accounts receivable - trade debtors<br>  (excluding dishonoured bills - see note 3) | 4 000 | 2 500 |
| Bills payable  (see note 2) | 4 200 | 5 000 |
| Debenture discount * | 400 | - |
| Receiver of Revenue (see note 8) | 1 000 credit | ? |
| Plant and machinery, at book value<br>  (see note 6) | 18 000 | 16 300 |
| Recommended dividends (see note 9) | 2 000 | See note 8 |
| Retained income | 700 | ? |
| Stock | 4 500 | 6 000 |

  * To be written off and treated as
    extraordinary item

# E51 CONTINUED

2.    All goods for resale have been bought on credit and the company has either paid accounts in full after the normal credit period of 60 days or has accepted bills at 90 days.    The stock figures given above had not been taken into account when determining the cost of goods sold per the above income statement.

3.    Sales have all been conducted on a credit basis.    Discounts of R900 were allowed to customers during the year for prompt payment.    Bills have been drawn on certain customers and immediately discounted with the bank. Bills totalling R1 000 were dishonoured during the year and this figure is included in the selling and administrative expenses.    In the opinion of the directors, R600 of this amount is irrecoverable.    The sales figure, per the income statement above, comprises receipts from debtors and proceeds on bills discounted at the bank.    Discounting charges may be ignored.

4.    The company redeemed its remaining 50 8% debentures of R100 each on 30 June 19x7, and paid interest to that date.

5.    When disposing of a surplus area of land during the year, the company had paid a sum equal to the cost of the land sold, directly to the holder of the mortgage, and the amount representing the profit on the transaction was banked.    In terms of its Articles, the company is not allowed to distribute capital profits as dividends.

6.    No other fixed assets were bought or sold during 19x7.

7.    Motor and travelling expenses consist of:

|  |  |
|---|---:|
| - leasing charges of R400 per month for vehicles leased on 1 February 19x7 | R4 800 |
| - travel allowance to the managing director | 2 000 |
| - refund of travelling expenses to the auditor | 500 |
|  | R7 300 |
|  | ===== |

8.    Tax payments during the year were for:

|  |  |
|---|---:|
| - balance of tax assessed for 19x6 | R1 500 |
| - first provisional payment for 19x7 | 1 500 |
|  | R3 000 |
|  | ===== |

The secretary calculated that the company had no taxable income for 19x7, and a second provisional tax payment for 19x7 was not made.    The auditor however calculated the tax for 19x7 at R2 700.    Ignore penalty for nonpayment of provisional tax.

# E51 CONTINUED

9.    A directors' minute dated 31 December 19x7 recorded that the following
      items should be provided in respect of 19x7

      -    directors' fees                                              R5 000
      -    first and final dividend for the current year                R2 000

<u>YOU ARE REQUIRED TO</u>:

prepare the revised income statement and notes thereto for Quail Limited for
the year ended 31 December 19x7.   The statement should disclose only that
information specifically required by the Companies Act 1973, as amended, and
Schedule 4 thereto, and its format should be in accordance with generally
accepted accounting practice.   NO BALANCE SHEET IS REQUIRED.

SHOW ALL WORKINGS CLEARLY.   IGNORE COMPARATIVE FIGURES.

**E52**

You have recently been appointed as the accountant of a listed trading
company, Getafix Ltd and have been presented with <u>an extract</u> of the trial
balance at 29 February 19x8.

|  | Dr | Cr |
|---|---|---|
| Retained income 1/3/x7 | | R160 000 |
| Share capital | | |
|   100 000 ordinary shares of R2,00 | | 200 000 |
|    80 000 12% redeemable preference shares | | |
|     of R1 each | | 80 000 |
| Sales | | 510 000 |
| Interest paid | R6 700 | |
| Audit fees (expenses of R3 000 included) | 14 000 | |
| Profit on sale of land and buildings | | 18 700 |
| Stock 1/3/x7 | 32 000 | |
| Dividends received (unlisted R2 000) | | 3 400 |
| Directors emoluments | 38 000 | |
| Investment - Tulip Limited | 21 550 | |
| Bad debts written off | 20 000 | |
| Loss on sale of investments | 12 500 | |
| Purchases | 300 000 | |
| Preference dividend declared | 9 600 | |
| Secretarial fees | 22 000 | |
| Depreciation | 18 050 | |
| Interest received | | 8 300 |
| Sales expenses | 20 000 | |
| Administrative expenses | 30 000 | |
| Fixed assets | | |
|   Land and buildings - at cost | 130 000 | |
|   Plant, machinery and vehicles - at book value | | |
|     at 29/2/x8 | 162 450 | |
| Goodwill | 35 000 | |
| Debentures | | 79 600 |
| Tax paid | 25 000 | |

The following additional information is provided:

(1)    The directors have since the trial balance was extracted decided to
change the depreciation on plant, machinery and vehicles from 10%
reducing balance to 10% straight line retrospectively to the date of
purchase.   Plant, machinery and vehicles were all acquired on the
incorporation of the company on 1 September 19x6 and have no residual
value.

(2)    In terms of the articles of association profits on the sale of land and
buildings is not distributable as dividends.

(3)     The taxable income of the company is R48 000 and tax is payable at 50c in the Rand.   Two provisional payments of R8 000 each were made during the year.   The latest tax assessment received on 27 February 19x8 indicated that the company had overprovided R3 000 for taxation in the previous year.   Foreign tax paid to Zimbabwe amounted to R9 000.

(4)     On 30 November 19x7 the company issued 20 000 ordinary shares at par.
(5)     An interim ordinary dividend of 3c per share was declared and paid on 31 August 19x7 and a final ordinary dividend of 3c per share was declared on 29 February 19x8.
(6)     The directors have decided to write goodwill off over five years.
(7)     The details of the directors emoluments are as follows:
As directors         6 000
Other               32 000
(8)     Included in bad debts is an amount of R15 000 from one debtor who has been liquidated.
(9)     Closing stock on 29 February 19x8 was R78 000.
(10)    All investments were acquired to ensure a regular supply of merchandise.


<u>YOU ARE REQUIRED TO PREPARE</u>:

the income statement of Getafix Limited for the year ended 29 February 19x8 in accordance with the requirements of the Companies Act and generally accepted accounting practice.

(Ignore tax implications for prior year adjustments, extraordinary items and abnormal items.)

# E53

Chipp (Pty) Ltd started trading on 1 March 19x1.    In the financial year ended
28 February 19x2 the following provisional tax payments were made:

|                      |          |
|----------------------|----------|
| 31 August 19x1       | R5 000   |
| 28 February 19x2     | 5 800    |

The Income Statement for the year ended 28 February 19x2
included a taxation charge at the tax rate of 42% amounting to     10 600

However, the Receiver of Revenue disallowed certain expenditure
and raised a final assessment of                                   10 700

This assessment was received in January 19x3.

In the financial year ended 28 February 19x3 provisional tax
payments were made as follows:

|                      |          |
|----------------------|----------|
| 31 August 19x2       | 9 000    |
| 28 February 19x3     | 9 000    |

The estimated taxable income for 19x3 was                          42 000
and the rate of tax to be provided was                                45%

<u>YOU ARE REQUIRED TO</u>:

(a)    Show how taxation would be shown in the published annual financial
       statements of Chipp (Pty) Ltd for the year ended 28 February 19x3.

(b)    Show the amount due to (or overpaid to) the Receiver of Revenue at
       28 February 19x3.

(c)    Suggest ways in which the company could have maximised their cash flow
       in respect of the above tax payments.

**E54**

Alpha Limited owns and leases the Omega Centre, a mixed use of property
development in Pretoria.  The main components of the complex are a 10 storey
office tower, the 15 storey Omega Hotel, a shopping centre and parking
undercover for 600 cars situated on Stand 465, Sunnyside, Pretoria.

The draft balance sheet prepared by the inexperienced bookkeeper for the year
ended 28 February is as follows:

Balance sheet at 28 February 19x9

| | | | |
|---|---:|---|---:|
| Ordinary shares | R200 000 | Land | R50 000 |
| Preference shares | 50 000 | Buildings | 235 400 |
| Share premium | 20 000 | Office equipment | 40 500 |
| Profit on revaluation of | | Debtors | 191 100 |
|   land | 40 000 | Bank | 37 000 |
| Provision for taxation | 23 500 | Ordinary share issue | |
| Mortgage loan | 45 000 |   expenses | 15 900 |
| Interest on mortgage loan | 4 500 | Prepaid expenses | 400 |
| Provision for doubtful debts | 9 000 | Preference shareholders | 55 000 |
| Dividend on ordinary shares | 14 200 | Investments | 36 000 |
| Retained income | 204 600 | | |
| Creditors | 50 500 | | |
| | R661 300 | | R661 300 |
| | ======= | | ======= |

Additional information:

1.   The authorised ordinary share capital consists of 200 000 ordinary
     shares of no par value of which 100 000 have been issued.

2.   The authorised preference share capital consists of 50 000 8%
     redeemable preference shares of R1 each.  These had all been issued at
     a premium of 40 cents per share in 19x5.  On 3 January 19x9 they were
     redeemed at a premium of 10 cents per share.  The directors decided
     that this redemption which did not include the issue of further shares,
     should now be treated so as to have minimum effect on retained income.

3.   Interest on the loan is paid on 1 September and 1 March each year. The
     loan is to be repaid on 28 February 19y5.

4.   The land was acquired on 1 March 19x2 and revalued in 19x4.  The hotel
     was completed on 30 November 19x3 at a cost of R140 000 and all other
     buildings on 28 February 19x4. Depreciation is not charged on land and
     buildings.

5.   The office equipment was acquired on 1 March 19x7.  No acquisitions or
     disposals of office equipment have taken place since that date.
     Depreciation on office equipment at rate of 10% p.a. using the reducing
     balance method has been provided.

# E54 CONTINUED

6.    Investments:

| COMPANY | No. of shares | Book value | COMMENTS |
|---|---|---|---|
| Gamma Limited | 8 000 | R16 000 | Price on the J.S.E. on 28.2.x9 was R4,10 per share |
| Delta (Proprietary) Ltd | 10 000 | 20 000 | Directors' valuation R24 000 Cost R20 000 |

7.    The "provision for taxation R23 500", represents the company's tax liability for the year.

8.    Share issue expenses are to be written off without affecting profits available for dividends.

9.    An amount of R700 000 has been authorised by the directors for further building expansion over the next three years. A contract for the first phase of this plan, to be completed by 30 November 19x9, has been signed. To date R50 000 has been certified by the architects as having been completed, but no entries have been made in the books. This expansion is to be financed out of the proceeds of an issue of shares.

<u>YOU ARE REQUIRED TO:</u>

Prepare the balance sheet of Alpha Limited at 28 February 19x9, for inclusion in their published annual statements.

The balance sheet must comply with generally accepted accounting practice and should include any necessary information which can be inferred from the question. (Comparative figures are not required.)

# E55

Alpha Limited acquired a controlling interest in Fiat Limited on 1 April 19x8. The new directors of Fiat Limited decided

(i)    that buildings should be depreciated at the annual rate of 2,5% on cost in order to bring the accounting policy of Fiat Limited into line with that of the group. Previously Fiat Limited had not depreciated buildings. The remaining useful life of the buildings is estimated at 36 years from 1 April 19x8. The accounting policy is to be applied retrospectively.

(ii)    plant should be written off over its remaining useful life of 5 years as determined on 1 April 19x8. The group provides for depreciation on all fixed assets except land which is not depreciated, using the straight line method. In the past Fiat Limited had written off depreciation on the straight line method.

The following information is available in respect of land, buildings and plant at 1/4/19x8:

| | Date of acquisition by Fiat Limited | Cost to Fiat Ltd | Accumulated depreciation |
|---|---|---|---|
| Land | 1/4/19x4 | R20 000 | - |
| Buildings | 1/4/19x4 | 80 000 | - |
| Plant | 1/4/19x6 | 84 000 | R28 000 |

There have been no additions to the above since 1/4/19x8

The following draft income statements of Fiat Ltd for the years end 31 March have been prepared by the bookkeeper who had not been told about the directors' decision.

| | 19x9 | 19x8 |
|---|---|---|
| Turnover | R225 000 | R200 000 |
| | ======= | ======= |
| Net operating income before depreciation | R176 000 | R141 000 |
| Depreciation - plant | 14 000 | 14 000 |
| Depreciation - other assets | 2 000 | 2 000 |
| Net operating income | 160 000 | 125 000 |
| Dividend declared | 75 000 | 50 000 |
| Retained income for the year | 85 000 | 75 000 |
| Retained income at beginning of year | 90 000 | 15 000 |
| Retained income per balance sheet | R175 000 | R90 000 |
| | ======== | ====== |

Ignore taxation.

# E55 CONTINUED

<u>YOU ARE REQUIRED TO</u>:

(i)   Redraft the income statements for publication, AND

(ii)  Prepare the relevant notes to the income statement
      Ignore taxation.

# E56

The net income after tax but before extraordinary items of Lear Manufacturing Limited was reported as R1 500 000.   Included in the income statement, or notes thereto, are the following items:

| | |
|---|---:|
| Dividend income | R10 000 |
| Interest income, including R7 500 not yet received | 20 000 |
| Amortisation of patents, based on arbitrary life of 5 years | 50 000 |
| Depreciation of fixed assets | 400 000 |
| Gain on disposal of equipment | 200 000 |
| Uninsured loss of stock by flood (net of tax) | 150 000 |
| Uninsured loss of cash from employee fraud | 100 000 |
| Bad debt arising on insolvency of major debtor | 15 000 |
| Write off of investment following insolvency of major supplier | 25 000 |

<u>YOU ARE REQUIRED TO</u>:

(1)　COMPUTE the proceeds from the insurance claim in respect of the flood damage if the stock on hand at the date of the flood was assessed to have been R5 000 000 and the stock was insured for R4 000 000 (subject to the average clause).   Assume a tax rate of 40%.

(2)　DISCUSS the nature of extraordinary and abnormal items using each of the items in the above income statement to illustrate your answer. Your answer must not exceed twenty lines.

**E57**

The trial balances of Oupa Limited after all closing entries had been put through contained, inter alia, the following:

|  | 31 December 19x5 | 31 December 19x6 |
|---|---|---|
| Share capital | R20 000 | R20 000 |
| Retained income | 4 820 | 6 500 |

During April 19x6 the company's stock was damaged by a flood.

Of the stock of R20 000 only R500 was completely untouched.    The damaged stock was sold for R1 500.

The company's stock was insured for R12 000 and the policy was subject to the average clause.

All entries had been correctly made in the books during 19x6.

Taxation is at the rate of 40 cents in the rand.

During 19x6 there were no dividends declared, proposed or paid, nor were any transfers made to or from reserves.


<u>YOU ARE REQUIRED TO</u>:

to give the income statement and notes thereto for the year ended 31 December 19x6.  (Comparative figures are not required.)

# E58

The following is an extract from the income statement of Spiderlegs Limited for the year ended 31 December 19x4:

| | |
|---|---:|
| Net operating profit | R68 000 |
| Bad debt written off | 10 000 |
| Net income before taxation and extraordinary item | 58 000 |
| Taxation | 29 000 |
| Net income before extraordinary item | 29 000 |
| Extraordinary item | 40 000 |
| Net income | 69 000 |
| Transfer to general reserve | 9 000 |
| | 60 000 |
| Dividends - ordinary | 10 000 |
|         - preference | 2 000 |
| Retained income for the year | 48 000 |
| Prior year adjustment | (6 000) |
| Retained income at the beginning of the year | 20 000 |
| Retained income per balance sheet | R62 000 |

The following information is available:

(1)    The bad debt was the amount owing by one of the company's largest customers whose estate had been sequestrated.

(2)    The tax rate is 50%.

(3)    The extraordinary item arises from the profit on sale of land and buildings. The sale arose due to the expropriation of the land by the government. The profit arising from the sale is taxable.

(4)    The prior year adjustment arises from the correction of a fundamental error made in the 19x3 accounts.

(5)    At 31 December 19x4 the company's issued share capital was:

        180 000 ordinary shares of R1 each      R180 000
        20 000 10% preference shares of R1 each    20 000

(6)    On 1 August 19x4 the company had offered to its shareholders the right to take up one share at R3 for every 2 shares held. The offer expired on 1 September 19x4 by which date all shares had been taken up.

(7)    The ordinary dividend was declared on 31 December 19x4.

# E58 CONTINUED

<u>YOU ARE REQUIRED TO</u>:

(a)   Calculate the earnings and dividends per share (correct to one decimal place of a cent) for the year ended 31 December 19x4.

(b)   Statements AC 103 "Extraordinary items and prior year adjustments" and AC 104 "Earnings per share" were published on the same date.

   (i)   Define an extraordinary item
   (ii)  What is the  difference between an extraordinary item and an abnormal item?
   (iii) In what circumstances does a prior year adjustment arise?
   (iv)  What impact do the following items have on the  earnings per share
         calculation?  (Give reasons)
                  - extraordinary items
                  - abnormal items
                  - prior year adjustments

(c)   Show the note that would appear in the financial statements in respect of the extraordinary item.

**E59**

Apex Limited owns 80% of Sphere LImited and 10% of Venus Limited.  The
following information relates to the directors of the three companies for the
year ended 31 December 19x8.

<u>Apex Limited</u>

Jones:        appointed 1 July 19x6
Smith:        director for whole year.  Appointed managing director in place of

              Green on 1 July 19x8.
Peters:       chairman throughout the year.
Cilliers:     appointed alternate to Peters from 1 July 19x8.
Green:        managing director until 30 June 19x8 and then retired.

Emoluments

Each director receives R200 per quarter as fees.
In addition to the above the chairman receives a company car valued at R4 000
p.a.
The chairman and the managing director each receive an entertainment allowance
of R30 per month.
The managing director draws a salary of R80 000 p.a.  His  pension fund
contributions of 20% of his basic salary are paid by the company.

When Green retired he withdrew R65 000 as a lump sum from the pension fund.
His monthly pension is R3 000 and the company augments this pension by R550
per month.

<u>Sphere  Limited</u>

Peters:       chairman throughout the year.
Green:        managing director until 30 June 19x8 and then retired.
White:        appointment managing director 1 July 19x8 - new to the board.
Cronje:       resigned 30 September 19x8.
Cilliers:     director throughout the year.

Emoluments

Fees    -     each director receives R1 000 p.a.
Salary  -     the managing director receives R50 000 p.a.  His pension fund
              contributions of 10% of basic salary are  paid by the company.

Cronje, who had been the factory manager for years, being paid at the rate of
R36 000 p.a.,  resigned  from  both  the company and the board.  He was paid
R55 000 in terms of a restraint of trade agreement.

The company did not contribute to the pension fund on his behalf.

The company is to pay Green a pension of R220 p.m. for the next 10 years.

# E59 CONTINUED

<u>Venus Limited</u>:    both directors nominated by Sphere Limited

Cronje:     chairman until resigned 30 June 19x8.
White:      director throughout the year.

Emoluments

Fees - each director receives R100 per month.

As a result of the restraint of trade placed on Cronje (see above) he was forced to resign as the chairman of Venus Limited.    Consequently Venus Limited paid him a lump sum of R5 000 as compensation for loss of office.


<u>YOU ARE REQUIRED TO</u>:

show how the directors' remuneration would be disclosed in the annual financial statements for the year ended 31 December 19x8 of:

1.    Apex Limited
2.    Sphere Limited

(a) Discuss the principle of "generally accepted accounting practice" as it relates to disclosure in the annual financial statements  of companies.

(b) What are the three main sources of disclosure requirements which affect the published  financial statements of South African companies?

(c) Discuss briefly how accounting standards are developed in South Africa.

Alcab Limited, whose financial year ends on 31 December 19X9 has for the whole of the year had four directors; M, N, O and P.  O and P are the chairman of the board and the managing director respectively.  T is the secretary of Alcab Limited.  M is the sales director and N the production director.

On 31 March 19X9 Alcab Limited acquired 60% of Cablet Limited whose directors at that date were Q (also chairman), R (the managing director) and S (secretary).  On 1 April 19X9 Q, whose term of office had expired, was replaced as director and chairman  by M. N was appointed as the alternate to M, R and S were re-elected.  Cablet Limited paid Q R60 000 in accordance with a restraint of trade agreement.

On 1 November 19X9 Alcab Limited acquired 25% of a newly formed company Alison Limited whose directors were P, S and W.  P is the chairman of the board, W is the managing director and S is the sales director.  Because of its shareholding, Alcab is entitled to appoint one director to the board of Alison Limited.

Directors' emoluments paid by the respective companies were as follows:

|  | Alcab Limited | Cablet Limited | Alison Limited |
|---|---|---|---|
| Director's fees (including alternates) each per annum | R6 000 | R4 000 | R3 000 |
| Chairman's entertainment allowance | 2 000 | 1 600 | 900 |
| Managing director's salary | 64 000 | 48 000 | 50 000 |
| Secretary's salary | 50 000 | 28 000 | - |
| Sales director's  salary | 54 000 | - | 38 000 |
| Production director's salary | 40 000 | - | - |

A company car is given to the following directors of Alcab Limited M, N and P.  The value of the company car is assessed at R2 500 per annum.

All salaried executives and staff of all companies contributed 8% of their salaries to a pension fund.  The companies contributed 10%.

On 24 December 19X9 Cablet Limited granted Q a pension supplement of R6 000 per annum back dated to the date he left the employment of the company.

On 27 December 19X9, P received an advance of R10 000 from Alcab Limited for a business trip to Europe.

Alcab Limited granted housing  loans at an interest rate of 3% to the following executives in terms of their employment agreements:

BALANCE AT 31 DECEMBER 19X9

| P | R80 000 |
|---|---|
| N | 65 000 |
| M | 70 000 |
| T | 90 000 |

# E61 CONTINUED

Interest is calculated monthly in arrears and all interest payments were received during the year. The following capital repayments were made during the year:

| | | | |
|---|---|---|---|
| P | R10 000 | on | 30/6/19X9 |
| N | 5 000 | on | 31/12/19X9 |
| M | 15 000 | on | 31/12/19X9 |
| T | 10 000 | on | 30/9/19X9 |

The market related interest rate on similar loans is 20%. Housing loans are secured by a first mortgage bond over the property. No further advances were made during the year.


<u>YOU ARE REQUIRED TO</u>:

Disclose the above information in the financial statements of Alcab Limited for the year ended 31 December 19X9 in compliance with the Companies Act and generally accepted accounting practice.

# E62

The new bookkeeper of Quantum (Pty) Ltd, a manufacturing company, prepared a post-closing trial balance for the year ended 30 June 19X9.

|  | Dr. | Cr. |
|---|---|---|
| Ordinary share capital |  | R360 000 |
| Share premium 1/7/19X8 |  | 68 000 |
| Preference share capital |  | 200 000 |
| Redeemable mortgage debentures (issued 1/10/X8) |  | 160 000 |
| Reserve for redemption of preference shares |  | 60 000 |
| Retained income |  | 212 000 |
| Fixed assets | R484 000 |  |
| Investments | 231 400 |  |
| Debtors | 100 600 |  |
| Creditors |  | 72 400 |
| Bank | 18 400 |  |
| Stock | 144 600 |  |
| Provision for taxation | 6 400 |  |
| Trade marks | 20 000 |  |
| Deferred expenses |  |  |
| - share issue expenses | 42 000 |  |
| - preliminary expenses | 40 000 |  |
| - underwriters commission - preference shares | 14 000 |  |
| - debenture discount | 10 000 |  |
| Suspense account | 21 000 |  |
|  | R1 132 400 | R1 132 400 |

1. From the memorandum of association and other documents, the following information is available:

   a. Authorised share capital  
      400 000 ordinary shares of R1,50 — R600 000  
      100 000 9% redeemable cumulative preference shares of R2,00 each — 200 000  
      R800 000

   b. Redeemable mortgage debentures consist of 1 600 12% debentures of R100 each, secured by a first mortgage bond over land and buildings.

   c. The directors have the authority to issue all unissued shares.

2. As a result of the bookkeeper's limited knowledge he omitted to process correctly certain entries. Where cash was received or paid for these entries, such amounts were entered in the cash book and posted to a suspense account in the general ledger.

# E62 CONTINUED

The list of items in the suspense account include:

a.  The board of directors passed a resolution on 28 December 19X8 to redeem all of the preference shares at a premium of 50c per share on 31 December 19X8. The redemption was to be <u>financed out of</u> the proceeds of:

- an 18% long term loan secured by a second mortgage bond over land and buildings and repayable in 19Y5 (interest is payable yearly in arrears. Refer to note 3(e).
- a new issue of 80 000 ordinary shares at R1,80 per share.

The shares were applied for and allotted and the loan obtained on 30 December 19X8. The redemption was to be affected in such a manner as to have the least impact on retained income.

b.  As the company was in a loss situation up to the commencement of the current year, dividends were last paid on 30 June 19X7.

During the current year an interim ordinary dividend of 5c per share was declared and paid on all shares registered on 31 December 19X8.

c.  The company sold investments costing R16 600 at a profit of R3 400 on 5 February 19X9.

d.  The provisional payment made to the Receiver of Revenue on 31 December 19X8 and 30 June 19X9 amounted to R12 500 each.

3.  You are aware of the following for which no entries have been made in the records:

a.  On 30 June 19X9 it was decided to write off all deferred expenses (with the exception of debenture discount) in such a manner so as to have the minimum impact on distributable reserves.

b.  The debenture discount expenses should be amortized over the life of the debentures. The debentures are redeemable on 30 September 19Y3 at 105%. The premium on redemption should be provided over the life of the debentures.

c.  A final ordinary dividend of 6c per share was declared on 30 June 19X9.

d.  Tax at a rate of 50c in the Rand based on taxable income of R64 000.

e.  Interest on the 18% loan borrowed on 28 December 19X8 has not yet been accrued.

# E62 CONTINUED

<u>YOU ARE REQUIRED TO</u>:

> Prepare the necessary journal entries in the records of Quantum (Pty) Ltd to record all the transactions not processed by the bookkeeper. (Narrations are not required).

Mr Frank, who has worked for many years in the chemical industry, has just started his own private company to import industrial chemicals. As Mr Frank has a very limited knowledge of accounting, he has approached you for advice on the following matters:

A       Mr Frank found that many expenses were incurred in the formation of his company. He assumed that these expenses would be treated on a similar basis as other expenses - as a reduction of income. You have extracted the following balances from the general ledger:

| | |
|---|---:|
| Preliminary expenses | R26 000 |
| Share issue expenses - ordinary shares | 6 700 |
| Underwriters commission - ordinary shares | 20 000 |
| Share issue expenses - preference shares | 15 000 |
| Underwriters commission - preference shares | 9 500 |
| Stated capital | 380 000 |
| Share premium | 15 000 |
| 10% redeemable preference shares | 150 000 |
| Net income (after 2 months of trading) | 85 000 |

YOU ARE REQUIRED TO:

<u>Explain</u> to Mr Frank the different accounting treatments for deferred expenses and <u>identify</u> the most appropriate treatment. <u>Motivate</u> your answer.

Illustrate further by way of a journal entry the application of Sections 76 and 77 of the Companies Act in writing off all deferred expenses. Mr Frank has indicated that he would prefer the profit figure to remain as high as possible.

B       Mr Frank is considering the issue of 1 000 15% redeemable mortgage debentures of R100 each at R97. He expects to incur debenture issue expenses of R12 000 and will redeem the debentures at R106 in 10 years time.

YOU ARE REQUIRED TO:

<u>Explain</u> to Mr Frank the alternative accounting treatments for the debenture discount, the debenture issue expenses and the debenture premium. <u>Identify</u> the most appropriate treatment and <u>motivate</u> your answer.

Illustrate furthermore, the disclosure requirements for debentures in terms of the Companies Act and generally accepted accounting practice drafting the extracts from the balance sheet and notes to the financial statements <u>one year</u> after the date of the issue of the debentures (Make assumptions where the information is insufficient).

# E64

On 1 October 19X5 Venus Limited purchased a building for R800 000.  It had
been the policy of the company not to provide depreciation on buildings.  On
30 September 19X0 the directors decided to provide for depreciation on the
buildings at the rate of 2% p.a. on cost retrospectively to 1 October 19X5.

The following draft income statements of Venus Limited had been prepared for
the years ended 30 September by the book keeper who had not been told of the
directors' decision.

The provision of depreciation on the buildings does not affect taxation.

|                                          | 19X0     | 19X9     |
|------------------------------------------|----------|----------|
| Turnover                                 | R900 000 | R800 000 |
|                                          | =======  | =======  |
| Net income before depreciation           | R168 000 | R140 000 |
| Depreciation                             | 24 000   | 24 000   |
| Net income before tax                    | 144 000  | 116 000  |
| Taxation                                 | 57 600   | 46 400   |
| Net income after tax                     | 86 400   | 69 600   |
| Dividends paid                           | 50 000   | 40 000   |
| Retained income for the year             | 36 400   | 29 600   |
| Retained income at beginning of the year | 75 200   | 45 600   |
| Retained income per balance sheet        | R111 600 | R75 200  |
|                                          | =======  | ======   |

<u>YOU ARE REQUIRED TO</u>:

1)    Redraft the income statements of Venus Limited for publication.

2)    Prepare the relevant notes to the financial statements.

# E65

The managing director of Radio Five (Pty) Ltd presented you with the following draft income statement in respect of the financial year ended 30 September 19x0:

```
                                                              R000's
Gross profit                                                  R6 700
Other income                                                   2 150
                                                               8 850
Expenses                                                       5 408
  General expenses                          R4 500
  Depreciation                                 620
  Auditors fees                                 88
  Technical fees                               200
Net income before taxation                                     3 442
Taxation                                                       1 541
Net income after taxation                                      1 901
Dividends on ordinary shares paid 2 February 19x0               240
Transfer to non-distributable reserve                            900
Retained income for the year                                     761
Retained income at 30 September 19x9                          10 110
Retained income per balance sheet                            R10 871
                                                              ======
```

You ascertain the following:

1.    The following items were included in general expenses:-

      a.    An amount of R350 000 paid to the auditors in respect of consulting fees on the installation of a computerised accounting system.

      b.    An amount of R1 800 000 relating to stock written off when the company's new managing director was appointed.

      c.    A loss of R300 000 sustained in respect of flood damage arising because the company was underinsured.

2.    Other income included R900 000 which represents a surplus on the revaluation of land.  The balance represents R800 000 in respect of dividends received from listed companies, R260 000 in respect of dividends received from a subsidiary company and R190 000 in respect of interest from the subsidiary company.

3.    The tax charge includes a credit for R50 000 in respect of an overprovision of normal tax for the 19x9 financial year.  The company tax rate is 50%.

4.    Technical fees expense comprises of R120 000 paid to Software Consultants Inc. and the technical manager's salary of R80 000.

# E65 CONTINUED

The new managing director wishing to make a good impression and to maximise
the earnings per share of the company has made the following proposals:

(i)    All the  usual items mentioned in (1) above should not appear in the
       determination of the net income before taxation but should appear as a
       special deduction before dividends paid.

(ii)   The surplus on the revaluation of land mentioned in (2) above should be
       included in the determination of net income before taxation.


<u>YOU ARE REQUIRED TO:</u>

1.     Comment on the proposals of the managing director.  Substantiate your
       answer.

2.     Prepare the income statement and relevant notes of Radio Five (Pty) Ltd
       for the year ended 30 September 19x0.  Only information specifically
       required by the Companies Act and GAAP should be disclosed.  All
       amounts are to be regarded as material.

# E66

AC 000, "Framework for the preparation and presentation of financial statements," identifies the users of financial statements and their different needs for information.


YOU ARE REQUIRED TO:

Identify the various users of financial statements and discuss the information each user would require to meet their needs for useful information.

# E67

AC101 entitled 'The disclosure of accounting policies' defines the following concepts:

  (i) going concern
 (ii) matching
(iii) consistency
 (iv) prudence

<u>YOU ARE REQUIRED TO</u>:


define and explain the accounting implications of the above concepts.  Give an example for each concept of an item which could appear on the balance sheet of a manufacturing or trading company (or as an accompanying note) and explain how it illustrates the application of that particular concept.

## E68

Accounting policy notes are now a feature of annual financial reports produced by companies.

<u>YOU ARE REQUIRED TO</u>:

(a)    outline the purpose and conceptual framework relating to notes on accounting policies.

(b)    specify 3 matters which are normally dealt with in such notes, giving an example of the type of information which you would expect to see provided in each of the 3 cases.

## E68

Accounting policy notes are now a feature of annual financial reports produced by companies.

<u>YOU ARE REQUIRED TO</u>:

(a)   outline the purpose and conceptual framework relating to notes on accounting policies.

(b)   specify 3 matters which are normally dealt with in such notes, giving an example of the type of information which you would expect to see provided in each of the 3 cases.

**E69**

a)  Discuss the four fundamental accounting concepts which are cited in
    AC101, and in each case give a specific example of how the concept is
    applied in financial accounting.

b)  In terms of AC103 prior year adjustments arise through two
    circumstances.  What are these circumstances and give an example of
    each.

# E70

The following information relates to Taxco Limited which commenced business on 1 January 19x1.  The financial year end of the company is 31 December.


FIRST YEAR
| | | |
|---|---|---|
| 30 June 19x1 | Provisional payment | R26 000 |
| 31 December 19x1 | Provisional payment | 28 000 |
| 31 December 19x1 | Provided taxation | 56 000 |
| 16 April 19x2 | Received assessment | 56 000 |
| 16 May 19x2 | Paid assessment | |

SECOND YEAR
| | | |
|---|---|---|
| 30 June 19x2 | Provisional payment | R29 000 |
| 31 December 19x2 | Provisional payment | 30 000 |
| 31 December 19x2 | Provided taxation | 58 000 |
| 19 May 19x3 | Received assessment | 59 500 |
| 19 June 19x3 | Paid assessment | |

THIRD YEAR
| | | |
|---|---|---|
| 30 June 19x3 | Provisional payment | R31 000 |
| 31 December 19x3 | Provisional payment | 31 500 |
| 31 December 19x3 | Provided taxation | 65 000 |
| 18 April 19x4 | Received assessment | 64 800 |
| 18 May 19x4 | Paid assessment | |

FOURTH YEAR
| | | |
|---|---|---|
| 30 June  19x4 | Provisional payment | R33 000 |
| 31 December 19x4 | Provisional payment | 34 000 |
| 31 December 19x4 | Provided taxation | 67 400 |


YOU ARE REQUIRED TO:

a)  prepare the ledger accounts of the Receiver of Revenue and taxation for the four years 19x1 to 19x4.

b)  give the relevant disclosure in the annual financial statements of Taxco Limited for the four years ended 31 December 19x1 to 19x4 in respect of the above.

**E71**

The following information relates to Poll Limited which commenced business on 1 January 19x5.  The financial year end of the company is 31 December.

<u>FIRST YEAR</u>
| | | |
|---|---|---:|
| 30 June 19x5 | Provisional payment | R30 000 |
| 31 December 19x5 | Provisional payment | 33 000 |
| 31 December 19x5 | Provided taxation | 66 000 |
| 21 May 19x6 | Received assessment | 66 000 |
| 21 June 19x6 | Paid assessment | |

<u>SECOND YEAR</u>
| | | |
|---|---|---:|
| 30 June 19x6 | Provisional payment | R34 000 |
| 31 December 19x6 | Provisional payment | 40 000 |
| 31 December 19x6 | Provided taxation | 72 000 |
| 15 April 19x7 | Received assessment | 75 200 |
| 15 May 19x7 | Paid assessment | |

<u>THIRD YEAR</u>
| | | |
|---|---|---:|
| 30 June 19x7 | Provisional payment | R41 000 |
| 31 December 19x7 | Provisional payment | 45 000 |
| 31 December 19x7 | Provided taxation | 87 000 |
| 2 May 19x8 | Received assessment | 86 400 |
| 2 June 19x8 | Paid assessment | |

<u>FOURTH YEAR</u>
| | | |
|---|---|---:|
| 30 June 19x8 | Provisional payment | R46 000 |
| 31 December 19x8 | Provisional payment | 47 000 |
| 31 December 19x8 | Provided taxation | 93 100 |

<u>YOU ARE REQUIRED TO</u>:

a)     prepare the ledger accounts of the Receiver of Revenue and taxation for the four years 19x5 to 19x8.

b)     give the relevant disclosure in the annual financial statements of Taxco Limited for the four years ended 31 December 19x5 to 19x8 in respect of the above.

# E72

The following relevant information was extracted from the books of Raven Limited at 31 March 19x2, the company's financial year end.

| | |
|---|---:|
| Share capital - R1 ordinary shares (in issue throughout the year) | R500 000 |
| Share capital - 15% redeemable preference shares (of R1 each) | 150 000 |
| 18% debentures | 100 000 |
| Retained income | 220 000 |
| Net income for the year before depreciation and taxation | 600 000 |
| Plant - cost | 800 000 |
| Plant - accumulated depreciation - 1 April 19x1 | 160 000 |
| Deferred tax - 1 April 19x1 | 52 000 |
| Hire purchase creditor - 31 March 19x2 | 260 000 |
| Interest suspense - 31 March 19x2 | 30 000 |
| Payment to preference shareholders | 187 500 |

<u>Additional informaiton</u>

1) <u>REDEEMABLE PREFERENCE SHARES</u>

   The redeemable preference shares were redeemed on 31 March 19x2 at a premium of 10 cents per share. The only entry made by the bookkeeper to record the redemption was to debit the preference shareholders and to credit bank with the amount paid to the preference shareholders. To finance the redemption in part the company issued the debentures on 31 March 19x2. It is the company's policy to issue all shares and debentures at par.

2) <u>HIRE PURCHASE</u>

   All the plant was purchased on 1 April 19x0 under a hire purchase agreement, the terms of which were as follows:

   a)   A deposit of 25% paid on 1 April 19x0
   b)   Three annual instalments of R260 000 each payable on 31 March each year.

3) <u>TAXATION</u>

   The company provides depreciation at the rate of 20% p.a. on cost. The Receiver of Revenue granted an initial allowance of 25% and an annual wear and tear allowance of 15% computed using the reducing balance method. The tax rate has remained constant at 40c in the Rand. The company has not made any provision for the current year's taxation charge.

4) <u>ORDINARY DIVIDENDS</u>

   The directors proposed an ordinary dividend of 10%, but no entries have been made to give effect to this proposal.

# E72 Continued

5)    <u>TURNOVER</u>

The turnover of the company for the current year was R2 500 000.

**YOU ARE REQUIRED TO:**

prepare the income statement of Raven Limited and the notes thereto, for the year ended 31 March 19x2, in accordance with the requirements of Schedule Four and generally accepted accounting practice.

Accounting policy notes are <u>NOT</u> required.

AC 101 requires a company to disclose its accounting policy by way of notes to its financial statements.

You are currently preparing an analysis of the annual financial statements of a large manufacturing company on the Johannesburg Stock Exchange.

**<u>YOU ARE REQUIRED TO</u>:**

give the extent to which you would investigate the company's accounting policies as part of your analysis and state how the information contained in the accounting policies would influence your analysis and interpretation of the annual financial statements.

ANSWER IN POINT FORM

# E74

On 1 January 19x3 Meridian Limited purchased plant for R500 000.  The company used the reducing balance method for calculating depreciation, the rate of depreciation being 20% p.a..   The Receiver of Revenue allowed an initial allowance of 25% and a wear and tear allowance of 20% p.a. on the reduced balance.

On 31 December 19x6 the directors decided to change to the straight line method of calculating depreciation for plant retrospectively to 1 January 19x3.  It was agreed that the estimated life of the plant was 6 years and the estimated residual value R20 000.

The tax rate has remained constant at 40c.

The following draft income statements had been prepared for the years ended 31 December by the bookkeeper who had not been told the directors decision:

|  | 19x6 |  | 19x5 |
|---|---|---|---|
| Turnover | R800 000 |  | R650 000 |
|  | ======= |  | ======= |
| Net operating income before depreciation | R380 200 |  | R300 000 |
| Depreciation - plant | 51 200 |  | 64 000 |
| Net income before tax | 329 000 |  | 236 000 |
| Taxation | 131 600 |  | 94 400 |
| Current | R136 720 | R100 800 |  |
| Deferred | (5 120) | (6 400) |  |
| Net income after tax | 197 400 |  | 141 600 |
| Dividend paid | 150 000 |  | 100 000 |
| Retained income for the year | 47 400 |  | 41 600 |
| Retained income at beginning of the year | 91 600 |  | 50 000 |
| Retained income per balance sheet | R139 000 |  | R91 600 |
|  | ======= |  | ====== |

<u>YOU ARE REQUIRED TO</u>:

i)    redraft the income statements for publication, AND

ii)   give the relevant notes to the financial statements.

# E75

The following is the income statement of Biondi Limited for the year ended 28 February 19x2.

|                                            | 19x2     | 19x1     |
|--------------------------------------------|----------|----------|
| Turnover                                   | R510 000 | R450 000 |
|                                            | =======  | =======  |
| Net income before taxation                 | R98 150  | R80 000  |
| Taxation                                   | 30 000   | 33 600   |
| Net income after taxation                  | 68 150   | 46 400   |
| Preference dividend                        | 9 600    | 9 600    |
| Net income                                 | 58 550   | 36 800   |
| Ordinary dividend                          | 5 400    | 3 000    |
|                                            | 53 150   | 33 800   |
| Transfer to non-distributable reserve      | 18 700   | -        |
| Retained income for year                   | 34 450   | 33 800   |
| Retained income at 28 February 19x1        | 160 000  | 126 200  |
| Retained income per balance sheet          | R194 450 | R160 000 |
|                                            | =======  | =======  |

The following information is provided:

1.  After the financial statements were prepared the directors decided to change the depreciation on plant and machinery from 10% p.a. on the reducing balance to 10% p.a. on the straight line basis retrospectively from 1 September 19w8.  This was done in order to bring the accounting policy of Biondi Limited  into line with that of its holding company.  The plant and machinery was purchased on 1 September 19w8 for R190 000.

2.  On investigation it was discovered that the following items had been included in the net income before taxation figure

|                                      |         |
|--------------------------------------|---------|
| Loss on sale of investments          | R12 500 |
| Bad debts (abnormal item)            | 22 500  |
| Profit on sale of land and buildings | 18 700  |

<u>YOU ARE REQUIRED TO:</u>

i)   redraft the income statements for publication

ii)  prepare the relevant notes to the income statement

IGNORE TAXATION

## E76

The following accounting policies were prepared for inclusion in the financial statements of Petite Manufacturers Limited, a company which manufactures lounge suites.

### FIXED ASSETS

Land and buildings are not depreciated.  Other fixed assets are depreciated using the reducing balance method at a rate of 20% p.a.  This is not consistent with the policy used in previous years.

### STOCK

The cost of stock is determined using the first in first out method.  This is consistent with previous years.

### LEASED ASSETS

The company conducts part of its operations with leased assets.

### DEFERRED TAXATION

Deferred taxation is provided at current tax rates in cases where timing differences arise between the depreciation rates used by the company and the wear and tear allowances granted by the receiver of revenue.

### CASH FLOW INFORMATION

A cash flow statement is prepared in accordance with the requirements of generally accepted accounting practice instead of the source and application of funds statement.

### EARNINGS AND DIVIDENDS PER SHARE

Earnings per share 19x2 88,7c (19x1 116c)
Dividends per share 19x2 19,8c (19x1 13,3c)
The calculation of earnings per share is based on net income of R155 200 [19x1 R174 000] and the weighted average of 175 000 ordinary shares in issue during the year (19x1 150 000 shares) after a new issue on 30 September 1992.


<u>YOU ARE REQUIRED TO</u>:

critically discuss the proposed accounting policy notes in terms of generally accepted accounting practice.  Where appropriate, correction and improvements should be suggested.

**YOU NEED NOT REWRITE THE ACCOUNTING POLICIES**

Properties Limited owns Stands 359 and 360 in Witbank, each of which contains a factory building. The stands were purchased with the factories for R50 000 each on 1 December 19w7. Extensions were made in 1991 to the factory on Stand 359 amounting to R20 000. Land and buildings are not depreciated.

In 1993 the directors decided to have the land and buildings independently valued. This was done by Mr Able, a sworn appraiser, on 20 March 19x3. He determined that based on sales of similar properties in the area, the book value of Stand 359 was fair, but Stand 360 was undervalued by R15 000. The directors wish to show land and buildings at the valuation amount and have asked Mr Able to revalue the properties every three years in the future.

<u>YOU ARE REQUIRED TO</u>:

show how the above would be reflected in the financial statements and notes of Properties Limited for the year ended 31 March 19x3 in terms of Schedule Four of the Companies Act and generally accepted accounting practice

**E78**

Treasure Limited recently purchased land for R120 000. The following transactions have taken place regarding the erection of a building on the land:

-   A contract for the clearing of land amounting to R20 000 was concluded. A progress report at 31 March 19x3 was received showing that one quarter of the land had been cleared, but no payments have yet been made.

-   An architect has been contracted for R10 000 to plan the new building. He will commence work in April 19x3.

-   The directors have approved the tender received from AB Builders Limited of R120 000 to erect the building, but the builders have not yet been notified.

-   The directors have also approved the issue of 100 000 R1 15% redeemable, unsecured debentures at 4% discount in order to finance the above expenditure. These debentures were issued on 31 March 19x3 and will be redeemed at par on 1 April 19x8. The balance of the funds required to pay for the building will be derived from cash generated by operations.

<u>YOU ARE REQUIRED TO</u>:

show how the above would appear in the financial statements and notes of Treasure Limited for the year ended 31 March 1993 in terms of Schedule Four of the Companies Act and generally accepted accounting practice. No accounting policy notes are required.

# E79

The following balances were extracted from the trial balance of Tiara Limited,
a retail company, at 28 February 19x3:

| | |
|---|---:|
| Retained income 1 March 1992 | R47 000 |
| Underprovision of taxation in prior years | 1 000 Debit |
| Net operating income | 145 000 |
| Loss of stock due to fire | 40 000 |

## ADDITIONAL INFORMATION

1.  Tiara's turnover for the year ended 28 February 19x3 amounted to
    R900 000.

2.  A bad debt of R35 000 has been deducted in arriving at net operating
    income.  Bad debts do not normally exceed R5 000 in any year.

3.  Taxation has to be provided at 40c in the Rand.  All expenses deducted
    from net operating income can be deducted for tax.

4.  The company does not provide for deferred tax.

## YOU ARE REQUIRED TO:

prepare for the year ended 28 February 19x3 the income statement of Tiara
Limited and the notes thereto in accordance with Schedule Four of the
Companies Act and generally accepted accounting practice.

No accounting policy notes are required.

**SECTION F**

# CLOSE CORPORATIONS

**F1**

The following is the audited balance sheet of X (Proprietary) Limited. All the shares are owned by Mr X:

<u>BALANCE SHEET OF X (PROPRIETARY) LIMITED AT 31 DECEMBER 19x4</u>

CAPITAL EMPLOYED

| | |
|---|---:|
| Share capital | R100 |
| Non-distributable reserves | 2 000 |
| Distributable reserves - retained income | 10 500 |
| | R12 600 |
| | ====== |

EMPLOYMENT OF CAPITAL

| | |
|---|---:|
| Fixed assets | R8 000 |
| Net current assets | 4 000 |
| | R12 600 |
| | ====== |

When discussing the 19x4 financial statements with his auditors in February 19x5, Mr X became aware of the Close Corporation Act which had recently been introduced. He is considering converting the company into a close corporation, but requires further information about close corporation before he makes his final decision. He therefore consults you, knowing that you have dealt with close corporations in your Accounting II course.

He provides you with the following information:

1. The non-distributable reserve arose in 19x0 when the land and buildings were revalued.
2. The retained income consists of revenue reserves only.
3. The business will be expanded in the future due to a new product line which he intends to introduce. The expansion will have to be financed from new sources of capital, either by borrowing funds from the bank, or by issuing further shares in the company.


<u>FURTHER INFORMATION</u>

1. The current tax rate is 50%.
2. Should he decide to convert, the members' contribution will be set at R100.


<u>YOU ARE REQUIRED TO</u>:

(a) Assist Mr X in making his decision, by setting out in point form, the advantages and disadvantages of converting to and operating through a close corporation. He also wishes to know what financial statements need to be prepared and whether compliance with generally accepted accounting practice is necessary. (Ignore any discussion about tax implications.)
(b) Show the journal entries that would be put through in the books, assuming the company was converted into a close corporation. Narrations need <u>not</u> be shown.

# F2

The following are the balance sheets of Perry (Pty) Ltd at:

|  | 31.12.19x4 | 1.3.19x5 |
|---|---|---|
|  | Audited | Unaudited |

### Capital employed

| | | |
|---|---|---|
| Share capital - 18 000 ordinary | | |
| R1 shares | R18 000 | R18 000 |
| Distributable reserves | 16 000 | 18 500 |
| | R34 000 | R36 500 |
| | ====== | ====== |

### Employment of capital

| | | |
|---|---|---|
| Equipment at cost | R15 000 | R15 000 |
| Accumulated depreciation | 4 500 | 5 000 |
| | 10 500 | 10 000 |
| Net current assets | 23 500 | 26 500 |
| | | |
| Current assets | | |
| Stock | R19 500 | R21 000 |
| Debtors | 6 400 | 8 500 |
| Bank | 3 200 | 4 000 |
| | R29 100 | R33 500 |
| | ====== | ====== |
| | | |
| Current liabilities | | |
| Creditors | R 5 600 | R 7 000 |
| | ====== | ====== |
| | | |
| | R34 000 | R36 500 |
| | ====== | ====== |

The company's financial year-end is 31 December and its latest year of assessment of income tax purposes was 31 December 19x4.

The five shareholders of the company decided to convert the company to a close corporation, each of them acquiring a 20% interest in the corporation.

The close corporation, Perry CC, was incorporated on 1 March 19x5.

The issued share capital in the company will become the members' contribution to the close corporation in equal proportions.

The corporation will continue to use the same set of books previously used by the company and its financial year-end will be 31 December.

<u>YOU ARE REQUIRED TO:</u>

prepare journal entries to record the conversion of Perry (Pty) Ltd to a close corporation.

# F3

Care and Full were equal partners in a firm of bookkeepers, providing various bookkeeping and secretarial services to small businesses in Johannesburg.

Their trial balance at 30 June 19x4 was as follows:

|  | DR | CR |
|---|---|---|
| Creditors | | R34 000 |
| Debtors | R96 000 | |
| Bank | 13 800 | |
| Capital - Care | | 40 000 |
| Capital - Full | | 40 000 |
| Current account - Care | | 15 000 |
| Current account - Full | | 8 000 |
| Motor vehicles, at cost | 37 400 | |
| Accumulated depreciation - vehicles | | 6 000 |
| Provision for doubtful debts | | 4 200 |
| | R147 200 | R147 200 |

On 1 July 19x4, Care and Full decided to merge with their main competitor, Steady and form a close corporation, Carefully CC, each of them acquiring a third interest.

In order to expedite the formation of the close corporation, it was agreed to initially merge the two businesses and rearrange their affairs as follows:

1.  They would continue to use the same set of books as previously used by Care and Full.

2.  The assets and liabilities of Care and Full were agreed to be fairly stated in the books, with the exception of debtors, which were considered to be overvalued by R1 500.

3.  Work-in-progress of Care and Full at 30 June 19x4 was valued at R40 000.

4.  Steady would contribute his assets and liabilities at the following agreed valuations:

    | | |
    |---|---|
    | Debtors (net of a 10% provision) | R38 700 |
    | Motor vehicle (original cost R18 000) | 11 000 |
    | Creditors | 16 000 |
    | Bank | 5 000 |
    | Work-in-progress | 18 000 |

# F3 CONTINUED

5.   It was agreed that there was no goodwill attributable to either of the
     two businesses.

     Thereafter Care drew up a founding statement for the registration of a
     close corporation on the basis that the members' contributions of
     himself, Full and Steady would be represented by their individual
     shares in the net assets of the two merged businesses.


<u>YOU ARE REQUIRED TO:</u>

a)   prepare journal entries to record the rearrangement of the affairs of
     Care, Full and Steady and the formation of the close corporation.

b)   prepare, in accordance with generally accepted accounting practice, the
     balance sheet of Carefully CC at 1 July 19x4.

# F4

Warrior CC was incorporated on 1 April 19x6 with each of its members, Arthur, Barry, Charles and Derek, having a 25% interest. Each member made an equal contribution to the corporation, and profits and losses are to be shared equally.

The corporation's financial year-end is 31 December, the first period ending on 31 December 19x6.

Warrior CC's final adjusted trial balance at 31 December 19x6 was as follows:

|  | R000's | |
| --- | ---: | ---: |
|  | DR | CR |
| Creditors |  | 40 |
| Debtors | 70 |  |
| Investment - listed | 70 |  |
|        - unlisted | 50 |  |
| Land and buildings, at cost | 480 |  |
| Loan - Arthur |  | 63 |
| Loan - Derek |  | 21 |
| Members' contributions |  | 400 |
| Mortgage bond | 56 |  |
| Net income |  | 140 |
| Stock | 40 |  |
|  | R720 | R720 |

The following additional information should be taken into account:

1. The unlisted investments are valued by the members at R50 000, and consist of 50 000 shares in Arrow (Pty) Limited.

2. The listed investment comprises 6 000 shares in Salvation Limited, and had a market value of R80 000 on 31 December 19x6.

3. The mortgage bond is secured over the land and buildings, bears interest at the rate of 13% per annum and is repayable over 15 years, commencing in 19x9.

4. The current year's net income represents the balance after a R10 000 distribution had been made to each member. The distributions to Arthur and Derek were credited to their loan accounts, whilst Barry and Charles used these funds to purchase new cars for their wives

5. Stock consists of finished goods R50 000 and is valued on the FIFO basis.


<u>YOU ARE REQUIRED TO</u>:

1. prepare, in compliance with generally accepted accounting practice, the balance sheet of Warrior CC at 31 December 19x6.

2. prepare the members' net investment statement of Warrior CC for the year ended 31 December 19x6.

# F5

Oaklane (Pty) Ltd was, in accordance with the Close Corporations Act, converted to a close corporation on 1 January 19x5.

The following trial balance was extracted from the books of Oaklane CC at 31 December 19x5:

|  | DR | CR |
|---|---|---|
| Share capital | | R50 000 |
| Share premium | | 12 500 |
| Retained income | | 25 000 |
| Shareholders' loan - Leaff | | 10 000 |
|              - Budd | | 22 500 |
| Land and buildings | R112 500 | |
| Office furniture, at cost | 12 500 | |
| Accumulated depreciation | | |
|   - office furniture | | 5 000 |
| Stock - 1 January 19x5 | 37 500 | |
| Debtors | 62 500 | |
| Bank | 5 000 | |
| Creditors | | 25 000 |
| Sales | | 700 000 |
| Purchases | 550 000 | |
| Administration fees | 10 000 | |
| Motor vehicle lease expenses | 6 250 | |
| Motor vehicle repairs and maintenance | 7 500 | |
| Printing | 5 000 | |
| Product research costs | 7 500 | |
| Salaries | 33 750 | |
| | R850 000 | R850 000 |

## Additional information

1. The corporation continued to use the same set of books as previously used by the company. However, no entries have been made in the books to record the conversion.

2. The shareholding of the company was in the following ratio:

   | | |
   |---|---|
   | Leaff | 75% |
   | Budd | 25% |

3. The members agreed to share the ownership and profits of the close corporation equally, and that their respective contributions to the corporation would be equal.

4. In terms of the conversion agreement, the assets of the company were to be revalued to the following amounts:

   | | |
   |---|---|
   | Land and buildings | R125 000 |
   | Office furniture | 10 000 |

# F5 CONTINUED

5.      On 1 July 19x5 the members each withdrew R15 000 from thecorporation, the effect thereof being recorded against their loan accounts.  There were no other movements on the loan accounts during the year ended 31 December 19x5.

6.      Interest at the rate of 12% per annum is to be provided on the opening balances on the members' loan accounts.

7.      Stock at 31 December 19x5 amounted to R26 000, and comprised finished goods valued on the FIFO basis.

8.      Members' salaries for the year to be provided are as follows:

          Leaff          R20 000
          Budd            15 000

9.      Office furniture is depreciated at the rate of 10% p.a. on cost.  There were no fixed asset acquisitions or disposals during the year.

10.     The members authorised a distribution for 19x5 of R25 000, payable on 15 January 19x6.

11.     The current tax rate is 50%

<u>YOU ARE REQUIRED TO</u>:

prepare, in compliance with general accepted accounting practice, the financial statements of Oaklane CC at 31 December 19x5.

Acton and Beaton are in partnership sharing profits and losses in the ratio 3:1 respectively.   Their trial balance at 31 May 19x4 is as follows:

```
Capital - Acton                                              R80 000
Capital - Beaton                                              60 000
Current account - Acton                                       28 000
Current account - Beaton                                      12 000
Accounts payable                                             135 000
Accounts receivable                            R158 000
Bank                                             35 000
Stock                                            90 000
Motor vehicles, at cost                          36 000
Fittings, at cost                                23 000
Accumulated depreciation - vehicles                           18 000
Accumulated depreciation - fittings                            9 000
                                               R342 000     R342 000
                                               =======      =======
```

On 1 June 19x4, Acton and Beaton agree to admit Crichton as a partner on the following terms and conditions:

1.   Crichton's capital contribution is to be R88 000, made up as follows:

```
         Land and buildings                    R81 000
         Payment for goodwill                    7 000
                                                R88 000
                                                ======
```

2.   The tangible assets of Acton and Beaton are to be valued as follows:

```
         Motor vehicles                         R9 000
         Fittings                                5 000
         Stock                                 144 000
```

        Accounts receivable         at book value, but 10% of the amount outstanding is considered to be doubtful.

3.   A joint life policy on the lives of Acton and Beaton is to be surrendered on 1 June 19x4 for R34 000.

4.   The profit sharing ratio of Acton, Beaton and Crichton is to be 2:2:1 respectively.

5.   The new partnership will continue to use the books previously used by Acton and Beaton.

6.   Goodwill is not to be shown in the partnership books at any stage at all.

# F6 CONTINUED

Immediately after the admission of Crichton to the partnership, Acton drew up a founding statement for the formation of a close corporation, in terms of which the three partners would each make an initial cash contribution of R1 000 and thereby become members of the corporation.

Thereafter, Acton, acting as agent for the corporation to be formed, entered into a written contract with the three partners for the acquisition of the tangible assets and liabilities of the partnership at net book value.  The purchase consideration was settled by the corporation securing loans from its members equal to their individual shares in the net tangible asset value of the partnership.

The corporation, Tons CC, was duly incorporated and the members ratified the pre-incorporation contract entered into for the acquisition of the partnership.  The corporation continued to use the same set of books previously used by the partnership.


<u>YOU ARE REQUIRED TO</u>:

prepare journal entries to record the admission of Crichton to the partnership of Acton and Beaton, the formation of the corporation and its acquisition of the partnership assets and liabilities.  (Narrations are not required.)

**F7**

Rice and Lamb, members of Howzat CC, who hold a 60% and 40% share
respectively, decide during 19x7 to develop an export market for the CC.
This will require additional capital and knowledge of international marketing
opportunities.   Accordingly they decide to pay in a further R2 000 each by
way of additional contributions on 1 January 19x8.   They also decide to admit
Wessels as a member with effect from 1 January 19x8.   Wessels is to pay in
R20 000 of which R4 000 is for his contribution.   For purposes of his
admission the following matters are agreed:

(1)    Land and buildings are to be valued at R50 000.
(2)    Goodwill is valued at R10 000 but the members do not wish to show
       goodwill in the books.
(3)    Members' percentage interests will be:   Rice - 40%, Lamb - 40% and
       Wessels - 20%.
(4)    The amount due to Rice on the admission of Wessels is to be left in the
       CC.

The balance sheet of the CC at 31 December 19x7 appeared as follows:

<u>HOWZAT CC (BK/34621/86)</u>

<u>BALANCE SHEET AT 31 DECEMBER 19x7</u>

<u>NOTES</u>

| | Cost | Accumulated depreciation | |
|---|---|---|---|
| **FUNDS EMPLOYED** | | | |
| Members' contributions | | | R4 000 |
| Undrawn income | | | <u>50 000</u> |
| Members' interest | | | 54 000 |
| Loans from members | | | <u>76 000</u> |
| | | | R130 000 |
| | | | ======= |
| | | | |
| **EMPLOYMENT OF FUNDS** | | | |
| Fixed assets | | | |
| Land and buildings | R30 000 | - | R30 000 |
| Motor vehicles | 46 000 | R14 800 | 31 200 |
| Shop fittings and equipment | <u>7 600</u> | <u>1 520</u> | <u>6 080</u> |
| | R83 600 | R16 320 | 67 280 |
| | ================= | | |
| Net current assets | | | 62 720 |
| Current assets | | | |
| Stock | | R33 000 | |
| Debtors | | 15 420 | |
| Bank | | <u>30 300</u> | |
| | | R78 720 | |
| | | ====== | |
| Current liabilities | | | |
| Creditors | | R16 000 | |
| | | ====== | |
| | | | <u>R130 000</u> |
| | | | ======= |

# F7 CONTINUED

<u>HOWZAT CC (BK/34621/86)</u>

<u>NOTES TO THE BALANCE SHEET AT 31 DECEMBER 19x7</u>

(2)   Statement of members' interests

|  | <u>Rice</u> | <u>Lamb</u> | <u>Total</u> |
|---|---|---|---|
| Members' interests | 60% | 40% | 100% |
| Closing balances at 31 December 19x7 | | | |
|   Members' contributions | R2 000 | R2 000 | R4 000 |
|   Undrawn income | 30 000 | 20 000 | 50 000 |
|   Loans from members | <u>48 000</u> | <u>28 000</u> | <u>76 000</u> |
| | R80 000 | R50 000 | R130 000 |

<u>YOU ARE REQUIRED TO</u>:

(a)   prepare the journal entries to record the adjustments and the admission of Wessels as a member.

(b)   prepare the balance sheet at 1 January 19x8, after recording the adjustments, as well as the statement of members' interests reflecting the effect of the changes.

**F8**

The following trial balances were extracted from the books of Grand Properties CC (BK/5689/86) at 28 February 19x8:

|  | 19x7 Debit | 19x7 Credit | 19x8 Debit | 19x8 Credit |
|---|---|---|---|---|
| Members contributions - Acre | R10 000 |  | R10 000 |  |
|               - Landsman | 15 000 |  | 15 000 |  |
| Members loans - Acre | 50 000 |  | 60 000 |  |
|           - Landsman | 40 000 |  | 100 000 |  |
| Revaluation of land and buildings | - |  | 50 000 |  |
| Undrawn income at 1 March | 100 000 |  | 140 000 |  |
| Loans secured by mortgage | 250 000 |  | 350 000 |  |
| Land and buildings |  | R500 000 |  | R700 000 |
| Furniture and equipment - cost |  | 20 000 |  | 25 000 |
| Furniture and equipment - accumulated depreciation |  | 4 000 |  | 6 500 |
| Debtors | 15 000 |  | 17 500 |  |
| Creditors |  | 2 000 |  | 3 000 |
| Receiver of Revenue |  | 12 000 |  | 8 000 |
| Members for distributions |  | 8 000 |  | 10 000 |
| Bank |  | 4 000 | 57 000 |  |
| Rents received |  | 150 000 |  | 190 000 |
| Depreciation | 2 000 |  | 2 500 |  |
| Property and administration expenses | 19 000 |  | 25 500 |  |
| Interest paid - members | 9 000 |  | 16 000 |  |
| Interest paid - long term loans | 30 000 |  | 39 000 |  |
| Salaries - members | 10 000 |  | 12 000 |  |
| Taxation charge for year | 32 000 |  | 38 000 |  |
| Distribution to members | 8 000 |  | 10 000 |  |
|  | R645 000 | R645 000 | R942 500 | R942 500 |

Additional information:

(1)    Members interests are:  Acre 50%, Landsman 50%.

(2)    No fixed assets have been sold during the year.

(3)    Distributions to members were declared on 15 February and paid on 31 March.

(4)    Movements on members' loans during the year were:

|  | Acre | Landsman |
|---|---|---|
| Advances | R20 000 | R80 000 |
| Withdrawals | (10 000) | (20 000) |

Repayment dates are not fixed.    Interest of approximately 10% is paid.

# F8 CONTINUED

(5)    Payments made to the Receiver of Revenue during the year were:

|                       | 19x7     | 19x8     |
|-----------------------|----------|----------|
| 1986 assessment       | R5 000   |          |
| 19x7 assessment       |          | R12 000  |
| Provisional payments  | 20 000   | 30 000   |

Tax provisions made for 19x6 and 19x7 were correctly estimated.

(6)    Land and buildings comprise a number of blocks of flats and industrial properties which are let by the CC.  A register is kept of the properties.

(7)    Long term loans are secured by mortgage of the land and buildings. They bear interest at 12%.  Monthly repayments of capital and interest are made.  Repayments of R50 000 are due to be made during 19x8/x9.

(8)    Transactions with members during the year were:

|                          | Acre   |        | Landsman |         |
|                          | 19x7   | 19x8   | 19x7     | 19x8    |
|--------------------------|--------|--------|----------|---------|
| Interest  paid           | R5 000 | R6 000 | R6 000   | R10 000 |
| Salaries paid            | 6 000  | 7 000  | 4 000    | 5 000   |
| Distributions declared   | 4 000  | 5 000  | 4 000    | 5 000   |

<u>YOU ARE REQUIRED TO</u>:

Prepare the annual financial statements for the year ended 28 February 19x8 in accordance with the needs of the members and generally accepted accounting practice.  You should include a balance sheet, income statement, notes to the balance sheet and income statement and a cash flow statement.

**F9**

You are the auditor of A (Proprietary) Limited, a private company with 5 shareholders, each owning 20 000 shares of R1 each.    Each member of the company participates actively in the running of the company and there is close co-operation among the members in the management of its affairs.

The members have asked you to advise them as to whether it would be beneficial for them to convert the company into a close corporation.

<u>YOU ARE REQUIRED TO</u>:

Briefly outline your advice under the following headings:

(i)   Whether the company qualifies for conversion to a close corporation;
(ii)  Whether it would be advantageous to convert;
(iii) Whether there are any drawbacks.

# F10

The following balances were obtained from the books of Electronic Games CC at
31 December 19x7:

| | | |
|---|---:|---:|
| Undrawn ncome 1 January 19x7 | | R19 475 |
| Members' contributions - M Metroman | | 56 250 |
|                      - P Pacman | | 28 125 |
|                      - R Robotman | | 28 125 |
| Equipment | R64 050 | |
| Accumulated depreciation - equipment | | 17 100 |
| Land and buildings | 105 000 | |
| Surplus on revaluation of land and buildings | | 15 000 |
| Investments at cost | 13 500 | |
| Loan from member P Pacman | | 7 500 |
| Loan to member M Metroman | 3 000 | |
| Stock at 31.12.19x7 | 15 225 | |
| Accounts receivable | 18 000 | |
| Accounts payable | | 13 900 |
| Provisional tax payments | 21 500 | |
| Gross profit | | 86 130 |
| Sundry expenses | 35 680 | |
| Rent received | | 9 300 |
| Dividends received | | 2 550 |
| Bank | 7 500 | |
| | R283 455 | R283 455 |

Additional information:

1.  Sundry expenses consist of:

| | | |
|---|---:|---:|
| Salaries to members - Metroman | R8 000 | |
|                     - Pacman | 11 000 | R19 000 |
| Interest paid on member's loan | | 750 |
| Remuneration to accounting officer | | 1 425 |
| Other interest paid | | 375 |
| Administrative and selling expenses<br>(including R225 relating to January 19x8) | | 7 725 |
| Depreciation - equipment | | 6 035 |
| | | R35 680 |

2.  A distribution of R22 500 of the undrawn income for 19x7 is to be made
    to members and credited to their loan accounts.

3.  A provision of R30 800 must be made for the 19x7 taxation.

4.  Interest of 10% per annum was paid on the member's loan from P Pacman.
    The CC repaid R600 on 1 January 19x7.

# F10 CONTINUED

5.    Stock is valued at the lower of cost and net realisable value on a first-in-first-out basis.

6.    The loan to M Metroman is interest free.   The CC advanced a further R1 050 during the year and he repaid R1 650 during the year.

7.    Turnover for the year comprised net sales to customers and amounted to R276 000.

8.    The three members of the CC are M Metroman, P Pacman, and R Robotman. Their members' contributions are in the same ratio as their interest, namely 50% : 25% : 25% respectively.

9.    Investments consist of:

      7 500 ordinary shares in Computech (Pty) Ltd purchased for R10 000 during 19x6.   (Members valuation of R10 000.)
      3 000 ordinary shares in Metro Industrial (Pty) Ltd purchased at a cost of R3 500 during 19x5.   (Members valuation R7 000.)   Both investments were acquired to ensure a continuity of supplies of raw materials.


<u>YOU ARE REQUIRED TO</u>:

prepare the financial statements for Electronic Games CC for the year ended 31 December 19x7 in accordance with generally accepted accounting practice. A cash flow statement is not required.

# F11

Proctor and Pollock are the sole shareholders in Cricket Promotions (Proprietary) Limited.  The issued share capital of 20 000 ordinary shares of R1 each is held equally by the 2 shareholders.  They decide on 1 March 19x8 to convert the company, whose financial year ends on 28 February, to a close corporation, Cricket Promotions CC.  They agree that their contributions in the close corporation will be:  Proctor R2 500 with a 25% interest and Pollock R7 500 with a 75% interest.

The balance sheet of the company at 28 February 19x8 was as follows:

<u>CRICKET PROMOTIONS (PROPRIETARY) LIMITED</u>

| CAPITAL EMPLOYED | | |
|---|---|---|
| Share capital | | R20 000 |
| Retained income | | 60 000 |
| Shareholders' loans | | |
|   Proctor | R5 000 | |
|   Pollock | <u>15 000</u> | <u>20 000</u> |
| | | R100 000 |
| | | ======= |

| EMPLOYMENT OF CAPITAL | | |
|---|---|---|
| Fixed assets | | |
|   Land and  buildings, at cost | | R25 000 |
|   Vehicles and furniture, at cost | R10 000 | 6 000 |
|   Accumulated depreciation | <u>4 000</u> | 31 000 |
| Net current assets | | 69 000 |
|   Current assets | | |
|     Stock | R45 000 | |
|     Debtors | 15 000 | |
|     Bank | <u>18 000</u> | |
| | R78 000 | |
| | ====== | |
|   Current liabilities | | |
|     Creditors | R9 000 | |
| | ====== | <u>R100 000</u> |
| | | ======= |

<u>YOU ARE REQUIRED</u>:

(a)    to give the journal entries to convert the company to a close corporation.  The corporation will continue to use the books of the company.

(b)    to prepare the balance sheet of Cricket Promotions CC at 1 March 19x8 together with the statement of members' interests.

# SECTION G

# BRANCH ACCOUNTING

# G1

The directors of a company with branches in Pretoria, Pietersburg and Bloemfontein consult you with regard to their system of bookkeeping.

They explain that the Johannesburg head office has to pay the following charges which are partly on account of branch activities:

(i)    London buying agent's salary.
(ii)   Interest on bank overdraft in London.
(iii) Rent of warehouse in Cape Town, where goods are stored pending dispatch to head office and branches.
(iv)   Bookkeepers' salaries.  Most of the financial books are kept at head office.
(v)    Salary of the managing director, whose duty is to supervise all branches as well as head office.

They are most anxious that their accounts should show accurate and comparable figures, and, to allow for the above, they propose to charge stock to branches at cost plus 10%.

Write them a letter setting out your views.

## G2

From the following particulars you are required to establish the branch
current account as it appears in the head office ledger of the PQ Trading Co.
Ltd.

Stock is charged to the branch at cost.

The account must show the balance due to head office at 30 June 19x4, as well
as the profit or loss made by the branch for the year ended on that date.

| | |
|---|---:|
| Branch stock 30 June 19x3 | R2 850 |
| Branch cash 30 June 19x3 | 120 |
| Branch debtors 30 June 19x3 | 2 142 |
| Goods to branch during year | 24 694 |
| Branch credit sales | 28 416 |
| Branch cash sales | 3 140 |
| Cash paid by customers at branch | 27 103 |
| Cash remitted to head office | 30 200 |
| Goods returned by customers to branch | 225 |
| Goods returned by branch to head office | 500 |
| Discounts allowed to customers at branch | 216 |
| Branch salaries paid by head office | 1 560 |
| Branch expenses paid by head office | 1 016 |
| Branch bad debts at 30 June 19x4 | 21 |
| Branch stock on hand at 30 June 19x4 | 3 619 |

Prepare in columnar form the branch, head office and "group" income statement
for the year ended 30 June 19x4 given the following information for head
office:

| | |
|---|---:|
| Sales | R50 000 |
| Stock at 30 June 19x3 | 4 500 |
| Purchases | 63 494 |
| Stock at 30 June 19x4 | 6 300 |
| Goods sent to branches (net) | 24 194 |
| Expenses | 4 500 |
| Net income from branch | 5 093 |

# G3

The following is the Durban branch current account as it appears in head office books at 30 June 19x4:

DURBAN BRANCH ACCOUNT

| 19x4 | | | | 19x4 | | | |
|---|---|---|---|---|---|---|---|
| June | 1 | Balance | R22 030 | June | 2 | Cash | R5 000 |
| | 8 | Goods sent to branches | 4 590 | | 11 | Goods returned from branches | 220 |
| | 11 | Advertising paid on Durban's behalf | 520 | | 15 | L Martin's balance transferred | 420 |
| | 13 | Advance to J Behr, Durban manager | 250 | | | | |
| | 28 | Goods sent to branches | 8 020 | | | | |

The following statement is received from Durban, but the Durban books have not yet been finally closed:

| 19x4 | | | | |
|---|---|---|---|---|
| June | 1 | Balance as per May account | | R17 030 |
| | 9 | Goods returned | R220 | |
| | 13 | Goods from head office | | 4 590 |
| | 28 | Motor car sent to head office | 5 250 | |
| | | Goods returned | 100 | |
| | 29 | Cash | 5 000 | |
| | 30 | Profit and loss account | 18 270 | |
| | | Balance | 29 320 | |
| | | | R39 890 | R39 890 |
| | | | ====== | ====== |

Give:

(a)   the necessary journal entries in head office books;
(b)   the necessary journal entries in Durban books;

so that the current accounts will be in complete agreement when the books are finally closed for the year.

**G4**

Close the branch books and pass the necessary journal entries in the head
office books so that the results of the branch operations for the quarter, and
the final branch figures may be incorporated in the head office balance sheet
at 31 December 19x4.

The relative figures are as follows:

HEAD OFFICE BOOKS

Summary of Wolseley branch account for the quarter ended
31 December 19x4

| | | | |
|---|---:|---|---:|
| Balance | R2 500 | Cash | R4 621 |
| Rent | 82 | Rebate on freight | |
| 9 | | | |
| Goods | 2 332 | Balance | 974 |
| Salaries | 162 | | |
| Sundry expenses | 48 | | |
| Advertising | 180 | | |
| Administration expenses | 300 | | |
| | R5 604 | | R5 604 |
| | ===== | | ===== |

WOLSELEY BRANCH BOOKS

Summary of head office account for the quarter ended
31 December 19x4

| | | | |
|---|---:|---|---:|
| Cash | R4 790 | Balance | R2 500 |
| Goods returned | 7 | Goods | 2 332 |
| Sale to head office customer | 6 | Rent | 82 |
| Balance | 318 | Sundry expenses | 48 |
| | | Salaries | 162 |
| | | Debtor's account collected | 4 |
| | R5 128 | | R5 128 |
| | ===== | | ===== |

TRIAL BALANCE OF WOLSELEY BRANCH AT 31 DECEMBER 19X4

| | | | |
|---|---:|---|---:|
| Stock at 30 September 19x4 | R729 | Head office | R318 |
| Debtors | 1 485 | Sales - cash | 1 592 |
| Furniture | 1 | Sales - credit | 3 035 |
| Cash | 183 | Provision for bad debts | 70 |
| Purchases | 2 325 | | |
| Expenses | 48 | | |
| Salaries | 162 | | |
| Rent | 82 | | |
| | R5 015 | | R5 015 |
| | ===== | | ===== |

Stock at branch at 31 December 19x4          R632

# G5

The following information was extracted from the Odendaalrus branch and head
office books before the books were finally closed for the year ended 30 June
19x4:

HEAD OFFICE BOOKS

ODENDAALRUS BRANCH ACCOUNT

| 19x3 | | | | 19x4 | | | | |
|---|---|---|---|---|---|---|---|---|
| July | 1 | Balance | R1 407 | June 30 | Cash | | | R2 138 |
| 19x4 | | | | " | " | Debtor's account | | |
| June 30 | Goods | | 2 278 | | | collected | | 20 |
| " | " | Rent | 120 | " | " | Balance | | 2 312 |
| " | " | Salaries | 480 | | | | | |
| " | " | Advertising | 20 | | | | | |
| " | " | Sundry expenses | 65 | | | | | |
| " | " | Managing director's | | | | | | |
| | | salary | 100 | | | | | |
| | | | R4 470 | | | | | R4 470 |
| | | | ===== | | | | | ===== |

| | | | | |
|---|---|---|---|---|
| June 30 | Balance | | R2 312 | |

ODENDAALRUS BRANCH BOOKS

HEAD OFFICE ACCOUNT

| 19x4 | | | | 19x3 | | | | |
|---|---|---|---|---|---|---|---|---|
| June 30 | Cash | | R2 638 | July | 1 | Balance | | R1 407 |
| " | " | Goods returned to | | 19x4 | | | | |
| | | head office | 7 | June 30 | Goods | | 2 100 |
| " | " | Balance | 1 527 | " | " | Rent | 120 |
| | | | | " | " | Salaries | 480 |
| | | | | " | " | Sundry expenses | 14 |
| | | | R4 172 | | | | R4 172 |
| | | | ===== | | | | ===== |
| | | | | June 30 | Balance | | R1 527 |

TRIAL BALANCE AT 30 JUNE 19X4

| | | | |
|---|---|---|---|
| Debtors | R1 106 | Head office | R1 527 |
| Stock at 1 July 19x3 | 623 | Sales | 3 839 |
| Cash | 329 | | |
| Goods from head office | 2 093 | | |
| Sundry expenses | 315 | | |
| Rent | 120 | | |
| Salaries | 780 | | |
| | R5 366 | | R5 366 |
| | ===== | | ===== |

Stock on hand at 30 June 19x4 was R796.

Goods to the value of R178 were dispatched by the head office on 28 June 19x4, but were not received by the branch until 3 July 19x4.

Give:

(a)    the closing journal entries in the Odendaalrus branch books showing the results of the branch operations for the year ended 30 June 19x4;  and

(b)    the journal entries necessary in the head office books in order that the branch and the head office current accounts may be in agreement at 30 June 19x4.

# G6

The following information was extracted from the Welkom branch and Pretoria head office books of Retailers Ltd before the books were finally closed for the year ended 30 June 19x4.

Stock is sent to the branch at cost plus 10%.

### HEAD OFFICE BOOKS

### WELKOM BRANCH ACCOUNT

| 19x3 | | | | 19x3 | | | |
|---|---|---|---|---|---|---|---|
| July 1 | Balance | | R4 275 | July 2 | Cash | | R500 |
| 19x4 | | | | 19x4 | | | |
| June 30 | Goods sent to branch | | 8 437 | June 30 | Cash | | 12 646 |
| | Rent | | 600 | | J Smyth - account | | |
| | Salaries | | 1 560 | | paid by branch | | 50 |
| | Administration fee | | 300 | | Balance | | 3 146 |
| | Sundry expenses | | 270 | | | | |
| | Managing director's | | | | | | |
| | salary | | 900 | | | | |
| | | | R16 342 | | | | R16 342 |
| | | | ====== | | | | ====== |

### WELKOM BRANCH BOOKS

### HEAD OFFICE ACCOUNT

| 19x4 | | | | 19x3 | | | |
|---|---|---|---|---|---|---|---|
| June 30 | Cash | | R13 646 | July 1 | Balance | | R3 775 |
| | Cash - payment to | | | 19x4 | | | |
| | local creditor on | | | June 30 | Goods received from | | |
| | behalf of head | | | | head office | | 8 107 |
| | office | | 50 | | Rent | | 600 |
| | Balance | | 560 | | Salaries | | 1 560 |
| | | | R14 042 | | | | R14 042 |
| | | | ====== | | | | ====== |

### TRIAL BALANCE AT 30 JUNE 19X4

| | | |
|---|---|---|
| Debtors | R574 | |
| Goods received from head office | 8 107 | |
| Local purchases | 429 | |
| Stock at 1 July 19x3 | 2 695 | |
| Rent | 600 | |
| Salaries | 1 560 | |
| Sales | | R14 262 |
| Head office | | 346 |
| Bank | | 100 |
| | R14 608 | R14 608 |
| | ====== | ====== |

# G6 CONTINUED

The following must be taken into account:

(a)  Stock on hand at Welkom at 30 June 19x4 amounted to R2 090.   All this
     stock (and all the stock on hand at 1 July 19x3) had been received from
     head office.
(b)  Stock priced at R330 was dispatched by head office on 29 June 19x4, but
     was not received at Welkom until 8 July 19x4.
(c)  A remittance of R1 000 sent by the branch on 30 June 19x4 was not
     received by head office until 2 July 19x4.
(d)  The debit notes from head office for administration fee, proportion of
     managing director's salary and sundry expenses were received by the
     branch after the above summary of the head office account was drawn up.


<u>YOU ARE REQUIRED TO GIVE</u>:

(a)  The closing journal entries in the Welkom branch books showing the
     results of the branch operations for the year ended 30 June 19x4.
(b)  Any journal entries which may be necessary in the head office books
     before the final accounts for the year can be drawn up.

## G7

The following information was extracted from the Newlands branch and head office books before the books were finally closed for the year ended 31 December 19x4:

<u>HEAD OFFICE BOOKS</u>

### NEWLANDS BRANCH ACCOUNT

| 19x4 | | | | 19x4 | | | |
|---|---|---|---|---|---|---|---|
| Jan 1 | Balance | R 3 907 | | Dec 31 | Cash | R6 759 | |
| Dec 31 | Goods sent to branch | 4 610 | | " " | Debtor's account collected | 29 | |
| " " | Rent | 202 | | " " | Balance | 3 286 | |
| " " | Salaries | 642 | | | | | |
| " " | Sundry expenses | 113 | | | | | |
| " " | Administration expenses | 400 | | | | | |
| " " | Advertising | 300 | | | | | |
| | | R10 074 | | | | R10 074 | |
| | | ====== | | | | ====== | |

| | | | |
|---|---|---|---|
| Dec 31 | Balance | R 3 286 | |

<u>NEWLANDS BRANCH BOOKS</u>

### HEAD OFFICE ACCOUNT

| 19x4 | | | | 19x4 | | | |
|---|---|---|---|---|---|---|---|
| Dec 31 | Cash | R7 436 | | Jan 1 | Balance | R3 907 | |
| " " | Goods returned to head office | 5 | | Dec 31 | Goods received from head office | 4 426 | |
| " " | Sales to head office customer | 4 | | " " | Rent | 202 | |
| " " | Balance | 1 845 | | " " | Salaries | 642 | |
| | | R9 290 | | " " | Sundry expenses | 112 | |
| | | ===== | | | | R9 290 | |
| | | | | | | ===== | |
| | | | | Dec 31 | Balance | R1 845 | |

### TRIAL BALANCE AT 31 DECEMBER 19x4

| | | | | |
|---|---|---|---|---|
| Cash | R 514 | | Head office current account | R1 845 |
| Goods received from head office | 4 426 | | Sales | 8 468 |
| Rent | 202 | | Provision for bad debts | 70 |
| Bad debts | 100 | | Goods returned to head office | 5 |
| Salaries | 642 | | Accumulated depreciation of motor vehicles to | |
| Debtors | 2 489 | | 31 December 19x3 | 1 000 |
| Sundry expenses | 163 | | | |
| Stock at 1 January 19x4 | 1 352 | | | |
| Motor vehicles at cost | 1 500 | | | |
| | R11 388 | | | R11 388 |
| | ====== | | | ====== |

(1)    Stock at 31 December 19x4 had cost R1 428.

(2)    Allow for depreciation of motor vehicles at the rate of 20% per annum on the reducing balance.

(3)    Increase the provision for bad debts to R80.


Give -

(a)    the closing journal entries in the Newlands branch books showing the results of the branch operations for the year ended 31 December 19x4.

(b)    the journal entries necessary in the head office books in order that the branch and head office current accounts may be in agreement at 31 December 19x4.

# G8

The following balances were extracted from the books of the head office (Johannesburg), and the two branches of the Anglo-African Property Co. Ltd at 30 June 19x4.

Prepare columnar and general income statements for the year and balance sheet at that date.

|  | Head office | Durban | Cape Town |
|---|---|---|---|
| Standard Bank of SA Ltd - overdraft | R1 060 | R270 | R960 |
| Debtors for rent | 170 | 830 | 50 |
| Creditors - trade | 12 100 | 570 | 910 |
| Rents receivable | 18 250 | 9 630 | 12 570 |
| Share capital - authorised and issued in R1 shares | 150 000 | | |
| Property - at cost | 190 000 | 50 000 | 50 000 |
| 6% mortgage debentures | 50 000 | | |
| Interest on debentures | 2 250 | | |
| Audit fees | 480 | 240 | 320 |
| Salaries and wages | 1 500 | 1 200 | 1 200 |
| Durban current account | Dr. 43 020 | | Cr. 300 |
| Cape Town current account | Dr. 38 470 | Dr. 400 | |
| Head office current account | | Cr. 43 140 | Cr. 37 470 |
| Maintenance and repairs | 1 600 | 940 | 640 |
| Retained income | Cr. 5 080 | | |
| General reserve | 50 000 | | |
| Provisional tax paid | 9 000 | | |

One quarter's debenture interest must be provided.  A remittance by letter transfer of R1 000 from Cape Town had been sent in June, but received by head office in July.

Durban branch had paid an account of R100 for maintenance and repairs on behalf of Cape Town, but the latter had not responded to the debit note, nor provided for the amount.

Durban branch had collected R120 on account of rent for July 19x4 from a Johannesburg tenant, but head office had not received advice of this transaction when this trial balance was extracted.

South African normal tax amounting to R10 000 must be provided.  The company owns six different buildings in Johannesburg.  Details of all buildings owned are recorded in a register at the head office in Johannesburg.

Omit comparative figures.

**G9**

The following balances were extracted from the books of the South African Trading Co. Ltd at 30 June 19x4, a company which owns three shops in Johannesburg, two in Cape Town and two in Durban.

|  | Head office | Cape Town | Durban |
|---|---|---|---|
| Audit fees | R2 000 | R1 000 | R800 |
| Bad debts | 15 000 | 12 000 | 9 000 |
| Cash at bank | 41 950 | 8 000 | 5 000 |
| Cape Town branch current account (debit) | 289 000 |  |  |
| Directors' fees | 10 000 |  |  |
| Durban branch current account (debit) | 255 050 |  |  |
| Furniture at cost | 35 000 | 24 000 | 20 000 |
| Accumulated depreciation - furniture to 30 June 19x3 | 5 000 | 4 000 | 2 000 |
| Gross profit for the year ended 30 June 19x4 | 300 000 | 200 000 | 120 000 |
| Head office current accounts (credit) | 286 000 | 253 750 |  |
| Interest paid | 5 000 |  |  |
| Land and buildings (cost) | 200 000 | 100 000 | 80 000 |
| Loan (secured by mortgage of land and buildings) | 100 000 |  |  |
| Provision for bad debts | 12 000 | 9 000 | 7 250 |
| General reserve | 50 000 |  |  |
| Salaries | 100 000 | 40 000 | 20 000 |
| Share capital (authorised and issued, in R1 shares) | 1 000 000 |  |  |
| Stock | 290 000 | 120 000 | 95 000 |
| Creditors | 32 000 | 5 000 | 3 000 |
| Debtors | 240 000 | 180 000 | 145 000 |
| Sundry expenses | 28 000 | 19 000 | 11 200 |
| Retained income at 30 June 19x3 | 12 000 |  |  |

Furniture must be depreciated at the rate of 5% per annum on the reducing balance.

All the old stock had been disposed of in May 19x4 and present stocks are all taken in at cost.

Stock to the value of R800 was sent to Durban by head office during the year was received, but no entries were made in the Durban books.

R3 000 was remitted from Cape Town to Johannesburg in June, but it was not received until July and no entries had yet been made in the Johannesburg books.

## G9 CONTINUED

Durban branch paid one of head office creditors the sum of R500, but head office had not yet responded to the entry.

R200 000 must be transferred to reserve.

Prepare a columnar and a general income statement and a balance sheet.  The last two named should not be in columnar form.

Ignore taxation and omit comparative figures.

# G10

From the following particulars, prepare the balance sheet of the YZ Company Limited at 31 December 19x2 and supporting income statements.

| | Bloemfontein | East London | Head office |
|---|---|---|---|
| Cash at bank | R6 500 | R4 500 | R100 200 |
| Share capital - authorised and issued (600 000 shares of 50c each) | | | 300 000 |
| Travelling expenses | 7 200 | 7 300 | 1 500 |
| Directors' fees | | | 6 000 |
| Sales, less returns | 313 000 | 282 000 | |
| Wages | 20 000 | 16 000 | |
| 6% debentures, secured by first mortgage over fixed property | | | 75 000 |
| General reserve | | | 50 000 |
| Carriage inwards | 8 000 | 800 | |
| Head office and branch accounts | 162 300 | 110 800 | B. 168 800 |
| | | | E.L. 114 800 |
| Sundry expenses | 29 800 | 26 700 | 1 500 |
| Land and buildings at cost | 33 000 | 17 500 | 75 000 |
| Rent received | | | 5 000 |
| Retained income at 1 January 19x2 | | | 22 000 |
| Stock 1 January 19x2 | 47 000 | 42 000 | |
| Debtors | 175 000 | 149 000 | |
| Creditors | 12 500 | 11 200 | |
| Discounts allowed | 4 500 | 3 000 | |
| Bad debts | 8 700 | 7 800 | |
| Bills payable | | | 29 000 |
| Purchases | 126 000 | 110 000 | |
| Furniture and fittings at cost | 2 000 | 2 700 | 1 400 |
| Motor vehicles at cost | 6 000 | 5 800 | |
| Salaries | 13 500 | 10 800 | 10 500 |
| Audit fees | 1 500 | 1 200 | 1 500 |
| Accumulated depreciation - furniture and fittings | 300 | 500 | 200 |
| Accumulated depreciation - motor vehicles | 600 | 600 | |

The cost of stock at 31 December 19x2 was: Bloemfontein R62 000; East London R49 000. All slow-moving stock had been disposed of in November. At 31 December 19x2 there was a remittance of R6 500 in transit from Bloemfontein branch to head office, and at this date East London had dispatched R4 000 worth of goods to Bloemfontein, which entry had not been responded to (the relative goods being received in January 19x3).

Provide 20% depreciation on the cost of the motor vehicles and 10% on the cost of furniture and fittings.

Make provision for the interest on debentures for the year.

Any further essential information may be assumed. Ignore taxation and omit comparative figures.

# G11

The XYZ Company Limited, having its head office in Johannesburg, and branches at Cape Town and Durban, submits the following trial balances (before the branch books have been closed to head office) at 31 December 19x2:

| | Head | Cape Town office | Durban | | Head | Cape Town office | Durban |
|---|---|---|---|---|---|---|---|
| Bank | | | R6 030 | Share capital | | | |
| Cash | R680 | R320 | 460 | – authorised | | | |
| Debtors | 421 680 | 66 000 | 62 480 | and issued: | | | |
| Premises at cost | 102 000 | 30 000 | 600 000 | Furniture and | | | |
| equipment at | | | | R1 each | R600 000 | | |
| cost | 100 000 | | | Bank | | 23 410 | R21 810 |
| Cape Town | | | | Creditors | 521 460 | 820 | 1 080 |
| branch | 145 160 | | | Retained | | | |
| Durban branch | 146 120 | | | income including | | | |
| Closing stocks | 286 500 | 44 000 | 69 300 | profit for | | | |
| Loss for the year | | 9 220 | | the year | 41 770 | 10 360 | |
| | | | | Head office | 126 910 | 126 830 | |
| | | | | Accumulated | | | |
| | | | | depreciation on | | | |
| | | | | furniture and | | | |
| | | | | equipment | | | |
| | | | | 31 December 19x2 | 15 500 | | |
| | R1 202 140 | R149 540 | R138 270 | | R1 202 140 | R149 540 | R138 270 |

# G11 CONTINUED

It was found:

(a)     That R10 000 remitted by Cape Town to head office on 30 December 19x2
        was not responded to until 2 January 19x3.
(b)     An invoice for R8 250 goods supplied by head office to Cape Town on 27
        December 19x2 was not responded to until January on receipt of the
        goods.
(c)     Goods invoiced by head office at R18 810 in December 19x2 had not
        arrived in Durban until January and the debit had not been responded to
        by Durban.
(d)     Owing to an error, an invoice dated 4 November 19x2 from head office
        for R480 was not responded to by Durban, the relative goods having been
        received 22 November 19x2.
(e)     All purchases are made and railages paid by head office.   Goods are
        invoiced to branches at 10% over cost of purchases and railage.
(f)     The premises consist of a shop building on freehold stand 7645
        Parkwood, Johannesburg, purchased for R102 000 in 19x0 and a shop
        building on freehold stand 1010 Lakeview, Cape Town, purchased for
        R30 000 in 19x1.

Pass the necessary journal entries in the head office books and prepare the
company's balance sheet at 31 December 19x2.

Any essential information not provided may be assumed.   Ignore taxation and
omit comparative figures.

# G12

D'arcy Limited carries on business as a wholesale merchant with a head office in Johannesburg and a branch in Pretoria.  Both the head office and branch operate independent accounting systems.

All purchases of merchandise are made by the head office and invoiced to the Pretoria branch at cost plus 5%.

The trial balances at 31 August 19x7 for the head office and branch are shown below:

|  | HEAD OFFICE | | BRANCH | |
|---|---|---|---|---|
|  | DR | CR | DR | CR |
| Share capital | | R90 000 | | |
| Retained income 1.9.19x6 | | 5 560 | | |
| Creditors | | 10 800 | | |
| Land and buildings, at cost | R44 000 | | R24 000 | |
| Furniture, at cost 1.9.19x6 | 4 000 | | 1 600 | |
| Accumulated depreciation - furniture 31.8.19x7 | | 2 000 | | R680 |
| Motor vans, at cost 1.9.19x6 | 8 800 | | 3 200 | |
| Accumulated depreciation - motor vans 31.8.19x7 | | 5 280 | | 1 440 |
| Stock 1.9.19x6 | 6 200 | | 4 410 | |
| Provision for unearned profit in branch stock 1.9.19x6 | | 210 | | |
| Debtors | 18 200 | | 5 200 | |
| Bank | 3 800 | | 3 600 | |
| Head office current account | | | | 34 890 |
| Branch current account | 35 720 | | | |
| Sale of motor van | | | | 3 000 |
| Sales | | 65 000 | | 36 600 |
| Purchases | 75 400 | | | |
| Goods received from head office | | | 27 720 | |
| Administration expenses | 10 000 | | 6 360 | |
| Goods sent to branch | | 28 350 | | |
| Depreciation | 180 | | 520 | |
| | R207 200 | R207 200 | R76 610 | R76 610 |

The following information is relevant:

1.   On 29 August 19x7 the head office despatched goods to the branch and invoiced the branch with R630.  The goods were not received or recorded by the branch until 2 September 19x7.

# G12 CONTINUED

2. On 24 August 19x7 the branch collected a cheque for R200 from a head office debtor.  This was deposited in the branch bank account and the head office current account credited.  The head office was advised of this transaction only 3 September 19x7.

3. On 30 August 19x7 the head office paid by cheque administration expenses amounting to R100 on behalf of the branch.  The branch was advised of this transaction only on 2 September 19x7.

4. A cheque for R300 remitted by the branch to the head office on 29 August 19x7 was not received or recorded by the head office until 1 September 19x7.

5. (i) On 1 September 19x6 a head office vehicle was sold to one of the branch's customers in Pretoria for R3 000 cash.  This sum had been received by the branch, deposited in the branch bank account and credited to "sale of vehicle" account.  No other entries have been recorded for this transaction by the branch or head office.

  (ii) The vehicle sold under (i) above had originally cost R3 800 and at the date of sale had been depreciated in total by R3 000.

  (iii) The annual depreciation for the year calculated at 20% per annum on the written down value has already been put through in both the head office and branch books.

   In computing and recording the depreciation of head office vehicles the bookkeeper had not considered the information given in (i) and (ii) above.

   Vehicles are depreciated at the rate of 20% per annum on the written down value.

6. At 31 August 19x7 the stock at head office was valued at R6 600 and the stock at branch at the transfer price of R3 612.

<u>YOU ARE REQUIRED TO GIVE</u>:

(i) the adjusting and closing journal entries in the Pretoria branch books showing  the results of the branch operations for the year ended 31 August 19x7.

(ii) any journal entries which may be necessary in the head office books before the final financial statements for the year can be drawn up.

# G13

Write up the necessary ledger accounts in the head office books to record the information set out below showing the net income of the branch for the six months and the amount owing by branch debtors.

Would you be satisfied with the results reflected?  If not, what investigations would you make?

Goods sent to the branch are invoiced at selling price, the rate of gross profit on selling price being 25%.

All expenses are paid by head office and all cash received by the branch is remitted daily to head office.

| | |
|---|---:|
| Debtors, 1 January 19x2 | R3 160 |
| Stock at selling price, 1 January 19x2 | 8 280 |
| Goods from head office | 82 120 |
| Returns to head office | 840 |
| Cash sales | 48 010 |
| Credit sales | 34 560 |
| Cash remitted to head office | 80 240 |
| Stock at selling price, 30 June 19x2 | 7 080 |
| Bad debts | 170 |
| Mark-ups | 110 |
| Mark-downs | 180 |
| Expenses paid by head office: | |
|   Salaries | 3 000 |
|   Rent | 1 380 |
|   Advertising | 640 |
|   Sundries | 1 090 |

Retailers Ltd of Johannesburg supplies its Parkview branch with goods and charges the branch at selling price which is cost plus 33 1/3%.

All expenses are paid by the head office and all cash sales and cash collected from debtors by the Parkview branch is banked to the credit of head office account immediately.

The following information relates to the Parkview branch for the six months ended 31 December 19x2:

| | |
|---|---:|
| Stock on hand at 1 July 19x2 at selling price | R7 200 |
| Stock on hand at 31 December 19x2 at selling price | 6 600 |
| Goods sent to branch at selling price | 86 400 |
| Debtors at 1 July 19x2 | 4 630 |
| Cash sales | 52 750 |
| Credit sales | 32 380 |
| Cash received from debtors | 29 210 |
| Goods returned to head office at cost price | 600 |
| Goods returned to branch by customers | 360 |
| Bad debts written off | 1 640 |
| Parkview branch - rent | 6 000 |
| salaries | 6 000 |
| expenses | 1 500 |

The branch manager has also advised head office that:

(a)  Goods whose selling price was R1 080 were stolen during the six months.
(b)  A sales assistant had inadvertently charged a cash customer R40 instead of R30 for some goods.
(c)  Some obsolete stock was sold at half price for R120 during September.

Record the above transactions in the books of the head office by means of ledger accounts and by means of these ledger accounts determine the profit of the branch for the six months ended 31 December 19x2.

# G15

The Boot and Shoe Co. Ltd has its head office at Johannesburg and a branch at Kimberley.

All goods are handled in two departments - A and B.

All goods sent to the branch are invoiced by head office at selling price, which in the case of Department A is cost plus 25% and in the case of Department B is cost plus 33 1/3%.  All expenses are paid from head office.

The branch keeps its own debtors' ledger and remits all cash collected to head office daily.

The following is a trial balance extracted from the branch books at 30 September 19x2:

| | | |
|---|--:|--:|
| Stock 1 April 19x2 at selling price - Dept. A | R1 200 | |
| Stock 1 April 19x2 at selling price - Dept. B | 1 600 | |
| Goods from head office at selling price - Dept. A | 10 500 | |
| Goods from head office at selling price - Dept. B | 11 500 | |
| Cash sales - Dept. A | | R4 500 |
| Cash sales - Dept. B | | 5 600 |
| Credit sales - Dept. A | | 5 750 |
| Credit sales - Dept. B | | 6 600 |
| Returns from customers - Dept. A | 250 | |
| Returns from customers - Dept. B | 200 | |
| Debtors | 5 000 | |
| Head office | 7 800 | |
| | R30 250 | R30 250 |

Stock 30 September 19x2 at selling price:  Dept. A - R1 500.
Stock 30 September 19x2 at selling price:  Dept. B - R1 200.

Prepare a trading account in the form usually adopted by concerns which do not charge stock at selling price showing the gross profit actually made in each department of the Kimberley branch.

Reconcile the profit shown in this trading account with the profit that would be expected on the turnover when taking the percentage which has been added to the cost into account.

# G16

The Dustbowl branch of the Golden City Retailers Ltd keeps its own debtors'
ledger and banks all cash collected by it to the credit of the head office
bank account.

Branch expenses are paid by head office and goods are supplied to the Dustbowl
branch at selling price which is cost plus 33 1/3%.

From the information given below in respect of the Dustbowl branch for the
year ended 31 March 19x2, prepare

(1)    the branch stock account,
(2)    the branch debtors' account,
(3)    the branch gross profit account, and
(4)    the branch profit and loss account,

as they would appear in the ledger of the Golden City Retailers Ltd.

| | |
|---|---:|
| Stock at Dustbowl branch at 1 April 19x1 (selling price) | R31 760 |
| Goods sent to the branch during the year (selling price) | 422 520 |
| Goods returned to head office during the year (selling price) | 3 800 |
| Branch cash sales for the year | 162 760 |
| Branch credit sales for the year | 244 800 |
| Branch debtors at 1 April 19x1 | 23 430 |
| Cash received from branch debtors during the year | 226 210 |
| Discount allowed to debtors | 3 840 |
| Branch rent | 8 100 |
| Branch salaries | 18 200 |
| Branch general expenses | 7 600 |

The branch manager informed the head office that:

(i)    Stock on hand at 31 March 19x2 (at selling price) was R28 720.
(ii)   Goods whose selling price was R1 200 were stolen during March 19x2.
(iii)  On instructions from head office a sale had been held during March 19x2
       and goods were marked down by 20% on selling prices.    The turnover
       during the period of the sale totalled R48 000 and is included in the
       sales figures above.
(iv)   During March he discovered that the cashier had stolen R520 by altering
       the amounts of cash sales dockets.

# G17

The Modern Wear Company Limited operates a branch in Pretoria which sells goods both for cash and on credit.

The head office supplies all goods to the branch at cost plus 33 1/3%, which is the price at which the goods are normally sold by the branch.

The head office pays all expenses of the branch and the branch banks daily for the credit of the head office account all cash received.

From the following information in respect of the Pretoria branch for the year to 31 December 19x3, prepare the accounts in the books of the head office reflecting the gross and net profits made by the branch and the branch debtors and branch stock accounts.

| | |
|---|---:|
| Debtors at 1 January 19x3 | R8 000 |
| Stock at normal selling price at 1 January 19x3 | 20 000 |
| Stock at normal selling price at 31 December 19x3 | 15 600 |
| Sales - credit | 43 000 |
| Sales - cash | 59 000 |
| Goods issued to branch at normal selling price | 112 000 |
| Goods returned by branch at normal selling price | 8 000 |
| Cash received from debtors | 41 000 |
| Discount allowed to debtors | 1 100 |
| Bad debts | 200 |
| Expenses paid by head office on behalf of branch: | |
|   Wages and salaries | 8 000 |
|   Expenses of delivery to customers | 1 000 |
|   Light and heat | 700 |
|   Selling expenses | 1 300 |
|   Rent | 3 000 |
|   General expenses | 600 |

During the year members of the branch staff were supplied with goods marked at R4 000, being the selling price. It is the practice of the company to allow members of the staff to purchase goods at cost price and to charge the difference between selling price and cost price of such goods to 'staff perquisites account'.

The figures given for cash and credit sales do not include purchases by members of staff.

During a sale in September 19x3 goods were marked down to cost plus 16 2/3%. The cost price of the goods sold during the sale was R12 000. The sales are included in the sales figures given above.

# G18

Tyrol Traders Limited operates a general dealers business at its head office in Johannesburg and a branch in Springs.

The branch keeps its own debtors, but all other records are kept by head office. Head office sends the branch all its goods for resale and charges the branch at selling price i.e. cost to head office plus 50%. It also pays all branch expenses and the branch banks all cash received daily for the credit of head office bank account.

The following information relates to the branch for the year ended 30 September 19x8:

| | |
|---|---:|
| Stock on hand 1 October 19x7 at selling price | R14 160 |
| Stock on hand 30 September 19x8 at selling price | 11 280 |
| Goods sent to branch at selling price | 169 920 |
| Goods returned to head office at selling price | 3 360 |
| Cash sales | 43 404 |
| Credit sales | 123 672 |
| Goods returned by debtors | 1 200 |
| Bad debts | 2 300 |
| Discount allowed | 720 |
| Branch expenses paid by head office | 16 600 |

<u>Additional information</u>

1. The previous cashier had stolen R900 from the proceeds of cash sales and had altered the invoices to hide the defalcation.
2. The head office cost of goods sold during a sale held by the branch in June 19x8 was R9 000. These goods had been marked down 20% on selling price and the proceeds are included in the above cash sales figure.
3. During the year goods, the selling price of which was R1 260, had been marked up a further 10% on selling price and sold by the branch manager contrary to head office policy.

<u>YOU ARE REQUIRED TO PREPARE</u>:

The following accounts as they would appear in the head office ledger for the year ended 30 September 19x8.

(a) Branch stock account.
(b) Branch gross profit account.
(c) Branch profit and loss account.

# G19

Outpost Limited has a central warehouse and head office and operates a number of retail shops, which are supplied by the central warehouse and charged by head office at cost prices. The accounts are kept at head office, which pays all shop expenses other than wages and small payments, which are paid by the shops out of their takings.

On 1 January 19x5 the shop accounts at head office for the Dargle branch showed the following:

| | |
|---|---:|
| Cash on hand at shop | 700 |
| Amounts owing by credit customers to shop | 1 300 |
| Stock on hand at shop | 24 500 |
| Fixtures at shop at cost less amounts written off | 12 000 |
| Shop rates and insurance paid in advance | 900 |

The transactions which relate to the shop for the year ended 31 December 19x5 were as follows:

| | |
|---|---:|
| Cash sales at shop | R620 740 |
| Credit sales at shop | 21 500 |
| Cash received by shop from credit customers | 18 600 |
| Remittance from shop to head office | 460 150 |
| Goods sent to shop from central warehouse | 340 000 |
| Allowance to credit customers for defective goods | 715 |
| Payments by head office on account of shop | |
|   Rent, rates, insurance | 30 180 |
|   Salaries | 47 000 |
|   General expenses | 5 180 |
|   Fixtures purchased (1 October 19x5) | 800 |
| Payments by shop | |
|   Wages | 169 000 |
|   Goods purchased | 5 000 |
|   General expenses | 3 500 |

At 31 December 19x5, the shop stocks were valued at R31 000. At that date, rates and insurance paid in advance amounted to R1 050. Customers' debts amounting to R120 were written off. Fixtures were depreciated on a reducing balance method at the rate of 20% per annum.

<u>YOU ARE REQUIRED TO PREPARE</u>:

1. The shop's income statement for the year ended 31 December 19x5, and
2. A list of the balances outstanding on the shop's accounts at 31 December 19x5.
3. The branch current account as it would appear in the head office ledger if the branch had maintained a self balancing ledger.

Fairdeal Limited has its head office in Johannesburg and a branch in Witbank. The branch is self-accounting and pays its own expenses except rent and salaries which are paid by head office.  All purchases are made by head office and stock sent to the branch is invoiced at cost.

The following trial balance was extracted from Witbank branch general ledger at the end of the financial year, 30 September 19x7:

| | | |
|---|---:|---:|
| Office furniture | R2 000 | |
| Shop fittings | 4 890 | |
| Stock - 30 September 19x6 | 21 600 | |
| Goods received from head office | 140 280 | |
| Goods returned to head office | | R760 |
| Branch debtors control | 27 200 | |
| Bad debts | 800 | |
| Accrued expenses | | 500 |
| Administration and selling expenses | 8 850 | |
| Cash at bank | 1 560 | |
| Sales (cash and credit) | | 250 780 |
| General ledger suspense account | 490 | |
| Head office current account | 44 730 | |
| | R252 040 | R252 040 |

<u>NOTES</u>:

1.    When the bookkeeper found that the general ledger did not balance he debited the difference to a general ledger suspense account.

2.    The following is a summary of the branch current account in the HEAD OFFICE books:

| | | |
|---|---:|---:|
| Balance at 30 September 19x6 | R38 060 | |
| Goods sent to branch | 142 400 | |
| Branch salaries paid | 25 000 | |
| Branch rent paid | 12 000 | |
| Cash received from branch debtor A | | R150 |
| Goods returned by branch | | 840 |
| Cash remittances received from branch | | 218 790 |
| Balance at 30 September 19x7 | 2 320 | |
| | R219 780 | R219 780 |

3.    A cash remittance of R3 000 made by the branch on 30 September 19x7 was not received by head office until 4 October 19x7 and stock costing R2 200 sent by head office was not received by the branch until 5 October 19x7.

4.    No entry had been put through the branch books to record the receipt of
      R150 by head office on 25 September 19x7 from branch debtor A.

5.    Stock costing R80 had been returned to head office during August 19x7.
      The correct  entry had been made in the branch journal and the debit
      correctly posted.  The credit side of the entry had, however, been
      incorrectly posted to debit of the goods received from head office.

6.    Shop fittings purchased on 1 February 19x6 for R900 were sold on 31
      January 19x7 for R650.  The receipt of the R650 had been entered in the
      cash sales column in the branch cash book.  Upon discovering the error,
      the branch bookkeeper deleted  the amount from the cash sales column
      and entered it in the sundries column from where it was posted  to
      credit of shop fittings, but he omitted to alter the total of the cash
      sales and sundries columns.  The cash sales column is posted in total
      monthly.  No other entries have been made in respect of this sale of
      shop fittings.

7.    No furniture was bought or sold during the year.

8.    Depreciation has always been provided by the branch on the reducing
      balance of fixed assets at the rate of 10% per annum and must be
      provided on the same basis for the year ended 30 September 19x7.


<u>YOU ARE REQUIRED</u>:

(i)   To journalise all the adjustments necessary in the books of the Witbank
      branch at 30 September 19x7.  Closing transfers are NOT required.

(ii)  To complete:

      (a)   Head office current account in the branch books.
      (b)   Branch current account in head office books.

The head office of Radcon Limited is situated in Johannesburg.  The company has a branch in Durban.  The head office purchases all stock for the branch and invoices it to the branch at cost.

The branch keeps its own set of books  and pays  all its own expenses, except rent and salaries, which are paid by head office.

On the last day of each quarter a cash remittance is made by the branch to head office.  A remittance of R3 000 made on 31 December 19x8 was not received by the head office until 3 January 19x9.

On 31 December 19x8 the following trial balance was extracted from the branch's general ledger:

| | | |
|---|---:|---:|
| Office furniture | R500 | |
| Shop fittings | 1 230 | |
| Stock at 1 January 19x8 | 5 400 | |
| Stock received from head office | 23 780 | |
| Stock returned to head office | | R190 |
| Debtors control | 6 800 | |
| Bad debts | 200 | |
| Creditors control | | 580 |
| Administration expenses | 750 | |
| Selling expenses | 380 | |
| Cash at bank | 390 | |
| Sales | | 47 720 |
| Creditors ledger suspense account | 120 | |
| General ledger suspense account | 490 | |
| Head office current account | 8 540 | |
| | R48 490 | R48 490 |

<u>NOTES</u>:

(1)    The list of balances extracted from the creditors ledger did not agree with the balance on the creditors control account in the general ledger.  The bookkeeper adjusted the control by transferring the difference to a creditors ledger suspense account.

(2)    As the general ledger did not balance the bookkeeper opened a general ledger suspense account and debited this account with difference on the trial balance.

## G21 CONTINUED

(3)    The following is a summary for the year ended 31 December 19x8 of the branch's account in head office books:

|  |  |  |
|---|---|---|
| Balance at 1 January 19x8 | R1 250 |  |
| Stock sent to branch | 25 900 |  |
| Branch salaries paid | 5 600 |  |
| Branch rent paid | 1 200 |  |
| Cash received from branch debtor - A. Smith |  | R150 |
| Set off of amount owing by A. Jones to branch against amount owing by head office to A. Jones |  | 60 |
| Stock returned by branch |  | 270 |
| Cash received from branch |  | 30 130 |
| Balance at 31 December 19x8 |  | 3 340 |
|  | R33 950 | R33 950 |
|  | ====== | ====== |

(4)    Stock costing R2 200 sent to the branch on 24 December 19x8 was not received by the branch until 7 January 19x9. No entry has yet been made in the branch books in respect of this amount.

(5)    Stock costing R80 had been returned to head office in October 19x8 and correctly journalised in the branch books. The credit side of the journal entry had been posted, incorrectly, to the debit side of stock received from head office account in the branch general ledger.

(6)    The entry put through in the branch books for the set off of A. Jones' debtors account in the branch books against his creditors account in head office books was:

|  |  |  |
|---|---|---|
| Creditors' control | R60 |  |
| A. Jones (creditors' ledger) | 60 |  |
| Debtors' control |  | R60 |
| A. Jones (debtors' ledger) |  | 60 |

The balance of R60 on A. Jones account in the branch creditors' ledger had been recorded on the list of creditors balances as a credit balance.

(7)    No entry had been put through the branch books to record the receipt of R150 by head office from the branch debtor, A. Smith.

(8)    Shop fittings which had been purchased for R800 on 1 July 19x7 were sold for R650 on 30 April 19x8. The receipt of R650 had been included in the cash book in the cash sales column, which is posted in total at the end of each month. On discovering this error, the branch bookkeeper deleted the amount from the cash sales column, entered it in the sundries column and posted it to the credit of shop fittings account. He omitted to alter the total of the cash sales column in the cash book. No other entries had been made in respect of this sale of shop fittings.

(9)    No furniture had been bought or sold during the year.

# G21 CONTINUED

(10)  Depreciation had been written off the depreciated value of the fixed
      assets at the rate of 5% per annum up to 31 December 19x7.
      Depreciation must be written off on the same basis for the year ended
      31 December 19x8.

<u>YOU ARE REQUIRED</u>:

1.    To journalise all the adjustments necessary in the books of the branch
      at 31 December 19x8 to correct them.

2.    To complete - (a)   the head office current account in the branch
      ledger

                      (b)   the branch current account in the head office ledger

      showing how the balances on these accounts would be reconciled <u>before</u>
      the closing entries are made.

<u>NOTE</u>:   THE CLOSING ENTRIES ARE NOT REQUIRED.

## G22

A trader commenced business on 1 January 19x8 with a head office and one branch.

All goods were purchased by the head office and goods sent to the branch were invoiced at a fixed selling price of 25% above cost. All sales, both by head office and the branch, were made at the fixed selling price.

The following trial balance was extracted from the books at the head office at 31 December 19x8:

| | | |
|---|---:|---:|
| Capital | | R52 000 |
| Drawings | R1 740 | |
| Purchases | 123 380 | |
| Sales | | 83 550 |
| Goods sent to branch (at selling price) | | 56 250 |
| Branch current account | 24 550 | |
| Fixed assets | 33 000 | |
| Debtors and creditors | 7 980 | 11 060 |
| General expenses | 8 470 | |
| Balance at bank | 3 740 | |
| | R202 860 | R202 860 |

No entries had been made in the head office books for cash in transit from the

branch to head office at 31 December 19x8 - R1 000.

When the balances shown below were extracted from the branch books at 31 December 19x8, no entries had been made in the books of the branch for goods in transit on that date from head office to branch R920 (selling price).

In addition to the balances which can be determined from the information given below the following balances appeared in the branch books at 31 December 19x8.

| | |
|---|---:|
| Fixed assets | R6 000 |
| General expenses | 6 070 |
| Debtors | 7 040 |
| Creditors (excluding head office) | 1 630 |
| Sales | 51 700 |
| Balance at bank | 1 520 |

When stock was taken on 31 December 19x8 it was found that there were no shortages at the head office, but at the branch there were shortages amounting to R300 at selling price.

<u>YOU ARE REQUIRED TO</u>:

to prepare the income statement for
(i)   head office
(ii)  the branch
as they would appear if goods sent to the branch had been invoiced at cost, and a balance sheet of the whole business at 31 December 19x8.

Head office and branch stocks are to be valued at cost.

Calderwoods Limitedoperates from a head office in Johannesburg and a branch in Durban, where separate books are kept.

Goods sent to the branch by the head office are charged at cost plus 10%.

The following trial balance was extracted from the head office books at 30 September 19x8.

| | | |
|---|---:|---:|
| Retained income  -  1 October 19x7 | | R8 840 |
| Audit fees | R1 000 | |
| Bank | 14 575 | |
| Branch current account | 19 170 | |
| Creditors | | 17 000 |
| Debtors | 25 000 | |
| Furniture - cost | 5 000 | |
| Furniture - accumulated depreciation 1 October 19x7 | | 1 500 |
| General expenses | 2 465 | |
| Goods sent to branch | | 47 300 |
| Interest on loan | 2 000 | |
| Land and buildings | 65 000 | |
| Loan | | 40 000 |
| Motor vehicles - cost | 25 000 | |
| Motor vehicles - accumulated depreciation 1 October 19x7 | | 10 000 |
| Purchases | 206 420 | |
| Provision for unearned profit on stock at 1 October 19x7 | | 500 |
| Provisional tax payments | 5 000 | |
| Salaries | 40 500 | |
| Sales | | 227 250 |
| Share capital | | 100 000 |
| Stock 1 October 19x7 | 41 260 | |
| | R452 390 | R452 390 |

In addition to the balances which can be deduced from the information given above, the following balances appeared in the branch books at 30 September 19x8:

| | |
|---|---:|
| Balance at bank | R1 520 |
| Creditors (excluding head office) | 960 |
| Debtors | 8 040 |
| Furniture - cost | 2 000 |
| Furniture - accumulated depreciation 1 October 19x7 | 300 |
| General expenses | 7 670 |
| Salaries | 8 400 |
| Sales | 60 000 |

# G23 CONTINUED



1.  The authorised share capital of Calderwoods Limited is R200 000 in shares of R1 each of which 100 000 have been issued.

2.  The 10% loan, secured by a mortgage over land and buildings, is repayable on 30 September 19y0. Interest is payable in arrear on 1 April and 1 October each year.

3.  The land and buildings consist of an office block and showroom situated on Stand 123 in Highveld Township. They were acquired on 30 November 19x5 at a cost a of R50 000. Additions costing R15 000 were completed in 19x6.

4.  At 30 September 19x8 the following stock was on hand:

    | | |
    |---|---|
    | At head office  -  at cost | R35 380 |
    | At the branch - at cost | 7 700 |

    Cost is determined by the head office using the weighted average of prices as per suppliers' invoices. The branch uses the weighted average of prices as per the invoices on which goods are charged to it by the head office.

    All stocks on hand have a net realisable value in excess of cost as determined above.

    On 28 September 19x8 stock, invoiced to the branch at R3 300, was dispatched. This stock was received by the branch early in October.

5.  Debtors include an amount of R450 owing by P Strauss, a director, in respect of goods purchased by him for R600 on 20 January 19x8. He paid R150 on account on 20 August 19x8. The company's normal terms of credit are 60 days.

6.  Included in the head office general expenses is R2 000 paid to the directors as fees. The managing director's salary of R15 000 is included in the head office salaries. In addition the managing director has the use of a company car. This benefit is assessed at R600 per annum.

7.  The branch general expenses include a leasing charge of R3 000 for motor vehicles and R2 400 for rent of the premises.

8.  Depreciation is to be provided on the assets of head office and the branch as follows:

    | | |
    |---|---|
    | Furniture       - | 5% p.a. on cost |
    | Motor vehicles - | 20% p.a. on cost |

9.  South African normal tax for the year amounted to R5 200.

# G23 CONTINUED

10.    A   dividend of 5% had been declared payable to the shareholders registered on 30 September 19x8, but no provision had been made  in the books for this dividend.

<u>YOU ARE REQUIRED TO PREPARE FOR CALDERWOODS LIMITED</u>:

(i)    the detailed balance sheet at 30 September 19x8.

(ii)   the detailed columnar income statement for the year ended 30 September 19x8.

      Notes to the financial statements are required.

# G24

J. Benson owns the Union Supply Company which carries on business as wholesale

merchants at head office in Johannesburg and at a branch in Durban.

Both the head office and the Durban branch keep complete set of books.

All purchases are made by the head office and goods are transferred to the
Durban branch at cost plus 5%.

From the following trial balances and notes appended prepare:

(1)    the journal entries necessary to close the branch books
(2)    the journal entries necessary to close the head office books
(3)    columnar income statement of Union Supply Company.

<u>TRIAL BALANCES AT 31 MARCH 19x5</u>

| | Head office Dr. | Head office Cr. | Branch Dr. | Branch Cr. |
|---|---|---|---|---|
| J. Benson, capital account | | R47 780 | | |
| Fixtures and fittings, at cost 1 April 19x4 | R2 000 | | R800 | |
| Fixtures and fittings - accumulated depreciation 1 April 19x4 | | 900 | | R300 |
| Motor vans at cost 1 April 19x4 | 4 400 | | 1 600 | |
| Motor vans - accumulated depreciation 1 April 19x4 | | 2 200 | | 500 |
| Sale of motor van on 1 April 19x4 | | 1 500 | | |
| Land and buildings at cost 1 April 19x4 | 22 000 | | 12 000 | |
| Sales (net) | | 31 000 | | 18 300 |
| Debtors | 5 100 | | 2 600 | |
| Bank | 1 900 | | 300 | |
| Stock, head office 1 April 19x4 | 3 100 | | | |
| Stock, branch 1 April 19x4 | | | 2 205 | |
| Purchases | 37 700 | | | |
| Creditors | | 5 400 | | |
| Wages | 3 800 | | 2 480 | |
| Expenses | 1 200 | | 700 | |
| Goods sent to branch | | 14 175 | | |
| Branch current account | 17 860 | | | |
| Goods received from head office | | | 13 860 | |
| Head office current account | | | | 17 445 |
| Provision for unearned profit on branch stock | | 105 | | |
| J. Benson - drawings | 4 400 | | | |
| | R103 060 | R103 060 | R36 545 | R36 545 |

329

# G24 CONTINUED

<u>NOTES</u>:

1. On 28 March 19x5 the head office dispatched goods to the branch and charged the branch R315 for them. The goods were not received by the branch until 2 April 19x5 and no entries had been made in the branch books.
2. On 20 March 19x5 the branch collected a cheque for R100 from a head office customer and deposited it in the branch account, crediting head office with the amount. They failed to notify the head office of this fact until 3 April 19x5 and no entries had been made in the head office books.
3. On 31 March 19x5 the head office paid by cheque sundry expenses amounting to R50 on behalf of the branch. The branch did not receive advice of this charge.
4. A cheque for R150 remitted by the branch to head office on 29 March 19x5 was not received by head office until 2 April 19x5 and no adjusting entry had been made.
5. At 31 March 19x5 the stock in the head office warehouse was valued at R3 300. At 31 March 19x5 the stock in the branch warehouse, valued at cost plus 5% was R1 806.
6. The motor van sold during the year cost R1 900 , and the depreciation provided thereon at 31 March 19x4 amounted to R1 500.
7. Depreciation is to be provided as follows:
   (a) on both head office and branch fixtures and fittings at 5% per annum on cost
   (b) on both head office and branch motor vans at 20% per annum on the written down value.

# G25

Tempest Limited, which has its head office in Johannesburg and branches in Cape Town and Durban, submits the following trial balances (before the branch books have been closed) at 31 December 19x8:

|  | Head office | Cape Town | Durban |
|---|---|---|---|
| Debits |  |  |  |
| Cash | R68 | R32 | R46 |
| Bank | - | - | 603 |
| Cape Town branch | 14 691 | - | - |
| Debtors | 42 168 | 6 600 | 6 248 |
| Durban branch | 14 612 | - | - |
| Land and buildings - cost | 10 200 | 3 000 | - |
| Machinery | 10 000 | - | - |
| Profit and loss account | - | 922 | - |
| Stocks | 28 650 | 4 400 | 6 300 |
|  | R120 389 | R14 954 | R13 827 |
|  | ======= | ====== | ====== |
| Credits |  |  |  |
| Bank | R2 341 | R2 181 | - |
| Creditors | 53 221 | 82 | R108 |
| Share capital (R1 shares) | 10 000 | - | - |
| Head office | - | 12 691 | 12 683 |
| Retained income at 1 January 19x7 | 49 100 |  |  |
| Profit and loss account | 4 177 | - | 1 036 |
| Accumulated depreciation - machinery at 31 December 19x8 | 1 550 |  |  |
|  | R120 389 | R14 954 | R13 827 |
|  | ======= | ====== | ====== |

It was found:

(a)   that most goods are purchased by head office and since 1 January 19x8 have been invoiced to branches at 10% above cost.  No goods purchased locally were on hand at the branches on 31 December 19x8.

(b)   that R2 000 remitted by Cape Town to head office on 29 December 19x8 was not received or responded to until 3 January 19x9.

(c)   that goods invoiced by head office at R1 881 on 28 December 19x8 did not arrive in Durban and were not recorded until 15 January 19x9.

(d)   that goods invoiced on 10 November 19x8 by head office to Durban for R48 were received on 15 November 19x8 but due to an error were not responded to until 8 January 19x9.


<u>YOU ARE REQUIRED TO</u>:

(i)    to show the reconciliations of the current accounts.
(ii)   to prepare the balance sheet of Tempest Limited at 31 December 19x8. (Any essential information which is not given should be supplied from your imagination.)

<u>TRIAL BALANCES AT 30 JUNE 19x2</u>

|                                          | HEAD OFFICE | BRANCH |
|------------------------------------------|-------------|--------|
| Branch current account                   | R19 400 Dr. | -      |
| Head office current  account             | -           | R16 400 Cr. |
| Stock 1 July 19x1                        | 5 000       | 3 300  |
| Goods to branch - from head office       | 22 000      | 20 900 |
| Purchases                                | 54 000      | -      |
| Sales                                    | 47 000      | 34 000 |
| Expenses                                 | 6 000       | 1 000  |
| Provision for unearned profit on stock   | 300         | -      |
| Debtors                                  | 8 000       | 5 000  |
| Cash                                     | 2 000       | 1 000  |
| Other assets                             | 4 300       | 19 200 |
| Capital                                  | 30 000      | -      |

1.   The branch had collected R100 from a head office debtor.  Head office had not recorded this receipt.

2.   The branch had sent cash of R600 to head office on 30 June 19x2.  This amount had not yet been received by head office.

3.   Head office had paid R1 400 in respect of branch expenses.  The branch has not responded to this payment.

4.   On 28 June 19x2 head office sent goods to the branch for R1 100.  These goods were received by the branch on 3 July 19x2.

5.   All goods are invoiced to the branch at cost plus 10%.  Stock on hand at 30 June 19x2 was:-

     At head office          R4 000
     At branch               R4 400

<u>YOU ARE REQUIRED TO</u>:

Draw up an  income statement in columnar form for the year ended 30 June 19x2.

The statement must show the actual cost of goods sold by the group, the actual cost of goods sold by head office and the invoiced cost of goods sold by the branch.

Diggers Trading Company operates a number of branches to which it supplies goods for resale at cost plus 5%. Inter-branch transfers of stock must be authorised by head office which passes debit and credit notes to the sending and receiving branches at the price at which the goods were originally invoiced to the branch. Branches respond by either debiting or crediting head office current account.

The following information has been extracted from the Pretoria branch books and records for the year ended 31 March 19x0:

<u>Assets at 1 April 19x9</u>

| | |
|---|---:|
| Stock at invoiced cost to the branch | R5 985 |
| Bank | 240 |
| Petty cash float | 50 |
| Debtors | 4 550 |

There were no liabilities on 1 April 19x9

<u>Summarised transactions during year ended 31 March 19x0</u>

| | |
|---|---:|
| Sales per sales journal (see notes 1 + 2) | R72 781 |
| Goods received from head office | 50 799 |
| Goods returned to head office | 1 449 |
| Goods received from other branches | 5 145 |
| Goods sent to other branches | 2 058 |
| Expenses paid by head office | 6 000 |
| Petty cash reimbursements received from head office | 630 |
| Payments of account by branch debtor direct to head office | 500 |
| Cash remitted to head office | 65 000 |
| Cash paid by debtors | 20 000 |
| Bad debts written off | 50 |

The following additional information is given:

1.  Summarised extract from branch sales journal (maintained in columnar form) for the year

| | Cash sales | Credit sales | Cash discount | General sales tax | Total |
|---|---|---|---|---|---|
| Retail customers | R15 075 | R8 200 | R1 675 | R931 | R25 881 |
| Wholesale customers | 30 780 | 12 700 | 3 420 | – | 46 900 |
| | R45 855 | R20 900 | R5 095 | R931 | R72 781 |

2.  During the year a wholesale cash customer purchased goods marked at R112. These were subsequently found to be faulty and were returned. The customer was refunded from that day's cash takings but no entry has been made in the sales journal to record this refund.

    All other returns were by credit customers who were given credit notes which were recorded in the sales journal.

# G27 CONTINUED

3.    Head office pays all branch expenses except petty expenses which are paid out of branch petty cash kept on the imprest system.  Head office periodically reimburses the petty cash to maintain the float at R50.

4.    Head office has paid the general sales tax of R931 to the revenue authorities.

5.    Branch managers have been instructed to mark up all goods for resale by 100% on the invoiced cost to the branch and to allow  the following discounts:

| | |
|---|---|
| Wholesalers | 37 1/2% trade discount |
| All cash customers | 10% cash discount. |

6.    Branch stock at 31 March  19x0 amounted to R8 400 at invoiced cost to the branch.

7.    The branch petty cash box contains R15 in cash and vouchers for expenses amounting to R35 which have not been reimbursed by head office.

8.    Branches are completely self-accounting and each branch produces a separate detailed income statement and balance sheet at the end  of the year.

<u>YOU ARE REQUIRED TO PREPARE</u>:

1.    The detailed income statement for the Pretoria branch for the year ended 31 March 19x0.

2.    The detailed balance sheet for  the Pretoria branch at 31 March 19x0.

3.    The head office current account in the Pretoria branch ledger for the year.

What would the branch net profit have been if:

-    No discounts had been allowed to any customers, AND
Head office had invoiced stock to all the branches at original cost?

# G28

The following balances were extracted from the books of head office (Randburg) and the branch (Vereeniging) of Republic Enterprise Limited at 30 September 19x3:

|  | Head office Randburg | Branch Vereeniging |
|---|---|---|
| Accumulated loss | R20 000 | - |
| Accounts payable | 24 896 | - |
| Accounts receivable | 25 500 | R13 000 |
| General expenses | 6 000 | 3 500 |
| Bank balance (debit) | 10 136 | 1 500 |
| Branch current account (debit) | 89 300 | - |
| Furniture and fittings - at cost 30 September 19x2 | 10 000 | 4 000 |
| Goods received from head office | - | 69 300 |
| Goods sent to branch | 70 875 | - |
| Head office current account (credit) | - | 87 225 |
| Motor vans - at cost 30 September 19x2 | 32 000 | 8 000 |
| Accumulated depreciation - 30 September 19x2: |  |  |
|   Furniture and fittings | 4 500 | 1 500 |
|   Motor vans | 15 240 | 2 500 |
| Proceeds from sale of motor van | 6 000 | - |
| Land and buildings - at cost | 105 000 | 60 000 |
| Purchases - goods for resale | 188 500 | - |
| Sales (net) | 155 000 | 91 500 |
| Share capital |  |  |
|   (Authorised and issued R1 shares) | 250 000 | - |
| Stock - 30 September 19x2 | 15 500 | 11 025 |
| Provision for unearned administration  fees 30 September 19x2 | 525 |  |
| Wages | 25 100 | 12 400 |

<u>NOTES</u>:

1.  The branch is self accounting and its books have not yet been closed.

2.  All purchases are made by head office and goods are sent to the branch at cost plus 5%.  This is added to cover estimated administration expenses incurred by head office on behalf  of the branch.

3.  A cheque for R750 remitted by branch to head office on 29 September 19x3 was not received by head office until 3 October 19x3.

4.  On 28 September 19x3 head office sent goods to the branch at an invoiced price  of R1 575.  These  goods  were  not received by the branch until 2 October 19x3, but head office wants this stock to be reported in the  branch balance sheet  the year end.

5. On 25 September 19x3 the branch collected R500 from a head office customer and deposited the amount in the branch account. The branch did not notify head office of this collection until 5 October 19x3 and head office has not yet responded to this transaction.

6. On 30 September 19x3 head office paid general expenses of R250 on behalf of the branch but did not advise the branch until 4 October 19x3.

7. On 30 June 19x3 head office sold a motor van for R6 000 and credited the proceeds to an account "proceeds on sale of motor van". No other entries have been made in respect of this transaction. At 30 September 19x2 this motor van stood in the books at a written down value of R5 760. The van had been purchased on 1 April 19x0 and had been depreciated at the rate of 20% per annum by the reducing balance method.

8. Depreciation for the year ended 30 September 19x3 must be provided as follows:

   (a) Furniture and fittings - both head office and branch at 10% per annum on cost.

   (b) Motor vans - both head office and branch at 20% per annum by the reducing balance method.

9. At 30 September 19x3 stock on hand was as follows:-

   Head office   -   R16 500 at cost
   Branch        -   R9 030 at invoiced prices.


<u>YOU ARE REQUIRED TO</u>:

(a) To prepare the journal entries necessary to close the BRANCH BOOKS at 30 September 19x3.

(b) To prepare a detailed income statement for the year ended 30 september 19x3 for management in columnar form showing the BOOK GROSS PROFIT earned by head office and branch and the TRUE GROSS PROFIT for the firm.

# G29

The following trial balances were extracted from the ledgers  of the head
office and Durban branch of the Nationwide Distributors Limited:

<u>TRIAL BALANCE AT 31 DECEMBER 19x6</u>

| | <u>HEAD OFFICE</u> | | <u>DURBAN</u> | |
|---|---:|---:|---:|---:|
| Share capital, authorised and issued in R1 shares | | R200 000 | | |
| Retained income - 1 January  19x6 | | 100 000 | | |
| Stock on hand at head office - 31 December  19x6 | R105 000 | | | |
| Stock on hand at Cape Town 1 January  19x6 | 25 000 | | | |
| Goods received from head office: | | | | |
| by Cape Town branch | 300 000 | | | |
| by Durban branch | | | R205 920 | |
| Goods returned to head office: | | | | |
| by Cape Town branch | | 5 000 | | |
| by Durban branch | | | | R17 160 |
| Purchases from suppliers: | | | | |
| by Cape Town branch | 18 400 | | | |
| by Durban branch | | | 51 480 | |
| Rent - head office | 23 000 | | | |
| - Cape Town\Durban | 12 000 | | 10 000 | |
| Salaries - head office | 75 000 | | | |
| Cape Town/Durban | 40 000 | | 35 000 | |
| Sundry expenses - head office | 15 000 | | | |
| - Cape Town/Durban | 8 000 | | 7 000 | |
| Managers' commission - payments on account - Cape Town/Durban | 5 000 | | 5 000 | |
| Administration fees | | 17 000 | | |
| Bank | 186 220 | | 5 000 | |
| Head office account | | | | 23 840 |
| Cash - head office | 2 000 | | | |
| - Cape Town/Durban | 400 | | 600 | |
| Gross profit on sales of R800 000 | | 200 000 | | |
| Debtors | 100 000 | | 25 000 | |
| Sales - Cape Town/Durban | | 400 000 | | 300 000 |
| Creditors | | 66 000 | | 4 000 |
| Provisional taxation payments | 45 100 | | | |
| Durban branch account | 27 880 | | | |
| | R988 000 | R988 000 | R345 000 | R345 000 |

# G29 CONTINUED

(1)    The closing entries in respect of the head office trading account only have already been made.

(2)    The ledger accounts in respect of the Cape Town branch are kept in the head office ledger.  The goods sent to the Cape Town branch are entered in the books at cost price.

(3)    The Durban branch was opened on 1 April 19x6, and goods are sent to it at cost plus 10%, the surcharge being treated in the head office ledger as an "administration fee".   This account is not used for any other purpose.

(4)    The branch managers are each to receive a commission  equal to 20% of the balance of "gross profit on sales" less those expenses (other than their commission) directly allocatable to their branch.   The Durban branch manager does not  know that the goods from head office have been charged at an inflated cost.

On examining the records the following matters are discovered:

(a)    Remittance of R300 made by Durban  on 29 December 19x6 to head office was received and recorded by the head office only on  4 January 19x7.

(b)    Goods returned to head office by Durban on 28 December 19x6 were  not received or recorded  by  head office until  13 January 19x7.   The issue  price of these goods was R4 290.

(c)    On the 14 October 19x6, goods sent from the Cape Town branch were received by the Durban branch.  No entries have been made in either the head office ledger or Durban branch ledger.   The issue price of these goods for  the Durban branch  manager's  accounts is R12 870 which includes the "administration fee".

(d)    Goods were returned to head office by Cape Town branch on the 23 December 19x6.   The entry for these returns - R1 500 - has not been recorded at all.   The goods arrived at the head office on 11 January 19x7.

(e)    An issue of goods by the head office to Durban on the 17 November 19x6 was correctly  recorded in  the  Durban  branch  ledger on arrival of the goods on 9 December 19x6.   The head office, however, in its own ledger recorded only the cost price of these goods and did not add the surcharge.  After allowing for this and the aforegoing errors the head office and Durban branch books are in agreement.

(f)    The closing stocks on hand at 31 December 19x6 were:
           Cape Town          R25 200
           Durban              42 900   (see note (g) below)
           Head office        105 000

# G29 CONTINUED

(g)   The Durban stocks on hand as per manager's certificate at 31 December 19x6 amount to R42 900. All these goods had been received from head office.

(h)   Taxation for the year, it is accurately estimated, will be assessed at R50 000

<u>YOU ARE REQUIRED TO</u>:

(1)   Prepare the head office account commencing with the balance as shown in the trial balance, the trading account and profit and loss account as they will appear in the Durban branch ledger, and its balance sheet for submission to the head office.

(2)   Prepare a trading account in respect of the Cape Town branch.

(3)   Prepare a columnar income statement (excluding the trading section) for the head office and Cape Town branch only.

(4)   Prepare the appropriation section of the retained income account for the whole company.

(5)   Show how the <u>stock</u> would appear in the balance sheet of the company at 31 December 19x6.

MNO Traders Limited invoices goods to its branch at cost plus 10 per cent. The branch manager is unaware of this agreement.

At 30 June 19x7, after the branch had closed its books, the following information was available:

(a)   The net profit according to the branch profit and loss account in the branch books was R28 300.

(b)   On 30 June 19x7 goods invoiced at R550 had been sent to the branch, but the branch did not respond to this entry until 5 July 19x7 when the goods arrived.

(c)   The branch had returned goods, invoiced to them at R33, to head office on 1 June 19x7. These goods were misappropriated by the head office store-man who has since disappeared. The theft was concealed by making no entry in the goods returned book. This loss was not covered by insurance.

(d)   A branch debtor for R120 was declared insolvent on 3 July 19x7. No dividend is expected from his estate, but no entry has been made in the books.

(e)   According to returns sent to head office by the branch, stock on hand at the branch premises (at prices invoiced by head office) was as follows:

        at 30 June 19x6 - R5 830
        at 30 June 19x7 - R4 730


<u>YOU ARE REQUIRED TO</u>:

to pass the necessary journal entries in the head office books.

**G31**

(a)     STATE the advantages and disadvantages of invoicing inter branch transfers at selling prices.

(b)     STATE what additional control procedures would be expected in such an accounting system.

341

# G32

A firm consistently adds 50% to the cost of all goods to arrive at their selling prices and invoices goods to its branches at selling prices.

The following information, relating to the Geldfontein branch for the year ended 30 June 19x4, was extracted from the head office books.

| | | | | |
|---|---|---|---|---|
| Stock 30 June 19x3 | cost price R4 000 | selling price | R6 000 |
| Goods sent to branch | cost price 20 000 | selling price | 30 000 |
| Goods returned by branch | cost price 400 | | |
| Cash sales (actual cash received) | | | 5 400 |
| Proceeds of sale of redundant stock | | | 1 900 |
| Credit sales | | | 20 500 |
| Goods returned by credit customers | cost price R800 | selling price | 1 200 |
| Debtors at 30 June 19x3 | | | 6 000 |
| Cash received from debtors | | | 16 000 |
| Bad debts written off | | | 500 |
| Branch expenses | | | 1 042 |
| Branch manager's salary | | | 1 800 |
| Stock on hand at branch at 30 June 19x4 | cost price R4 000 | selling price | 6 000 |

<u>The following information is available</u>

1.  It is the policy of the firm to allow a deduction of 10% off the normal selling price to cash customers. During the year to 30 June 19x4 advantage was taken of this mark-down in respect of all cash sales. This discount is regarded as a trade discount.

2.  The redundant stock was sold to an auctioneer, for cash, for R800 less than it would have been sold to a normal cash customer taking advantage of the 10% mark-down.

3.  During the year a "special sale" was held for credit customers only. All goods selected during the sale were marked down by 20%. The total of invoices issued during the sale amounted to R2 720 and this amount is included in credit sales.

4.  A customer who had purchased goods during the "special sale" for R240 returned them to the head office as they were unsuitable. The head office agreed to accept the return of the goods on behalf of the branch subject to the arrangement that the branch be entitled to charge the customer a 5% handling fee. The fee was based on the normal selling price of the goods and not on the price charged during the "special sale". At 30 June 19x4 these goods were still held in stock by the head office. No entries have been made in the books to record the return of the goods nor the charging of the handling fee.

5.  Allash was accounted for except for an amount of R270 which was misappropriated out of cash received from cash sales.

# G32 CONTINUED

6.      The branch manager is entitled to a commission of 50% of the branch net
        profit after allowing for his commission.


<u>YOU ARE REQUIRED TO</u>:

show the following ledger accounts in the head office books in respect of the
Geldfontein branch for the year ended 30 June 19x4.

     (a)  Branch stock account

     (b)  Branch gross profit account

     (c)  Branch debtors account

     (d)  Branch profit and loss account

# G33

Cobra Limited has a head office in Johannesburg and a branch in Pofadder. Goods are supplied by head office to the branch at selling price which is cost plus 33 1/3%. Branch books are kept at head office.

The following is an extract of the branch stock account for the year ended 31 December 19x1:

BRANCH STOCK ACCOUNT

| 19x1 | | | | 19x1 | | |
|---|---|---|---|---|---|---|
| Jan 1 | Balance b/f | R6 320,00 | | | Goods returned from branch | R1 300,00 |
| | Goods to branch | 84 640,00 | | | Cash sales | 32 400,00 |
| | | | | | Debtors | 48 800,00 |
| | | | | | Mark downs | 700,00 |
| | | | | 19x1 | | |
| | | | | Dec 31 | Balance c/f | 7 760,00 |
| | | R90 960,00 | | | | R90 960,00 |
| | | ========= | | | | ========= |

Stock was taken at the branch on 31 December 19x1, but the total value of the stock did not agree with the balance on the branch stock account. Investigation revealed the following:

(1)   The cashier had stolen R260,00 during December 19x1 and had concealed the theft by altering the cash sales dockets. This amount is not recoverable.

(2)   Head office had not been advised of an amount of R40,00 representing a special reduction of selling prices in respect of goods sold to the branch staff.

(3)   Stock valued at R100,00, at selling price, could not be accounted for.

(4)   Goods sent to branch by head office amounting to R800 at selling price, and debited to the branch did not arrive at the branch until 7 January 19x2.

<u>YOU ARE REQUIRED TO</u>:

(a)   List briefly the objectives, advantages and circumstances in which a head office maintains the accounting records of a branch including keeping a stock account at selling prices. (Your answer must be limited to 10 lines.)

(b)   Calculate the value of stock taken at the branch on 31 December 19x1 before any adjustments had been put through.

(c)   Journalise the entries required to adjust the branch stock account in head office books. (Narrations are <u>not</u> required.)

# G34

AB Retailers Limited has  a head office in Johannesburg and a branch in Goldfontein.

The branch keeps its own debtors' ledger and banks all cash collected by it to the credit of the head office bank account.  Branch expenses are paid by head office and goods are supplied to the branch at selling price which is cost plus 33 1/3%.

From the information given below in respect of the Goldfontein branch for the year ended 31 December 19x3 prepare:

      the branch stock account
      the branch debtors' account
      the branch gross profit account
      the branch profit and loss account

as they would appear in the ledger of AB Retailers Limited.

| | |
|---|---:|
| Stock at the Goldfontein branch at 1 January 19x3, at selling price | R6 320 |
| Goods sent to the branch during the year, at selling price | 84 000 |
| Goods returned to head office during the year, at selling price | 800 |
| Goods returned by debtors | 120 |
| Branch cash sales for the year | 32 406 |
| Branch credit sales for the year | 48 800 |
| Branch debtors at 1 January 19x3 | 5 200 |
| Cash received from branch debtors during the year | 45 300 |
| Discount allowed to debtors | 500 |
| Branch rent | 4 800 |
| Branch salaries | 8 600 |
| Branch general expenses | 3 300 |

The following additional information is available:

(a)   The branch stocktaking on 31 December 19x3 revealed a shortage, at selling price, of R1 200.  An investigation revealed that
   (i)   The cashier had stolen R260 during December 19x3 and had concealed the theft by altering the cash sales dockets.  This amount is not recoverable.
   (ii)   Head office had not been advised of an amount of R40 representing a special reduction of selling prices in respect of goods sold on credit to the branch staff.
   (iii) Stock valued at R100, at selling price, could not be accounted for.
   (iv)   Goods sent to branch by head office amounting to R800 at selling price, and debited to branch, did not arrive at the branch until 7 January 19x4.

(c)   An amount of R180 owing by debtors is irrecoverable and must be written off.

(d)   The branch manager's commission of 5% of the branch income, after allowing for his commission, must be provided for.  (Work to the nearest rand).

# G35

Casuals Limited of Springs supplies its Delmas branch with goods and charges them out at selling price.  All expenses are paid by head office and the branch banks all cash collected from debtors and cash sales to the credit of head office bank account daily.

The following account it in the head office books:-

BRANCH STOCK ACCOUNT

| 19x3 | | | | 19x3 | | |
|---|---|---|---|---|---|---|
| Jan 1 | | Balance | R4 500 | Jan 1 - Dec 31 | Cash sales | R9 463 |
| Jan 1 - Dec 31 | | Goods to branch | 10 000 | | Debtors | 6 031 |
| | | Branch gross profit a/c | 5 000 | | | |

The following information relates to the branch for the year ended 31 December 19x3 :-

1. Stock on hand at 31 December 19x3, at selling price, amounted to R3 240.
2. A sale, at which normal selling prices were reduced by 20%, was held. Turnover at the sale amounted to R984.
3. The cashier had stolen cash amounting to  R124  by altering cash sale slips.  The amount is irrecoverable.
   No entry in respect of the theft has been made in the books.
4. It was known that there had been a pilferage of stock from the branch.


<u>YOU ARE REQUIRED TO</u>:

complete the branch stock account and branch gross profit account, showing the true gross profit for the year ended 31 December 19x3.

Narrations in the accounts should clearly indicate the origin of the entries.

Retailers Limited is a company with a head office in Johannesburg and a branch in Springs.  All goods are supplied to the branch by Head Office and charged at selling prices.  Head Office remits R10 on the first day of each month to the branch to be used as petty cash.  The Head Office pays all other expenses. The following information relates to the branch for the period from 1 July 19x4 to the 31 January 19x5 during which period all goods were marked up to realise a gross profit of 33 1/3% on turnover.

|  |  |
|---|---:|
| Stock, at selling price at 1 July 19x4 | R1 470 |
| Goods sent to branch, at selling price | 5 220 |
| Goods returned by branch, at selling price | 210 |
| Credit notes issued to credit customers for good returned | 75 |
| Cash refunds out of petty cash to cash customers for goods returned | 30 |
| Goods stolen in transit to a customer in September and replaced free of charge, at selling price | 12 |
| Cash stolen by salesman who had covered up his theft by altering cash sales dockets | 32 |
| Cash sales (excluding the amount of R32 mentioned above) | 2 121 |
| Stock at selling price at 31 January 19x5 | 1 680 |
| Unexplained stock shortage at 31 January 19x5 at selling price | 150 |

On the 1 February 19x5, the selling price of all goods was reduced so that the percentage of gross profit to turnover would be only 30%.  On 1 March 19x5, the selling price of certain slow moving stocks which had been invoiced  to the branch in 19x3 at R315 were marked down by a uniform percentage to R252.

The following information relates to the period from the 1 February 19x5 to the 30   June 19x5:

|  |  |
|---|---:|
| Goods sent to branch, at selling price | R3 460 |
| Goods returned by branch, at selling price | 140 |
| Credit notes issued to credit customers for goods returned | 40 |
| Cash refunded out of petty cash to cash customer for goods returned | 20 |
| Cash recovered from salesman (the balance of R22 being irrecoverable) | 10 |
| Cash sales | 1 269 |
| Sales of slow moving stock (included in the cash sales figure above) | 168 |
| Stock, at selling price, at 30 June 19x5 | 1 664 |

# G36 CONTINUED

The following information relates to the whole financial year:
|  |  |
|---|---:|
| Cash discount allowed to debtors | R54 |
| Bad debts written off | 45 |
| Cash received from debtors | 4 345 |
| Petty cash on hand at 1 July 19x4 | 6 |
| Petty cash on hand at 30 June 19x5 | 4 |
| Debtors, 1 July 19x4 | 1 680 |
| Debtors, 30 June 19x5 | 1 670 |
| Rent paid, by head office | 360 |
| Salaries paid by head office | 1 280 |
| General expenses, paid by head office | 245 |

At 30 June 19x5 there were no shortages of the slow moving stocks

<u>YOU ARE REQUIRED TO</u>:

Prepare the following ledger accounts in the head office books for the financial year ended 30 June 19x5.

(a)      Branch stock account.
(b)      Branch gross profit account.
(c)      Branch debtors account.
(d)      Branch profit and loss account.

# G37

The Springfield branch of Riverside Retailers keeps its own debtors ledger and banks all cash collected by it to the credit of head office bank account.

A petty cash account, periodically reimbursed by head office, is kept by the branch for petty disbursements.

All other branch expenses are paid by head office.

Goods are supplied to the branch at selling price which will give a gross profit of 25%.

The following information relates to the Springfield branch for the year ended 31 March 19x7:

| | |
|---|---:|
| Stock at 1 April 19x6 (selling price) | R12 708 |
| Goods sent to branch (selling price) | 169 008 |
| Goods returned to head office (selling price) | 1 548 |
| Cash received  from cash sales | 64 698 |
| Credit sales | 97 911 |
| Debtors at 1 April 19x6 | 9 372 |
| Cash received from  debtors | 90 484 |
| Discount allowed to debtors | 384 |
| Discount allowed  on cash sales | 202 |
| Petty cash on hand 1 April 19x6 | 110 |
| Petty cash reimbursements by head office | 112 |
| Petty cash on hand 31 March 19x7 | 2 |
| Rent | 2 000 |
| Salaries | 5 200 |
| General expenses | 1 760 |

The following further information is available:

(a)    Stock on at hand 31 March 19x7 (at selling price) was R16 460.
(b)    Goods with a selling price of R120 were stolen during March 19x7.
(c)    During March it was discovered that the cashier had stolen R96 and concealed  the theft  by altering the amounts of cash sales dockets.
(d)    The temporary cashier had charged one cash customer R5 instead of R6 and another cash customer R14 instead of R10.  The second customer had subsequently complained  and been paid R4 out of petty cash.   No further entries have been made concerning these items.


<u>YOU ARE REQUIRED TO PREPARE</u>:

(a)    The branch stock account
(b)    The branch debtors account
(c)    The branch gross profit account
(d)    The branch profit and loss account.

# G38

The following accounts appear in the head office ledger of Worth's Limited:

<u>SANDTON BRANCH STOCK ACCOUNT</u>

| 19x6 | | | 19x6 | | |
|---|---|---|---|---|---|
| Jul | Balance | R24 928 | Jul - Oct | Cash sales | R17 130 |
| Jul - Oct | Goods sent to branch | 41 928 | | | |

<u>SANDTON BRANCH GROSS PROFIT ACCOUNT</u>

| | | | 19x6 | | |
|---|---|---|---|---|---|
| | | | Jul 1 | Balance | R6 232 |
| | | | Jul - Oct | Goods sent to branch | 10 482 |

A fire occurred at the branch on 31 October 19x6. Stock invoiced to the branch totalling R8 120 was salvaged in perfect condition together with the branch records. but the rest of the stock at the branch at the date of the fire was completely destroyed.

Branch stocks had been insured for R18 000 and the insurance policy contained the usual 'average clause'.

Upon investigation of head office and branch records you discover that the following had not yet been recorded in the above accounts:

(i)   Markdowns totalling R792 allowed during a sale held at the branch August 19x6.
(ii)  Markdowns resulting from a sale (cash only) held during October 19x6, when all selling prices were reduced by 20%. Sales during this sale period amounted to R6 536, which amount is included in the cash sales total of R17 130 shown above in the branch stock account.
(iii) The theft of R200 by the cashier who concealed the misappropriation by altering cash sales dockets.
(iv)  The theft of stock the selling price of which was R320.
(v)   Staff purchases amounting to R2 310. The staff is allowed to purchase goods at cost plus ten per cent. The markdown on normal selling prices is shown as staff perquisites in the income statement. All staff purchases are paid in cash and are not included in the cash sales of R17 130.

At 31 July 19x6 debtors owed R3 200 and during the period 1 July to 31 October 19x6 they made payments totalling R14 230 and had been allowed cash discounts amounting to R300. They had returned goods to the branch amounting to R150 and R800 had been written off as bad debts. Items affecting branch stock and gross profit had not yet been entered in the relevant accounts. The balance owing by debtors at 31 October 19x5 was R3 850.

<u>YOU ARE REQUIRED TO</u>:

(a)   complete the writing up of the Sandton branch stock account and gross profit account to the date of the fire, and

(b)   write up the insurance claim account.

# G39

Target Limited of Cape Town supplies its Paarl branch with goods and charges them at selling price.  All expenses are paid by the head office and all cash collected by the Paarl branch is banked daily to the credit of head office account.

The following information related to the Paarl branch for the year ended 30 April 19x9.

| | |
|---|---:|
| Stock on hand at 1 May 19x8 at selling price | R21 600 |
| Stock on hand at 30 April 19x9 at selling price | 14 850 |
| Goods sent to branch at selling price - 1 May to 15 October 19x8 | 63 200 |
| Goods sent to branch at selling price - 1 Nov. 19x8 to 30 April 19x9 | 50 000 |
| Cash sales - 1 May to 31 October 19x8 | 14 000 |
| Cash sales - 1 November 19x8 to 30 April 19x9 | 12 400 |
| Credit sales - 1 May to 31 October 19x8 | 53 120 |
| Credit sales - 1 November 19x8 to 30 April 19x9 | 38 000 |
| Goods returned to head office at cost price - 1 May  to 15 Oct. 19x8 | 600 |
| Goods returned to branch by customers - 1 May to 31 October 19x8 | 240 |
| Bad debts written off | 1 640 |
| Rent | 6 000 |
| Salaries | 12 000 |
| Expenses | 5 000 |

<u>NOTES</u>:

1.  Up to 15 October 19x8 goods had always been marked up by 33 1/3% on cost.
2.  Head office decided, with effect from 1 November 19x8, to reduce selling prices in order to achieve a gross profit of 20% on selling price.
    The prices of goods in stock were to be adjusted accordingly.
3.  Stock was taken on 16 October 19x8, and at selling price (cost plus 33 1/3%) amounted to R22 800.  No goods were sent to or returned by the Paarl branch during the period 16 October to 31 October 19x8.  Sales less returns for that period amounted to R6 000.
4.  Stock which had been charged to branch at R400 was sold for R480 on 3 July 19x8.
5.  The cashier misappropriated R300 cash during the period 1 March 19x9 to 30 April 19x9 and altered the cash sale dockets accordingly.  The cashier had left at the end of April 19x9 and could not be traced.
6.  On head office instructions goods marked at R200 were donated by the Paarl branch to the Paarl Senior Citizens Club on 16 April 19x9.
7.  It was suspected that there had been petty pilfering of stock from the branch.

<u>YOU ARE REQUIRED TO</u>:

to prepare for the year ended 30 April 19x9

the branch stock account
the branch gross profit account
the branch profit and loss account.

# G40

Wholesalers Limited of Johannesburg supplies its Brixton branch with goods and charges them at selling price which is cost plus 33 1/3%.

The branch does not keep its own books.  All expenses are paid by the head office and all cash sales and cash collected from debtors by the Brixton branch are immediately banked for the credit of head office.

The Brixton branch was destroyed by fire on 24 August 19x3.  Some stock, invoiced to the branch at R416, was salvaged.

The following information relates to the Brixton branch for the period 1 July 19x3 to 24 August 19x3:

| | |
|---|---:|
| Stock on hand at 1 July 19x3 at selling price | R4 820 |
| Goods sent to branch at selling price | 4 600 |
| Debtors at 1 July 19x3 | 3 710 |
| Cash sales | 4 210 |
| Credit sales | 2 680 |
| Cash received from debtors | 2 010 |
| Goods returned to head office, at cost price | 315 |
| Goods returned to branch by customers, at selling price | 82 |
| Bad debts written off | 115 |

You established that:

1.    Goods which had cost R162 were stolen from the branch during July.  The insurance company settled a claim during September 19x3 for R180 being the replacement cost of the goods.

2.    The branch had a 'stocktaking sale' during July 19x3.  All goods sold were marked down by 10% of the normal selling price.  Sales during this period (included in the figures above) amounted to:

      | | |
      |---|---|
      | Cash sales | R660 |
      | Credit sales | R204 |

3.    During August a cashier had stolen R104 and concealed the theft by altering cash sales dockets.  This amount was irrecoverable and the loss was uninsured.

4.    The stocks at the branch were adequately insured against fire.


<u>YOU ARE REQUIRED TO:</u>

show the following accounts for the period 1 July 19x3 to 24 August 19x3 as they would appear in the books of the head office:

    Branch stock account,
    Branch gross profit account,
    Branch profit and loss account,
    Branch debtors control account.

## G41

Vaal Stores Limited has its head office in Johannesburg and operates six branches in the Southern Transvaal and one branch in Potchefstroom. All transactions are reflected in the head office books from returns submitted by the branches.

Head office does all the purchasing of goods for resale and charges goods sent to the Potchefstroom branch at cost plus 30% and in the case of all other branches at cost plus 25%. Branches sell only for cash and bank all receipts (less refunds made to customers) daily for transfer to head office.

The following information relates to the Potchefstroom branch for the year ended 31 March 19x5:

19x4

1.     1 April     Stock on hand, at selling price     R195 000

2.     1 April to
14 December -Goods sent to branch, at selling price     286 000

3.     "     -Goods returned by branch to head office
at cost price     28 800

4.     "     -Sales     335 660

5.     You glean the following:

    (a)    8 August    Included in the above (2) is stock which had been sent to Florida branch having been costed Florida but had been recorded in the ledger as having been sent to the Potchefstroom branch R6 500

    (b)    9 October    Stock sent to the Potchefstroom branch was costed as Sandton and recorded in the ledger as having gone to the Sandton branch R18 750

    (c)    31 October    Certain goods which had originally been marked at R3 750 were sold for R4 140, which amount is included in the sales figure of R335 660 (see above)

    (d)    30 November    In addition to (3) all old and redundant stock at the branch was withdrawn by head office and sold by public auction.This stock had originally cost R13 000 and realised R7 500 at the auction.

    (e)    14 December    A fire broke out in the branch premises and destroyed all stock with the exception of stock amounting to R8 190 at selling price which was salvaged undamaged. At the date of the fire, stock at the branch had been insured for R72 270 (at cost). The insurance policy contained an "average" clause and the amount due by the insurance company was received by the head office on 10 February 19x5.

# G41 CONTINUED

From 15 December 19x4 to 31 March 19x5 the following transactions took place:

(a)   Goods sent by head office to branch, at selling price          R260 000

(b)   Refunds made to customers in respect of goods returned
      to the branch                                                    5 200

(c)   Sales for the period amounted to                                184 990

(d)   A pre-stocktaking allowance sale was held at the branch.
      During the sales period all selling prices were reduced by
      20% and sales during the "clearance sale" period amounted
      to (included in (8) above)                                      41 600


<u>YOU ARE REQUIRED TO</u>:

Show how the following accounts in respect of the Potchefstroom branch would
appear in the  head office ledger:

a.    branch stock account
b.    branch gross profit account
c.    insurance claim account

Motor Spares (Proprietary) Limited sells new and reconditioned motor vehicle spares to the general public from its trading outlet in Johannesburg and a branch in Pretoria.

The head office at Johannesburg purchases all stocks for its own requirements as well as for the Pretoria branch.
Sales to customers, from both outlets, are at a mark-up of 40% on the original cost. Goods sent to the branch are charged to the branch at selling price less 20%.

The following information is given:

1.  The trial balance extracted from the head office books at 1 July 19x4 was as follows:

| | | |
|---|---:|---:|
| Capital - authorised and issued | | |
|   400 000 shares of R1 each | | R400 000 |
| Retained income | | 31 800 |
| Creditors for purchases | | 130 000 |
| Provision for unearned profit on stock | | 1 200 |
| Land and buildings - at cost | R280 000 | |
| Pretoria branch current account | 75 200 | |
| Stock, at cost | 87 000 | |
| Debtors | 115 500 | |
| Bank | 5 300 | |
| | R563 000 | R563 000 |

2.  The only assets of the branch at 1 July 19x4 consisted of:

| | |
|---|---:|
| Stock | R11 200 |
| Debtors | 64 000 |
| | R75 200 |

3.  The following information relates to the year ended 30 June 19x5:

| | Head office | Pretoria |
|---|---:|---:|
| Payments to suppliers for purchases | R528 400 | |
| Cash received from customers | 328 900 | |
| Cash remitted to head office via | | |
| Pretoria bankers | | R243 560 |
| Cash discounts received from suppliers | | 30 000 |
| Goods invoiced to branch | | 268 800 |
| Purchases | 550 000 | |
| Salesmens' salaries and commission | 32 740 | 17 460 |
| Sales to customers, less returns | | |
| Cash | 43 200 | 39 100 |
| Credit | 316 740 | 268 060 |
| Administration expenses | 59 040 | 19 780 |

# G42 CONTINUED

4. (i)      The stocks at head office are always recorded at actual cost.

   (ii)     The stocks at the branch are recorded at the price which they were invoiced from head office and it is this price at which they should be recorded in the income statement

  (iii)    Included in purchases is an amount of R4 250 which was spent on the acquisition of early model vehicles.   These vehicles were stripped and all usable parts were reconditioned.   The cost of stripping and reconditioning the spares, estimated at R3 400, is included in head office administration expenses.   These reconditioned spares were on hand at 30 June 19x5.

  (iv)    There were no stock shortages.

   (v)     Included in "sales to customers" in Pretoria is the disposal of shop soiled goods which had been marked down by R840.   All other sales both in Johannesburg and Pretoria were at normal selling prices.

  (vi)    The branch remitted all cash received to head office after paying selling and administration expenses.   An amount of R1 500 remitted by Pretoria on 30 June 19x5 was only received at head office on 2 July 19x5.

  (vii)   A Pretoria branch debtor paid R1 400 at head office where it was included in "Cash received from customers".   This amount has not been recorded in the branch books.

 (viii)   There were no creditors for selling and administration expenses at 30 June 19x4 or 30 June 19x5.


<u>YOU ARE REQUIRED TO PREPEARE</u>:

(a)    Income statement for the year ended 30 June 19x5, showing the results in columnar form for head office and the branch.

(b)    Branch debtor control account showing the balance on that account at 30 June 19x5.

(c)    Branch current account for the year ended 30 June 19x5 after all closing entries have been passed.

Variety Stores Limited has a head office in Johannesburg and a branch in Alberton.  Head office remits R25 on the first day of each month to the branch

for it to meet petty expenses and disbursements.  All other branch expenses are paid by head office.

The following information relates to the branch for the period from 1 January 19x3 to 30 June 19x3, during which period goods sent to the branch were marked up by 50% on cost:

| | |
|---|---:|
| Stock at selling prices 1 January 19x3 | R5 289 |
| Goods sent to branch at selling prices | 30 210 |
| Goods returned by branch at selling prices | 210 |
| Credit notes issued to branch debtors for goods returned | 25 |
| Cash refunded out of petty cash to cash customers for goods returned | 90 |
| Goods lost in transit to a customer and replaced free of charge | 12 |
| Shortage in cash sales, irrecoverable | 32 |
| Cash sales (excluding amount of R32 above) | 12 726 |
| Credit sales | 17 194 |
| Unexplained stock shortage at 30 June 19x3 | 450 |
| Stock at selling prices at 30 June 19x3 | 5 040 |

On 1 July 19x3 the selling prices of all goods were reduced  so that the gross profit percentage to turnover would be 25% and certain slow moving stocks were marked down by an additional amount of R50.  All slow moving stock had been sold by 31 December 19x3.

The following information relates to the period from 1 July 19x3 to 31 December 19x3:

| | |
|---|---:|
| Goods sent to branch at selling prices | R44 000 |
| Goods returned by branch at selling prices | 240 |
| Credit notes issued to branch debtors for goods returned | 140 |
| Cash sales | 15 614 |
| Stock at selling prices at 31 December 19x3 | 7 520 |

The following information related to the whole financial year from 1 January to 31 December 19x3:

| | |
|---|---:|
| Cash discounts allowed to branch debtors | R270 |
| Bad debts written off | 322 |
| Cash received from branch debtors | 41 319 |
| Petty cash on hand 1 January 19x3 | 10 |
| Petty cash on hand 31 December 19x3 | 20 |
| Branch debtors outstanding 1 January 19x3 | 5 999 |
| Branch debtors outstanding 31 December 19x3 | 6 223 |
| Rent | 2 400 |
| Salaries | 6 000 |
| General expenses | 487 |

<u>YOU ARE REQUIRED TO</u>:

to write up theaccounts in the books of head office recording the branch stock, gross profit, net profit and debtors.

# G44

A company has a head office and one branch which keeps a complete set of books.

After the branch books had been closed at 30 September 19x3, it was discovered that the balance on the head office current account in the branch books did not agree with the balance on the branch current account in the head office books.

The difference can be accounted for as follows:

1.      Stock costing R1 000 had been sent to the branch but had not been recorded by the branch.  This stock was on hand at 30 September 19x3 and had been included in the branch stock sheets.

2.      Head office had charged the branch an administration fee of R500 which the branch had not taken  into account.

3.      Head office had received R200 from a branch debtor and had credited this amount to the branch current account but had not informed the branch of the receipt.

4.      Head office had not recorded the branch net profit of R15 600 in its books.

Assuming that it is not intended to re-open the branch  profit and loss account.


<u>YOU ARE REQUIRED TO</u>:


Draft the journal entry necessary to correct the head office current account in the <u>branch books</u>.

## G45

The following information was extracted from the Wolwehoek branch and the head office books of the Geelbek Trading Company, before the books were finally closed, for the year ended 30 June 19x8. The ledger accounts and balances given below are as they appeared in the books at the close of business on 30 June 19x8.

<u>HEAD OFFICE BOOKS</u>

<u>SUMMARY OF WOLWEHOEK BRANCH ACCOUNT</u>

| 19x7 | | | | 19x8 | | | |
|---|---|---|---|---|---|---|---|
| Jul 1 | Balance | R12 672 | | Jun 30 | Cash | | R19 688 |
| 19x8 | | | | 30 | Goods returned | | |
| Jun 30 | Goods sent to | | | | by branch | | 88 |
| | branch | 23 172 | | 30 | Branch debtor's | | |
| 30 | Rent | 1 080 | | | account collected | | 120 |
| 30 | Advertising | 130 | | | | | |
| 30 | Administrative | | | | | | |
| | expenses | 2 052 | | | | | |

<u>WOLWEHOEK BRANCH BOOKS</u>

<u>SUMMARY OF HEAD OFFICE ACCOUNT</u>

| 19x8 | | | | 19x7 | | | |
|---|---|---|---|---|---|---|---|
| Jun 30 | Cash | R25 288 | | Jul 1 | Balance | | R12 672 |
| 30 | Goods returned | | | 19x8 | | | |
| | to head office | 156 | | Jun 30 | Goods received | | |
| 30 | Head office creditor | | | | from head office | 21 048 | |
| | paid | 52 | | 30 | Rent | 988 | |
| 30 | Advance to head | | | 30 | Advertising | 120 | |
| | office manager for | | | | | | |
| | travelling expenses | 60 | | | | | |

<u>OTHER LEDGER BALANCES AT 30 JUNE 19x8</u>

| | Dr. | | Cr. |
|---|---|---|---|
| Advertising | R240 | Sales | R27 560 |
| Cash | 260 | Creditors | 224 |
| Goods from head office | 20 892 | | |
| Rent | 988 | | |
| Salaries | 4 280 | | |
| Stock at 1 July 19x7 | 2 600 | | |
| Debtors | 7 796 | | |

# G45 CONTINUED

1.   Stock on hand at the branch amounted to R1 680 at 30 June 19x8.
2.   Goods to the value of R68 had been returned to head office by the branch  on 30 June 19x8, but were not received by head office until July.  Head office has not responded to the branch entry.
3.   Goods to the value of R2 124 were despatched to the branch by head office on 29 June 19x8, but were not received by the branch until July. The branch has not responded to the head office entry.
4.   A remittance  of R5 600 was made by the branch to head office on 30 June 19x8.  This amount was received by head office in July.  Head office has not responded to the branch entry.
5.   The advance to the head office manager was not spent by him until July.
6.   Head office credits 'advertising account' and debits the branch with R10 for advertising each month, but an error had been made by the head office bookkeeper who had duplicated the June 19x8 journal entry.
7.   The Head office debit notes for the June, 19x8 branch rent and for administrative expenses have not been responded to by the branch.


<u>YOU ARE REQUIRED TO GIVE</u>:


(a)   The adjusting and closing journal entries in the branch books for the year ended 30 June 19x8.

(b)   The journal entries relating to the branch necessary in the head office books before the final accounts of the business for the year can be prepared.

# G46

The Ritz Company Limited has its head office in Johannesburg and its branch in Durban.  Separate sets of books are kept by the branch and head office. The company's year ends on 30 September.  Before closing entries had been put through at 30 September 19x9 the current accounts in the respective books were as follows:

<u>HEAD OFFICE BOOKS</u>

BRANCH CURRENT ACCOUNT

| 19x9 | | | 19x9 | | | |
|------|------|------|------|------|------|------|
| Sept 1 | Balance | R3 000 | Sept 2 | Cash | | R800 |
| Sept 5 | Goods | 1 200 | Sept 18 | Cash | | 1 000 |
| | | | Sept 23 | Cash | | 1 000 |
| | | | Sept 30 | Balance | | 1 400 |
| | | R4 200 | | | | R4 200 |

<u>BRANCH BOOKS</u>

HEAD OFFICE CURRENT ACCOUNT

| 19x9 | | | 19x9 | | | |
|------|------|------|------|------|------|------|
| Sept 15 | Cash | R1 000 | Sept 1 | Balance | | R1 700 |
| Sept 15 | Goods | 30 | Sept 3 | Goods | | 500 |
| Sept 18 | Cash | 1 000 | Sept 8 | Goods | | 1 200 |
| Sept 30 | Balance | 1 385 | Sept 30 | Cash received from head office debtors | | 15 |
| | | R3 415 | | | | R3 415 |

(1)    The goods returned to head office on 15 September were lost in transit. The carrier repudiated liability for the loss and the goods were not insured.  It is the company's policy that the true gross profit of branch and head office be shown and that the sender will bear the loss if goods are lost in transit.

(2)    In July 19x8 the  branch had debited the head office with R180 for goods returned.  These goods were never despatched to the head office which therefore did not respond to the entry.  At 30 September 19x8, these goods,  which were not insured were considered as lost in transit and the correct adjustments made;  however,  they were erroneously included in stock on hand at the branch at that date.  On 15 December 19x8, after the financial accounts had been completed, the error was discovered and the goods immediately despatched to head office but no entries were made in either the books of the branch or those of the head office.  The head office received these goods on 21 December 19x8.

<u>YOU ARE REQUIRED TO</u>:

show the journal entries which will be made in the head office and branch books at 30 September 19x9 to reconcile the current accounts and to give effect to the company's policy as outlined above.

# G47

Rhodes and Barnato are in partnership and operate under the name of Flame Lily Jewellers.  The partnership manufactures high class South African styled jewellery for the Cape tourist trade, using local precious and semi-precious stones.  The factory, warehouse and head office are situated in Kimberley and all sales are conducted through a retail branch in Cape Town and a sub-branch in Sea Point.  The head office and Cape Town branch keep separate sets of books and the Cape Town branch also records the transactions of the Sea Point sub-branch.

Jewellery is manufactured in the factory and is  invoiced to the warehouse at factory cost plus 10%.  Goods are invoiced at the same price to the Cape Town branch, which then invoices part of the stock to the  Sea Point sub-branch at selling price.  All jewellery is sold at a standard mark up of 150% on head office invoice price.

Rhodes and Barnato share profits and losses equally.

On 31 December 19x8 the following trial balances were extracted from the head office and Cape Town branch books:

| | Kimberley branch | | Cape Town branch | |
|---|---|---|---|---|
| | Dr. | Cr. | Dr. | Cr. |
| Administration and selling expenses | R2 583 | | R5 871 | |
| Cash at bank | 6 059 | | 18 927 | |
| Cape Town branch current account | 28 470 | | | |
| Capital - Rhodes | | R40 000 | | |
|       - Barnato | | 40 000 | | |
| Creditors | | 8 462 | | |
| Debtors | | | 14 921 | |
| Drawings - Rhodes | 12 500 | | | |
|       - Barnato | 12 500 | | | |
| Factory wages paid | 18 100 | | | |
| Factory overheads (including depreciation of plant and machinery) | 5 040 | | | |
| Goods sent to Cape Town branch | | 36 740 | | |
| Goods sent to Sea Point | | | | R14 300 |
| Goods received from head office | | | 27 830 | |
| Head office current account | | | | 13 400 |
| Plant and machinery,at cost less depreciation to 31.12.x8 | 16 500 | | | |
| Raw materials used | 11 300 | | | |
| Sales - Cape Town branch | | | | 34 320 |
| Sea Point sub branch:- | | | | |
|   Expenses | | | 7 341 | |
|   Gross profit | | | | 21 945 |
|   Stock, at selling price | | | 3 575 | |
| Stock of raw materials 31.12.x8 | 6 436 | | | |
| Stock at 1.1.x8 | | | 5 500 | |
|   Finished goods | 2 310 | | | |
|   Work in progress | 4 144 | | | |
| Unearned factory profit 1.1.x8 | | 400 | | |
| | R125 942 | R125 942 | R83 965 | R83 965 |

# G47 CONTINUED

<u>NOTES</u>

1.  Stock on hand at Sea Point sub branch at selling price at 1 January
    19x8 was R825.

2.  The following are the current accounts for the month of December 19x8.

Head office current account (Cape Town branch books)

| 19x8 |    |                |         | 19x8 |    |                       |         |
|------|----|----------------|---------|------|----|-----------------------|---------|
| Dec  | 13 | Bank           | R4 320  | Dec  | 1  | Balance               | R15 360 |
|      | 27 | Goods returned | 2 200   |      | 4  | Goods ex head office  | 2 640   |
|      | 30 | Bank           | 6 160   |      | 24 | Goods ex head office  | 2 810   |
|      | 31 | Balance        | 13 400  |      | 29 | Goods ex head office  | 5 270   |
|      |    |                | R26 080 |      |    |                       | R26 080 |

Cape Town branch current account (head office books)

| 19x8 |    |                  |         | 19x8 |    |         |         |
|------|----|------------------|---------|------|----|---------|---------|
| Dec  | 1  | Balance          | R19 000 | Dec  | 3  | Bank    | R1 000  |
|      | 20 | Goods to branch  | 2 810   |      | 15 | Bank    | 4 320   |
|      | 23 | Goods to branch  | 5 270   |      | 31 | Balance | 28 470  |
|      | 28 | Goods to branch  | 6 710   |      |    |         |         |
|      |    |                  | R33 790 |      |    |         | R33 790 |

3.  Stock on hand at 31 December 19x8

    | | | |
    |---|---|---:|
    | Finished goods | - at head office warehouse | R1 980 |
    |                | - at Cape Town branch      | 5 302 |
    | Work-in-progress | | 5 484 |

4.  A physical stock count at the Sea Point sub-branch, after the close of
    business on 31 December 19x8, revealed a closing stock figure of R3 245
    at selling price. Goods with a selling price of R330 had been
    stolen on 16 December 9x8, and a claim for the cost of stolen goods
    had been admitted, but not yet paid, by the firm's insurance company.
    The loss had not been recorded in the Cape Town branch books. There
    were no other stock shortages.

5.  The manager of the Cape Town branch is entitled to a commission of 5%
    of the net profit attributable to the Cape Town branch operations
    (excluding the profit of the Sea Point sub- branch) <u>after</u> deducting his
    commission.

<u>REQUIRED</u>:

Prepare journal entries to:

(a)  reconcile the Cape Town branch and head office current accounts;
(b)  adjust and close the Cape Town branch books in such a way as to show
     separately the Sea Point sub-branch profit;
(c)  incorporate the branch profits or losses into the head office books;
(d)  close the head office books.

Narrations are not required. Indicate clearly whether your journal entries
relate to the branch or head office books.

# G48

The head office of Geneva Groceries charges goods to its Clarens branch at a mark up of 50% on cost i.e. selling price.  On 1 October 19X8 some of the balances in the head office ledger relating to that branch were as follows:

| | |
|---|---:|
| Stock account at selling price | R33 375 |
| Cash | 1 000 |
| Debtors | 17 900 |
| Furniture at cost | 52 000 |
| Accumulated depreciation - furniture | 10 135 |

There were no other assets and liabilities relating to the branch.

On 1 October 19X8 it was decided that the branch would keep its own records and head office made all the transfers necessary in its ledger in respect of entries relating to the branch.

A summary of branch transactions for the year ended 30 September 19X9 reveals:

| | |
|---|---:|
| Credit sales | R225 465 |
| Cash sales | 33 750 |
| Cash paid by debtors | 224 160 |
| Cash remitted to head office | 255 000 |
| Goods returned by credit customers | 3 000 |
| Goods returned to head office, at selling price | 7 500 |
| Discount allowed to debtors | 1 935 |
| Bad debts written off | 845 |
| Goods received from head office, at selling price | 273 000 |
| Closing stock at selling price per physical count at branch | 39 660 |

According to the head office records R230 000 cash was received from the branch and goods costing head office R200 000 were sent to Clarens during the year.  It was found that both discrepancies are due to items in transit on 30 September 19X9.  Branch salaries and expenses paid by head office amounted to R19 225 and R10 750 respectively.  Depreciation on furniture for the year amounted to R2 550.

Both head office and branch use the perpetual method for recording stock.

The records for stock at the branch are maintained at selling price.

<u>YOU ARE REQUIRED TO</u>:

(1)   Record in the head office ledger the branch transactions (including adjustments and closing entries) for the year ended 30 September 19X9 in the relevant accounts which relate to the branch.

(2)   Give the actual gross profit and net income made by the branch.

ALL WORKINGS MUST BE SHOWN

# G49

Oribi commenced a wholesale business on 1 January 19x9 with his head office situated in Johannesburg and one branch in Sabie.  All goods are purchased in bulk by head office and are normally repackaged into smaller units immediately, but at 31 December 19x9 goods costing R3 002 had not been repackaged.  The cost of the packing material amounted to 1% of the selling price.

Only repackaged goods are sent to branch and the branch is invoiced at selling price less 10%.

The branch maintains its own self balancing ledger recording all items affecting stock at invoiced cost.

The following trial balances were extracted at 31 December 19x9 before adjusting for matters to in the notes:

| | Head office | | Branch | |
| --- | --- | --- | --- | --- |
| | Dr. | Cr. | Dr. | Cr. |
| Capital - Oribi | | R400 000 | | |
| Drawings | R10 000 | | | |
| Purchases | 319 002 | | | |
| Packing materials | 4 070 | | | |
| Sales | | 240 000 | | R90 000 |
| Packed goods sent to branch | | 95 400 | | |
| Selling and admin expenses | 36 002 | | R3 960 | |
| Debtors | 28 000 | | 4 200 | |
| Creditors | | 41 072 | | 650 |
| Packed goods received from Head Office | | | 92 700 | |
| Current accounts | | | | |
| Head office | | | | 11 100 |
| Branch | 15 400 | | | |
| Bank | 3 998 | | 890 | |
| | R416 472 | R416 472 | R101 750 | R101 750 |

<u>NOTES</u>:

1. All sales were made at the fixed selling price which yields a fixed gross profit on turnover of 20%.
2. Goods despatched and invoiced by head office to the branch in December for R2 700 were not received until after the year end.  Notification of a cash remittance of R1 600 from the branch in December to head office was only received in January.

# G49 CONTINUED

3.    The branch stock taking disclosed a shortage of goods with a normal
      sales value of R500.  Other goods with a normal sales value of R2 000
      had been damaged and require to be written down by R1 090 below
      invoiced price to the branch.  The loss in value was due to negligence
      on the part of the employees and neither loss is covered by insurance.

      Apart from the foregoing all stocks at 31 December 19x9 had a
      realisable value in excess of cost.

4.    There were no shortages of packing materials or stocks at head office.

5.    Packing materials on hand cost R70.


<u>YOU ARE REQUIRED TO</u>:

(i)    prepare, in columnar form, the detailed income statement for the year
       ended 31 December 19x9 for the branch, head office and group.

(ii)   show, in detail, the net assets represented by the adjusted branch
       current account at the year end.

# G50

Constellation Limited has its head office in Johannesburg and branches in Benoni and Springs.  Part of the company's accounting system has been decentralised and the Benoni branch now operates its own double entry system and also records in its ledger all the transactions of the Springs branch.

All the merchandise sold by the company is purchased by head office.  Goods sent to the Benoni branch are invoiced by head office at cost plus 20% .  Head office credits "goods sent to branch" with the full invoice price.  Both Benoni and Springs  branches sell at a standard selling price determined by adding 50% to the head office invoice price to the Benoni branch.

The Benoni branch supplies merchandise to the Springs branch and invoices all goods sent to the latter at standard selling prices.

1.   The following is the Benoni branch trial balance at 31 October 1990.

|  | Dr | Cr |
|---|---|---|
| Head office current account | | R64 500 |
| Furniture at cost | R31 000 | |
| Accumulated depreciation – 31 October 1990 | | 3 100 |
| Stock 1 November 1989 | 21 000 | |
| Debtors | 19 000 | |
| Bank | 5 200 | |
| Sales | | 199 500 |
| Goods from head office | 240 000 | |
| Goods sent to Springs branch | | 81 000 |
| Stock account – Springs branch | 19 800 | |
| Gross profit account – Springs branch | | 47 900 |
| Administration and selling expenses | 60 000 | |
| | R396 000 | R396 000 |

2.   Stock with a selling price of R1 800 had been destroyed by fire at the Springs branch on 10 October 1990.  The company's insurers have agreed to pay R600 in full settlement for the loss, but no entries have been recorded for the loss or for the amount receivable from the insurers.  There were no other stock shortages at the Springs branch during the current financial year.

3.   Stock on hand at Benoni on 31 October 1990 at head office invoice price was R48 000.

# G50 CONTINUED

4.    An analysis of head office current account for October 1990 showed the
following:

HEAD OFFICE CURRENT ACCOUNT

| 1990 | | | 1990 | | |
|---|---|---|---|---|---|
| Oct 3 | Bank | R 5 500 | Oct 1 | Balance b/d | R55 000 |
| 12 | Goods to H.O. | 5 000 | 16 | Goods from H.O. | 35 000 |
| 29 | Bank | 15 000 | | | |
| 31 | Balance c/d | 64 500 | | | |
| | | R90 000 | | | R90 000 |
| | | ====== | | | ====== |

A statement received from Head Office was as follows:

BENONI BRANCH CURRENT ACCOUNT

| 1990 | | | 1990 | | |
|---|---|---|---|---|---|
| Oct 1 | Balance b/d | R62 500 | Oct 2 | Bank | R 7 500 |
| 14 | Goods to branch | 35 000 | 5 | Bank | 5 500 |
| 28 | Goods to branch | 43 500 | 12 | Goods from branch | 5 000 |
| | | | 31 | Balance c/d | 123 000 |
| | | R141 000 | | | R141 000 |
| | | ======= | | | ======= |

<u>YOU ARE REQUIRED TO PREPARE</u>:

i)    The adjusting and closing journal entries in the Benoni books showing
the results of the branches' operations for the year ended 31 October
1990.

ii)    Any journal entries which may be necessary in the head office books
before the final accounts for the year can be drawn up.

    NARRATIONS ARE REQUIRED

# G51

Budapest Limited of Durban supplies its Pinetown branch with goods and charges them at selling price.

All expenses are paid by head office and all cash collected by the Pinetown branch is banked to the credit of head office daily.

The following information relates to the Pinetown branch for the year ended 30 September 19x1:

| | |
|---|---:|
| Stock on hand at 1 October 19x0 at selling price | R86 400 |
| Stock on hand at 30 September 19x1 at selling price | 58 000 |
| Goods sent to branch at selling price – | |
|   1 October 19x0 to 15 March 19x1 | 252 800 |
| Goods sent to branch at selling price– | |
|   1 April to 30 September 19x1 | 200 000 |
| Cash sales – 1 October 19x0 to 31 March 19x1 | 56 000 |
| Cash sales – 1 April to 30 September 19x1 | 49 800 |
| Credit sales – 1 October 19x0 to 31 March 19x1 | 212 400 |
| Credit sales – 1 April to 30 September 19x1 | 152 000 |
| Goods returned to head office at cost price – | |
|   1 October 19x0 to 15 March 19x1 | 2 400 |
| Goods returned to head office at cost price – | |
|   1 April to 30 September 19x1 | 800 |
| Goods returned to branch by customers – | |
|   1 October 19x0 to 31 March 19x1 | 1 000 |
| Goods returned to branch by customers – | |
|   1 April to 30 September 19x1 | 800 |
| Bad debts written off for year | 6 500 |
| Rent for the year | 24 000 |
| Salaries for the year | 48 000 |
| Expenses for the year | 20 000 |

1. Up to 16 March 19x1 goods had always been marked up by $33^1/_3\%$ on cost.

2. In order to meet the increased competition in the retail trade, head office decided, with effect from 1 April 19x1, to reduce selling prices by marking goods up by 25% on cost. The prices of goods in stock were to be adjusted accordingly.

3. Stock was taken on 16 March 19x1 and at selling price (cost plus $33^1/_3\%$) it amounted to R91 200. No goods were sent to or returned by the Pinetown branch during the period 16 March to 31 March 19x1. Sales less returns by customers for that period amounted to R24 000.

4. Stock which had been charged to the branch at R1 600 was, on head office instructions, sold for R1 800 on 5 December 19x0.

5. On head office instructions goods marked at R500 were donated by the Pinetown branch to the Pinetown Rotary Club on 19 September 19x1.

<u>YOU ARE REQUIRED TO PREPARE FOR THE YEAR ENDED 30 SEPTEMBER 19X1</u>:

(a)    the branch stock account
(b)    the branch gross profit account
(c)    the branch profit and loss account

       Dates may be omitted.

# G52

Artists Limited, a radio distributor, operates a head office in Durban and a branch in Pinetown.  The branch is fully autonomous except that it purchases all its stocks from the head office at cost plus 10%.

The following trial balances were extracted at 31 October 19x1:

| | Head office | | Branch | |
| --- | --- | --- | --- | --- |
| | Dr | Cr | Dr | Cr |
| Retained income 1 November 19x0 | - | R8 840 | - | - |
| Audit fees | R1 000 | - | - | - |
| Branch current account | 19 170 | - | - | - |
| Head office current account | - | - | - | R19 070 |
| Bank | 39 575 | - | R1 520 | - |
| Debtors | 25 000 | - | 8 040 | - |
| Creditors | - | 17 000 | - | 960 |
| Interest paid | 3 000 | - | - | - |
| General expenses | 2 465 | - | 7 670 | - |
| Goods received from H.O. | - | - | 41 800 | - |
| Goods sent to branch | - | 47 300 | - | - |
| Salaries | 40 500 | - | 8 400 | - |
| Sales | - | 227 250 | - | 55 000 |
| Stock - 1 November 19x0 | 41 260 | - | 5 500 | - |
| Share capital (R1 shares) | - | 100 000 | - | - |
| Stationery and printing | 5 000 | - | 400 | - |
| Purchases | 206 420 | - | - | - |
| Furniture | 5 000 | - | 2 000 | - |
| Motor vehicles | 25 000 | - | - | - |
| Land and buildings | 124 000 | - | - | - |
| Accumulated depreciation | | | | |
| - furniture | - | 1 500 | - | 300 |
| - motor vehicles | - | 10 000 | - | - |
| Building Society loan | - | 100 000 | - | - |
| Provision for unearned profit in stock - 1 November 19x0 | - | 500 | - | - |
| Sundry income | - | 25 000 | - | - |
| | R537 390 | R537 390 | R75 330 | R75 330 |

## Notes

1.  The building society loan, borrowed in 19w7, is secured by a mortgage bond over the land and buildings.  Interest is payable once a year in arrear on 31 January at 12% p.a.  The mortgage bond is repayable in 10 equal instalments, the first instalment falling due on 31 January 19x2.

2.  The land and buildings consist of an office block situated on Stand No. 4276 Mobeni and were purchased on 1 January 19w8 for R124 000.

"

# G52 CONTINUED

3.    A review of the head office bank account and bank statement revealed a salary cheque for R1 560 which had been processed by the bank but which accidentally had not been entered in the cash book. This omission has not been rectified.

4.    Goods which had cost head office R5 000 had been dispatched to the branch prior to the year end by the head office. At 31 October 19x1 the goods had not been received by the branch and consequently had not been included in the branch stock count.

5.    Closing stock figures were:

| | |
|---|---|
| Head office - at cost | R40 900 |
| Branch - at cost plus 10% | R7 700 |

Stocks are valued at the lower of cost or net realisable value where cost has been determined on the FIFO basis.

6.    Included in general expenses is R1 500 in respect of a lease of a photocopying machine.

7.    No entries have been passed in respect of depreciation. The rates applicable are:

| | |
|---|---|
| Furniture | - 5% p.a. on cost |
| Motor vehicles | - 20% p.a. on cost |

8.    Cash of R5 400 had been received from debtors by the branch on behalf of head office. The head office bookkeeper had been informed telephonically but no entries had been passed in this regard.

9.    Included in general expenses is an amount of R300 paid to a director as fees. The other director, who is also the managing director, gets no fee but receives a salary of R20 000 which is included in head office salaries. The managing director also has the use of a company car. The cost to the company of running the car is R2 500 p.a. but the benefit to the director is assessed at R920 p.a.

10.   A vintage van, used by head office for promotional purposes, was sold on 29 October 19x1 for R25 000. The van, which had a book value of R2 000 at the date of sale, had originally cost R6 000. The receipt of the R25 000 has been credited to sundry income. No other entries have been passed with regard to this transaction.

<u>YOU ARE REQUIRED TO PREPARE</u>:

the balance sheet and income statement of Artists Limited for the year ended 31 October 19x1 in accordance with Schedule 4 and generally accepted accounting practice.
Ignore taxation.

# G53

Afro Weavers, a craft and curio business, operates from its head office in Nelspruit.  On 1 July 19x1, Afro Weavers opened a branch at the Satara Rest Camp in the Kruger National Park.  The branch maintains its own bank account and accounting records.  The stock account is kept at selling price using the perpetual stock method and an account is kept for all expenses including those paid by head office.  Head office supplies goods to the branch at selling price, using a mark up of 25% on cost.  The head office also maintains its own stock records using the perpetual stock method at cost and a record of the branch's gross profit in its ledger.

The following transactions, relating to the Satara Branch, took place  during the year ended 30 June 19x2.

| | |
|---|---:|
| Goods received by Satara branch at selling price | R185 000 |
| Goods sold by the branch for cash | 160 000 |
| Goods returned to Nelspruit by Satara branch at cost price | 6 000 |
| Cash received from Satara branch | 145 000 |
| Administration expenses paid by Satara branch | 8 000 |
| Salaries of Satara branch paid by head office | 12 000 |

The following additional information is available:

1.    The head office records  reflect that goods  costing R4 000 were sent by the head office to the branch on 30 June 19x2.  These goods were received in Satara on 2 July 19x2.

2.    Goods marked at R2 000 were donated by the branch as Christmas gifts to Kruger National Park wardens.  No entry had been made in respect of this transaction.

3.    Head office records reveal that of the goods returned by the branch during the year ended 30 June 19x2 goods costing R300 had been completely destroyed at the head office while they were being offloaded from a delivery truck.  No entry had been made in respect of the loss. The loss was not covered by insurance.

4.    There was no stock shortage at the Satara branch at 30 June 19x2.


<u>YOU ARE REQUIRED TO</u>:

a.    record the relevant transactions in the head office account and trading stock account in the ledger of the Satara branch.

b.    record the above transactions (including adjustments and closing entries) in the accounts that relate to the branch in the ledger of the head office.

# SECTION H

# HOLDING COMPANY ACCOUNTING

# H1

Maxi Limited bought all the shares in Mini Ltd on 1 July 19x7 for R260 000 cash.

The balance sheet of Mini Ltd at 1 January 19x7 in summarised form was:

| | | | |
|---|---|---|---|
| Capital in R1 shares | R200 000 | Assets | R220 000 |
| Retained income | 20 000 | | |
| | R220 000 | | R220 000 |
| | ======= | | ======= |

The following figures have been  extracted from the financial statements of Mini Ltd:

| | | |
|---|---|---|
| Retained income | 1 January 19x7 | R20 000 |
| Net income | 31 December 19x7 | 60 000 |
| | | 80 000 |
| | | |
| Dividends paid 2 July 19x7 | R40 000 | |
| Dividends paid 31 December 19x7 | 20 000 | 60 000 |
| Retained income 31 December 19x7 | | 20 000 |
| Loss 31 December 19x8 | | 16 000 |
| Retained income 31 December 19x8 | | 4 000 |
| Net income 31 December 19x9 | | 12 000 |
| | | 16 000 |
| Dividends paid 31 December 19x9 | | 7 000 |
| Retained income 31 December 19x9 | | R9 000 |
| | | ===== |

Profits are deemed to have been earned evenly throughout each year.


<u>YOU ARE REQUIRED TO</u>:

give all the journal entries relating to the above in the books of Maxi Ltd for the years ended 31 December 19x7, 19x8 and 19x9.

# H2

Investment Limited was incorporated with a capital of R200 000 made up of 200 000 ordinary shares of R1 each. The company purchased the total issued capital of the B Company Limited from the existing shareholders on 1 January 19x4. The purchase price of the 100 000 shares was R200 000 which was satisfied by the issue of shares in Investment Limited, issued at a premium of 25c per share.

The following was the summarised balance sheet of B Company Limited at 1 January 19x4:

| | | | |
|---|---|---|---|
| Share capital | | Fixed property | R200 000 |
|   Authorised and issued | | Sundry assets | 24 000 |
|     100 00 shares of R1 each | R100 000 | | |
| Retained income | 30 000 | | |
| Creditors | 94 000 | | |
| | R224 000 | | R224 000 |
| | ======= | | ======= |

The net income of B Company Limited for the year ended 30 June 19x4 was R37 000 and a dividend of R30 000 was declared out of these profits in June 19x4 and paid during July. The fixed property was sold for R250 000 on 31 October 19x4. For the purpose of valuing the shares of the B Company Limited the property was valued at R270 000 but the book value was not adjusted. B Company Limited made a trading profit of R20 000 for the year ended 30 June 19x5 and this amount, together with the profit on the sale of property was declared as a dividend on 30 June 19x5 and distributed in July 19x5.

<u>YOU ARE REQUIRED TO</u>:

show, by means of journal entries, how the purchase of the shares in B Company Limited and the receipt of dividends should be treated in the books of Investment Limited. You should also include any other adjustments which you consider advisable.

You should assume that the profits have been earned evenly throughout the period.

# H3

Holdings Limited bought all the shares in Subsidiary Limited on 31 December 19x3 for R50 000 cash.

The balance sheet of Subsidiary Limited at 30 June 19x4 in  summarised form was:

| | | | | |
|---|---|---|---|---|
| Share capital | | | Land and buildings | R28 000 |
|   Authorised and issued | | | Payments in advance | 1 000 |
|    200 000 shares of R1 each | R20 000 | | Bank | 3 000 |
| Retained income | 9 000 | | | |
| Creditors | 3 000 | | | |
| | R32 000 | | | R32 000 |

The summarised income statement was as follows:

| | | |
|---|---|---|
| Retained income at 30 June 19x3 | | R8 000 |
| Net income from rents for the year (earned at a constant rate) | | 5 000 |
| | | 13 000 |
| Dividends paid | | |
|   2 January  19x4 | R1 000 | |
|   30 June   19x4 | 3 000 | 4 000 |
| | | R9 000 |
| Retained income at 30 June 19x4 | | |

The summarised income statement for the year ended 30 June 19x5 was a follows:

| | | |
|---|---|---|
| Net income from rents for the year (earned at a constant rate) | | R8 000 |
| Profit on the sale of land and buildings   June 19x5 | | 18 000 |
| | | 26 000 |
| Dividends paid | | |
|   2 January 19x5 | R5 000 | |
|   30 June 19x5 | 10 000 | 15 000 |
| | | 11 000 |
| Retained income at 30 June 19x4 | | 9 000 |
| Retained income at 30 June 19x5 | | R20 000 |

Give the journal entries in Holdings Limited's books for:

(a)    the purchase of the shares
(b)    the receipt of the dividends
(c)    any  other  related  matters,  including  the  transfers  to  the  income statement.

# H4

On 1 January 19x3 Aye Limited purchased all the shares in Bee Limited for R125 000. The issued capital of Bee Limited was 100 000 shares of R1 each and the retained income at that date R20 000. All the tangible assets of Bee Limited were considered to be fairly valued.

The results reflected by the financial statements of Bee Limited were as follows:

|  |  |  |  |
|---|---|---|---|
| 19x3 (profit) | R10 000 | 19x4 (loss) | R2 000 |
| 19x5 (profit) | R12 000 | | |

Bee Limited declared and paid the following dividends:

|  |  |  |  |
|---|---|---|---|
| 2 January 19x3 | 15% | 31 December 19x3 | 12% |
| 31 December 19x5 | 4% | | |

Aye Limited decides to take credit in its income statement for the profits earned Bee Limited only to the extent that dividends have actually been declared.

<u>YOU ARE REQUIRED TO</u>:

(a)   give all the journal entries relating to the above in the books of Aye Limited for the years ended 31 December 19x3, 19x4 and 19x5.

(b)   show the relevant portion of the balance sheet of Aye Limited for the 3 years.

# H5

The following figures have been extracted from the accounts of Subs Limited:

| | | |
|---|---:|---:|
| <u>Retained income 1 July 19x1</u> | | R15 000 |
| Net profit from rents for the year ended 30 June 19x2 | | <u>10 000</u> |
| | | R25 000 |
| Dividend paid 2 January 19x2 | R6 000 | |
| Dividend paid 30 June 19x2 | <u>12 000</u> | <u>18 000</u> |
| <u>Retained income 30 June 19x2</u> | | 7 000 |
| Profit on sale of Property A, 10 September 19x2 | 8 000 | |
| Net profit from rents for the year ended 30 June 19x3 | <u>10 000</u> | <u>18 000</u> |
| | | 25 000 |
| Dividend paid on 18 November 19x2 out of profit on sale | | |
|   of Property A | 8 000 | |
| Dividend paid 30 June 19x3 | <u>10 000</u> | <u>18 000</u> |
| <u>Retained income 30 June 19x3</u> | | 7 000 |
| Profit on sale of Property C, 31 August 19x3 | 3 000 | |
| Net profit from rents for the year ended 30 June 19x4 | <u>8 000</u> | <u>11 000</u> |
| | | 18 000 |
| Dividend paid 30 June 19x4 | | <u>6 000</u> |
| <u>Retained income 30 June 19x4</u> | | R12 000 |

Note: The profits from rents were earned evenly throughout each year.

On 1 January 19x2 Holdings Limited acquired all the shares in Subs Limited for
R94 600. In determining the purchase price of the shares, Holdings Limited
considered all the assets to be worth their book values with the exception of
land and buildings which were considered to be worth 40% more than the book
value.  Land and buildings in the balance sheet at the date of acquisition
of the shares consisted of the following properties:

| | |
|---|---:|
| Property A - book value | R14 000 |
| Property B - book value | 16 000 |
| Property C - book value | <u>9 000</u> |
| | R39 000 |

On 1 January 19x2 Subs Limited had a balance of R6 000 on general reserve and
a balance of R3 000 on non-distributable reserve.

There were no other reserves.

It has always been the practice of Holdings Limited to take credit for income
from subsidiary companies only to the extent that dividends are declared.


<u>YOU ARE REQUIRED</u>:

To prepare all the journal entries to give effect to the above transactions
in the books of Holdings Limited for the years ended 30 June 19x2, 19x3 and
19x4.

# H6

On 1 January 19x7 Hamish Limited bought all the shares of R1 each in Scott Limited for R135 000.

The purchase price was settled by the issue of 110 000 shares of R1 each in Hamish Limited.

At the time of the purchase of the shares, the issued capital of Scott Limited was 100 000 shares of R1 each and its reserves (all of which were described as distributable) were R20 000.  The directors of Hamish Limited considered that the balance sheet of Scott Limited at 31 December 19x6 reflected the fair value of its assets with the exception of one building shown in the balance sheet at R50 000.  No adjustment was made in the books of Scott Limited.

The building was sold on 15 June 19x9 for R59 000 and the profit declared as a special on 1 July 19x9.

The profits and losses from trading, after taxation, shown by Scott Limited in its financial statements were:

|  | R |
|---|---|
| Year ended 31 December 19x7 | 10 000 profit |
| Year ended 31 December 19x8 | 3 000 loss |
| Year ended 31 December 19x9 | 8 000 profit |

The following dividends were paid by Scott Limited:

|  | R |
|---|---|
| 31 December 19x7 | 10 000 |
| 31 December 19x8 | 5 000 |
| 1 July 19X9 (special dividend) | 9 000 |
| 31 December 19x9 | Nil |

Hamish Limited takes credit for the income from subsidiary companies only to the extent that dividends are received.

<u>YOU ARE REQUIRED</u>:

to show, in journal entry form, in the books of Hamish Limited, all entries, including cash, to record the foregoing

(A)   from 1 January 19x7 to 31 December 19x9;

(B)   during 19x9, if Scott Limited had sold the buildings for R67 500 and paid a special dividend of R17 500.

# H7

On 1 July 19x3 Areberg Limited purchased all the shares in Fuchsia Limited for R200 000.

The purchase price was settled by the issue of 90 000 shares of no par value in Areberg Limited.

On 1 July 19x3 Fuchsia Limited had an issued share capital of 100 000 shares of R1 each and retained income of R60 000.  The directors of Areberg Limited considered that the balance sheet of Fuchsia Limited at 30 June 19x3 fairly reflected the value of the assets with the exception of one building.

The building shown in the balance sheet at a cost of R110 000 was considered to be worth R170 000.  No adjustment was made in the books of Fuchsia Limited to adjust for this increase in value.

The building was sold on 31 December 19x5 for R160 000 and the profit declared as a special dividend on 19 January 19x6.

The profits and losses after taxation of Fuchsia Limited are summarised as follows:-

| | |
|---|---|
| Year ended 30 June 19x4 | R60 000 profit |
| Year ended 30 June 19x5 | 8 000 loss |
| Year ended 30 June 19x6 | 40 000 profit |

The following dividends were paid by Fuchsia Limited.

| | |
|---|---|
| 30 June 19x4 | R70 000 |
| 30 June 19x5 | 10 000 |
| 19 January 19x6 (special) | 50 000 |
| 30 June 19x6 | 40 000 |

It has always been the practice of Areberg Limited to take credit for income from its subsidiary companies only to the extent that dividends are declared.


<u>YOU ARE REQUIRED:</u>

(a)    to give the journal entries (including cash transactions) relating to the above in the books of Areberg Limited.

(b)    to show how the information relating to Fuchsia Limited would be disclosed in the balance sheet of Areberg Limited at 30 June 19x6.

# H8

A Company Limited bought all the shares in B Company Limited on 30 September 19x1, the price paid being based on a valuation of the tangible assets.

The balance sheet of B Company Limited at 30 June 19x1, in summarised form, was as follows:

| Share capital | | | Land and buildings, at cost | |
|---|---|---|---|---|
| Authorised and issued | | | Property A | R30 000 |
| 50 000 shares of R1 each | R50 000 | | Property B | 24 000 |
| Retained income | 5 000 | | Bank | 3 000 |
| | | | | |
| Creditors | 2 000 | | | |
| | R57 000 | | | R57 000 |
| | ====== | | | ====== |

A Company Limited's valuations of the properties at the date of acquisition were:

Property A     R40 000              Property B     R29 000

The retained income of B Company Limited was as follows:

| | | |
|---|---|---|
| Retained income 1 July 19x1 | | R5 000 |
| Net income from rents for the year ended 30 June 19x2 | | 6 000 |
| | | 11 000 |
| Dividend paid 2 October 19x1 | R3 000 | |
| Dividend paid 30 June 19x2 | 3 000 | 6 000 |
| Retained income 30 June 19x2 | | 5 000 |
| Net income from rents for the year ended 30 June 19x3 | | 8 000 |
| Profit on sale of Property A, 24 November 19x2 | | 7 000 |
| | | 20 000 |
| Dividend paid 2 January 19x3 | 8 000 | |
| Bonus paid on 31 January 19x3 out of profit on sale of Property A | 7 000 | 15 000 |
| Retained income 30 June 19x3 | | 5 000 |
| Net income from rents for the year ended 30 June 19x4 | | 4 000 |
| | | 9 000 |
| Dividend paid 30 June 19x4 | | 8 000 |
| Retained income 30 June 19x4 | | R1 000 |
| | | ===== |

The net income from rents was earned evenly during each financial year.

You are required to give all the journal entries relating to the above in the books of A Company Limited for the years ended 30 June 19x2, 19x3 and 19x4, assuming that A Company Limited takes credit for the profits of subsidiary companies only to the extent that dividends are declared.

Cash transactions are to be journalised.

# H9

H Limited bought all the shares in S Limited for cash on 1 January 19x1.   At the date of acquisition the balance sheet of S Limited in summarised form was as follows:

S LIMITED

| | | | |
|---|---|---|---|
| Share capital | | Land and buildings | |
|   Issued 20 000 shares of R1 each | R20 000 | | |
| Retained income | 3 000 | Property A | R10 000 |
| Loan account 6% | 6 000 | Property B | 20 000 |
| Overdraft | 1 000 | | |
| | R30 000 | | R30 000 |

The purchase price of the shares was based on a valuation of the tangible assets.   For the purpose of calculating the purchase price, the land and buildings were valued as follows:

|  |  |
|---|---|
| Property A | R15 000 |
| Property B | 22 000 |
| | R37 000 |

H Limited agreed to take over the loan from 1 January 19x1 with the understanding that it could be converted into fully paid 7% preference shares of R1 each at any time during the period 1 January 19x1 to 31 December 19x2.

H Limited paid the creditor for the loan in full on 2 January 19x1.   On 31 December 19x1 S Limited paid the interest on the loan for the year ended 31 December 19x1.

The loan was converted into 7% preference shares on 31 December 19x1.

# H9 CONTINUED

The retained income of S Limited for the period 1 January 19x1 to 31 December 19x4 is as follows:

| | | |
|---|---:|---:|
| Retained income 1 January 19x1 | | R3 000 |
| Net income for the year ended 31 December 19x1 | | 4 800 |
| | | 7 800 |
| Dividend paid 2 January 19x1 | R2 000 | |
| Dividend paid 31 December 19x1 | 2 000 | 4 000 |
| Retained income 1 January 19x2 | | 3 800 |
| Net income for the year ended 31 December 19x2 | | 4 800 |
| | | 8 600 |
| Dividend paid preference shares 31 December 19x2 | 420 | |
| Dividend paid ordinary shares 31 December 19x2 | 2 000 | 2 420 |
| Retained income 1 January 19x3 | | 6 180 |
| Net income for the year ended 31 December 19x3 | | 3 800 |
| Profit on sale of Property A - 30 June 19x3 | | 4 000 |
| | | 13 980 |
| Dividend paid out of profit on sale of Property A - 15 July 19x3 | 4 000 | |
| Dividend paid preference shares 31 December 19x3 | 420 | 4 420 |
| Retained income 1 January 19x4 | | 9 560 |
| Net income for the year ended 31 December 19x4 | | 3 600 |
| | | 13 160 |
| Dividend paid ordinary shares 31 March 19x4 | 3 000 | |
| Dividend paid ordinary shares 31 December 19x4 | 3 600 | |
| Dividend paid preference shares 31 December 19x4 | 420 | 7 020 |
| Retained income 1 January 19x5 | | R6 140 |

The net income was earned evenly throughout each year.

The directors of H Limited wish to credit to the cost of the investment any dividends declared out of profits earned prior to the acquisition of such shares.

<u>YOU ARE REQUIRED TO:</u>

Journalise the above in the books of H Limited (including cash transactions).

# H10

Apple Ltd bought all the shares in Pie Ltd on 1 January 19x7 for R390 000 cash

The balance sheet of Pie Ltd at 30 June 19x6 in summarised form was:

| Capital in R1 shares | R300 000 | Assets | R330 000 |
|---|---|---|---|
| Retained income | 30 000 | | |
| | R330 000 | | R330 000 |
| | ======= | | ======= |

The following figures have been extracted from  the financial  statements of Pie Ltd:

| | | | |
|---|---|---|---|
| Retained income | 1 July 19x6 | | R30 000 |
| Net income | 30 June 19x7 | | 90 000 |
| | | | 120 000 |
| Dividends paid 2 January 19x7 | | R60 000 | |
| Dividends paid 30 June 19x7 | | 30 000 | 90 000 |
| Retained income 30 June 19x7 | | | 30 000 |
| Net income 30 June 19x8 | | | 32 000 |
| Retained income 30 June 19x8 | | | 62 000 |
| Net income 30 June 19x9 | | | 18 000 |
| | | | 80 000 |
| Dividend paid 30 June 19x9 | | | 70 000 |
| Retained income 30 June 19x9 | | | R10 000 |
| | | | ====== |

Profits are deemed to have been earned evenly throughout each year.

You are required to give all the journal entries relating to the above in the books of Apple Ltd for the years ended 30 June 19x7, 19x8 and 19x9.

# H11

The following is the trial balance of Buildings (Pty) Limited at 31 December 19x2:

|                                            |         |         | R5      |
|--------------------------------------------|---------|---------|---------|
| Share capital                              |         |         | R5      |
| Land and buildings, at cost                | R10 000 |         |         |
| Debtors for rent                           |      51 |         |         |
| Rents received in advance                  |         |         |     100 |
| Unexpired assessment rates and insurance   |     110 |         |         |
| Trade creditors                            |         |         |     204 |
| Bank                                       |     150 |         |         |
| Loan account - Black                       |         |         |   8 000 |
| Retained income                            |         |         |   2 002 |
|                                            | R10 311 |         | R10 311 |

The authorised capital of the company is R2 000 in R1 shares.

All the issued shares are held by Black.

Brown agrees to buy these shares from him at a price to be determined on the basis of the land and buildings being worth R25 000.  He also agrees to lend R8 000 to Buildings (Pty) Limited to enable the company to repay Black's loan.

Brown subscribed for the remaining shares in the company and utilises portion of his loan account to pay for the shares subscribed for.

The company immediately declares a dividend of R2 000, Brown's loan account being utilised.  Show how these transactions, including cash transactions, would be reflected in Brown's journal.

# H12

On 1 July 19x5 H Limited purchased all the shares in S Limited for R115 000.
The issued capital of S Limited is 100 000 shares of R1 each and the retained
income at that date was R15 000.

The results reflected by the accounts of S Limited at 30 June each year were
as follows:

19x6 (profit)  R16 000        19x7(loss)  R3 000     19x8  (profit)  R14 000.

On 30 June 19x6, S Limited paid a dividend of 20% and on 30 June 19x8 it paid
a dividend of 12%.

H Limited decides to take credit in its income statement for the profits
earned by S Limited only to the extent to which dividends have actually been
declared.


<u>YOU ARE REQUIRED</u>:

(a)     to give all the journal entries relating to the above in the books of
        H Limited for the years ended 30 June 19x6, 19x7 and 19x8.

(b)     show the relative portion of the balance sheet of H Limited for the
        three years ended 30 June.

# H13

On 1 July 19x2 Romeo Holdings Limited bought for cash all the shares in Juliet Limited, the price paid being based on a sworn valuation of the tangible assets.

The balance sheet of Juliet Limited at 30 June 19x2 was as follows:

| Share capital | | | Land and buildings, at cost | | | |
|---|---|---|---|---|---|---|
| Authorised and issued | | | | | | |
| 100 000 shares of R1 each | R100 000 | | Property A | R50 000 | | |
| Retained income | 15 000 | | Property B | 20 000 | | |
| Sundry creditors | 5 000 | | Property C | 30 000 | R100 000 | |
| | | | Cash at bank | | 20 000 | |
| | R120 000 | | | | R120 000 | |
| | ======= | | | | ======= | |

Sworn valuations of the properties at the date of purchase were:

Property A  R80 000;      Property B  R40 000;      Property C  R65 000.

The following figures have been extracted from the accounts of Juliet Limited:

| | | |
|---|---|---|
| Retained income 1 July 19x2 | | R15 000 |
| Net profit from rents for the year ended 30 June 19x3 | | 10 000 |
| | | 25 000 |
| Dividend paid 2 July 19x2 | R10 000 | |
| Dividend paid 30 June 19x3 | 10 000 | 20 000 |
| Retained income 30 June 19x3 | | 5 000 |
| Net income from rents for the year ended 30 June 19x4 | | 15 000 |
| | | 20 000 |
| Profit on sale of property A | | 25 000 |
| | | 45 000 |
| Dividend paid 30 June 19x4 | 10 000 | |
| Bonus paid on 30 June 19x4 out of profit on sale of property A | 25 000 | 35 000 |
| Retained income 30 June 19x4 | | 10 000 |
| Net income from rents for the year ended 30 June 19x5 | | 12 000 |
| | | 22 000 |
| Profit on sale of property C | | 40 000 |
| | | 62 000 |
| Dividend paid 30 June 19x5 | | 12 000 |
| Bonus paid on 30 June 19x5 out of profit on sale of property C | 40 000 | 52 000 |
| Retained income 30 June 19x5 | | R10 000 |
| | | ====== |

Romeo Holdings Limited takes credit for the profits of subsidiary companies only to the extent that dividends are declared.

<u>YOU ARE REQUIRED TO</u>:

give all the entries relating to the above for the years ended 30 June 19x3, 19x4 and 19x5.   Journalise all cash transactions.

# H14

On 1 July 19X7 Roan Limited purchased all the shares in Springbok Limited.
The balance sheet of Springbok Limited at 31 December 19X7 was as follows:-

| Share capital | R100 000 | Land and buildings | |
|---|---|---|---|
| Retained income | 30 000 | Property A | R75 000 |
| | | Property B | 50 000 |
| | | Bank | 5 000 |
| | R130 000 | | R130 000 |

Roan Limited considered each of Springbok Limited's properties to be worth 20%
more than its book value.  There was no goodwill.

A summary of the retained income of Springbok Limited is as follows:-

| | | |
|---|---|---|
| Retained income 1 January 19X7 | | R15 000 |
| Net income for the year ended 31 December 19X7 | | 36 000 |
| | | 51 000 |
| Dividend paid 31 December 19X7 | | 21 000 |
| | | 30 000 |
| Net income for the year ended 31 December 19X8 | | 48 000 |
| | | 78 000 |
| Dividend paid 30 June 19X8 | R28 000 | |
| Dividend paid 31 December 19X8 | 16 000 | 44 000 |
| | | 34 000 |
| Profit on sale Property B 28 May 19X9 | 6 000 | |
| Net income for the year ended 31 December 19X9 | 60 000 | |
| | | 100 000 |
| Dividend paid 30 June 19X9 out of proceeds of sale of Property B | | 6 000 |
| Retained income 31 December 19X9 | | R94 000 |

The net income of Springbok Limited was earned evenly throughout each year.

It has always been the policy of Roan Limited to take credit for income from
its subsidiary companies only to the extend that dividends are declared.


<u>YOU ARE REQUIRED:</u>


To give the journal entries in the books of Roan Limited relating to its
holding in Springbok Limited from and including the purchase of the shares on
1 July 19X7 until 31 December 19X9.  (Narrations to journal entries are not
required.)

# SECTION I

# ELEMENTARY GROUP FINANCIAL STATEMENTS – WHOLLY-OWNED

SECTION 1

ELEMENTARY GROUP
FINANCIAL STATEMENTS
– WHOLLY-OWNED

On 30 June 19x4 Alpha Limited purchased all the shares in Omega Limited.  At that date the balance sheets of the two companies were as follows:



### BALANCE SHEETS AT 30 JUNE 19x4

|  | ALPHA LTD | | OMEGA LTD | |
|---|---|---|---|---|
| SHARE CAPITAL | | | | |
| Authorised and issued | | | | |
| in R1 shares | | R350 000 | | R100 000 |
| DISTRIBUTABLE RESERVES | | | | |
| General reserve | R70 000 | | R10 000 | |
| Retained income | 30 000 | 100 000 | 10 000 | 20 000 |
| LOAN FROM HOLDING COMPANY | | | | |
| Alpha Limited | | | | 10 000 |
| CURRENT LIABILITIES | | | | |
| Creditors | | 35 000 | | 15 000 |
| Shareholders for dividends | | | | |
| declared 15 June 19x4 | | 5 000 | | 10 000 |
| | | R490 000 | | R155 000 |
| | | ======= | | ======= |

|  | ALPHA LTD | | OMEGA LTD | |
|---|---|---|---|---|
| FIXED ASSETS | | | | |
| Land and buildings, | | | | |
| at cost | | R120 000 | | R50 000 |
| Fixtures, at cost | R30 000 | | R10 000 | |
| Accumulated depreciation | 10 000 | 20 000 | 5 000 | 5 000 |
| | | 140 000 | | 55 000 |
| INVESTMENT IN SUBSI-DIARY COMPANY | | | | |
| Shares in Omega Ltd. | | | | |
| at cost | 150 000 | | | |
| Loan in Omega Ltd | 10 000 | 160 000 | | |
| CURRENT ASSETS | | | | |
| Stock | 80 000 | | 50 000 | |
| Debtors | 60 000 | | 30 000 | |
| Bank | 50 000 | 190 000 | 20 000 | 100 000 |
| | | R490 000 | | R155 000 |
| | | ======= | | ======= |

The purchase price of the shares was based on the book values of the tangible assets with the exception of the land and buildings which were considered to be worth R60 000, and fixtures R15 000.  At 30 June 19x4 Omega Ltd owed Alpha Ltd R12 000 for goods supplied during the year.

Prepare the consolidated balance sheet at 30 June 19x4 and show your workings.

I2

H Limited purchased all the shares in S Limited on 1 July 19x3.

The following are the income statements of the two companies for the year ended 30 June 19x4 and the balance sheets at 30 June 19x4:

<u>INCOME STATEMENTS FOR THE YEAR ENDED 30 JUNE 19x4</u>

|  | H LTD. | S LTD. |  | H LTD. | S LTD. |
|---|---|---|---|---|---|
| Property expenses |  | R12 000 | Gross profit | R80 000 |  |
| Selling and administration expenses | R25 000 |  | Rent receivable |  | R22 000 |
| Rent of premises paid to S Limited | 15 000 |  | Interest on loan to |  |  |
| Depreciation of furniture | 600 | 200 | S Limited | 500 |  |
| Audit fees and expenses | 400 | 100 |  |  |  |
| Interest on loan from H Ltd |  | 500 |  |  |  |
|  | 41 000 | 12 800 |  |  |  |
| Net income carried down | 39 500 | 9 200 |  |  |  |
|  | R80 500 | R22 000 |  | R80 500 | R22 000 |
|  | ====== | ====== |  | ====== | ====== |
|  |  |  |  |  |  |
| Balance per balance sheet | R79 500 | R19 200 | Balance at 1 July 19x3 | R40 000 | R10 000 |
|  |  |  | Net income for the year |  |  |
|  |  |  | ended 30 June 19x4 | 39 500 | 9 200 |
|  | R79 500 | R19 200 |  | R79 500 | R19 200 |
|  | ====== | ====== |  | ====== | ====== |

<u>NOTE</u>:  No depreciation has been allowed in respect of buildings.

## 12 CONTINUED

<u>BALANCE SHEETS AT 30 JUNE 19x4</u>

| | H LTD. | S LTD. | | H LTD. | | S LTD. | |
|---|---|---|---|---|---|---|---|
| SHARE CAPITAL | | | FIXED ASSETS | | | | |
| Authorised and issued | | | Land and buildings, at cost | | R35 000 | | R110 000 |
| in R1 shares | R200 000 | R100 000 | Furniture at cost | R6 000 | | R2 000 | |
| | | | Accumulated depreciation | 1 800 | 4 200 | 600 | 1 400 |
| DISTRIBUTABLE RESERVE | | | | | 39 200 | | 111 400 |
| Retained income | 79 500 | 19 200 | INVESTMENT IN SUBSIDIARY COMPANY | | | | |
| | 279 500 | 119 200 | Shares in S Limited at cost | 120 000 | | | |
| | | | Loan to S Limited | 10 000 | 130 000 | | |
| LOAN FROM HOLDING COMPANY | | | | | | | |
| H Limited | | 10 000 | CURRENT ASSETS | | | | |
| | | | Stock | 80 000 | | | |
| CURRENT LIABILITIES | | | Debtors | 30 000 | | 3 600 | |
| Creditors | 20 000 | 5 800 | Bank | 20 300 | 130 300 | 20 000 | 23 600 |
| | R299 500 | R135 000 | | | R299 500 | | R135 000 |

When the shares were bought it was considered that furniture was worth its book value.

Prepare for submission to the directors, the detailed consolidated income statement for the year ended 30 June 19x4 and the consolidated balance sheet at that date.  Show your workings using a work sheet.

X Limited purchased all the shares in Y Limited on 31 March 19x4 at which date the summarised balance sheets of the two companies were:

<u>BALANCE SHEETS AT 31 MARCH 19X4</u>

| | <u>X Limited</u> | <u>Y Limited</u> | | <u>X Limited</u> | | <u>Y Limited</u> | |
|---|---|---|---|---|---|---|---|
| <u>SHARE CAPITAL</u> | | | <u>FIXED ASSETS</u> | | | | |
| Authorised and | | | Land and buildings | | | | |
| issued in | | |   at cost | | R10 000 | | R6 000 |
| R1 shares | R30 000 | R10 000 | Plant at cost | R8 000 | | R4 000 | |
| | | | Accumulated | | | | |
| | | |   depreciation | 3 000 | 5 000 | 2 000 | 2 000 |
| <u>DISTRIBUTABLE</u> | | | | | 15 000 | | 8 000 |
| <u>RESERVES</u> | | | | | | | |
| Retained income | 13 000 | 4 000 | <u>INVESTMENT IN</u> | | | | |
| | | | <u>SUBSIDIARY COMPANY</u> | | | | |
| <u>CURRENT LIABILITIES</u> | | | Shares in Y Limited | | | | |
| Creditors | 5 000 | 2 000 |   at cost | | 16 000 | | - |
| | | | | | | | |
| | | | <u>CURRENT ASSETS</u> | | | | |
| | | | Stock | 7 000 | | 4 000 | |
| | | | Debtors | 6 000 | | 3 000 | |
| | | | Bank | 4 000 | 17 000 | 1 000 | 8 000 |
| | R48 000 | R16 000 | | | 48 000 | | R16 000 |
| | ====== | ====== | | | ====== | | ====== |

When the shares were bought it was considered that:

(i)   Y Limited's land and buildings were worth R7 000.
(ii)  The other tangible assets of Y Limited were stated at fair values in the balance sheet.

<u>YOU ARE REQUIRED TO</u>:

Prepare the consolidated balance sheet at 31 March 19x4

**14**

Doll Limited acquired a 100% interest in Howzit Limited on 1 January 19x1 for
R125 000.  The directors considered the assets to be fairly valued on that
date.  On 1 January 19x1 the retained income of Howzit Limited was R15 000.

The trial balances of the two companies on 31 December 19x5 were as follows:

|  | Doll Limited | Howzit Limited |
|---|---|---|
| Cash | R25 000 | R15 000 |
| Debtors | 27 000 | 20 000 |
| Stock | 32 000 | 25 000 |
| Investment in Howzit Limited | 125 000 | - |
| Plant and equipment  (net) | 45 000 | 40 000 |
| Land and buildings | 60 000 | 45 000 |
| Dividends | 10 000 | 5 000 |
| Purchases | 40 000 | 35 000 |
| Operating expenses (including tax) | 15 000 | 10 000 |
|  | R379 000 | R195 000 |
|  | ======= | ======= |
| Creditors | R39 000 | R20 000 |
| Capital  (R1 shares) | 200 000 | 75 000 |
| Retained income 1.1.19x5 | 71 000 | 45 000 |
| Sales | 64 000 | 55 000 |
| Dividends from subsidiary | 5 000 | - |
|  | R379 000 | R195 000 |
|  | ======= | ======= |
| Stock 31 December 19x5 | R38 000 | R25 000 |

<u>YOU ARE REQUIRED TO</u>:

1. Prepare a consolidated work sheet at 31 December 19x5.
2. Prepare a consolidated income statement for the year ended 31 December
   19x5 and a consolidated balance sheet at that date.

## 15

On 1 January 19x4 Big Limited purchased all the shares in Small Limited. When the shares were bought it was considered that the book figures for the tangible assets in Small Limited fairly stated their present values with the exception of plant which was valued at R36 000.  The balance sheet at the date of purchase of the shares showed plant as follows:

| | | |
|---|---|---|
| Plant at cost | R50 000 | |
| Accumulated depreciation | 20 000 | R30 000 |

Depreciation is written off at 10% per annum on cost.

The following are the income statements of the two companies for the year ended 31 December 19x4 and the balance sheets at 31 December 19x4.

### INCOME STATEMENTS FOR THE YEAR ENDED 31 DECEMBER 19x4

| | Big Limited | Small Limited | | Big Limited | Small Limited |
|---|---|---|---|---|---|
| Director's emoluments and fees | R30 000 | R11 000 | Trading profit | R192 000 | R40 000 |
| Depreciation | 12 000 | 5 000 | Interest on loan to Small Limited | 3 000 | – |
| Interest on loan from Big Limited | – | 3 000 | | | |
| Audit fees | 3 000 | 1 000 | | | |
| Net income carried down | 150 000 | 20 000 | | | |
| | R195 000 | R40 000 | | R95 000 | R40 000 |
| | ======= | ====== | | ======= | ====== |
| Dividends declared in January 19x4 | R65 000 | R30 000 | Balance at 1 Jan 19x4 | R185 000 | R50 000 |
| Balance per balance sheet | 270 000 | 40 000 | Net income for year ended 31 Dec 19x4 | 150 000 | 20 000 |
| | R335 000 | R70 000 | | R335 000 | R70 000 |
| | ======= | ====== | | ======= | ====== |

No depreciation has been allowed on buildings.

# 15 CONTINUED



BALANCE SHEETS AT 31 DECEMBER 19x4

| | Big Limited | Small Limited | | Big Limited | Small Limited |
|---|---|---|---|---|---|
| SHARE CAPITAL | | | FIXED ASSETS | | |
| Authorised and issued in R1 shares | R400 000 | R60 000 | Land and buildings at cost | R200 000 | R60 000 |
| DISTRIBUTABLE RESERVE | | | Plant, at cost R120 000 | R50 000 | |
| Retained income | 270 000 | 40 000 | Accumulated depreciation 36 000 | 84 000 / 25 000 | 25 000 |
| | | | | 284 000 | 85 000 |
| LOAN FROM HOLDING COMPANY | | | INVESTMENT IN SUBSIDIARY COMPANY | | |
| Big Limited | | 60 000 | Shares in Small Limited 120 000 | | |
| | | | Dividend received 30 000 | | |
| | | | 90 000 | | |
| CURRENT LIABILITIES | | | Loan to Small Limited 60 000 | 150 000 | |
| Creditors | 54 000 | 13 000 | | | |
| | | | CURRENT ASSETS | | |
| | | | Stock | 140 000 | 30 000 |
| | | | Debtors | 80 000 | 30 000 |
| | | | Bank | 70 000 / 290 000 | 28 000 / 88 000 |
| | R724 000 | R173 000 | | R724 000 | R173 000 |

YOU ARE REQUIRED:

Prepare the detailed consolidated income statement for the year ended 31 December 19x4 and the consolidated balance sheet at that date.

## 16

On 31 March 19x4, Fish Limited acquired all the shares in Hoek Limited. At that date the tangible assets of Hoek Limited were considered to be fairly valued. The income statements of the two companies for the year ended 31 March 19x5 and the balance sheets at that date were as follows:

INCOME STATEMENTS

|                                        | FISH LIMITED | HOEK LIMITED |
|----------------------------------------|-------------:|-------------:|
| TRADING PROFIT FOR THE YEAR            |      R42 000 |      R16 000 |
| DIVIDENDS RECEIVED                     |        2 500 |            - |
| INTEREST RECEIVED (PAID)               |        1 500 |      (1 500) |
| NET INCOME BEFORE TAXATION             |       46 000 |       14 500 |
| TAXATION                               |       19 000 |        5 500 |
| NET INCOME AFTER TAXATION              |       27 000 |        9 000 |
| DIVIDENDS PAID                         |       16 000 |        2 500 |
| RETAINED INCOME FOR THE YEAR           |       11 000 |        6 500 |
| RETAINED INCOME AT 31 MARCH 19x4       |       29 000 |       12 000 |
| RETAINED INCOME PER BALANCE SHEET      |      R40 000 |      R18 500 |

BALANCE SHEETS

|                            | FISH LIMITED | HOEK LIMITED |
|----------------------------|-------------:|-------------:|
| SHARE CAPITAL              |     R100 000 |      R30 000 |
| RETAINED INCOME            |       40 000 |       18 500 |
| SHAREHOLDERS' EQUITY       |      140 000 |       48 500 |
| LONG TERM LOAN             |       60 000 |       12 500 |
| CURRENT LIABILITIES        |       50 000 |        9 000 |
|                            |     R250 000 |      R70 000 |

|                            |            |         | FISH LIMITED |         | HOEK LIMITED |
|----------------------------|-----------:|--------:|-------------:|--------:|-------------:|
| FIXED ASSETS               |            |         |              |         |              |
| Land and building at cost  |            |         |     R110 000 |         |      R40 000 |
| INVESTMENT IN SUBSIDIARY   |            |         |              |         |              |
| Shares at cost             |    R45 000 |         |              |         |            - |
| Loan                       |     12 500 |         |       57 500 |         |              |
| CURRENT ASSETS             |            |         |              |         |              |
| Stock                      |     45 000 |         |              | R18 000 |              |
| Debtors                    |     26 000 |         |              |   9 000 |              |
| Bank                       |     11 500 |  82 500 |              |   3 000 |       30 000 |
|                            |            |         |     R250 000 |         |      R70 000 |

YOU ARE REQUIRED TO:

prepare the consolidated annual financial statements for the year ended 31 March 19x5.

Use a work sheet.

(A consolidated cash flow statement is not required).

## 17

Hintertux Limited purchased all the shares in Seefeld Limited on 1 July 19x4 when Seefeld Limited's retained income had a debit balance of R10 000.

The following are the trial balances of Hintertux Limited and Seefeld Limited at 30 June 19x8.

|  | Hintertux Limited | | Seefeld Limited | |
|---|---|---|---|---|
|  | Dr | Cr | Dr | Cr |
| Share capital (R1 shares) |  | R140 000 |  | R80 000 |
| Retained income 1 July 19x7 |  | 110 000 |  | 48 000 |
| General reserve |  | 30 000 |  | - |
| Loan - Hintertux Limited |  | - |  | 2 400 |
| Land and buildings at cost | R120 000 |  | R70 000 |  |
| Plant and machinery at cost | 150 000 |  | 60 000 |  |
| Accumulated depreciation - plant and machinery |  | 62 000 |  | 42 000 |
| Investment in Seefeld Limited | 104 000 |  | - |  |
| Stock | 30 000 |  | 42 000 |  |
| Debtors | 26 000 |  | 34 400 |  |
| Loan - Seefeld Limited | 2 400 |  | - |  |
| Bank | 9 000 |  | 44 800 |  |
| Creditors |  | 58 000 |  | 36 400 |
| Net income before tax |  | 85 600 |  | 32 800 |
| Profit on sale of land |  | - |  | 30 000 |
| Dividends paid | 10 000 |  | 7 200 |  |
| Taxation | 34 200 |  | 13 200 |  |
|  | R485 600 | R485 600 | R271 600 | R271 600 |

## Additional information

1. On 1 July 19x4 when purchasing the shares in Seefeld Limited, Hintertux Limited valued the land at R20 000 above original cost to Seefeld Limited. It valued plant and machinery at R14 000 more than book value at the date of purchase. It did however agree with Seefeld's estimate of the remaining useful life of the plant. All other assets and liabilities were considered to be fairly valued.

2. No adjustments were made in the books of Seefeld Limited in respect of the land or the plant.

3. In January 19x8 Seefeld Limited sold half the land. No other sales or purchases of land or plant have taken place.

4. Seefeld Limited has neither purchased nor sold plant since it originally purchased plant costing R60 000.

5. Depreciation is provided by Seefeld Limited at the rate of 10% p.a. on cost.

6.     Seefeld Limited's articles prohibit the declaration of a dividend out
       of the profit on sale of land.

<u>YOU ARE REQUIRED TO:</u>

prepare the consolidated income statement of Hintertux Limited and its
subsidiary for the year ended 30 June 19x8 and the consolidated balance sheet
at the same date.

Notes to the financial statements are not required.

## 18

On 1 January 19x1 H Ltd acquired 200 000 ordinary shares of R1 each and 60 000 10% preference shares of R1 each in S Ltd.

The cost of the shares were:

Ordinary shares                 R2,50c each
10% preference shares       80c each.

On 1 January 19x1 the following balances appeared in the books of H Ltd and S Ltd.

|  | H Ltd | S Ltd |
|---|---|---|
| Ordinary share capital (R1 each) | R2 500 000 | R200 000 |
| 6% preference share capital (R1 each) | 250 000 | - |
| 10% preference shares capital (R1 each) | - | 10 000 |
| Retained income | 870 000 | 250 000 |

The directors of H Ltd considered the assets of S Ltd to be fairly valued.

During 19x1:

(1)     H Ltd reported a net income after tax, but before dividends received, of R1 000 000.
H Ltd paid its preference dividends for the year and an ordinary dividend of 14 cents per share.

(2)     S Ltd reported a net income after tax of R120 000.
S Ltd paid its preference dividends for the year and an ordinary dividend of 20 cents per share.

<u>YOU ARE REQUIRED TO</u>:

prepare consolidating journal entries to record the above.

On 1/1/19x4 a holding company acquired all the shares in the subsidiary company for R126 000.  The share capital of the subsidiary was R100 000 and its retained income was R10 000.   The plant stood in its books at a cost of R50 000 and accumulated depreciation to date was R10 000.   This plant had been bought two years previously when its estimated life was 10 years.  When the holding company acquired the shares it considered that the plant had a remaining life of 8 years but that, as replacement costs had increased, the plant was worth more than its book value.

## YOU ARE REQUIRED TO:

give the proforma consolidation journal entries for the year ended 31/12/19x6 in respect of the above.

On 1 July 19x7 Cessna Limited acquired all the shares in Piper Limited. At that date all the tangible assets and liabilities of Piper Limited were considered by Cessna Limited to be fairly valued except for plant and machinery which was valued at R8 000 more than book value.

Piper Limited provides for depreciation on plant machinery at 10% per annum.

## BALANCE SHEETS AT 30 JUNE 19x9

| | Cessna Limited | Piper Limited | | Cessna Limited | Piper Limited |
|---|---|---|---|---|---|
| Share capital | R225 000 | R50 000 | Land and buildings | R83 000 | R42 800 |
| Retained income | 52 850 | 33 500 | Plant and machinery | 135 000 | 70 000 |
| | | | Accumulated depn | 40 500 | 28 000 |
| | 277 850 | 83 500 | | 94 500 | 42 000 |
| 10% debentures | - | 25 000 | | | |
| | 277 850 | 108 500 | | 177 500 | 84 800 |
| Current liabilities | | | Investments | | |
| Creditors | 61 350 | 27 700 | 50 000 shares in | | |
| Receiver of Revenue | 14 500 | 9 500 | Piper Limited | 89 000 | - |
| | | | 10 000 10% debentures | | |
| | | | in Pipers Ltd | 10 000 | - |
| | | | Current assets | 77 200 | 60 900 |
| | | | Stock | 54 800 | 45 000 |
| | | | Debtors | 21 300 | 15 000 |
| | | | Bank | 1 100 | 900 |
| | R353 700 | R145 700 | | R353 700 | R145 700 |

## INCOME STATEMENTS FOR THE YEAR ENDED 30 JUNE 19x9

| | Cessna | Piper |
|---|---|---|
| Net income before tax | R44 750 | R25 000 |
| Taxation | 17 900 | 9 500 |
| Net income | 26 850 | 15 500 |
| Dividends paid | 11 000 | 10 000 |
| Retained income for the year | 15 850 | 5 500 |
| Retained income at 30 June 19x8 | 37 000 | 28 000 |
| Retained income per balance sheet | R52 850 | R33 500 |

NOTES:

(1)   At 1 July 19x7 the retained income of Piper Limited was R25 000.

(2)   Cessna Limited agreed with the estimated life of the plant of Piper Limited.

(3)   Piper Limited and Cessna Limited have not made any purchases or sales of plant and machinery since acquisition date.

YOU ARE REQUIRED TO:

Prepare the detailed consolidated income statement of the group for  the year ended 30 June 19x9, and the consolidated balance sheet at that date.

**I11**

On 1 July 19x1 H Limited acquired 50 000 shares in S Limited.

The following balances were extracted from the books of the two companies at
30 June 19x2:

|                                                    | H Limited | S Limited |
|----------------------------------------------------|-----------|-----------|
| Capital, authorised and issued in R1 shares        | R100 000  | R50 000   |
| General reserve                                    | 65 000    | -         |
| Share premium                                      | -         | 20 000    |
| Retained income at 30 June 19x1                    | 10 000    | 2 000     |
| Net income for the year                            | 18 400    | 8 000     |
| Creditors                                          | 10 000    | 2 000     |
| Dividends paid                                     | 3 000     | 2 000     |
| Loan from buildings society, secured by mortgage   |           |           |
|   of land and buildings and guaranteed by H Limited | -  | 10 000    |
| Land and buildings, at cost                        | 25 000    | 15 000    |
| Furniture, at cost less depreciation               |           |           |
|   (cost R6 000 and R5 500)               | 5 000     | 5 000     |
| Stock                                              | 70 000    | 45 000    |
| Debtors                                            | 15 600    | 20 000    |
| Investment in S Limited                            | 72 000    | -         |
| Bank                                               | 12 800    | 5 000     |

At 30 June 19x2 S limited owed H Limited R1 500.

S Limited has written off R200 in respect of depreciation of furniture for the
year ended 30 June 19x2.

Prepare a detailed consolidated balance sheet at 30 June 19x2.

On 1 January 19x5 X Limited purchased all the shares in Y Limited for R120 000.  On that date the summarised balance sheet at Y Limited was:

| Share capital | R100 000 | Land and buildings - at cost | |
|---|---|---|---|
| Retained income | 6 000 | Property A purchased 19x0 | R45 000 |
| | | Property B purchased 19x4 | 55 000 |
| | | Debtors for rent | 1 000 |
| | | Bank | 5 000 |
| | R106 000 | | R106 000 |
| | ======= | | ======= |

Since Property B had been purchased recently it was considered to be worth its book value.  Property A was considered to be worth R59 000.  Y Limited did not adjust the value of Property A in its books.

Immediately after acquisition of the shares X Limited occupied the entire building on Property B.

The summarised income statement of the two companies for the year ended 30 June 19x6 are:

| | X Limited | Y Limited |
|---|---|---|
| Trading profit | R100 000 | - |
| Rent received - Property A | - | R12 000 |
|           - Property B | - | 8 000 |
| | 100 000 | 20 000 |
| Expenses | 80 000 | 30 000 |
| Net income | 20 000 | (10 000) |
| Profit on sale of Property A | - | 16 000 |
| Retained income for the year | 20 000 | 6 000 |
| Retained income at 30 June 19x5 | 13 000 | 8 000 |
| Retained income per balance sheet | R33 000 | R14 000 |
| | ====== | ====== |

No dividends have been declared by either company for two years.

<u>YOU ARE REQUIRED TO</u>:

prepare the consolidated income statement for the year ended 30 June 19x6.

On 1 January 19x7 H Limited acquired all the shares in S Limited.  At that date S Limited's balance sheet was summarised as follows:

| Share capital | R75 000 | Plant at cost | R60 000 |
|---|---|---|---|
| Retained income | 25 000 | Accumulated depreciation | 24 000 |
| Creditors | 10 000 | | 36 000 |
| | | Stock | 29 000 |
| | | Debtors | 27 000 |
| | | Bank | 18 000 |
| | R110 000 | | R110 000 |

In determining  the purchase price of R126 000 H Limited considered that all the tangible assets and liabilities to be worth their book values with the exception of plant which was considered to be worth R42 000 and had a remaining life of six years.  When the plant was acquired on 1 January 19x3 it was thought that it would last for ten years when it would have no scrap value.

The following of list balances were extracted from the books of two companies at 31 December 19x9:

| | H Limited | S limited |
|---|---|---|
| Bank (debit balances) | R21 700 | R21 200 |
| Creditors | 20 000 | 12 500 |
| Debtors | 35 000 | 45 600 |
| Dividends paid | 50 000 | 30 000 |
| H Limited - current account | - | 21 600 Cr. |
| Land and buildings | 350 000 | - |
| Net income for the year | 190 000 | 46 200 |
| Plant at cost | 73 000 | 60 000 |
| Accumulated depreciation - plant | 36 500 | 42 000 |
| Retained income 1 January 19x9 | 170 000 | 25 800 |
| Share capital (authorised and issued in R1 shares) | 300 000 | 75 000 |
| Shares in S Limited | 111 000 | - |
| S Limited - current account | 21 600 Dr. | - |
| Stock | 54 200 | 66 300 |

<u>Note</u>:

S Limited has not changed its basis of calculating depreciation nor has it purchased or sold any plant during the past three years.


<u>YOU ARE REQUIRED TO</u>:

prepare a detailed consolidated balance sheet at 31 December 19x9 and consolidated income statement for the year ended on that date for H Limited and its subsidiary.

Ignore taxation and comparative figures.  Notes to the financial statements are not required.

The following are extracts from the trial balances of H Limited and its wholly owned subsidiary S Limited at 31 December 19x9:

|  | H Limited | S Limited |
|---|---|---|
| Share capital | R200 000 | R50 000 |
| General reserve | 15 000 | |
| Retained income 1 January 19x9 | 35 000 | |
| Net income for the year | 18 500 | |
| Provision for loss in subsidiary 31 December 19x9 | 23 600 | |
| Accumulated loss 1 January 19x9 | | 16 000 |
| Net loss for year | | 3 400 |
| Dividends paid | 10 000 | |

When H Limited acquired the shares in S Limited the retained income of S Limited was R4 200.


<u>YOU ARE REQUIRED TO</u>:

calculate the distributable reserves appearing in the consolidated balance sheet at 31 December 19x9.

**I15**

On 28 February 19x5 Base Limited acquired 100% of the shares and assumed the loan in Ball Limited for R145 000.

The capital employed of Ball Limited at 28 February 19x5 was as follows:

| | |
|---|---:|
| Share capital | R10 000 |
| Retained income | 10 000 |
| | 20 000 |
| Shareholders' loan | 120 000 |
| | R140 000 |

In determining the purchase consideration the balance sheet values of all assets were accepted as fairly valued.

The following preliminary trial balances were extracted at 28 February 19x7:

| | BASE LIMITED | | BALL LIMITED | |
|---|---|---|---|---|
| | Dr. | Cr. | Dr. | Cr. |
| Share capital | | R155 000 | | R10 000 |
| Retained income - 1 March 19x6 | | 41 000 | | 19 000 |
| Loan account - Base Limited | | 120 000 | | |
| Plant - at cost | R10 000 | | | |
|     - accumulated depreciation 1 March 19x6 | 4 000 | | | |
| Investment in subsidiary | | | R25 000 | |
| Loan account - Ball Limited | 120 000 | | | |
| Current account - Ball Limited | 21 000 | | | |
| Stock 1 March 19x6 | 45 000 | | 270 000 | |
| Debtors | 10 000 | | 42 000 | |
| Cash at bank | | 17 000 | | |
| Creditors | | 16 000 | | 43 000 |
| Bank overdraft | | 2 000 | | |
| Current account - Base Limited | | | | 12 000 |
| Sales | | 120 000 | | 720 000 |
| Purchases | | 98 000 | | 561 000 |
| Interest payable on loan account | | 12 000 | | |
| Rent | 4 000 | | 15 000 | |
| Advertising | 3 000 | | | |
| Wages and salaries | | 7 000 | | 20 000 |
| Administration fee | 6 000 | | | |
| Interest receivable on loan account | | 12 000 | | |
| | R350 000 | R350 000 | R930 000 | R930 000 |

NOTES:

i)    Depreciation is provided on plant at R1 000 p.a.   No plant was purchased during the year.

ii)   Advertising for the year was R6 000, all paid for by Base Limited but to be borne by the two companies equally.

iii)  Base Limited charged Ball Limited an administration fee of R6 000 for the current year.

iv)   A dividend of R10 000 was declared by Ball Limited on 28 February 19x7 but no entries have yet been passed.

v)    Stock at cost at 28 February 19x7 - Base Limited          R55 000
                                          Ball Limited          R285 000

vi)   Provide for company taxation as follows:  Base Limited    R14 400
                                                Ball Limited    R46 800

<u>YOU ARE REQUIRED TO</u>:

1) Prepare for Base Limited and its subsidiary company the detailed consolidated income statement for the year ended 28 February 19x7.

2) Show how plant would appear in the consolidated balance sheet at 28 February 19x7.

H Ltd purchased all the shares in B Ltd on 1 January 19x2 for R50 000.  The summarised balance sheet of B Ltd at 31 December 19x1 was as follows:

| | |
|---|---|
| Share capital - R1 shares | R1 000 |
| Retained income | 35 000 |
| Loan | 9 000 |
| | R45 000 |
| | ====== |
| | |
| Land and buildings | R20 000 |
| Furniture and fixtures | 10 000 |
| Net current assets | 15 000 |
| | R45 000 |
| | ====== |

At the date of purchase H Ltd considered B Ltd's assets with the exception of land and buildings to be fairly valued.  There was no goodwill.

The following facts are available:

1.    During the year ended 31 December 19x2 B Ltd made a profit of R10 000.

2.    On 5 January 19x2 B Ltd declared and paid a dividend of R10 000.

3.    On 1 September 19x2 B Ltd sold its land and buildings for R35 000.

4.    On 2 September 19x2 B Ltd declared a dividend of R15 000 out of the proceeds of the sale of land and buildings.

5.    On 31 December 19x2 B Ltd declared a dividend of R6 000 which was paid on 10 January 19x3.


<u>YOU ARE REQUIRED TO</u>:

a)    Show how the relevant information would be disclosed in H Ltd's financial statements for the year ended 31 December 19x2.

b)    Prepare the proforma journal entries necessary to consolidate H Ltd and its subsidiary company for the year ended 31 December 19x2.

In January 19x1 Y Limited purchased all the shares in W Limited for R110 000. At that date W Limited's retained income was R20 000. The directors of Y Limited considered that all the tangible assets of W Limited were fairly valued.

The following lists of balances were extracted at 31 December 19x2:

|  | Y LIMITED | W LIMITED |
|---|---|---|
| Bank (debit balances) | R9 000 | R6 000 |
| Creditors | 117 000 | 32 000 |
| Debtors | 102 000 | 48 000 |
| Plant at cost | 90 000 | 50 000 |
| Profit on sale of shares in R Limited | 12 000 | |
| Investment in W Limited | | 103 000 |
| Share capital | 250 000 | 100 000 |
| Stock | 220 000 | 84 000 |
| Trading profit before depreciation and tax | 60 000 | 26 000 |
| Retained income 31 December 19x1 | 79 000 | 16 000 |
| Accumulated depreciation - plant | | |
| at 31 December 19x1 | 18 000 | 20 000 |
| Provisional tax payments | 12 000 | 6 000 |

The following information is available:

1.	Provision for depreciation of plant at the rate of 10% p.a. on a straight line basis has yet to be made. No plant has been purchased or sold by either of the companies since the acquisition of the shares in W Limited by Y Limited.

2.	No entries have been made in respect of the provision for taxation on the profits for the year 19x2 of R15 000 for Y Limited and R6 000 for W Limited.

3.	Each company has declared a dividend of 10c per share to shareholders registered on 31 December 19x2, but no entries have been made in the books.

<u>YOU ARE REQUIRED TO PREPARE</u>:

the consolidated balance sheet of Y Limited and its subsidiary company at 31 December 19x2 and the consolidated income statement for the year ended on that date.

A Ltd purchased all the shares in B Ltd for R120 000 on 1 July 19x3.  At the date the shares were acquired the share capital of B Ltd was R100 000 and its retained income was R8 000.  B Ltd's plant stood in the books at R40 000 and its accumulated depreciation at R10 000.  This plant had been purchased two years previously with an estimated life of 8 years.  When determining the purchase price of the shares A Ltd considered that:

(1)    the plant had a remaining life of 7 years

(2)    since the cost of replacement had increased, the plant was worth more than its net book value

(3)    that all the remaining assets were worth their book values

(4)    that no goodwill attached to the business.


<u>YOU ARE REQUIRED TO</u>:

prepare the proforma journal entries necessary to consolidate A Ltd and its subsidiary company for the year ended 30 June 19x6.

On 1 January 19x1 H Limited purchased all the shares in S Limited for R300 000.

The directors of H Limited accepted that the book values of the tangible assets of S Limited approximated to fair market values on the date the shares were purchased.

The abridged balance sheets of the two companies on 1 January 19x1, before H Limited purchased the shares were as follows:

<u>H LIMITED</u>

<u>BALANCE SHEET AT 1 JANUARY 19X1</u>

| | | |
|---|---|---|
| CAPITAL EMPLOYED | | |
| Share capital - ordinary R1 shares | | R700 000 |
| Retained income | | 350 000 |
| | | 1 050 000 |
| Long term loan | | 180 000 |
| | | R1 230 000 |
| | | ========= |
| | | |
| EMPLOYMENT OF CAPITAL | | |
| Fixed assets | | 650 000 |
| | | |
| Net current assets | | 580 000 |
| Current assets | | |
| | | |
| Stock | R230 000 | |
| Bank | 400 000 | |
| | R630 000 | |
| | ======= | |
| | | |
| Current liabilities | | |
| Accounts payable | R50 000 | |
| | ======= | |
| | | |
| | | R1 230 000 |
| | | ========= |

**I19 CONTINUED**

<u>S LIMITED</u>

<u>BALANCE SHEET AT 1 JANUARY 19X1</u>

```
CAPITAL EMPLOYED
Share capital ordinary R1 shares                        R100 000
Share premium                                             20 000
Non-distributable reserve                                 25 000
Retained income                                           75 000
                                                         220 000
Long term loan                                            90 000
                                                        R310 000
                                                        =======


EMPLOYMENT OF CAPITAL
Fixed assets                                            R240 000

Net current assets                                       70 000
   Current assets
      Stock                           R60 000
      Bank                             30 000
                                      R90 000
                                      ======

   Current liabilities
      Accounts payable                R20 000
                                      ======              R310 000
                                                        =======
```

You are required to prepare the consolidated balance sheet of H Limited and
its subsidiary company at 1 January 19x1.

Operations Limited acquired Premises Limited many years ago when Operations Limited required additional space for its factory operations. At 30 June 19x0 (the date of acquisition) the summarised balance sheet of Premises Limited was as follows.

| | | | |
|---|---|---|---|
| Share capital | R50 000 | Land and buildings | R105 000 |
| Retained income | 30 000 | Current assets | 5 000 |
| | 80 000 | | |
| Long term loan | 20 000 | | |
| Current liabilities | 10 000 | | |
| | R110 000 | | R110 000 |

At 30 June 19x0 the land and buildings were considered to be worth R125 000.

At 31 December 19x8 Premises Limited sold the land and buildings for R175 000 as the manufacturing operations of the group had moved to larger premises. The profit on sale of R70 000 had been transferred to a non-distributable reserve as the company's memorandum of association prohibited the distribution of this type of profit to shareholders by way of dividend. No dividends have been paid by the subsidiary.

At 30 June 19x9 the balance sheet of each company was as follows:-

| | Operations Ltd | Premises Ltd |
|---|---|---|
| CAPITAL EMPLOYED | | |
| SHARE CAPITAL | R2 000 000 | R50 000 |
| NON DISTRIBUTABLE RESERVE | - | 70 000 |
| RETAINED INCOME | 450 000 | 130 000 |
| | 2 450 000 | 250 000 |
| LONG TERM LOAN | 600 000 | 245 000 |
| | R3 050 000 | R495 000 |
| | | |
| EMPLOYMENT OF CAPITAL | | |
| FIXED ASSETS - Land and buildings | - | R500 000 |
| Plant and equipment | R2 500 000 | - |
| INVESTMENT IN SUBSIDIARY | 200 000 | - |
| CURRENT ASSETS | 800 000 | 5 000 |
| Stock | 250 000 | - |
| Debtors | 400 000 | - |
| Bank | 150 000 | 5 000 |
| CURRENT LIABILITIES | 450 000 | 10 000 |
| Creditors | 450 000 | 10 000 |
| NET CURRENT ASSETS (LIABILITIES) | 350 000 | (5 000) |
| | R3 050 000 | R495 000 |

The holding company had advanced Premises Limited R100 000 to finance the purchase of land.

You are required to prepare the consolidated balance sheet of Operations Limited (without notes etc.) at 30 June 19x9.

On 1 January 19x1 H Company bought all the shares in S Company.  In arriving at the purchase price the directors of H Company considered that the book values of the net assets of S Company approximated to fair market values.  The balance sheets of the two companies immediately after the purchase of the shares by H Company were:

|  | H Company | S Company |
|---|---|---|
| Share capital - R1 shares | R2 500 000 | R400 000 |
| Non-distributable reserves | 2 000 000 | 600 000 |
| Distributable reserves | 300 000 | 200 000 |
|  | 4 800 000 | 1 200 000 |
| Long term loans | 500 000 | - |
|  | R5 300 000 | R1 200 000 |
|  |  |  |
| Fixed assets |  |  |
| Cost | R4 800 000 | R1 000 000 |
| Accumulated depreciation | 1 200 000 | 300 000 |
|  | 3 600 000 | 700 000 |
| Investment in S Company | 1 000 000 | - |
| Current assets |  |  |
| Stock | 800 000 | 500 000 |
| Accounts receivable | 300 000 | 200 000 |
| Loan to S Company | 10 000 | - |
| Cash at bank | 300 000 | - |
|  | 1 500 000 | 700 000 |
| Current liabilities |  |  |
| Accounts payable | 800 000 | 100 000 |
| Loan from H Company | - | 10 000 |
| Bank overdraft | - | 90 000 |
|  | 800 000 | 200 000 |
| NET CURRENT ASSETS | 700 000 | 500 000 |
|  | R5 300 000 | R1 200 000 |

<u>YOU ARE REQUIRED TO</u>:

prepare the consoldiated balance sheet of H Company and its subsidiary company at 1 January 19x1.

Gander Limited purchased all the issued share capital of Small Limited on 1 July 19x1 for R34 000 at which date the summarised balance sheet of Small Limited was as follows:

| SHARE CAPITAL | | | | |
|---|---|---|---|---|
| 20 000 ordinary shares of | | Land and buildings, | | |
| R1 each | R20 000 | at cost | | R26 000 |
| 5 000 preference shares of | | Bank | | 10 000 |
| R2 each | 10 000 | | | |

Note: The preference shares are
      redeemable at R2,20 per
      share on or after
      30 June 19x9

| RETAINED INCOME | 6 000 | | | |
|---|---|---|---|---|
| | R36 000 | | | R36 000 |

(a)   On 2 July 19x1 Small Limited declared and paid a dividend on the ordinary shares of R6 000.
(b)   In 19x7 Small Limited sold the fixed property in the above balance sheet at a profit of R10 000.  In the terms of the articles of both companies profits of this nature are not available for distribution to shareholders as dividend.

The following lists of balances at 20 June 19x9 were extracted from the books of the two companies:

|  | Gander Limited | Small Limited |
|---|---|---|
| Retained income | R6 200 | R1 700 |
| Bank (debit) | 8 000 | 5 600 |
| Non-distributable reserve | - | 10 000 |
| Creditors | 4 000 | 100 000 |
| Debtors | - | 6 000 |
| General reserve | 12 000 | 6 000 |
| Goodwill, at cost | 4 000 | - |
| Investment in Small Limited - ordinary shares | 18 000 | - |
| Investment in Small Limited - preference shares | 10 000 | - |
| Land and buildings, at cost | 50 000 | 20 000 |
| Motor vehicles, at cost | 3 000 | 8 400 |
| Plant and equipment, at cost | 75 000 | - |
| Accumulated depreciation - plant and equipment | 21 000 | - |
|                       - motor vehicles | 800 | 2 200 |
| Share capital - ordinary shares of R1 each | 130 000 | 20 000 |
| Share capital - preference shares of R2 each | - | 10 000 |
| Stock | 6 000 | 10 000 |

<u>NOTES</u>:

(1)   On 2 January 19x8 Small Limited became responsible for selling all products manufactured by Gander Limited.  Stocks were transferred to Small Limited at their manufactured cost of R12 000.  All these stocks had been sold by the end of the year.

(2)   Turnover for the year ended 30 June 19x9 was as follows:

|                | |
|----------------|----------|
| Gander Limited | R40 000  |
| Small Limited  | 35 000   |

(3)   On 1 July 19x8 Gander Limited transferred to Small Limited at net book value of R8 400 a number of motor vehicles which had cost R12 000.

All the transactions involved were completed before the close of business on 30 June 19x9.

<u>YOU ARE REQUIRED</u>:

(i)    to show the pro forma journal entries necessary for consolidation.
(ii)   to prepare the consolidated balance sheet at 30 June 19x9.

**SECTION J**

# ELEMENTARY GROUP FINANCIAL STATEMENTS – PARTLY-OWNED

SECTION 1

ELEMENTARY GROUP
FINANCIAL STATEMENTS
– PARTLY-OWNED

**J1**

H Ltd acquired 60% of the shares in S Ltd when the latter's abridged balance
sheet was:

| | | | |
|---|---|---|---|
| Share capital | R400 000 | Plant at cost | R180 000 |
| Retained income | 50 000 | Accumulated depreciation | 20 000 |
| | | | 160 000 |
| | | Other net assets | 290 000 |
| | R450 000 | | R450 000 |

The directors of H Limited valued the assets at their respective book values.

At 31 December 19x9 the trial balances of H Ltd and S Ltd were as follows:

| | H Ltd | S Ltd |
|---|---|---|
| | R000's | R000's |
| Share capital | R1 000 | R400 |
| Retained income 1 January 19x9 | 640 | 220 |
| Creditors | 130 | 100 |
| Accumulated depreciation - plant | 600 | 180 |
| Sales | 2 000 | 800 |
| Dividends received | 30 | - |
| | R4 400 | R1 700 |
| | | |
| Cost of sales | R1 400 | R500 |
| Operating expenses | 300 | 200 |
| Taxation | 120 | 40 |
| Stock | 350 | 190 |
| Debtors | 500 | 110 |
| Bank | 110 | 70 |
| Investment in S Ltd | 320 | - |
| Plant | 1 210 | 540 |
| Dividends paid | 90 | 50 |
| | R4 400 | R1 700 |

During the year S Ltd had sold stock at cost of R25 000 to H Ltd.

<u>YOU ARE REQUIRED TO PREPARE</u>:

(a)   Consolidated balance sheet at 31 December 19x9.
(b)   Consolidated income statement for the year ended 31 December 19x9.

USE A WORK SHEET.

Rhodes Limited bought 75% of the shares in Beit Limited on 2 January 19x5 for R111 000.

At that date the directors of Rhodes Limited considered that all tangible assets other than land and buildings were fairly valued in Beit Limited's balance sheet.  Land and buildings was considered to be worth R50 000.

The following are the balance sheets and income statements of Rhodes Limited and Beit Limited at 31 December 19x5:

<u>BALANCE SHEETS AT 31 DECEMBER 19x5</u>

|  | <u>RHODES LIMITED</u> | <u>BEIT LIMITED</u> |
|---|---|---|
| Share capital (shares of R1 each) | R400 000 | R80 000 |
| Non-distributable reserve | 40 000 | 25 000 |
| Distributable reserves |  |  |
| General reserve | 125 000 | 15 000 |
| Retained income | 81 000 | 49 000 |
|  | R646 000 | R169 000 |
|  | ======= | ======= |
| Fixed assets |  |  |
| Land and buildings (at valuation) | R225 000 | R65 000 |
| Machinery (cost) | 100 000 | 60 000 |
| (accumulated depreciation) | (40 000) | (15 000) |
|  | 60 000 | 45 000 |
| Investment in Beit Limited | 105 000 | - |
| Net current assets | 256 000 | 59 000 |
| Current assets | 410 000 | 100 000 |
| Current liabilities | (154 000) | (41 000) |
|  | R646 000 | R169 000 |
|  | ======= | ======= |

# J2 CONTINUED

<u>INCOME STATEMENTS FOR THE YEAR ENDED 31 DECEMBER 19x5</u>

|  | RHODES LIMITED | BEIT LIMITED |
|---|---|---|
| Turnover | R980 000 | R520 000 |
|  | ======= | ======= |
| Trading profit before depreciation | 185 000 | 118 000 |
| Depreciation of machinery | 11 000 | 6 000 |
|  | 174 000 | 112 000 |
| Dividend received from Beit Limited | 9 000 | - |
|  | 183 000 | 112 000 |
| Taxation | 87 000 | 56 000 |
|  | 96 000 | 56 000 |
| Dividends paid | 40 000 | 20 000 |
|  | 56 000 | 36 000 |
| Transfer to general reserve | 25 000 | - |
| Retained income for the year | 31 000 | 36 000 |
| Retained income at 31 December 19x4 | 50 000 | 13 000 |
| Retained income per balance sheet | R81 000 | R49 000 |
|  | ====== | ====== |

<u>Additional information</u>:

1. Beit Limited neither bought nor sold land and buildings during the year.
   They did, however, revalue the land and buildings during 19x5, to current market values, resulting in a non-distributable reserve of R25 000.
   Rhodes Limited also revalued their land and buildings during the year.

2. Included in the turnover of Rhodes Limited is R100 000 representing sales to Beit Limited during the year. Rhodes Limited does not mark-up these goods when transferring them to Beit Limited.

3. Beit Limited declared and paid two dividends during the year. The first on 2 January 19x5 and the other during December 19x5.


<u>YOU ARE REQUIRED TO</u>:

prepare the consolidated income statement of Rhodes Limited and its subsidiary company for the year ended 31 December 19x5 and the consolidated balance sheet at that date.


<u>USE A WORKSHEET</u>

## J3

On 1 July 19x1 H Limited acquired 40 000 shares in S Limited.

The following balances were extracted from the books of the two companies at 30 June 19x2:

|  | H Limited | S Limited |
|---|---|---|
| Capital, authorised and issued in R1 shares | R100 000 | R50 000 |
| General reserve | 65 000 | - |
| Share premium | - | 20 000 |
| Retained income at 30 June 19x1 | 10 000 | 2 000 |
| Net income for the year | 18 000 | 8 000 |
| Creditors | 10 000 | 2 000 |
| Dividends paid | 3 000 | 2 000 |
| Loan from building society, secured by mortgage over land and buildings and guarantee by H Limited | - | 10 000 |
| Land and buildings, at cost | 25 000 | 15 000 |
| Furniture, at cost less depreciation (cost R6 000 and R5 500) | 5 000 | 5 000 |
| Stock | 70 000 | 45 000 |
| Debtors | 30 000 | 20 000 |
| Investment in S Limited | 57 600 | - |
| Bank | 12 400 | 5 000 |

At 30 June 19x2 S Limited owed H Limited R1 500.

S Limited has written off R200 in respect of depreciation of furniture for the year ended 30 June 19x2.

Prepare a detailed consolidated balance sheet at 30 June 19x2.

**J4**

The following are the trial balances of Ferrari Limited and its subsidiary company Dino Limited at 30 June 19x6:

|                                                              | Ferrari Limited | Dino Limited |
|--------------------------------------------------------------|----------------:|-------------:|
| Share capital (R1 each)                                      |         R50 000 |      R20 000 |
| General reserve                                              |          15 000 |        6 000 |
| Retained income 1 July 19x5                                  |          20 000 |        5 000 |
| Net income for the year before taxation and interest         |          24 720 |        8 000 |
| Accumulated depreciation - motor vehicles - 30 June 19x6     |          10 000 |        7 000 |
| 8% debentures                                                |          15 000 |       10 000 |
| Creditors                                                    |           8 000 |        3 000 |
|                                                              |        R142 720 |      R59 000 |
|                                                              |         ======= |       ====== |
| Land and buildings at cost                                   |         R50 000 |      R21 000 |
| Motor vehicles at cost                                       |          20 000 |       15 000 |
| Investment in Dino Limited at cost (18 000 shares)           |          23 000 |            - |
| Investment in Dino Limited at cost (900 debentures)          |           9 000 |            - |
| Stock                                                        |          22 000 |       17 000 |
| Bank                                                         |           8 520 |        2 200 |
| Interest paid                                                |           1 200 |          800 |
| Provisional tax payments                                     |           9 000 |        3 000 |
|                                                              |        R142 720 |      R59 000 |
|                                                              |         ======= |       ====== |

<u>Additional information</u>

1. Ferrari Limited acquired the investment in Dino Limited on 1 July 19x1 when its retained income (the only distributable reserve at the date of acquisition) amounted to R3 000.
2. There has been no change in the issued share capital of either company since 1 July 19x1.
3. All tangible assets of Dino Limited were considered to be fairly valued at 1 July 19x1.
4. The directors of Ferrari Limited wish to declare a dividend of 10% of its net income for the year to 30 June 19x6. Ferrari Limited takes account of dividends from investments when they are declared.
5. The directors of Dino Limited wish to declare a dividend of 25% of its net income for the year to 30 June 19x6.
6. Taxation for the year is estimated at R9 900 for Ferrari Limited and R3 200 for Dino Limited.
7. Depreciation has been charged at the rate of 25% (straight line) on cost. Both companies have a strict policy of replacing a vehicle after 3 years' use.
8. Turnover for the year for Ferrari Limited and Dino Limited was R100 000 and R35 000 respectively.

<u>YOU ARE REQUIRED TO</u>:

(a) Prepare the consolidated balance sheet for Ferrari Limited and its subsidiary company at 30 June 19x6.

(b) Prepare the consolidated income statement for Ferrari Limited and its subsidiary company for the year ended 30 June 19x6.

### Trial balances at 31 December 19x9

|  | H Limited | S Limited |
|---|---|---|
| Share capital (R1 shares) | R500 000 | R100 000 |
| Share premium | 25 000 | 20 000 |
| General reserve | 40 000 | 15 000 |
| Retained income - 1 January 19x9 | 120 000 | 85 000 |
| 10% debentures | 100 000 | 50 000 |
| Net income before tax | 64 000 | 43 000 |
| Dividends received from S Ltd | 12 000 | - |
| Other dividends received | 9 000 | 4 000 |
| Creditors | 72 000 | 23 000 |
| Receiver of Revenue (creditors) | 6 000 | 4 500 |
| Shareholders for dividends declared | 30 000 | 9 000 |
| Land, at cost | 235 000 | 60 000 |
| Investment in S Ltd, at cost | 160 000 | - |
| Other investments, at cost | 120 000 | 50 000 |
| Dividends receivable from S Ltd (debtor) | 7 200 | - |
| Debtors | 172 800 | 30 000 |
| Bank | 88 000 | 95 500 |
| Stock | 125 000 | 85 000 |
| Dividends declared - final | 30 000 | 9 000 |
| Dividends paid - interim | 15 000 | 6 000 |
| Taxation | 25 000 | 18 000 |
|  | - | - |
|  | ======= | ====== |

### Additional information:

1.  H Ltd acquired 80 000 shares in S Ltd on 1 January 19x7.  With the exception of S Ltd's land, H Ltd considered all the assets of S Ltd to be fairly valued in S Ltd's balance sheet at the date of acquisition.

2.  On 1 January 19x7 S Ltd's capital and reserves were:

| | |
|---|---|
| Share capital | R100 000 |
| Share premium | 20 000 |
| General reserve | 10 000 |
| Retained income | 50 000 |
| | R180 000 |
| | ======= |

3.  Taxation has been accurately estimated.

4.  The following transfers to reserves are to made:

| | |
|---|---|
| H Ltd | R10 000 |
| S Ltd | R6 000 |

Prepare a consolidated income statement for the year ended 31 December 19x9 and a consolidated balance sheet at that date.

# J6

On 1 October 19x2 Green Limited purchased 60% of the shares in Gold Limited for R74 400.  At that date the retained income of Gold Limited was R15 000 and all the tangible assets of Gold Limited were considered to be fairly valued with the exception of plant.  There was no goodwill.  Gold Limited had purchased the plant on 1 October 19x1 for R50 000 and provided depreciation thereon at 10% p.a. using the straight line method. Green Limited agreed with the estimated life of the plant.

The following is an extract from the trial balance of Gold Limited at 30 September 19x5.

| | |
|---|---:|
| Share capital - R1 shares | R100 000 |
| Retained income 1 October 19x4 | 24 000 |
| Net income before tax and depreciation | 30 000 |
| Accumulated depreciation - plant | 20 000 |
| Plant at cost | 50 000 |
| Depreciation - plant | 5 000 |
| Taxation | 10 000 |

Give the proforma consolidation journal entries for the year ended 30 September 19x5.

# J7

The following are the trial balances of H Limited and S Limited at 31 December
19x1:

|  | H Limited | S Limited |
|---|---|---|
| Capital - ordinary | R500 000 | R200 000 |
|       - preference | 100 000 | 50 000 |
| Retained income 1 January 19x1 | 300 000 | 60 000 |
| Operating profit before tax | 200 000 | 170 000 |
| 12% debentures | - | 100 000 |
| Interest received | 3 600 | - |
| Dividends received - ordinary | 32 000 | - |
|       - preference | 2 000 | - |
| Accumulated depreciation | 62 400 | 20 000 |
| | R1 200 000 | R600 000 |
| | ========= | ======= |
| Plant | R362 000 | R200 000 |
| Stock | 190 000 | 140 000 |
| Debtors | 176 000 | 80 000 |
| Cash | 70 000 | 59 000 |
| Investment in S Limited - ordinary shares | 170 000 | - |
|       - preference shares | 20 000 | - |
|       - debentures | 60 000 | - |
| Interest paid | - | 6 000 |
| Depreciation | 24 000 | 10 000 |
| Taxation | 72 000 | 60 000 |
| Dividends paid - ordinary | 50 000 | 40 000 |
|       - preference | 6 000 | 5 000 |
| | R1 200 000 | R600 000 |
| | ========= | ======= |

1.  H Limited acquired 80% of the ordinary share capital and 40% of the
    preference share capital of S Limited on 1 January 19x1.
2.  H Limited subscribed for 60% of the 12% debentures which were issued at
    par on 1 July 19x1.


<u>YOU ARE REQUIRED TO</u>:

Prepare for submission to the directors a consolidated income statement for
the year ended 31 December 19x1 and a consolidated balance sheet at
31 December 19x1.

## J8

Pin Limited  acquired 80% of the issued share capital of Needle Limited for
R16 000 on 31 December 19x6 when Needle Limited's balance sheet was:

| | |
|---|---:|
| Share capital | R10 000 |
| Retained income | 8 000 |
| Long term liability | 5 000 |
| | R23 000 |
| | ====== |

| | | |
|---|---:|---:|
| Plant | R12 000 | |
| Accumulated depreciation | 4 000 | R8 000 |
| Net current assets | | 15 000 |
| | | R23 000 |
| | | ====== |

Needle Limited writes off its plant over 6 years using the straight line
method.  Pin Limited agrees with this method and agrees with the remaining
life of the plant.  Needle Limited's net income after tax for the years ended
31 December 19x7, 19x8 and 19x9 amounted to R6 000, R9 000 and R10 000
respectively.  The net current assets were considered to be fairly valued.

The following dividends were received by Pin Limited Needle Limited:

    R2 400 on 21 December 19x7
    R3 200 on 15 November 19x8
    R4 000 on  3 December 19x9


<u>YOU ARE REQUIRED TO</u>:

(a)   calculate the outside shareholders' interest in Needle Limited at the
      date of acquisition.

(b)   calculate Needle Limited's portion of the consolidated accumulated
      depreciation at 31 December 19x8.

(c)   calculate the outside shareholders' interest in Needle Limited at
      31 December 19x9.

# J9

The following lists of balances were extracted from the books of Alpha Limited and Beta Limited at 31 December 19x6.

|  | Alpha Limited | Beta Limited |
|---|---|---|
| Share capital in R1 shares | R100 000 | R30 000 |
| Retained income - 1 January 19x6 | 55 000 | 6 000 |
| Creditors | 19 000 | 14 800 |
| Net income for the year | 23 000 | 6 000 |
| Accumulated depreciation - furniture | 2 000 | 1 000 |
| Bills payable | - | 17 000 |
|  | R199 000 | R74 800 |
| Land and buildings, at cost | R30 000 | - |
| Furniture, at cost | 5 000 | R3 000 |
| Stock | 70 000 | 45 000 |
| Debtors | 30 000 | 18 000 |
| Bank | 6 700 | 3 700 |
| S.A. normal tax | 10 300 | 2 700 |
| Dividends paid on 31 December 19x6 | 12 000 | 2 400 |
| Shares in Beta Limited (25 000 at cost) | 35 000 | - |
|  | R199 000 | R74 800 |

The shares in Beta Limited were purchased in 19x2 when Beta Limited's retained income was R5 400. When the shares were purchased the tangible assets of Beta Limited were considered to be fairly valued in the books. Furniture appeared in the books at its cost of R2 000 and there was accumulated depreciation of R500. No furniture has since been sold or scrapped by Beta Limited.

Prepare the consolidated income statement and consolidated balance sheet.

# J10

H Limited purchased 75% of the shares in S Limited for R82 500 on 1 October
19x6.  At that date the share capital of S Limited was R80 000 and its
distributable reserves were R17 000.  S Limited's plant stood in the books at
R48 000 cost and there was accumulated depreciation of R12 000.  The plant had
been purchased 2 years previously at which date it had an estimated life of
8 years.  When determining the purchase price of shares H Limited considered
that:

1.      all tangible assets except plant were worth their book values
2.      there was no goodwill
3.      the plant had a remaining life of 7 years
4.      depreciation on plant is provided on the fixed instalment method.


<u>YOU ARE REQUIRED TO</u>:

calculate the accumulated depreciation in respect of this plant as it would
be shown in the consolidated financial statements of H Limited and its
subsidiary at 30 September 19x9.

The following are the trial balances of H Limited and S Limited at 31 December 19x8:

|                                          | H Limited | S Limited |
|------------------------------------------|-----------|-----------|
| Share capital in R1 shares               | R50 000   | R20 000   |
| Share premium                            | -         | 2 000     |
| Retained income 1 January 19x8           | 10 000    | 5 000     |
| Rent received                            | -         | 15 000    |
| Gross profit                             | 60 000    | -         |
| Accumulated depreciation- equipment      | 12 000    | -         |
| Creditors                                | 2 000     | -         |
|                                          | R134 000  | R42 000   |
|                                          | =======   | ======    |
| Land and buildings, at cost              | -         | R34 000   |
| Equipment, at cost                       | R40 000   | -         |
| Investment in S Limited                  | 33 000    | -         |
| Administration expenses                  | 35 000    | 3 000     |
| Selling expenses                         | 3 000     | -         |
| Taxation                                 | 8 800     | 4 800     |
| Stock                                    | 9 000     | -         |
| Debtors                                  | 4 000     | -         |
| Bank                                     | 1 200     | 200       |
|                                          | R134 000  | R42 000   |
|                                          | =======   | ======    |

<u>NOTES</u>

1. On 1 October 19x8 H Limited acquired 16 000 shares in S Limited in order to ensure their tenancy of the building owned by S Limited. The rent payable by H Limited was immediately doubled. H Limited was the only tenant in the building.
2. The administration expenses of S Limited were incurred evenly throughout the year.
3. Included in H Limited's administration expenses is an amount of R4 000 for depreciation on equipment.
4. H Limited marks up its merchandise to realise a gross profit of 25% on turnover.
5. Both companies have recommended a dividend of 10%.
6. Both companies pay tax at the rate of 40c in the R. There are no items in either companies net income before tax, which do not form part of their taxable income.

<u>YOU ARE REQUIRED TO</u>:

draw up the consolidated balance sheet of H Limited and its subsidiary at 31 December 19x8 and a DETAILED consolidated income statement for the year ended on that date.

Notes to the financial statements are not required.

# J12

The following trial balances were extracted from the books of Helvetia Limited and St Moritz Limited at 30 June 19X9 as if there was no connection between the two companies:

|                                         | Helvetia Limited | St Moritz Limited |
|-----------------------------------------|-----------------:|------------------:|
| Share capital                           | R200 000         | R100 000          |
| General reserve                         | 50 000           | -                 |
| Retained income 1 July 19X8             | 12 000           | 10 000            |
| Net income for the year                 | 67 500           | 24 000            |
| Accumulated depreciation - plant        | 14 000           | 18 000            |
|                         - furniture     | 2 500            | 1 000             |
| Loan from Helvetia Limited              | -                | 30 000            |
| Creditors                               | 15 000           | 9 000             |
|                                         | R361 000         | R192 000          |
|                                         | =======          | =======           |
|                                         |                  |                   |
| Land and buildings at cost              | R130 000         | R 80 000          |
| Plant at cost                           | 35 000           | 60 000            |
| Furniture at cost                       | 5 000            | 4 000             |
| Investment in St Moritz Limited         | 105 000          | -                 |
| Loan to St Moritz Limited               | 30 000           | -                 |
| Stock                                   | 18 000           | 13 000            |
| Debtors                                 | 13 000           | 11 000            |
| Bank                                    | 5 000            | 14 000            |
| Dividends paid                          | 20 000           | 10 000            |
|                                         | R361 000         | R192 000          |
|                                         | =======          | =======           |

<u>NOTES</u>

1.  On 1 July 19X8 Helvetia Limited purchased 75% of the shares in St Moritz Limited.  For the purposes of valuing the shares:

    (a)  It was considered that plant was worth 20% <u>less</u> than its book value and had a remaining life of 8 years with no residual value - see note 2.

    (b)  Land and buildings were worth double their book values - see note 5.

    (c)  All other tangable assets were considered to be worth their book values.

2.  St Moritz Limited had purchased its plant on 1 July 19X6 when it was considered that the plant had a life of 10 years and no estimated residual value.

3.  Furniture is depreciated by St Moritz Limited at the rate of R200 p.a. using the straight line method.

4.  No furniture or plant had been sold by either company during the current financial year.

# J12 CONTINUED

5.    St Moritz Limited had purchased the land adjoining its present factory for R50 000 on 1 April 19X9.

6.    It was decided that each company would transfer R10 000 to general reserve.  No entries have been put through in either set of books for these transfers.

<u>YOU ARE REQUIRED TO</u>:

Prepare the consolidated balance sheet of Helvetia Limited and its subsidiary company at 30 June 19X9 and the consolidated income statement for the year ended on that date.

Notes to the financial statements are not required.

# J13

The following lists of balances were extracted from the books of H Limited and
S Limited at 30 June 19x1:

|                                                          | H Limited | S Limited |
|----------------------------------------------------------|-----------|-----------|
| Retained income at 30 June 19x0                          | R10 000   | R2 000    |
| Depreciation - furniture                                 | 200       | 100       |
| Furniture, at cost                                       | 4 000     | 2 500     |
| Goodwill, at cost                                        | 3 000     | -         |
| Profit for the year before charging depreciation or tax  | 14 200    | 4 100     |
| Share capital, authorised and issued in R1 shares        | 50 000    | 10 000    |
| Shares in S Limited, 8 000 at cost                       | 10 000    | -         |
| Stock                                                    | 30 000    | 7 000     |
| Creditors                                                | 5 400     | 3 000     |
| Debtors                                                  | 20 000    | 6 400     |
| Accumulated depreciation - furniture                     | 1 000     | 500       |
| Tax                                                      | 5 600     | 1 600     |
| Bank (debit balances)                                    | 7 800     | 2 000     |

S Limited's trade is not seasonal and turnover was more or less constant
throughout the year.

H Limited acquired the shares in S Limited on 30 September 19x0, at which date
it was considered that the true values of S Limited's  tangible assets
corresponded with their book values.

The directors of both companies recommended a dividend of 10 per cent.

Prepare a detailed consolidated balance sheet at 30 June 19x1 and a detailed
consolidated income statement for the year ended on that date.

# J14

On 1 July 19x7 H Limited acquired 80% of the shares in S Limited.  At that date the retained income of S Limited was R1 000 and all the asset, except land and buildings, were fairly valued in the books of S Limited.

The following are the trial balances at 31 December 19x8 of:

|                                                        | H Limited | S Limited |
|--------------------------------------------------------|----------:|----------:|
| Share capital (R1 shares)                              | R50 000   | R20 000   |
| Retained income - 1 January 19x8                       | 5 000     | 4 000     |
| Gross profit                                           | 60 000    | 30 000    |
| Interest on loan                                       | 1 000     | -         |
| Dividend received                                      | 4 000     | -         |
| Loan from H Limited                                    | -         | 10 000    |
| Accumulated depreciation - furniture & equipment       | 6 000     | 2 000     |
| Bills payable                                          | -         | 3 000     |
| Creditors                                              | 3 000     | 1 000     |
|                                                        | R129 000  | R70 000   |
|                                                        | =======   | ======    |
| Land and buildings, at cost                            | R12 000   | R25 000   |
| Investment in S Limited, at cost                       | 20 000    | -         |
| Furniture and equipment, at cost                       | 10 000    | 5 000     |
| Loan to S Limited                                      | 10 000    | -         |
| Administration expenses                                | 17 000    | 9 500     |
| Selling expenses                                       | 13 000    | 7 000     |
| Interest on loan                                       | -         | 1 000     |
| Depreciation - furniture and equipment                 | 1 000     | 500       |
| Dividends paid                                         | 8 000     | 5 000     |
| Stock                                                  | 7 000     | 6 000     |
| Debtors                                                | 16 000    | 7 000     |
| Bills receivable                                       | 5 000     | -         |
| Provisional tax payments                               | 10 000    | 4 000     |
|                                                        | R129 000  | R70 000   |
|                                                        | =======   | ======    |

## NOTES

1.  H Limited had drawn bills on S Limited for goods sold to them at normal selling prices.  R2 000 of these bills are due in January 19x9.
2.  Both companies write off depreciation on furniture and equipment at the rate of 10% per annum on cost.  S Limited has neither purchased nor sold any furniture and equipment since 19x6.
3.  Taxation for the year ended 31 December 19x8 is:

|            |         |
|------------|---------|
| H Limited  | R12 000 |
| S Limited  | 4 800   |

## YOU ARE REQUIRED TO:

prepare the detailed consolidated financial statements of H Limited and its subsidiary company for management for the year ended 31 December 19x8.

Prior to 1 July 19x1, Tall Limited held no shares in Short Limited, but on that day it subscribed for 40 000 shares of R1 each at a premium of 50c per share.

The following balances were extracted from the books of the two companies at 30 June 19x2:-

|  | Tall Limited | Short Limited |
|---|---|---|
| Share capital, R1 shares | R100 000 | R50 000 |
| General reserve | 65 000 | - |
| Share premium | - | 20 000 |
| Retained income at 30 June 19x1 | 10 000 | 2 000 |
| Net income before tax | 21 600 | 10 200 |
| Creditors | 10 000 | 2 000 |
| Dividends paid | 3 000 | 2 000 |
| Loan secured by mortgage of land and buildings and guaranteed by Tall Limited | - | 10 000 |
| Land and buildings, at cost | 25 000 | 15 000 |
| Furniture, at cost less depreciation (cost R6 000 and R5 500) | 5 000 | 5 000 |
| Stock | 70 000 | 45 000 |
| Debtors | 25 600 | 18 200 |
| Investment in Short Limited | 60 000 | - |
| Bank | 10 000 | 5 000 |
| Taxation | 8 000 | 4 000 |

At the time the shares were subscribed for the directors of Tall Limited considered that the book values of Short Limited's assets fairly represented their true values.

At 30 June 19x2 Short Limited owed Tall Limited R1 500.

Short Limited has written off R200 in respect of depreciation of furniture for the year ended 30 June 19x2.

<u>YOU ARE REQUIRED TO</u>:

prepare the consolidated income statement for the year ended 30 June 19x2 and the consolidated balance of Tall Limited and its subsidiary at that date.

# J16

On 1 January 19x2, A Company Limited bought 6 000 ordinary shares and 4 000 6% preference shares in B Company Limited.

Before agreeing to the prices of the shares, the directors of A Company Limited obtained sworn valuations of the tangible assets of B Company Limited and land and buildings were valued at R5 000 and the remaining tangible assets were valued at their book values.

The preference shares in B Company Limited carry a preferent right to dividends. On winding up they are preferent as to return of capital and arrears of dividend, whether declared or not, but not participate further in any profits.

The following trial balances were extracted from the books of the two companies at 31 December 19x2

|  | A Company Limited |  | B Company Limited |  |
|---|---|---|---|---|
| Share capital, authorised and issued |  |  |  |  |
|   ordinary shares of R1 each | R50 000 |  | R10 000 |  |
|   6% preference share of R1 each | - |  | 5 000 |  |
| General reserve | 25 000 |  | 4 000 |  |
| Retained income - 1 January 19x2 | 5 000 |  | 1 000 |  |
| Net income for the year | 8 240 |  | 6 300 |  |
| Creditors | 3 000 |  | 2 000 |  |
| Preference dividend paid to |  |  |  |  |
|   31 December 19x2 |  |  | R300 |  |
| Land and buildings | R5 000 |  | 1 000 |  |
| Plant, at cost less depreciation |  |  |  |  |
|   (cost R20 000) | 16 500 |  | - |  |
| Furniture, at cost less depreciation |  |  |  |  |
|   (cost R5 000 and R2 000) | 3 500 |  | 1 500 |  |
| Stock | 32 240 |  | 11 000 |  |
| Debtors | 19 000 |  | 9 500 |  |
| Bank |  | 4 000 | 5 000 |  |
| Shares in B Company limited - |  |  |  |  |
|   ordinary shares, at cost | 15 000 |  | - |  |
|   6% preference shares, at cost | 4 000 |  | - |  |
|  | R95 240 | R95 240 | R28 300 | R28 300 |

At 31 December 19x2, B Company Limited owed A Company Limited R1 200 which is included in the figures for debtors and creditors in the above trial balances. B Company Limited has neither purchased nor sold furniture during the year and is depreciating furniture at the rate of 10% per annum on cost.

Prepare a detailed consolidated balance sheet at 31 December 19x2 and a consolidated income statement for the year ended on that date.


(Ignore taxation.)

# J17

The summarised balance sheets at 31 December 19x4  and supporting income statements include the following information:

<u>Balance sheet</u>

|  | X Ltd | P Ltd |  | X Ltd | P Ltd |
|---|---|---|---|---|---|
| Share capital |  |  | Property - cost | R18 500 | R7 000 |
| R1 shares | R40 000 | R8 000 | Machinery - cost | 10 000 | 8 000 |
| Reserves |  |  | Less accumulated |  |  |
| Non-distributable | 17 500 | 5 500 | depreciation | 5 800 | 2 300 |
| Distributable | 10 150 | 4 700 |  | 4 200 | 5 700 |
| X Limited |  | 4 500 |  | 22 700 | 12 700 |
| Creditors | 6 000 | 3 000 | Shares in P Ltd at |  |  |
| Bank |  | 2 500 | net cost | 10 500 |  |
| Proposed dividends | 2 500 | 1 600 | P Ltd | 5 700 |  |
|  |  |  | Stock | 17 000 | 12 000 |
|  |  |  | Debtors | 14 500 | 5 000 |
|  |  |  | Bank and cash | 5 750 | 100 |
|  | R76 150 | R29 800 |  | R76 150 | R29 800 |
|  | ====== | ====== |  | ====== | ====== |

<u>Income statements for the year ended 31 December 19x4</u>

|  | X Ltd | P Ltd |  | X Ltd | P Ltd |
|---|---|---|---|---|---|
| Depreciation of |  |  | Trading profit | R20 000 | R12 000 |
| machinery | R1 800 | R800 | Dividends from  P Ltd | 1 950 |  |
| Profit before |  |  |  |  |  |
| taxation | 20 150 | 11 200 |  |  |  |
|  | R21 950 | R12 000 |  | R21 950 | R12 000 |
|  | ====== | ====== |  | ====== | ====== |
| Taxation | 8 600 | 4 800 | Profit for the year, |  |  |
| Dividend paid | 2 000 | 1 000 | before taxation | 20 150 | 11 200 |
| Dividend proposed | 2 500 | 1 600 | Retained income from |  |  |
| Transfer to non- |  |  | previous year | 8 100 | 2 900 |
| distributable |  |  |  |  |  |
| reserve | 5 000 | 2 000 |  |  |  |
| Retained income | 10 150 | 4 700 |  |  |  |
|  | R28 250 | R14 100 |  | R28 250 | R14 100 |
|  | ====== | ====== |  | ====== | ====== |

1.    X limited bought 75% of the shares in P Limited on 2 January 19x3 for
      R11 100.   At that time the directors of X Limited   conidered that,
      except for property which they valued at R5 000, but which, at that
      date, appeared in the books at R4 000, the net figures at which the
      tangible assets appeared in the balance sheet of P Limited were a true
      reflection of their current values.   On 2 January 19x3 the non-
      distributable reserves of P Limited stood at R1 500 and the
      distributable reserves at R1 300.   On 2 January the machinery stood in
      the books of P Limited as follows:

| | |
|---|---:|
| Cost | R6 000 |
| Accumulated depreciation | 900 |
| Net book value | R5 100 |

2.    P Limited has not sold any fixed assets since 2 January 19x3.


<u>YOU ARE REQUIRED TO</u>:

prepare the consolidated income statements of X Limited and its subsidiary
company for the year ended 31 December 19x4 and the consolidated balance sheet
at that date.

# J18

You are the auditor of Headleys Limited.  At 31 December 19x7 the accountant presents  you with the following financial statements for all of the group companies which were prepared as if there was no connection  between  them. The accountant asks you to assist him in the preparation of the group financial statements.

<u>BALANCE SHEETS AT 31 DECEMBER 19x7</u>

| | HEADLEYS LTD | ALLANDALE (PTY) LTD | BEAVERON (PTY) LTD |
|---|---|---|---|
| <u>CAPITAL EMPLOYED</u> | | | |
| Ordinary share capital | R100 000 | R10 000 | R5 000 |
| Preference share capital | - | 5 000 | - |
| Distributable reserve | | | |
|   Retained income | <u>203 000</u> | <u>46 000</u> | <u>32 000</u> |
| | 303 000 | 61 000 | 37 000 |
| Long term liabilities | | | |
|   Debentures | 40 000 | 15 000 | - |
|   Headleys Ltd - Loan | - | 10 000 | - |
|   Standard Bank Limited - Loan | <u>-</u> | <u>-</u> | <u>15 000</u> |
| | R343 000 | R86 000 | R52 000 |
| | ======= | ====== | ====== |
| <u>EMPLOYMENT OF CAPITAL</u> | | | |
| Fixed assets | | | |
|   Land and buildings - at cost | R150 000 | R50 000 | R40 000 |
|   Plant - at cost less | | | |
|     depreciation | <u>60 000</u> | <u>30 000</u> | <u>10 000</u> |
| | 210 000 | 80 000 | 50 000 |
| Investment in subsidiaries | | | |
|   Allandale (Pty) Ltd | | | |
|     - ordinary shares | 40 000 | - | - |
|     - preference shares | 5 000 | - | - |
|     - debentures | 5 000 | - | - |
|     - loan | 10 000 | - | - |
|   Beaveron (Pty) Ltd | | | |
|     - ordinary shares | 12 000 | - | - |
| Net current assets | <u>61 000</u> | <u>6 000</u> | <u>2 000</u> |
| | R343 000 | R86 000 | R52 000 |
| | ======= | ====== | ====== |

<u>INCOME STATEMENT FOR THE YEAR ENDED 31 DECEMBER 19x7</u>

| | | | |
|---|---:|---:|---:|
| Turnover | R2 000 000 | R400 000 | R250 000 |
| | ========== | ======= | ======= |
| Net income before tax | R162 000 | R66 000 | R45 000 |
| Taxation | 65 000 | 26 000 | 18 000 |
| Net income after tax | 97 000 | 40 000 | 27 000 |
| Dividends paid | | | |
|   - ordinary | 10 000 | 20 000 | 10 000 |
|   - preference | - | 1 000 | - |
| Retained income for the year | 87 000 | 19 000 | 17 000 |
| Retained income at 31 December 19x6 | 116 000 | 27 000 | 15 000 |
| Retained income per balance sheet | R203 000 | R46 000 | R32 000 |
| | ======= | ====== | ====== |

You are able to ascertain the following:

1.    <u>Allandale (Pty) Ltd</u>

    Headleys Limited, owns 100% of the ordinary and preference share capital of Allandale (Pty) Ltd.  These shares were bought on 1 January 19x4 when Allandale (Pty) Ltd's retained income was R15 000.  Land and buildings which had cost R50 000 were considered to be worth R60 000.  Certain items of plant, with a book value of R9 000, were considered to be worth R10 000.  The remaining life of these assets according the management of Allandale (Pty) Ltd was estimated to be 5 years.  The directors of Headleys Limited agreed with this estimate.

2.    <u>Beaveron (Pty) Ltd</u>

    Headleys Limited bought 75% of the shares of Beaveron (Pty) Ltd some years ago when the retained income of Beaveron (Pty) Ltd was R7 000.  All the assets of Beaveron (Pty) Ltd were considered to be fairly valued except for the land and buildings.

<u>YOU ARE REQUIRED TO</u>:

prepare the consolidated income statement for the year ended 31 December 19x7 and the consolidated balance sheet at that date for the group.  Neither a cash flow statement nor notes to the financial statements are required.

## J19

The following trial balances were extracted at 31 December 19x9:

|                                              | H Limited | S Limited |
|----------------------------------------------|-----------|-----------|
| Share capital (R1 shares)                    | R10 000   | R5 000    |
| Retained income - 1 January 19x8             | 12 000    | 4 000     |
| Net income before depreciation               | 3 200     | 8 000     |
| Dividends received                           | 1 000     | -         |
| Accumulated depreciation - furniture         | 2 900     | -         |
|            - plant | -         | 6 000     |
|                                              | R29 100   | R23 000   |
|                                              |           |           |
| Furniture at cost                            | R4 000    | -         |
| Plant at cost                                | -         | R10 000   |
| Depreciation                                 | 200       | 1 000     |
| Investment in S Limited (3 000 shares)       | 6 000     | -         |
| Dividends paid                               | 7 000     | 1 000     |
| Stock                                        | 2 000     | 3 600     |
| Investments (listed)                         | 1 000     | -         |
| Bank                                         | 8 900     | 7 400     |
|                                              | R29 100   | R23 000   |

The shares in S Limited were acquired by H Limited on 1 January 19x6. At that date the retained income of S Limited was R1 000 and plant was the only asset in S Limited's balance sheet which was not considered fairly valued. S Limited had no goodwill.

At the date of acquisition of the shares H Limited considered that the plant had a remaining life of 8 years with no residual value. Both companies use the straight line method of calculating depreciation.

No plant was purchased or sold by S Limited since 1 January 19x6.

Prepare a consolidated balance sheet at 31 December 19x9 and a consolidated income statement for the year ended on that date.

# J20

H Limited holds 90% of the issued share capital of S1 Limited and 60% of the issued share capital of S2 Limited.

H Limited accounts for its subsidiaries using the cost basis of accounting. H Limited acquired its interests in the subsidiary companies when the retained income in S1 Limited was R5 000 and when S2 Limited was floated.

The summarised balances of the companies at 31 December 19x1 were as follows:

| Debits | H Limited | S1 Limited | S2 Limited |
|---|---|---|---|
| Assets | R145 700 | R90 000 | R30 000 |
| Investment in subsidiaries | 54 300 | - | - |
| Dividends paid | 20 000 | - | 2 000 |
|  | R220 000 | R90 000 | R32 000 |

| Credits | H Limited | S1 Limited | S2 Limited |
|---|---|---|---|
| Share capital | R60 000 | R50 000 | R8 000 |
| Retained income at 1 January 19x1 | 25 000 | 30 000 | 2 000 |
| Net income/(loss) for the year | 35 000 | (10 000) | 17 000 |
| Liabilities | 100 000 | 20 000 | 5 000 |
|  | R220 000 | R90 000 | R32 000 |

<u>YOU ARE REQUIRED TO</u>:

(a)  prepare the summarised consolidated balance sheet of H Limited and its subsidiary companies at 31 December 19x1.

(b)  prepare the summarised income statement of H Limited and its subsidiary companies for the year ended 31 December 19x1.

# J21

The following are the trial balances of P Limited, Q Limited and R Limited at 31 December 19x4

|                                                                     | P Ltd      | Q Ltd     | R Ltd     |
|---------------------------------------------------------------------|------------|-----------|-----------|
| Share capital - authorised and issued-                              |            |           |           |
|   ordinary share of R1 each                               | R150 000   | R30 000   | R50 000   |
|   five per cent preference shares                         |            |           |           |
|    of R1 each                                        | -          | -         | 10 000    |
| Loans from P Limited                                                |            | 5 000     | 10 000    |
| Interest on loans                                                   | 750        | -         | -         |
| Rent                                                                | -          | 3 000     | 6 000     |
| Retained income at 1 January 19x4                                   | 6 000      | 3 000     | 6 000     |
| Administration expenses recovered from                              |            |           |           |
|   subsidiary company                                      | 500        | -         | -         |
| Accumulated depreciation - furniture                                | 500        | -         | -         |
| Dividends received from subsidiary company                          | 3 900      | -         | -         |
| Dividends received from other listed                                |            |           |           |
|   investments                                             | 2 350      | -         | -         |
|                                                                     | R164 000   | R41 000   | R82 000   |
| Land and buildings, cost                                            | -          | R38 000   | R75 000   |
| Loans to Q Limited and R Limited                                    | R15 000    |           |           |
| Interest on loans                                                   | -          | 250       | 500       |
| Rent                                                                | 100        | -         | -         |
| Debtors                                                             | 500        | 200       | 100       |
| Property expenses                                                   | -          | 500       | 900       |
| Administration expenses                                             | 1 000      | 300       | 500       |
| Furniture, cost                                                     | 1 000      | -         | -         |
| Depreciation - furniture                                            | 100        | -         | -         |
| Bank                                                                | 1 000      | 750       | 2 000     |
| Shares in Q Limited (27 000), cost                                  | 36 000     | -         | -         |
| Ordinary shares in R Limited (50 000), cost                         | 70 000     | -         | -         |
| Preference shares in R Limited (10 000), cost                       | 10 000     | -         | -         |
| Dividends - preference shares, paid                                 |            |           |           |
|   31 December 19x4                                        | -          | -         | 500       |
| Dividends - ordinary shares, paid                                   |            |           |           |
|   31 December 19x4                                        | 3 000      | 1 000     | 2 500     |
| Other listed investments, cost (market value                        |            |           |           |
|   (R30 000)                                               | 26 300     | -         | -         |
|                                                                     | R164 000   | R41 000   | R82 000   |

The loans to Q Limited and R Limited were made by P Limited on 1 January 19x4.

The ordinary and preference shares in R Limited were acquired on 1 January 19x4.

The shares in Q Limited were acquired on 31 December 19x1 when the retained income of Q Limited was R4 000.

The "other listed investments" are trade investments.

# J21 CONTINUED

R Limited lets two offices in its building to P Limited  at a rental of R100 per annum.

Prepare the detailed consolidated income statement for  the year ended 31 December 19x4 and the consolidated balance sheet at that date of P Limited and its subsidiary companies.

The preference shares are preferent as to capital and dividend but do not participate further in the profits.

Ignore taxation.

## J22

Bennett Limited purchased 75% of the shares in Collins Limited on 1 July 19x7 for R150 000.  At that date all the tangible assets of Collins Limited were considered to be fairly valued.  The following are the trial balances of the two companies at 31 September 19x7:

|  | Bennett Limited | Collins Limited |
|---|---|---|
| Share capital | R400 000 | R80 000 |
| Non-distributable reserve | 150 000 | 10 000 |
| Retained income - 1 October 19x6 | 42 000 | 9 000 |
| Trading profit for the year | 230 000 | 160 000 |
| Rent received from Collins | 24 000 | - |
| Proposed dividends | 40 000 | - |
| Current account - Bennett | - | 8 000 |
| Accumulated depreciation - furniture | 16 000 | 20 000 |
| Creditors | 181 000 | 41 000 |
|  | R1 083 000 | R328 000 |
|  | ========= | ======= |
| Investment in CoLlins Limited | R150 000 | - |
| Land and buildings | 350 000 | - |
| Furniture, at cost | 80 000 | R40 000 |
| Stock | 105 000 | 76 000 |
| Debtors | 107 000 | 51 000 |
| Bank | 77 800 | 43 400 |
| Rent paid | - | 24 000 |
| General expenses | 108 000 | 48 000 |
| Taxation | 55 200 | 33 600 |
| Depreciation - furniture | 8 000 | 4 000 |
| Dividend proposed | 40 000 | 8 000 |
| Current accounts - Collins | 2 000 | - |
|  | R1 083 000 | R328 000 |
|  | ========= | ======= |

Collins Limited occupied the building owned by Bennett Limited for the year at a rental of R2 000 per month.

Collins Limited's profit is not seasonal and is deemed to have been earned evenly throughout the year.

On 30 September 19x7 the directors of each company recommended a dividend of 10%.  The outside shareholders' share of the subsidiary's proposed dividend is included in creditors.

The non-distributable reserve in Collins Limited arose in 19x5.

No fixed assets have been purchased or sold by Collins Limited since 1 July 19x7.

# J22 CONTINUED

<u>YOU ARE REQUIRED TO</u>:

prepare the detailed consolidated income statement of Bennett Limited and its subsidiary for the year ended 30 September 19x7 and the consolidated balance sheet at that date.

Notes to the financial statements are not required.

## J23

Omega Limited purchased 80% of the issued share capital of Citizen Limited on 1 July 19X9.  At that date the directors of Omega Limited considered all tangible assets other than land and buildings to be fairly valued in Citizen Limited's balance sheet.  Land and buildings were considered to be understated by R100 000.

The following are the balance sheets and income statements of Omega Limited and Citizen Limited:

<u>BALANCE SHEETS AT 30 JUNE 19X0</u>

|  | <u>Omega Limited</u> | <u>Citizen Limited</u> |
|---|---|---|
| Share capital | R400 000 | R300 000 |
| Non distributable reserve | 360 000 | 150 000 |
| - revaluation of land and buildings | | |
| Distributable reserves | | |
|   General reserve | 500 000 | 250 000 |
|   Retained income | 904 000 | 490 000 |
| Long-term liabilities | 486 000 | 470 000 |
| | R2 650 000 | R1 660 000 |
| | ========= | ========= |
| Fixed assets | | |
|   Land and buildings | R920 000 | R850 000 |
|   Plant and machinery | 550 000 | 380 000 |
|     Cost | 850 000 | 560 000 |
|     Accumulated depreciation | 300 000 | 180 000 |
|   Furniture and fittings | - | 90 000 |
|     Cost | - | 150 000 |
|     Accumulated depreciation | - | 60 000 |
| Investment in Citizen Limited | 788 000 | - |
| Net current assets | 392 000 | 340 000 |
|   Current assets | 620 000 | 495 000 |
|   Current liabilities | 228 000 | 155 000 |
| | R2 650 000 | R1 660 000 |
| | ========= | ========= |

<u>INCOME STATEMENTS FOR THE YEAR</u>
<u>ENDED 30 JUNE 19X0</u>

|                                          | Omega Limited | Citizen Limited |
|------------------------------------------|--------------:|----------------:|
| Turnover                                 | R2 260 000    | R1 280 000      |
|                                          | =========     | =========       |
| Operation profit                         | R760 000      | R568 000        |
| Depreciation                             |               |                 |
|   plant                        | 128 000       | 80 000          |
|   furniture                    | -             | 18 000          |
|                                          | 632 000       | 470 000         |
| Dividends received from Citizen Limited  | 24 000        | -               |
| Net income before taxation               | 656 000       | 470 000         |
| Taxation                                 | 304 000       | 235 000         |
| Net income after taxation                | 352 000       | 235 000         |
| Dividends paid                           | 60 000        | 45 000          |
|                                          | 292 000       | 190 000         |
| Transfer to general reserve              | 60 000        | 50 000          |
| Retained income for the year             | 232 000       | 140 000         |
| Retained income at beginning of year     | 672 000       | 350 000         |
| Retained income per balance sheet        | R904 000      | R490 000        |
|                                          | =======       | =======         |

<u>ADDITIONAL INFORMATION:</u>

1.    Citizen Limited revalued land and buildings to current values in May 19X0 resulting in a non-distributable reserve of R150 000. Citizen Limited has neither bought nor sold any land and buildings since 1 July 19X9.

2.    Citizen Limited declared and paid two dividends during the year - the interim divident of R15 000 on 5 July 19X9 and a final dividend on 29 June 19X0.

3.    It is the policy of Omega Limited to reduce its investments in subsidiaries by the amount of dividends received out of the acquisition profits.

4.    Omega Limited wishes to write off any goodwill on the acquisition of subsidiaries over a period of four years.

<u>YOU ARE REQUIRED:</u>

To prepare the consolidated balance sheet at 30 June 19X0 and consolidated income statement of Omega Limited and its subsidiary company for the year ended on this date. (Notes to the financial statements are not required).

# J23 CONTINUED

<u>WORKSHEET</u>

| | Omega<br>Limited | Citizen<br>Limited | Consolidated<br>Adjustments<br>Dr    Cr | Consolidated<br>Balances |
|---|---|---|---|---|
| Share capital | 400 000 | 300 000 | | |
| Non-distributable reserve | 360 000 | 150 000 | | |
| General reserve | 500 000 | 250 000 | | |
| Retained income | 904 000 | 490 000 | | |
| Long-term liabilities | 486 000 | 470 000 | | |
| | <u>R2 650 000</u><br>========= | <u>R1 660 000</u><br>========= | | |
| Fixed assets | | | | |
|   Land and buildings | 920 000 | 850 000 | | |
|   Plant + machinery | <u>550 000</u> | <u>380 000</u> | | |
|     Cost | 850 000 | 560 000 | | |
|     Acc. Depreciation | <u>300 000</u> | <u>180 000</u> | | |
|   Furniture + fittings | | <u>90 000</u> | | |
|     Cost | | 150 000 | | |
|     Acc. Depreciation | | <u>60 000</u> | | |
| Investment in Citizen Ltd | 788 000 | - | | |
| Net current assets | <u>392 000</u> | <u>340 000</u> | | |
|   Current assets | 620 000 | 495 000 | | |
|   Current liabilities | <u>228 000</u> | <u>155 000</u> | | |

should this be deleted

| | | |
|---|---|---|
| <u>R2 650 000</u><br>========= | <u>R1 660 000</u><br>========= | |

# J24

Galaxy Limited purchased 80% of the shares in Mars Limited on 1 July 19X0 for R240 000. At that date all the tangible assets of Mars Limited were considered to be fairly valued. The following are the trial balances of the two companies at 30 September 19X0:

| | Galaxy Limited | Mars Limited |
|---|---|---|
| Share capital (in R1 shares) | R800 000 | R160 000 |
| Non-distributable reserve - 1 October 19X9 | 300 000 | 20 000 |
| Retained income - 1 October 19X9 | 84 000 | 18 000 |
| Trading profit for the year | 460 000 | 320 000 |
| Rent received from Mars Limited | 48 000 | - |
| Proposed dividend | 80 000 | 4 000 |
| Current account - Galaxy Limited | - | 20 000 |
| Accumulated depreciation - furniture | 32 000 | 40 000 |
| Creditors | 302 000 | 78 000 |
| | R2 106 000 | R660 000 |
| | ========= | ======= |
| Investment in Mars Limited | R240 000 | - |
| Land and buildings | 700 000 | - |
| Furniture at cost | 160 000 | R80 000 |
| Stock | 210 000 | 152 000 |
| Debtors | 214 000 | 102 000 |
| Bank | 150 000 | 82 000 |
| Rent paid | - | 48 000 |
| General expenses | 220 000 | 104 000 |
| Taxation | 112 000 | 64 000 |
| Depreciation - furniture | 16 000 | 8 000 |
| Dividend proposed | 80 000 | 20 000 |
| Current account - Mars Limited | 4 000 | - |
| | R2 106 000 | R660 000 |
| | ========= | ======= |

Mars Limited had occupied the building owned by Galaxy Limited at a rental of R4 000 per month from 1 October 19X9.

Mars Limited's profit is not seasonal and is deemed to have been earned evenly throughout the year.

On 30 September 19X0 the directors of each company recommended a dividend of R80 000 for Galaxy Limited and R20 000 for Mars Limited. Galaxy Limited had not accounted for the dividend to be received from Mars Limited.

<u>YOU ARE REQUIRED TO PREPARE</u>:

The detailed consolidated income statement of Galaxy Limited and its subsidiary company for the year ended 30 September 19X0 and the consolidated balance sheet at that date.

Notes to the financial statements are not required.

# J25

The following are the trial balances of Poland Limited and its subsidiary company Warsaw Limited at 31 August 19x1, drawn up as if there was no relationship between the two companies.

|  | Poland Limited | Warsaw Limited |
|---|---|---|
| Ordinary share capital (R1 shares) | R150 000 | R100 000 |
| 12% preference share capital (R1 shares) | - | 50 000 |
| General reserve | 35 000 | 10 000 |
| Retained income - 1 September 19x0 | 40 000 | 24 000 |
| Operating income for year | 57 300 | 31 000 |
| Interest received | 3 600 | 4 200 |
| Preference dividend received | 1 200 | - |
| 9% loan from Poland Limited | - | 40 000 |
| 14% debentures of R100 each | 45 000 | - |
| Creditors | 8 900 | 3 800 |
| Proposed dividends - ordinary | 15 000 | 6 000 |
| Shareholders for dividends - preference | - | 3 000 |
|  | R356 000 | R272 000 |
|  | ======= | ======= |
| Land and buildings | R129 000 | R199 000 |
| Shares in Warsaw Limited |  |  |
|   75 000 ordinary | 105 000 | - |
|   20 000 preference | 20 000 | - |
| 9% loan to Warsaw Limited | 40 000 | - |
| 300 debentures in Poland Limited | - | 30 000 |
| Bank | 19 600 | 16 000 |
| Interest paid - debentures | 6 300 | - |
|              - loan Poland Limited | - | 3 600 |
| Taxation | 21 100 | 11 400 |
| Dividends - preference - paid | - | 3 000 |
|          - preference - declared | - | 3 000 |
|          - ordinary - proposed | 15 000 | 6 000 |
|  | R356 000 | R272 000 |
|  | ======= | ======= |

<u>ADDITIONAL NOTES</u>

1.    Poland Limited purchased its ordinary shares in Warsaw Limited, a property company, on 1 September 19w4 when the general reserve was R4 000 and the retained income was R16 000.

2.    Poland Limited purchased its preference shares in Warsaw Limited on 1 September 19w7. The preference dividend has never been in arrear.

3.    Warsaw Limited has not sold any land and buildings since its shares were acquired by Poland Limited. It purchased the debentures in Poland Limited on 1 September 19w9.

# J25 CONTINUED

4.  Both companies proposed their respective ordinary dividends on 31 August 19x1.  Poland Limited has not responded to either the proposed ordinary dividend of Warsaw Limited or its declared preference dividend.


<u>YOU ARE REQUIRED TO PREPARE</u>:

the <u>detailed</u> consolidated income statement of Poland Limited and its subsidiary company for the year ended 31 August 19x1 and the consolidated balance sheet at that date.

Notes to the consolidated financial statements are NOT required.

The following are the trial balances of Impressionists Limited, Monet Limited and Renoir Limited at 30 November 19x7:

|  | Impressionists Limited | Monet Limited | Renoir Limited |
|---|---|---|---|
| Share capital (in R1 shares) | R200 000 | R50 000 | R25 000 |
| Retained income | 80 000 | 15 000 | - |
| Net income before tax | 128 000 | 60 000 | - |
| Provision for loss in subsidiary - 30 November 19x7 | 19 000 | - | - |
| Accumulated depreciation - plant | 45 000 | 20 000 | - |
|  | R472 000 | R145 000 | R25 000 |
|  | ======= | ======= | ====== |
| Plant | R150 000 | R50 000 | - |
| Investment in Monet Limited | 52 000 | - | - |
| Investment in Renoir Limited | 28 000 | - | - |
| Net current assets | 140 000 | 61 000 | 9 000 |
| Taxation | 48 000 | 24 000 | - |
| Dividend paid | 50 000 | 10 000 | - |
| Transfer to provision for loss in subsidiary | 4 000 | - | - |
| Accumulated loss - 1 December 19x6 | - | - | 12 000 |
| Net loss for year | - | - | 4 000 |
|  | R472 000 | R145 000 | R25 000 |
|  | ======= | ======= | ====== |

<u>Notes</u>

1)   On 1 December 19x4 Impressionists Limited purchased 80% of the shares in Monet Limited.  At that date the retained income of Monet Limited was R6 000.  All the tangible assets of Monet Limited were considered to be fairly valued except for plant which was considered to be worth R9 000 more than its book value.  Monet Limited had been providing depreciation on plant at 10% p.a. using the straight line method.  The directors of Impressionists Limited agreed with the estimated life of the plant.  Monet Limited has neither purchased nor sold any plant since 1 December 19x4.

2)   On 1 December 19x3 Impressionist Limited purchased all the shares in Renoir Limited when the retained income of Renoir Limited was R3 000.

3)   The turnover of the three companies for year ended 30 November 19x7 was as follows:

        Impressionists Limited  R650 000
        Monet Limited            300 000
        Renoir Limited            20 000

     Included in  Impressionists Limited's  turnover  figure are sales of R70 000 made to Monet Limited at cost.

# J26 CONTINUED

<u>YOU ARE REQUIRED TO PREPARE</u>:

the consolidated income statement of Impressionists Limited and its subsidiaries for the year ended 30 November 19x7 and the consolidated balance sheet at that date.

Notes to the consolidated financial statements are NOT required.

At 31 December 19x1 you are presented with the following financial statements
of Meyer Limited and Tulu Limited.

<u>BALANCE SHEETS AT 31 DECEMBER 19x1</u>

| | Note | Meyer Limited | Tulu Limited |
|---|---|---|---|
| **CAPITAL EMPLOYED** | | | |
| Ordinary share capital | | R200 000 | R200 000 |
| Non-distributable reserves | 1 | 470 000 | 400 000 |
| Distributable reserves | 2 | 1 108 000 | 830 000 |
| Ordinary shareholders' interest | | 1 778 000 | 1 430 000 |
| Preference share capital | | 100 000 | 100 000 |
| | | 1 878 000 | 1 530 000 |
| Long term liabilities | 3 | 400 000 | 300 000 |
| | | R2 278 000 | R1 830 000 |
| | | | |
| **EMPLOYMENT OF CAPITAL** | | | |
| Fixed assets | 4 | R1 310 000 | R1 450 000 |
| Investment in subsidiary | | 550 000 | |
| Loan - Tulu Limited | | 150 000 | |
| Current Assets | | 483 000 | 610 000 |
| Stock | | 250 000 | 300 000 |
| Debtors | | 175 000 | 225 000 |
| Bank | | 58 000 | 85 000 |
| Current liabilities | | 215 000 | 230 000 |
| Creditors | | 205 000 | 220 000 |
| Dividend proposed | | 10 000 | 10 000 |
| | | R2 278 000 | R1 830 000 |

# J27 CONTINUED

<u>INCOME STATEMENTS FOR THE YEAR ENDED 31 DECEMBER 19x1</u>

|  | Note | Meyer Limited | Tulu Limited |
|---|---|---|---|
| Turnover | | R2 500 000 | R1 800 000 |
| | | ========= | ========= |
| Net operating income | | R451 000 | R366 000 |
| Interest paid | | | 36 000 |
| | | 451 000 | 330 000 |
| Other income | 5 | 17 000 | - |
| Net income before tax | | 468 000 | 330 000 |
| Taxation | | 230 000 | 165 000 |
| Net income after tax | | 238 000 | 165 000 |
| Preference dividend | | 10 000 | 10 000 |
| Net income attributable to ordinary shareholders | | 228 000 | 155 000 |
| Transfer to general reserve | | 60 000 | 40 000 |
| Ordinary dividends | | 30 000 | 20 000 |
| Paid | | 20 000 | 10 000 |
| Proposed | | 10 000 | 10 000 |
| Retained income for year | | 138 000 | 95 000 |
| Retained income at 31 December 19x0 | | 610 000 | 600 000 |
| Retained income per balance sheet | | R748 000 | R695 000 |
| | | ========= | ========= |

<u>NOTES TO THE FINANCIAL STATEMENTS</u>

|  | Meyer Limited | Tulu Limited |
|---|---|---|
| 1.   <u>Non-distributable reserves</u> | | |
|     Revaluation of land and buildings | R330 000 | R275 000 |
|     Capital redemption reserve fund | 140 000 | 125 000 |
| | R470 000 | R400 000 |
| | ======= | ======= |
| 2.   <u>Distributable reserves</u> | | |
|     Retained income | R748 000 | R695 000 |
|     General reserve | 360 000 | 135 000 |
| | R1 108 000 | R830 000 |
| | ========= | ======= |
| 3.   <u>Long term liabilities</u> | | |
|     Unsecured loan - Spanish Loan Company | | |
|     Repayable on 31 December 19x8 | | |
|     Interest rate 18% p.a. | R400 000 | |
|     Unsecured loan - Barcelona Bank | | |
|     Repayable 31 December 19x7 | | |
|     Interest rate 18% p.a. | | R150 000 |
|     Unsecured loan - Meyer Limited | | |
|     Interest rate 6% p.a. | | 150 000 |
| | R400 000 | R300 000 |
| | ======= | ======= |

# J27 CONTINUED

4.  <u>Fixed assets</u>

| | Valuation | Cost | Accumulated depreciation | Book value |
|---|---|---|---|---|
| **Meyer Limited** | | | | |
| Land and buildings | R800 000 | | - | R800 000 |
| Plant and equipment | | R780 000 | R270 000 | 510 000 |
| | R800 000 | R780 000 | R270 000 | R1 310 000 |
| **Tulu Limited** | | | | |
| Land and buildings | R950 000 | | | R950 000 |
| Plant and equipment | | R700 000 | R200 000 | 500 000 |
| | R950 000 | R700 000 | R200 000 | R1 450 000 |

5.  <u>Other income</u>

| | Meyer Limited |
|---|---|
| Interest - Tulu Limited | R9 000 |
| Dividends received | 8 000 |
| | R17 000 |

<u>ADDITIONAL INFORMATION</u>

1.  On 1 January 19x0 Meyer Limited purchased 80% of Tulu Limited's shares for R550 000.  At the acquisition date Tulu Limited's reserves consisted of

    | | |
    |---|---|
    | Capital redemption reserve fund | R125 000 |
    | General reserve | 50 000 |
    | Retained income | 250 000 |

    The tangible assets, with the exception of land and buildings, were considered to be fairly valued.

2.  During 19x1 Tulu Limited revalued its land and buildings by R275 000. This amount was credited to a non-distributable reserve.

3.  Meyer Limited holds no preference shares in Tulu Limited.

4.  Tulu Limited has not purchased any plant and equipment since 1 January 19x0, and depreciates plant and equipment at 10% p.a. on cost.

5.  Meyer Limited has not accounted for the dividend proposed by Tulu Limited.

<u>YOU ARE REQUIRED TO:</u>

prepare the consolidated income statement of Meyer Limited and its subsidiary for the year ended 31 December 19x1 and the consolidated balance sheet at that date.

NOTES TO THE FINANCIAL STATEMENTS ARE NOT REQUIRED

Spegash Limited purchased 80% of the shares in Montani Limited on 1 July 19x8 when Montani Limited's retained income had a debit balance of R20 000.

The following are the trial balances of Spegash Limited and Montani Limited at 30 June 19x2.

| | SPEGASH LIMITED | | MONTANI LIMITED | |
|---|---|---|---|---|
| | Debit | Credit | Debit | Credit |
| Share capital (R1 shares) | | R280 000 | | R160 000 |
| Retained income 1/7/19x1 | | 220 000 | | 96 000 |
| General reserve | | 60 000 | | |
| Loan - Spegash Limited | | | | 4 800 |
| Investment in Montani Limited | R166 400 | | | |
| Land and buildings at cost | 240 000 | | R140 000 | |
| Plant at cost | 300 000 | | 120 000 | |
| Accumulated depreciation - plant | | 124 000 | | 84 000 |
| Stock | 60 000 | | 84 000 | |
| Debtors | 93 600 | | 68 800 | |
| Loan - Montani Limited | 4 800 | | | |
| Bank | 18 000 | | 89 600 | |
| Creditors | | 116 000 | | 72 800 |
| Net income before tax | | 171 200 | | 65 600 |
| Profit on sale of land | | | | 60 000 |
| Dividend paid | 20 000 | | 14 400 | |
| Taxation | 68 400 | | 26 400 | |
| | R971 200 | R971 200 | R543 200 | R543 200 |

Additional information

1. On 1 July 19w8 when Spegash Limited bought the shares in Montani Limited, land and buildings were valued at R40 000 above the original cost to Montani Limited.  Plant was valued at R28 000 more than book value at the date of purchase, Spegash Limited agreed with Montani Limited's estimate of the remaining useful life of the plant.  All the other assets and liabilities were considered to be fairly valued.

2. No adjustments were made in the books of Montani Limited in respect of the revaluations of land and buildings or plant.

3. In January 19x2 Montani Limited sold half the land and buildings.  No other purchases or sales of land and buildings had taken place.

4. Montani Limited has neither purchased nor sold plant since it originally purchased the plant for R120 000.

5. Depreciation is provided by Montani Limited at 10% p.a. on cost.

6. Montani Limited's articles prohibit the declaration of a dividend out of the profits on the sale of land.

<u>YOU ARE REQUIRED TO:</u>

prepare the consolidated income statement of Spegash Limited and its subsidiary for the year ended 30 June 19x2 and the consolidated balance sheet at that date.

**Notes to the financial statements are not required.**

# SECTION K

# COMPANY ACCOUNTING – REDEMPTION OF PREFERENCE SHARES

SECTION K

COMPANY ACCOUNTING –
REDEMPTION OF
PREFERENCE SHARES

# K1

The Johannesburg Investment Company Limited has an authorised and issued share capital of:

> 10 000 redeemable six per cent cumulative preference shares of R2 each
> 40 000 ordinary shares of R1 each.

The redeemable preference shares may be redeemed at a premium of 25c per share at any time before 30 June 19x9.

On 31 March 19x5 there is a credit balance on retained income of R30 000 and it is decided to redeem the shares out of profits.

GIVE the relevant portions of the financial statements before and after the shares are redeemed and the entries (in the form of journal entries) which it would be necessary to pass.

# K2

A Limited makes an issue of R100 000 in 6% preference shares of R1 each, redeemable in 10 years at a premium of 5%.   On the expiry of the 10 years, the company decides to redeem 40 000 shares out of its then current funds and the remainder out of the proceeds of an issue at par of 60 000 R1 5% preference shares made for the purpose.   It further decides to issue as a free bonus to the ordinary shareholders 40 000 ordinary shares of R1 each at par in place of the preference shares redeemed out of current funds.

DRAFT in journal form the entries to give effect to the above transactions.

# K3

The following is an extract from the draft balance sheet of Portulacca Limited
at 30 November 19x8 :-

<u>Share capital</u>
  <u>Authorised</u>

| | |
|---|---:|
| 650 000 ordinary shares of R1 each | R650 000 |
| 250 000 6% redeemable preference shares of R1 each | 250 000 |
| | ======= |

  <u>Issued and fully paid</u>

| | |
|---|---:|
| 450 000 ordinary shares of R1 each | R450 000 |
| 100 000 6% redeemable preference shares of R1 each | 100 000 |
| | R550 000 |
| | ======= |

NOTE: The preference shares are redeemable not later than 31 December 19x8 at
a premium of 10 cents per share.

<u>Share premium</u>       R100 000
         =======

<u>Distributable reserves</u>

| | |
|---|---:|
| General reserve | R400 000 |
| Retained income | 25 000 |
| | R425 000 |
| | ====== |

The directors of Portulacca Limited have arranged to redeem the preference
shares on 31 December 19x8 its year end in accordance with  the provisions of
the Company Act 1973, as follows:-

a)    out of the proceeds of the issue on 15 December 19x8 of 6 000 5%
debentures of R10 each at par.

b)    out of the proceeds of the issue on 20 December 19x8 to existing
shareholders of 40 000 ordinary shares of R1 each at par.

The directors wish to maintain the distributable reserves at the  maximum
possible amount.

The annual preference share dividend was paid on 23 December 19x8.


<u>YOU ARE REQUIRED TO</u>:

give the journal entries relating to the redemption of the preference shares
and the issue of the new shares and debentures.  Cash transactions should be
journalised.

# K4

The following is an extract from the financial statements of Invention Limited at 30 June 19x5:-

SHARE CAPITAL
Authorised

|  |  |
|---|---:|
| 40 000 ordinary shares of R1 each | R40 000 |
| 10 000 six per cent redeemable preference shares of R1 each | 10 000 |
| 10 000 unclassified shares of R1 each | 10 000 |
|  | R60 000 |

Issued

|  |  |
|---|---:|
| 40 000 ordinary shares of R1 each, 75c paid | R30 000 |
| 10 000 six per cent redeemable preference shares of R1 each, fully paid | 10 000 |
|  | R40 000 |

> (Redeemable at any time at the option of the company, after 1 January 19x5 at R1,05 per share)

| SHARE PREMIUM | R 2 500 |
|---|---:|

| NON-DISTRIBUTABLE RESERVE | R10 000 |
|---|---:|

Capital redemption reserve

DISTRIBUTABLE RESERVES

|  |  |
|---|---:|
| General reserve | R10 000 |
| Retained income | 10 000 |
|  | R20 000 |

Preliminary expenses not yet written off amount to R2 000 and there are ample cash resources. The directors ask you whether it will be in order for them to:

(1)  write off the preliminary expenses.

(2)  redeem the 10 000 six  per cent redeemable preference shares otherwise than out of a fresh issue of shares.

(3)  utilise any profit that may be available for the purpose of making the ordinary shares fully paid up.

(4)  issue, as fully paid, 20 000 ordinary shares as a bonus to the ordinary shareholders.

State what advice you would give the directors and give the entries (in the form of journal entries) for the transactions which would result from your advice being accepted.  The narrations must indicate what authority is necessary for each transaction.

# K5

The following is extracted from the financial statements of Finance Limited at 30 June 19x5:

SHARE CAPITAL

Authorised

| | |
|---|---:|
| 100 000 ordinary shares of R1 each | R100 000 |
| 50 000 6% redeemable preference shares of R1 each | 50 000 |
| | ======= |

Issued

| | |
|---|---:|
| 60 000 ordinary shares of R1 each, fully paid | R60 000 |
| 10 000 ordinary shares of R1 each, 50c paid | 5 000 |
| 20 000 redeemable preference shares of R1 each, fully paid | 20 000 |
| | R85 000 |
| | ====== |

(Redeemable by the company at any time before 30 June 19x7 at R1,05 per share)

SHARE PREMIUM ........................................... R30 000

NON-DISTRIBUTABLE RESERVE

Capital redemption reserve ............................. R20 000

DISTRIBUTABLE RESERVES

| | |
|---|---:|
| General reserve | R17 000 |
| Retained income | 30 000 |
| | R47 000 |
| | ====== |

Goodwill stands in the books at R6 000 and share issue expenses at R1 000.

The directors wish to:

(1)  write off goodwill
(2)  write off share issue expenses
(3)  redeem the 20 000 6% redeemable preference shares
(4)  issue 10 000 fully paid ordinary shares to the members as bonus shares
(5)  have the unpaid portion of the 10 000 partly paid ordinary shares paid up.


YOU ARE REQUIRED TO:

to advise them on the best way of achieving the above so that the maximum amount remains to the credit of distributable reserves.

<u>STEELDALE LIMITED</u>

<u>EXTRACTS FROM DETAILED MONTHLY BALANCE SHEET AT 30 SEPTEMBER 19X0</u>

| | |
|---|---:|
| Stated capital account - 399 500 ordinary shares | R799 000 |
| 10% redeemable preference shares | 300 000 |
| Share premium | 10 000 |
| Retained income at 30 September 19x0 | 500 000 |
| | |
| Debentures in Black Mac Limited | 150 000 |
| Preference share issue expenses | 1 500 |

<u>ADDITIONAL INFORMATION:</u>

1. The company's authorised share capital comprises 500 000 ordinary shares of no par value and 50 000 preference shares of R10 each.
2. The directors have given notice to the preference shareholders that the preference shares will be redeemed at a premium of 5% on 1 October 19x0.
3. Dividends on these preference shares have been paid regularly on 30 June and 31 December each year.
4. The redemption is to be financed partly from the proceeds of a fresh issue of 100 500 shares on no par value at the lowest price possible without the need for passing a special resolution. The balance of the funds will be made available from the redemption at par of debentures Steeldale Limited holds in Black Mac Limited.
5. The share issue is to be underwritten and administered by Bartrust Merchant Bank for an all inclusive 1% commission to be settled half in cash and half by issue, as fully paid, of shares of no par value.
6. Issue expenses incurred by Bartrust Merchant Bank amounted to R1 500.
7. Bartrust Merchant Bank received applications for 70 000 shares from the public and applied for 10 000 shares in its own name.
8. The directors wish to write off all share issue expenses in such a way as to maintain distributable reserves at a maximum amount.


<u>YOU ARE REQUIRED TO</u>:

(a) journalise all the above transactions (including cash transactions) in the books of  STEELDALE LIMITED.

(b) show how the detailed shareholders' funds in the balance sheet of STEELDALE LIMITED would appear after the redemption of the preference shares and related transactions.

# K7

The following data was extracted from the balance sheet at 30 June 19x8 of Lawnmowers Limited:

<u>Share capital</u>
  <u>Authorised</u>

| | |
|---|---:|
| 1 000 000 ordinary shares of R1 each | R1 000 000 |
| 200 000 8% redeemable preference shares of R1 each | 200 000 |
| | 1 200 000 |
| | ========= |

  <u>Issued</u>

| | |
|---|---:|
| 800 000 ordinary shares of R1 each | 800 000 |
| 100 000 8% redeemable preference shares of R1 each | 100 000 |

| | | |
|---|---|---:|
| Share premium | | 80 000 |
| Capital redemption reserve | | 40 000 |
| Surplus on revaluation of land and buildings | | 100 000 |
| General reserve | | 200 000 |
| Retained income | (Cr.) | 50 000 |
| Dividend equalisation fund | | 40 000 |

The preference shares are redeemable at the option of the company, after 1 August 19x7, at a premium of 10 cents per share.

On 15 August 19x8 the redemption of 100 000 preference shares is to be arranged as follows:

    (i)   from the proceeds of the issue of 40 000 ordinary shares at R1,70 each.

    (ii)  from the proceeds of the issue of R100 000 10% debentures at par.

The above transactions were completed by 31 October 19x8. The directors decided to issue, on 15 November 19x8, as fully paid bonus shares, to all existing shareholders, one share for every eight shares held.

<u>Note</u>:

The preference dividends were paid up to date of redemption.

Share and debenture issue expenses of R6 000 were incurred. These are to be written off immediately. The directors wish to maintain the distributable reserves at the maximum possible amount.

<u>YOU ARE REQUIRED TO</u>:

Show the balances on the relevant accounts mentioned above on 31 December 19x8

after all the above transactions have been carried out. (Ignore the cashbook balances).

**K8**

On 28 February 19x5 RFK Limited had, inter alia, the following balances in its
accounting records:

|  | R |
| --- | --- |
| Ordinary share capital (shares of R1,00 each) | 400 000 |
| 12% redeemable preference share capital<br>  (shares of R2 each) | 150 000 |
| Share premium | 480 000 |
| Retained income | 215 000 |
| Bank overdraft | 30 000 |

Additional information:

(1)    The redeemable preference shares were redeemed at R2,10 per share on
        1 March 19x5.

(2)    The redemption was financed out of the following issues:
        -     100 debentures of R250 each
        -     as many ordinary shares at R1,25 each as were necessary to have
              sufficient cash for the redemption.

(3)    The costs involved in connection with the above were:
        -     debentures issue expenses        R2 000
        -     share issue expenses           R9 000

(4)    The expenses must be written off, and the redemption of preference
        shares effected in such a way as to maintain the distributable reserves
        at the maximum possible amount.

(5)    The directors have been granted a general authority by the annual
        general meeting to issue shares at their discretion.

(6)    The authorised share capital of the company is 1 000 000 ordinary
        shares of R1 each, and 100 000 preference shares of R2 each.


YOU ARE REQUIRED TO:

(a)    Show the shareholders' equity as it will appear in the balance sheet,
        after accounting for the above transactions.

(b)    Show an extract of the notes to the financial statements in respect of
        the shareholders' equity in compliance with the Companies Act.

        Show all workings.

**K9**

The following is an extract from the notes to the financial statements of
Gerber Limited for the year ended 30 June 19x9:

1.    SHARE CAPITAL
      Authorised
          200 000 ordinary shares of R1 each                     R200 000
          100 000 10% redeemable preference shares of R1 each      100 000
                                                                   R300 000
                                                                   =======

      Issued
          150 000 ordinary shares of R1 each                      R150 000
          100 000 10% redeemable preference shares of R1 each      100 000
                                                                   R250 000
                                                                   =======

      The redeemable preference shares are redeemable at the option of the
      directors at a premium of 20c per share.

2.    SHARE PREMIUM                                                R25 000
                                                                   ======

3.    DISTRIBUTABLE RESERVE
      Retained income                                             R146 000
                                                                   =======

      The directors decide to redeem the preference shares on 1 July 19x9.

      The funds necessary for redemption will be provided by:

      (a)   the issue of 800 R100 8% debentures at par
      (b)   raising a bank overdraft.

      The directors wish to retain the maximum amount on distributable
      reserves.


<u>YOU ARE REQUIRED TO</u>:

give the journal entries (including cash transactions) to record the above on
1 July 19x9.

Green Ltd. company has an authorised share capital of R300 000 in shares of R1 each.  The issued capital, all of which  is fully paid,  is 200 000 ordinary shares of R1 each and 100 000 six per cent cumulative preference shares of R1 each.

The preference shares are redeemable at a premium of 5c per share at any time before 30 June 19x5.

The company redeems 20 000 shares out of profits and 80 000 shares out  of the proceeds of a fresh issue at par of 80 000 ordinary shares.


<u>YOU ARE REQUIRED TO</u>:

(a)    the capital of the company as it would appear in its balance sheet before and after the redemption of a the preference shares and the fresh issue of the ordinary shares.

(b)    the journal entries relating to the redemption and the fresh issue.

# K11

The memorandum of the Alpha Company Limited stated that the authorised share capital was R150 000 in R1 shares.  The issued and paid capital was 50 000 5% preference shares, redeemable at any time between 30 June 19x4 and 30 June 19x8, at a premium of 5c per share, and 100 000 ordinary shares.  On 30 June 19x4 the company  decided to redeem 25 000 shares out of profits and 25 000 shares out of the proceeds of an issue, at par,  of 25 000 shares of R1 each.

<u>YOU ARE REQUIRED TO GIVE</u>:

(i)     the relevant portions of the company's financial statements before and after redemption.

(ii)    the journal entries relating to the redemption and the new issue. (Journalise cash transactions.)

# K12

The following is the summarised balance sheet of Partridge Limited at 30 September 19x7, its financial year end.

<u>CAPITAL EMPLOYED</u>

SHARE CAPITAL  
  Authorised                                            R580 000  
  2 000 000 ordinary shares of 50c each  
  130 000 10% redeemable preference  
    shares of R1 each  
  Issued  
  900 000 ordinary shares of 50c each       450 000  
  130 000 10% redeemable preference  
    shares of R1 each              <u>130 000</u>  
DISTRIBUTABLE RESERVE  
  Retained income                       <u>84 000</u>  
                                    R664 000  
                                    =======


<u>EMPLOYMENT OF CAPITAL</u>

FIXED ASSETS                                R305 000

NET CURRENT ASSETS                       359 000  
  CURRENT ASSETS  
    Stock                       R224 800  
    Debtors                  175 200  
    Investments              35 000  
    Bank                     <u>60 000</u>  
                      R495 000  
                      =======

  CURRENT LIABILITIES  
    Trade creditors               91 000  
    Shareholders for ordinary dividend    <u>45 000</u>  
                      R136 000  
                      =======

                                   <u>R664 000</u>  
                                    =======

# K12 CONTINUED

As the redeemable preference shares are redeemable at the option of the company at any time between 1 January 19x7 and 31 March 19x8 the directors have resolved the following:

1. The redeemable preference shares are to be redeemed on 31 December 19x7 at a premium of 10%.
2. The redemption is to be made partly out of profits leaving a balance of R20 000 in retained income and the balance out of a fresh issue of ordinary shares at a premium of 20%.
3. In order to raise funds
   (i)   the investments are to be sold and
   (ii)  sufficient ordinary shares are to be issued at a premium of 20%.
4. The share premium arising on the issue of the ordinary shares is to be utilised to the fullest extent permitted by the Companies Act 1973.


The above resolutions were carried out as follows:

1. The investments were sold for R30 000 cash on 5 December 19x7.
2. Allotment of the ordinary shares was made on 20 December 19x7, by which date all moneys had been received.
3. The preference shares were redeemed and the preference shareholders paid the amounts due to them on 31 December 19x7.

The net income for the 3 months to 31 December 19x7 amounted to R3 250 before taking into account the sale of the investments.


<u>YOU ARE REQUIRED TO GIVE</u>:

(a)  the journal entries (including cash transactions) to record the above transactions.

(b)  show the capital employed section of the balance sheet of Partridge Limited at 31 December 19x7 after the redemption of the preference shares.

# K13

On 30 June 19x8, Aranda Limited had the following balances in their accounting records:

|  | R |
| --- | --- |
| Ordinary shares of 50c each | 150 000 |
| 12% redeemable cumulative preference | |
|   shares of R2,00 each (Note 1) | 60 000 |
| Share premium | 12 000 |
| Capital redemption reserve | 40 000 |
| Reserve for redeeming preference shares | 4 000 |
| Retained income | 280 000 |
| Preliminary expenses | 15 000 |
| Share issue expenses | 8 000 |
| Bank overdraft (limited to R57 700) | 50 000 |

Additional information not yet taken into account:

1. The preference shares are redeemable at a premium of 30c per share before 1 July 19x9 provided all preference dividends have been paid to the date of the redemption.

2. At a meeting of the board of directors of Aranda Limited held on 30 May 19x8 it was decided:

   (a) To redeem the 12% redeemable cumulative preference shares of the company on 30 June 19x8 at a premium of 30c per share.
   (b) To <u>finance</u> this redemption by:
       - a private placing of 3 000 19% unsecured convertible debentures of R10,00 each at 110% and
       - by offering ordinary shares to the public at a premium of 25c on 30 June 19x8.
   (c) To write off all deferred expenditure immediately after the fresh issue of shares.
   (d) That the above decision should be effected in such a manner as to have the minimum impact on the distributable reserves.

3. The authorised share capital of the company comprises:
   380 000 ordinary shares of 50c each
     60 000 12% redeemable cumulative preference shares of R2,00 each

4. No preference dividend has been paid since 31 December 19x5.

5. The new share issue was underwritten by AB Underwriters Limited for a commission of 5%. All the shares were applied for and allotted to the public and the commission was paid to AB Underwriters. Share issue expenses of R5 000 were incurred and paid.

6. The directors have the authority to issue all unissued shares. This authority pertains until the next annual general meeting.

7.    The debentures will be convertible on 30 June 19y0 at the option of the debentureholders in the ratio of 4 shares for every debenture held. All unconverted debentures will be redeemed on 30 June 19y2 at a premium of 8%.

8.    The directors have in the past set aside out of profits an amount of R2 000 per annum to provide for the redemption of the preference shares.


<u>YOU ARE REQUIRED TO</u>:

(a)    prepare the journal entries in the books of Aranda Limited to record the above transactions.  (Narrations are not required.)  No notes are required.

(b)    prepare the capital employed section of the balance sheet on 30 June 19x8 in accordance with the requirements of Schedule 4 of the Companies Act and generally accepted accounting practice.  No notes are required.

# K14

The following information was extracted from the books and records of Century Limited at 29 April 19x9:

<u>Authorised share capital</u>

| | |
|---|---|
| 300 000 ordinary shares of R2 each | R600 000 |
| 120 000 15% redeemable preference shares of 50c each | 60 000 |
| | R660 000 |

<u>Issued share capital</u>

| | |
|---|---|
| 220 000 ordinary shares of R2 each | R440 000 |
| 120 000 15% redeemable preference shares of 50c each | 60 000 |
| | R500 000 |

| | |
|---|---|
| Retained income | R120 000 |
| Cash at bank | R8 000 |

On 1 March 19x9, a resolution had been passed by the board of directors of Century Limited in terms of which the preference shares were to be redeemed on 30 April 19x9 at a premium of 5c per share.   The redemption was to be financed out of:

(a)     a fresh issue of ordinary shares at an issue price of R2,50
(b)     a secured loan of R40 000 at 14%
(c)     the balance from the cash account.

The directors have indicated that they would like a balance of R3 000 to remain in the cash account and a balance of at least R70 000 to remain on the retained income.  Share issue expenses of R1 200 incurred will be written off against retained income.   The financial year end is 31 December when the annual preference dividend is declared. The preference dividend will be paid to the date of redemption.   The directors have resolved further that the redemption was to be effected in such a manner as to have the least impact on retained income.


<u>YOU ARE REQUIRED TO</u>:

(a)     calculate the number of ordinary shares that the company will issue.

(b)     prove that your scheme will fulfil the directors' requirements by showing the retained income and cash accounts.

# K15

1.    Emnet (Pty) Ltd was incorporated on 1 January 19x5 with an authorised share capital of 500 000 no par value ordinary shares and 50 000 10% redeemable preference shares of R2 each.

2.    During January 19x5 all the preference shares were issued at par and 300 000 ordinary shares were issued for R300 000.  Share issue expenses of R1 000 were incurred in respect of the issue of the preference shares.  Share issue expenses in respect of the ordinary shares issued amounted to R2 000.  On 2 January 19x8 an additional 100 000 ordinary shares were issued for R145 000.  Share issue expenses amounted to R3 000.  On 2nd January 19x8 the directors resolved to write off all share issue expenses incurred.  They wished to retain the maximum possible balance on the retained income account.

3.    Emnet (Pty) Ltd's financial year ends on 31 December.  Preference dividends are paid annually on 31 December.

4.    On 25 June 19x0 the directors resolved to redeem the preference shares on 30 June 19x0 at a premium of 20c per share.  The redemption of the preference shares must be effected in such a way as to maintain a balance of R100 000 on retained income. At 30 June 19x0 retained income reflected a credit balance of R171 000, the bank account reflected a debit balance of R20 000.

5.    The redemption of the preference shares will be partially financed by the issue of ordinary shares.  The directors wish to issue the minimum number of shares possible to comply with the requirements of Section 98 of  the Companies Act of 1973.  The required number of shares were subscribed for and allotted.  The balance of the funds needed to finance the redemption will be obtained from the issue of 10% debentures of R10 each.


YOU ARE REQUIRED TO:


Prepare the journal entries (including cash transactions) to record the transactions in the books of Emnet (Pty) Ltd for the year ended 31 December 19x0.

# K16

The following is an extract from the notes to the financial statements of Blackwood Limited for the year ended 31 December 19x7.

<pre>
1       SHARE CAPITAL
        Authorised
          300 000 ordinary shares of R1 each                    R300 000
          200 000 15% redeemable preference shares of R2 each    400 000
                                                                R700 000
                                                                =======

        Issued
          150 000 ordinary shares of R1 each                    R150 000
           60 000 15% redeemable preference shares of R2 each    120 000
                                                                R270 000
                                                                =======
</pre>

     The redeemable preference shares were issued after 1 July 1992 and are redeemable at the option of the directors at a premium of 10% per share.

<pre>
2       ORDINARY SHARE PREMIUM                                   R5 000
                                                                =====


3       DISTRIBUTABLE RESERVE
        Retained income                                        R147 000
                                                                =======
</pre>

The directors decide to redeem the preference shares on 1 January 19x8 at a premium of 12% per share.

In order to provide for the redemption, 100 000 ordinary shares were to be issued at a premium of 20c per share.

The distributable reserves were to be maintained at the maximum amount.

The ordinary share issue was fully subscribed.


<u>YOU ARE REQUIRED TO:</u>

give the journal entries (including cash transactions) to record the above on 1 January 19x8, if

(i)    permission is obtained from the court to utilise the share premium account to provide for the excess premium payable on redemption.

(ii)   permission is not obtained from the court.

# K17

The following balances appear in the books of a company:

| | |
|---|---:|
| Stated capital - 50 000 ordinary shares | R100 000 |
| Preference share capital - 30 000 8% cumulative preference shares of R1 each | 30 000 |
| Share premium | 8 000 |
| Capital redemption reserve fund | 50 000 |
| Retained income | 40 000 |
| Preliminary and issue expenses | 10 000 |
| Net income before tax | 9 000 |

<u>NOTES</u>

The preliminary and issue expenses account is made up as follows:

| | |
|---|---:|
| Preliminary expenses | R3 000 |
| Share issue expenses - ordinary shares | 3 500 |
|                 - preference shares | 1 500 |
| Debenture issue expenses | 2 000 |
| | R10 000 |

The directors wish to write off all the preliminary and issue expenses this year. They also want to issue 25 000 capitalisation shares in order to bring the ordinary stated capital account to R160 000. However, they would like to minimise the effect of all the above transactions on the retained income.

<u>YOU ARE REQUIRED TO</u>:

write a letter to the directors, informing them of the extent to which they may utilise S76, S77 and S98 of the Companies Act, to give effect to the above.

# SECTION L

# COMPANY ACCOUNTING – ELEMENTARY DEBENTURES

# L1

On 1 January 19x2 a company issued 1 200 9% debentures of R500 each at par. The debentures are repayable by annual drawings over three years at a premium of 4 1/2%, the first payment being due on 31 December 19x3.

Interest is payable yearly at 31 December.

Give the relative journal entries (including those for the payment of interest) in the books of the company for the years ended 31 December 19x3, 19x4 and 19x5.

On 1 April 19x3 a  company issued debentures to the value of R400 000 at par. Debenture issue expenses amounted to R2 400.

Interest at the rate of 10 1/2% per annum was payable half-yearly on 31 March and 30 September.

The debentures were redeemable at a premium of 4% by equal annual drawings, the first drawing of debentures to the nominal value of R80 000 being due on 31 March 19x4 one year after the date of issue.

Give the entries relating to the debentures in the company's books for the financial years ended 30 June 19x3, 19x4 and 19x5.

**L3**

The Excelsior Company Limited, whose financial year ends on 31 March, issued 120 10% debentures of R1 000 each at a discount of R4 per debenture, repayable at a premium of R2 per debenture.   The issue price was payable in full on application.   Applications were received for the 120 debentures on 30 September 19x1, and allotment took place on the same date.

Repayment was to be by drawings of 30 debentures on 31 March of each year, the first drawing to be on 31 March two and a half years after the date of issue.

Interest on the debentures was to be paid on 31 March and 30 September each year.

Show:

(a)    The journal entries for the issue of the debentures.
(b)    All journal entries relating to the debentures for the year ended 31 March 19x7.
(c)    The debenture premium accrued account as it would appear in the ledger of the Excelsior Company Limited from 1 October 19x1 to 31 March 19x7. (Journalise all cash transactions.)

# L4

Carter and Sons Ltd invited subscriptions for 200 10 1/2% debentures of R1 000 each which they were issuing at a discount of 2% payable in full on application.    Interest was payable on 30 June each year.

All the debentures were applied for and allotment took place on 1 July 19x1.

The debentures are to be redeemed at a premium of 4%.    Redemption is to take place by equal annual drawings over a period of five years, the first draw to be made on 30 June three years after the allotment date.

You are required to give all the entries, in the form of journal entries, which would be made in the books relating to these debentures during the years ended 30 June 19x4 and 30 June 19x5.

# L5

A company issued R100 000 of 10% debentures at R98 per cent on 1 January 19x1.
They were redeemable at R101 per cent by annual drawings of R20 000 (nominal
value) starting on 31 December 19x3.   Debenture issue expenses totalled R325.

Show the following accounts in the company's ledger for the years 19x3, 19x4
and 19x5.

(a)     Debentures.
(b)     Premium accrued on debentures.
(c)     Debenture discount.
(d)     Debenture interest.
(e)     Debenture issue expenses.

Interest is payable yearly on 31 December.

# L6

The Valhalla Manufacturing Co. Ltd issued 200 9 1/2% debentures of R1 000 each at 98 1/2% on 1 January 19x0.    They are redeemable at 101 1/2% by annual drawings of R20 000 (20 debentures of R1 000 each) starting on 31 December 19x2.

Debenture issue expenses amounted to R3 000.

Interest is payable yearly on 31 December.

Show the following accounts in the company's ledger for the years 19x2 and 19x3:

(a)    Debentures.
(b)    Premium accrued on debentures.
(c)    Debenture interest.
(d)    Debenture discount.
(e)    Debenture issue expenses.

# L7

On 1 January 19x3 a company issued debentures to the nominal value of R100 000 at par. They were redeemable at par on 31 December twenty years later.  The company decided to raise a sinking fund to be invested outside the business at 8% per annum.  Interest on this investment is received in cash annually on 31 December.  Give the relative ledger accounts in the books of the company for the financial years 19x3, 19x4 and 19x5.  (R0,021852 invested annually at 8% per annum for 20 years will amount to R1.)

**L8**

On 1 January 19x2 the Alpha Company Limited issued 100 R1 000 10% debentures
at par redeemable at par on 31 December 19x4.   The company provided for the
redemption of the debentures by the sinking fund method and invested the
necessary sum at the end of each financial year which together with interest
at 8% per annum received and reinvested would amount to the required sum on
31 December 19x4.

The investment was realised at its book value on 31 December 19x4.

The interest on the debentures was payable half-yearly on 30 June and 31
December.

<u>YOU ARE REQUIRED TO</u>:

(a)   The debenture redemption fund account for the three years.
(b)   The interest on investment account for the three years.
(c)   The journal entries required at 31 December 19x4 in respect of the
      debentures.  (Journalise any cash transactions.)

Note: R0,308033 invested annually at 8% per annum for three years amounts to
      R1.

**L9**

On 1 January 19x2 a limited liability company allotted 200 10% debentures, nominal value R100 each, at R95.   The issue price was received on allotment.

The debentures are redeemable at par, on 31 December ten years later.

Discount on debentures is to be written off over the life of the debentures.

It is decided to raise a redemption fund and to invest the fund outside the business in 10% Government Stock, which can be bought at par, and interest on which is payable annually on 31 December.

Prepare the ledger accounts in the books of the company in respect of these transactions for the two years ended 31 December 19x3.

R0,062745 invested each year at 10% compound interest will produce R1 in ten years.

Spring and Co. Ltd invited subscriptions for 1 000 10% debentures of R100 each which they were issuing at a discount of 4% payable in full on application.

All the debentures were applied for and allotment took place on 1 July 19x1.

The debentures are to be redeemed at par on 30 June 19x9.

In order to provide the necessary funds for redemption, the directors decide to invest a sum at 8% outside the business on 30 June of each year, the first investment being made on 30 June 19x2.

Interest is not received in cash, but is reinvested automatically.

<u>YOU ARE REQUIRED TO GIVE</u>:

(1)    The entries, in the form of journal entries, relating to the issue of the debentures.

(2)    The following ledger accounts for the years ended 30 June 19x2, 19x3 and 19x4:
    (a)    debenture redemption fund;
    (b)    debenture redemption fund investments;
    (c)    debenture discount.

(3)    The entries in the form of journal entries relating to the redemption of the debentures which would be made in the books on 30 June 19x9.

R0,094015 invested each year at 8% compound interest will produce R1 in eight years.

# L11

On 1 January 19x3 a company issued debentures to the nominal value of R100 000 at par. They were redeemable at a premium of 3% on 31 December ten years later.

Debenture issue expenses amounted to R600.

In order to provide the necessary funds for redemption, the directors decided to invest a sum at 8% per annum outside the business on 31 December of each year.   Interest on this investment is not received in cash, but is automatically reinvested, the entries being put through on 31 December of every year.

Give the relative ledger accounts in the company's books for the financial years 19x3, 19x4 and 19x5.

(R0,069029 invested annually at 8% per annum for ten years will amount to R1.)

## SECTION M

# CHANGES IN FINANCIAL POSITION

# M1

<u>BOND AND SON LIMITED</u>

<u>BALANCE SHEET AT 30 SEPTEMBER 19X8</u>

|  | 19X8 | 19X7 |
|---|---|---|
| <u>CAPITAL EMPLOYED</u> | | |
| Share capital | R40 000 | R40 000 |
| Retained income | 74 000 | 14 000 |
| Long term loan | 8 000 | 10 000 |
| | R122 000 | R64 000 |
| | ======= | ====== |
| <u>EMPLOYMENT OF CAPITAL</u> | | |
| Fixed assets | | |
| Land and buildings | R55 000 | R30 000 |
| Plant | 20 000 | 12 000 |
| Cost | 27 000 | 18 000 |
| Accumulated depreciation | 7 000 | 6 000 |
| Vehicles | 15 000 | 3 000 |
| Cost | 24 000 | 12 000 |
| Accumulated depreciation | 9 000 | 9 000 |
| | 90 000 | 45 000 |
| Investments | 25 000 | 15 000 |
| Current assets | 16 000 | 11 000 |
| Stock | 12 000 | 9 000 |
| Accounts receivable | 4 000 | 2 000 |
| Current liabilities | 9 000 | 7 000 |
| Accounts payable | 6 000 | 5 000 |
| Bank overdraft | 3 000 | 2 000 |
| Net current assets | 7 000 | 4 000 |
| | R122 000 | R64 000 |
| | ======= | ====== |

<u>NOTES:</u>

1.  During the year plant with a book value of R4 000 and accumulated depreciation of R2 000 thereon was sold at a profit of R1 000. No other plant was sold during the year.

2.  A vehicle costing R7 000 with accumulated depreciation of R5 000 was sold at a loss of R500. There were no other vehicle sales.

3.  The tax charge for the year was R12 500.

# M1 CONTINUED

4. Included in creditors were amounts owing to the Receiver of Revenue as
   follows:
           30 September 19x7       R800
           30 September 19x8       R900

5. Income received from investments amounted to R4 000 and R1 000 interest
   was paid during the year.

6. Dividends totalling R8 000 were paid during the year.

<u>YOU ARE REQUIRED TO PREPARE:</u>

A cash flow statement for the year ended 30 September 19x8 for Bond and Son
Limited.

## M2

From the following information relating to Trueform Manufacturing Limited you are required to prepare a cash flow statement for the year ended 30 June 19x5

<u>DETAILED BALANCE SHEETS AT 30 JUNE 19x4 AND 19x5</u>

|  | 19x4 | | 19x5 | |
|---|---|---|---|---|
| <u>CAPITAL EMPLOYED</u> | | | | |
| SHARE CAPITAL | | | | |
|   Authorised and issued | | R100 000 | | R100 000 |
| NON-DISTRIBUTABLE RESERVE | | | | |
|   Profit on sale of land and investments | | 2 000 | | 8 000 |
| DISTRIBUTABLE RESERVE | | | | |
|   Retained income | | 3 500 | | 5 500 |
| LONG TERM LIABILITY | | <u>30 000</u> | | <u>-</u> |
|   Loan | | R135 500 | | R113 500 |
| | | ======= | | ======= |
| <u>EMPLOYMENT OF CAPITAL</u> | | | | |
| FIXED ASSETS | | | | |
|   Goodwill, at cost less written off | | R3 000 | | - |
|   Land, at cost | | 20 000 | | R15 000 |
|   Buildings, at cost | R27 000 | | R27 000 | |
|   Accumulated depreciation | <u>3 000</u> | 24 000 | <u>3 500</u> | 23 500 |
|   Plant, at cost | 32 000 | | 40 000 | |
|   Accumulated depreciation | <u>8 000</u> | 24 000 | <u>10 500</u> | 29 500 |
|   Fixtures, at cost | 4 600 | | 4 600 | |
|   Accumulated depreciation | <u>1 500</u> | <u>3 100</u> | <u>1 800</u> | <u>2 800</u> |
| | | 74 100 | | 70 800 |
| INVESTMENTS | | <u>34 000</u> | | <u>20 000</u> |
| | | 108 100 | | 90 800 |
| NET CURRENT ASSETS | | 27 400 | | 22 700 |
|   CURRENT ASSETS | | | | |
|     Stock | R23 000 | | R21 000 | |
|     Debtors | 19 000 | | 20 000 | |
|     Bank | <u>15 600</u> | | <u>12 200</u> | |
| | R57 600 | | R53 200 | |
| | ====== | | ====== | |
|   CURRENT LIABILITIES | | | | |
|     Creditors | R18 200 | | R20 500 | |
|     Dividends | <u>12 000</u> | | <u>10 000</u> | |
| | R30 200 | | R30 500 | |
| | ====== | | ====== | |
| | | <u>R135 500</u> | | <u>R113 500</u> |
| | | ======= | | ======= |

<u>INCOME STATEMENTS FOR THE YEARS ENDED 30 JUNE 19x4 AND 19x5</u>

|  | 19x4 | 19x5 |  | 19x4 | 19x5 |
|---|---|---|---|---|---|
| Directors' fees | R1 000 | R1 500 | Trading profit | R27 500 | R29 250 |
| Interest on loan | 1 500 | 750 |  |  |  |
| Loss on sale of plant | - | 800 |  |  |  |
| Depreciation of plant | 2 000 | 2 500 |  |  |  |
| Depreciation of fixtures | 300 | 300 |  |  |  |
| Depreciation of buildings | 500 | 500 |  |  |  |
| Goodwill written off | 3 000 | 3 000 |  |  |  |
| Net income before tax | 19 200 | 19 900 |  |  |  |
|  | R27 500 | R29 250 |  | R27 500 | R29 250 |
|  | ======= | ====== |  | ====== | ====== |
|  |  |  |  |  |  |
| Taxation - S A normal | R7 200 | R8 400 | Balance brought |  |  |
| Transfer to reserve | 2 000 | 6 000 | forward | R3 500 | R3 500 |
| Dividends recommended | 12 000 | 10 000 | Net income | 19 200 | 19 900 |
| Balance per balance sheet | 3 500 | 5 500 | Taxation over- |  |  |
|  |  |  | provided for 19x4 | - | 500 |
|  |  |  | Profit on sale |  |  |
|  |  |  | of land | 2 000 | 5 000 |
|  |  |  | Profit on sale |  |  |
|  |  |  | of investments | - | 1 000 |
|  | R24 700 | R29 900 |  | R24 700 | R29 900 |
|  | ====== | ====== |  | ====== | ====== |

NOTE: Plant purchased during the year has cost R11 000.  Plant was sold during the year for R2 200.   Income from investments of R6 500 is included in the trading profit for the year ended 30 June 19x5.   Included in creditors at 30 June 19x4 was R500 owing to the Receiver of Revenue.

**M3**

The following balances were extracted from the books of Corona Limited at
30 September 19x5 and 19x6 after all the closing entries had been put through:

|  | 19x5 | 19x6 |
|---|---|---|
| Cash on hand and at bank | R30 000 | R28 000 |
| Creditors | 19 000 | 23 500 |
| Debtors | 40 000 | 51 250 |
| Debentures - 7% | 30 000 | - |
| Debentures - 10% | - | 60 000 |
| General reserve | - | 10 000 |
| Investments - listed | 40 000 | 30 000 |
| Land and buildings | 55 000 | 180 000 |
| Non-distributable reserve | - | 45 000 |
| Plant - cost | 30 000 | 45 000 |
| Accumulated depreciation - plant | 5 000 | 6 250 |
| Share premium | 25 000 | - |
| Share capital issued - ordinary shares of R1 each | 100 000 | - |
| Stated capital account | - | 175 000 |
| Stock | 60 000 | 62 000 |
| Receiver of Revenue | 1 000 | 1 500 |
| Retained income | 75 000 | 75 000 |

The following additional information is given:

1. On 1 October 19x5 existing members were offered one ordinary share at
   par for each four held.  The offer was fully subscribed and the shares
   were allotted on 31 October 19x5.  Immediately thereafter a
   capitalisation issue of one ordinary share for every five held was made
   out of distributable reserves.  On 1 July 19x6 the company converted
   its shares into shares of no par value.

2. During the year the 7% debentures were redeemed and new 10% debentures
   were issued.

3. On 1 July 19x6 existing land and buildings were revalued at R100 000.
   Extensions to the factory buildings were commenced during the current
   year and the final payment under the contract was made on 31 July 19x6.

4. Plant which had cost R10 000 and in respect of which depreciation
   amounting to R2 000 had been provided to the date of the sale was sold
   for R11 000 and new plant was purchased.

5. Investments costing R10 000 were purchased during the year and certain
   other investments were sold at a profit of R2 000.  The value of
   investments held at 30 September 19x6 was written down to market value
   and this resulted in a charge of R3 000 being made in the income
   statement.  The investments are not held for speculative purposes.

6. Taxation for the year ended 30 September 19x6 was R6 000.

# M3 CONTINUED

7.   A dividend of ten cents per share was paid to shareholders on
     29 September 19x6.

8.   Interest paid during the year amounted to R10 000.

9.   Income of R8 000 was received from listed investments.


<u>YOU ARE REQUIRED TO</u>:

prepare a cash flow statement for Corona Limited for the year ended
30 September 19x5.

# M4

The following lists of balances were extracted from the books of Fugi Limited at 30 June 19x5 and 31 December 19x5:

|  | 30 June 19x5 | 31 December 19x5 |
|---|---|---|
| Retained income | R3 100 | R3 500 |
| Capital redemption reserve fund | 12 500 | - |
| Cash at bank | 10 800 | 8 000 |
| 10% debentures | 10 000 | 8 000 |
| Freehold property at cost | 20 000 | 15 000 |
| Furniture - at cost | 8 000 | 8 000 |
| General reserve | 1 500 | 2 500 |
| Plant - at cost | 30 000 | 20 000 |
| Profit on sale of freehold property | - | 3 000 |
| Proposed dividend | - | 1 000 |
| Provision for bad debts | 2 000 | 2 000 |
| Accumulated depreciation - furniture | 6 200 | 6 400 |
|                        - plant | 18 000 | 10 600 |
| Provision for discount | 500 | 500 |
| Share capital - R1 shares | 25 000 | 37 500 |
| Share premium | 2 000 | 2 000 |
| Stock | 10 000 | 22 000 |
| Creditors | 10 000 | 5 000 |
| Debtors | 12 000 | 9 000 |

## NOTES:

1.  Certain plant was sold on 1 July 19x5 and a loss of R900 sustained. Plant is depreciated at 10% per annum on cost.

2.  No fixed assets have been purchased since 30 June 19x5.

3.  The debentures were issued on 1 January 19x1 and are redeemable in five equal drawings at par.  The first drawing took place on 31 December 19x5.

4.  It was realised after the balances were extracted that the provision for bad debts and the provision for discount should have been reduced at 31 December 19x5 to R1 500 and R300 respectively.

5.  Debenture interest is payable on 31 December each year and debenture interest accrued at 30 June has been included in sundry creditors.

6.  No dividends have been paid during the six months.

7.  In terms of the company's articles of association, the profit on sale of fixed property is not available for distribution to shareholders.


## YOU ARE REQUIRED TO:

prepare a cash flow statement for the six months ended 31 December 19x5. Ignore taxation.

# M5

The following lists of balances were extracted from the books of Skukuza
Limited at 30 September 19x2 and 19x3:

|  | 19x2 | | 19x3 | |
|---|---|---|---|---|
| Retained income | | R328 000 | | R400 500 |
| Bank | R12 000 | | R62 750 | |
| Capital redemption reserve fund | | 100 000 | | |
| Creditors | | 99 500 | | 47 000 |
| Non-distributable reserve – profit on sale of property | | | | 30 000 |
| Debentures | | 100 000 | | 100 000 |
| Debenture premium accrued | | 1 000 | | 1 500 |
| Debenture discount | 1 500 | | 1 250 | |
| Debtors | 175 000 | | 154 000 | |
| Investments | 200 000 | | 240 000 | |
| Plant, at cost | 400 000 | | 400 000 | |
| Property, at cost | 240 000 | | 230 000 | |
| Proposed dividend on ordinary shares | | | | 20 000 |
| Provision for doubtful debts | | 10 000 | | 12 000 |
| Accumulated depreciation – plant | | 160 000 | | 215 000 |
| Provision for discount | | 5 000 | | 4 000 |
| Receiver of Revenue | | 5 000 | | 2 000 |
| Share capital (R1 shares) | | | | |
| Ordinary | | 200 000 | | 400 000 |
| Preference | | 100 000 | | |
| Share premium | | 20 000 | | 40 000 |
| Stock | 100 000 | | 180 000 | |
| | R1 128 500 | R1 128 500 | R1 270 000 | R1 270 000 |

The following additional information is available:

1. No property has been purchased since 30 September 19x2.
2. Certain plant was sold on 2 October 19x2 at a loss of R6 000.
3. New plant costing R90 000 was purchased and brought into use on
   3 October 19x2.
4. Plant has always been depreciated at 20% per annum on cost.
5. The debentures were issued at a discount on 1 October 19x0 and are
   redeemable, at a premium of 4%, on 30 September 19x8.
6. No dividend on the ordinary shares was paid during the year.
7. The 7% preference shares were redeemed on 30 September 19x3 at a
   premium of 5% out of the proceeds of an issue of ordinary shares at a
   premium of 25 cents per share. The directors wished to retain the
   maximum amount as revenue reserves and had, therefore, debited the
   premium on the redemption of the preference shares to the share premium
   account.

# M5 CONTINUED

8.     The preference share dividend was paid to the date of redemption.
9.     Taxation for the year has been accurately estimated at R85 000.
10.    At 30 September 19x2 the investments consisted entirely of  investments subscribed for at par.  During January 19x3 these were sold at 102%.
11.    In May 19x3 the company purchased additional investments of R240 000.
12.    All adjustments and closing entries have been made.
13.    Interest of R18 000 was paid and income of R16 000 was received from investments.


<u>YOU ARE REQUIRED TO:</u>

prepare a cash flow statement for Skukuza Limited for the year ended 30 September 19x3.

**M6**

The following are the unclassified balance sheets of Albany Manufacturers
Limited at 31 December:

|                                                      | 19x6     | 19x7     |
|------------------------------------------------------|----------|----------|
| Creditors                                            | R20 000  | R60 000  |
| Bank overdraft                                       | 10 000   | 31 000   |
| Capital redemption reserve fund                      | -        | 10 000   |
| General reserve                                      | 30 000   | 20 000   |
| Mortgage debentures - R100 each                      | 50 000   | 100 000  |
| Ordinary shares of no par value                      | 150 000  | 197 600  |
| Accumulated depreciation - plant and machinery       | 55 100   | 56 245   |
|          - vehicles | 11 220   | 15 100   |
| Provision for taxation                               | 680      | 9 680    |
| Proposed dividends                                   | 3 000    | 8 500    |
| Redeemable preference shares - R1 each               | 100 000  | 40 000   |
| Retained income                                      | 10 000   | 13 400   |
| Surplus on revaluation of land and buildings         | -        | 33 000   |
|                                                      | R440 000 | R594 525 |
|                                                      | ======== | ======== |
| Debtors                                              | R31 000  | R41 000  |
| Debenture discount                                   | -        | 3 000    |
| Investments                                          | 21 000   | 25 000   |
| Land and buildings                                   | 227 000  | 272 000  |
| Plant and machinery, at cost                         | 111 100  | 153 000  |
| Preliminary expenses                                 | 3 000    | 1 600    |
| Stock                                                | 23 800   | 74 825   |
| Vehicles, at cost                                    | 23 100   | 24 100   |
|                                                      | R440 000 | R594 525 |
|                                                      | ======== | ======== |

<u>NOTES</u>:

(1)    In addition to the final dividends which were proposed and accrued on
31 December 19x7, the company paid interim dividends totalling R3 000
during the year.  The company's liability for taxation for the 19x7 tax
year was R13 600.

(2)    On 30 June 19x7 the company redeemed 60 000 of its R1 redeemable
preference shares at a premium of 4c per shares.  Part of the funds
required came from the proceeds of an issue of 30 000 no par value
shares at R1 per share and the remainder from the issue of mortgage
debentures.  The latter issues were also made on 30 June 19x7.

(3)    On 31 December 19x7, the directors authorised a capitalisation issue to
existing shareholders of 20 000 no par value shares at R1 each and
resolved that the capital redemption reserve fund be used for this
purpose.  On the same date the premium on the redemption of the
preference shares, certain preliminary expenses and share issue
expenses of R1 000 were written off either against net income or, where
appropriate, against stated capital.

## M6 CONTINUED

(4)    During 19x7 plant and machinery which had cost R6 000, and had been depreciated by R4 100, was traded in at a profit of R600 in part payment of new plant and machinery costing R51 150. Later in the year a machine with a book value of R620 was scrapped.

(5)    Two motor vehicles were also traded in at a loss of R750 during 19x7 against a new vehicle costing R4 250. The year's total depreciation of vehicles and plant and machinery was R12 755.

(6)    Interest totalling R10 000 was paid during the year and income from investments amounted to R5 400,

<u>YOU ARE REQUIRED TO</u>:

prepare the cash flow statement of Albany Manufacturers Ltd for the year ended 31 December 19x7.

The following are the abridged balance sheets of Drakensberg Limited at 31 December 19x1 and 31 December 19x2.

| | 31 Dec 19x3 | 31 Dec 19x2 | | 31 Dec 19x1 | 31 Dec 19x2 |
|---|---|---|---|---|---|
| | R000 | R000 | | R000 | R000 |
| SHARE CAPITAL | | | FIXED ASSETS | | |
| Ordinary shares | | | At cost or valuation | 1 000 | 1 200 |
| of R1 each | 225 | 360 | Accumulated depre- | | |
| 15% redeemable | | | ciation | 535 | 585 |
| preference shares | | | | 465 | 615 |
| of R1 each | 200 | 160 | INVESTMENTS | 170 | 195 |
| NON-DISTRIBUTABLE | | | | | |
| RESERVE | - | 200 | CURRENT ASSETS | | |
| | | | Stock | 250 | 300 |
| DISTRIBUTABLE RESERVES | | | Debtors | 300 | 150 |
| Equipment replacement | 60 | 40 | Bills receivable | 100 | 200 |
| Retained income | 300 | 210 | Cash | 10 | 10 |
| SHAREHOLDERS' FUNDS | 785 | 970 | | | |
| LONG-TERM LIABILITIES | | | | | |
| 12,5% debentures | - | 100 | | | |
| | | | | | |
| CURRENT LIABILITIES | | | | | |
| Creditors | 300 | 300 | | | |
| Overdraft | 60 | 20 | | | |
| Shareholders for | | | | | |
| ordinary dividend | 50 | 80 | | | |
| | R1 195 | R1 470 | | R1 195 | R1 470 |
| | ===== | ===== | | ===== | ===== |

The following information is available:

(a)  The following transactions occurred in respect of fixed assets:

    (i)   A R200 000 upward revaluation was made on 1 April 19x2;
    (ii)  Plant costing R250 000 was sold for R60 000, resulting in a book loss of R30 000.
    (iii) Various new items were purchased during the year.

(b)  The redeemable preference dividend is payable on 30 June of each year, and on 30 June 19x2 the relevant preference dividend was paid.  No interim ordinary dividend was paid.  Proper accruals were made for the preference dividends which are included in accounts payable.

(c)  The preference shares are being redeemed at par in instalments on 30 June each year.

(d)  60 000 ordinary R1 shares were issued at par on a 1 for 5 basis on 31 May 19x2 following a 1 for 3 capitalisation issue.

# M7 CONTINUED

(e)     No investments were sold during the year.

(f)     Interest paid amounted to R12 000 and dividends totalling R15 000 were
        received.


<u>YOU ARE REQUIRED</u>:

to prepare a cash flow statement for Drakensberg Limited for the year ended
31 December 19x2.

Taxation is to be ignored.

**M8**

The following are the summarised balance sheet of Eastern Limited at 30 June:

|  | 19x7 | | 19x8 | |
|---|---:|---:|---:|---:|
| **Share capital** | | | | |
| Authorised - shares of R1 each | | 200 000 | | 200 000 |
| | | ======= | | ======= |
| Issued - shares of R1 each | R90 000 | | R140 000 | |
| Share premium | 20 000 | R110 000 | 15 000 | R155 000 |
| **Distributable reserves** | | | | |
| General reserve | 40 000 | | 54 000 | |
| Retained income | 60 000 | 100 000 | 62 000 | 116 000 |
| | | 210 000 | | 271 000 |
| Long-term liabilities | | 58 000 | | 70 000 |
| | | R268 000 | | R341 000 |
| | | ======= | | ======= |
| **Fixed assets** | | | | |
| Cost | R250 000 | | R274 000 | |
| Accumulated depreciation | 90 000 | R160 000 | 114 000 | R160 000 |
| Unlisted investments - at cost | | 26 000 | | 29 125 |
| Net current assets | | 82 000 | | 151 875 |
| Current assets | | | | |
| Stock | 80 000 | | 100 875 | |
| Debtors | 90 000 | | 114 000 | |
| Bank | 24 000 | | 40 000 | |
| | R194 000 | | R254 875 | |
| | ======= | | ======= | |
| Current liabilities | | | | |
| Creditors (including taxation owing) | 100 000 | | 89 000 | |
| Proposed dividend | 12 000 | | 14 000 | |
| | R112 000 | | R103 000 | |
| | ======= | | ======= | |
| | | R268 000 | | R341 000 |
| | | ======= | | ======= |

# M8 CONTINUED

The following additional information is available:

1. On 30 June 19x8 fixed assets costing R10 000 and in respect of which R6 000 had been provided for depreciation to the date of sale were sold for R2 000.

2. Unlisted investments include loan portion of tax of R6 000 at 30 June 19x7 and R9 125 at 30 June 19x8.

3. The investments held at 30 June 19x7 (other than loan portion of tax) were sold in October 19x7 for R30 000. In January 19x8 investments were purchased at a cost of R20 000.

4. During the 19x8 financial year an amount of R30 000, being part of the balance of retained income, was capitalised by the issue of 30 000 fully paid shares to members at par.

5. During the 19x8 financial year the company made a capitalisation issue of 10 000 fully paid shares out of the share premium account.

6. The dividend proposed for 19x7 was paid in October 19x7 and an interim dividend of R7 000 was paid in March 19x8.

7. Taxation for the year amounted to R28 125 (including loan portion of tax R3 125).

8. During the 19x8 financial year R22 000 of the long-term loan was repaid. A further loan was negotiated in May 19x8.

9. Taxation owing at 30 June 19x7 was R4 000 and at 30 June 19x8 R6 000.

10. Interest paid during the year amounted to R8 000 and R5 000 was received as dividends from the unlisted investments.

<u>YOU ARE REQUIRED</u>:

To prepare a cash flow statement for Eastern Limited for the year ended 30 June 19x8.

# M9

The following balances were extracted from the books of the Johannesburg Trading Company Limited at 30 June 19x1 and 30 June 19x2 respectively:

|  | 19x1 |  | 19x2 |  |
|---|---|---|---|---|
| Share capital, in R1 shares |  |  |  |  |
|   ordinary |  | R50 000 |  | R60 000 |
|   redeemable preference |  | 20 000 |  | - |
| Share premium |  | - |  | 1 000 |
| Capital redemption reserve |  | - |  | 10 000 |
| General reserve |  | 7 000 |  | - |
| Retained income at 1 July |  | 4 000 |  | 2 900 |
| Profit on trading |  | 8 000 |  | 20 500 |
| Depreciation on furniture | R100 |  | R150 |  |
| Accumulated depreciation - furniture |  | 500 |  | 650 |
| Land and buildings, cost | 12 000 |  | 12 000 |  |
| rniture, cost | 1 200 |  | 1 600 |  |
| Stock | 6 000 |  | 55 600 |  |
| Debtors | 23 000 |  | 26 200 |  |
| Bank | 9 500 |  | 2 200 |  |
| Creditors |  | 6 300 |  | 4 200 |
| Debentures |  | 2 000 |  | - |
| Dividend - |  |  |  |  |
|   ordinary | 5 000 |  | - |  |
|   preference | 1 000 |  | 500 |  |
| Premium on redemption of preference |  | - |  |  |
|   shares |  |  |  | 1 000 |
|  | R97 800 | R97 800 | R99 250 | R99 250 |

The redeemable preference shares had been redeemed on 31 December 19x1.

(a)    Prepare a cash flow statement.

(b)    Advise the directors on the advisability of declaring a dividend on the ordinary shares.

Ignore taxation.

## M10

The following are the balance sheets of J.P. Dubbel Limited at 30 June 19x8
and 30 June 19x9:

| 30 June 19x8 | | 30 June 19x9 |
|---|---|---|
| R400 000 | Share capital | R800 000 |
| | 800 000 R1 ordinary shares | |
| - | Non-distributable reserve | 80 000 |
| | Surplus on revaluation of land | |
| 60 000 | Distributable reserve | 60 000 |
| 460 000 | Retained income | 940 000 |
| 400 000 | Long-term liability | - |
| R860 000 | 8% debentures | R940 000 |
| | Fixed assets | |
| R20 000 | Goodwill, at cost | - |
| 200 000 | Land and buildings, at valuation | R240 000 |
| 292 000 | Plant and equipment | 316 000 |
| 352 000 | - cost | 394 000 |
| 60 000 | - accumulated depreciation | 78 000 |
| 26 000 | Motor vehicles | 43 000 |
| 42 000 | - cost | 61 000 |
| 16 000 | - accumulated depreciation | 18 000 |
| 538 000 | | 599 000 |
| 200 000 | Listed investments, at cost | 197 000 |
| 204 000 | Current assets | 276 000 |
| 140 000 | Stock | 180 000 |
| 60 000 | Debtors | 80 000 |
| 4 000 | Bank | 16 000 |
| 82 000 | Current liabilities | 132 000 |
| 70 000 | Creditors | 108 000 |
| 10 000 | Proposed dividends | 20 000 |
| 2 000 | Taxation | 4 000 |
| 122 000 | Net current assets | 144 000 |
| R860 000 | | R940 000 |

# M10 CONTINUED

The following additional information is available:

(1)  The debenture repayments took place on 31 December 19x8 the date on which the ordinary shares were issued at a premium of 3%.  The debentures were redeemed at par.

(2)  Taxation  on the income  for  the year ended 30 June 19x8 amounted to R24 000.

(3)  During the year the following sales of fixed assets took place:

|  | Cost | Accumulated depreciation to date of sale | Sale price |
|---|---|---|---|
| Land and buildings | R40 000 | - | R60 000 |
| Plant and equipment | 40 000 | R20 000 | 16 000 trade-in |
| Motor vehicles | 10 000 | 6 000 | 2 000 |

(4)  Share issue expenses amounted to R3 760.  Underwriters commission was 2% on the total issue price.

(5)  During the year 300 shares in J.J. Company Limited were sold for R4 600.

(6)  Interest paid during the year was R16 000 and R25 000 dividends were received from  the listed investments.


<u>YOU ARE REQUIRED TO</u>:


prepare  a  cash flow statement for J.P. Dubbel Limited for the year ended 30 June 19x9.

# M11

The abridged trial balances of Tap-Tap Limited at 28 February 19x8 and 28 February 19x9 are as follows:

TAP-TAP LIMITED

Trial balances at

|  | 28 February 19x8 | 28 February 19x9 |
|---|---|---|
| Land and buildings - at valuation | R218 000 | R169 000 |
| Plant - at cost | 104 000 | 109 000 |
| Furniture - at cost | 50 000 | 54 000 |
| Investments | 17 000 | 13 000 |
| Stock | 34 000 | 53 000 |
| Debtors | 32 000 | 51 000 |
| Share issue expenses | 3 000 | - |
|  | R458 000 | R449 000 |
|  | ======= | ======= |
| Creditors | R39 000 | R27 000 |
| Receiver of Revenue | 15 000 | 2 000 |
| Ordinary dividends due | 10 000 | 18 000 |
| Bank overdraft | 16 000 | 1 000 |
| Provision for doubtful debts | 3 000 | 4 000 |
| Accumulated depreciation - plant | 31 000 | 13 000 |
|       - furniture | 24 000 | 15 000 |
| Stated capital account -<br>  ordinary shares | 100 000 | 148 000 |
| Preference share capital<br>  (R1 shares) | 110 000 | 50 000 |
| Capital redemption reserve fund | - | 8 000 |
| Revaluation of assets reserve | 45 000 | 93 000 |
| General reserve | 40 000 | 50 000 |
| Retained income | 25 000 | 20 000 |
|  | R458 000 | R449 000 |
|  | ======= | ======= |

Additional information:

1. Building extensions for the year to 28 February 19x9 cost R28 000. A certain piece of land was sold during the year for R135 000.

2. Plant purchased some years ago for R61 000, with a net book value of R32 000, was traded in during the year for R7 000. No other plant was sold or scrapped during the year.

3. Certain items of furniture, which had cost R15 000 (net book value R3 000), were completely destroyed by fire. The insurance company paid R2 000 in full settlement of the claim. No other furniture was disposed of during the year.

4. The preference shares have been redeemable at the option of the company, at a premium of 10%, since 1 January 19x9.

5.      "Share issue expenses" were incurred as follows:

     1 January 19x8   - preference share issue        R3 000
     28 February 19x9  - ordinary share issue         R4 000

It was decided to write off the balance in "share issue expenses" account at 28 February 19x9, but that, wherever possible, the distributable reserves should not be reduced.

6.      "Receiver of Revenue - amount due" account was credited at 28 February 19x9 with normal tax R34 000.

7.      All preference dividends due, amounting to R12 000, were declared and paid during the year.   The only ordinary dividends _paid_ were those declared in the previous year.

8.      During the year certain investments were sold at a profit of R6 000 and dividends of R2 000 were received.   No new investments were purchased.


<u>YOU ARE REQUIRED TO</u>:

prepare a cash flow statement for the company for the year ended 28 February 19x9, in a form suitable for publication.

## M12

The following information was extracted from "Against all Odds" (Proprietary)
Limited's balance sheet at 30 June 19x3 and its draft balance sheet at 30 June
19x4:

|                                                              | 19x4 | | 19x3 | |
|--------------------------------------------------------------|---------|---------|---------|---------|
| Furniture and fittings at cost                               | R35 000 |         | R20 000 |         |
| Furniture and fittings - accumulated depreciation            |         | R6 000  |         | R15 000 |
| Retained income                                              |         | 60 000  | 50 000  |         |
| Share capital - ordinary of R1 each                          |         | 200 000 |         | 100 000 |
| Share premium - ordinary shares                              |         |         |         | 20 000  |
| 10% Preference shares of R1 each                             |         |         |         | 100 000 |
| Capital redemption reserve                                   |         | 100 000 |         |         |
| Land                                                         |         |         | 100 000 |         |
| Shareholders for dividends                                   |         | 10 000  |         |         |
| Net current assets (excluding shareholders for dividend)     |         | 341 000 |         | 65 000  |
|                                                              | R376 000 | R376 000 | R235 000 | R235 000 |

### Notes

(1)  The only transaction involving furniture occurred on 2 January 19x4
     when old furniture costing R15 000 was traded in for new.  The
     furniture company allowed R1 000 on the old furniture and the
     difference was paid in cash.
(2)  Depreciation is provided on the straight line basis at the rate of 20%
     per annum.
(3)  In order to redeem the preference shares there was a fresh issue of
     ordinary shares at R1,20 per share.
(4)  The preference shares were redeemed on 1 July 19x3 at a premium of R1
     per share.  The directors retained the maximum in distributable
     reserves when doing so.
(5)  The interim dividend of R10 000 was paid out on 2 January 19x4 and the
     final dividend was paid on 31 July 19x4.
(6)  Against all Odds" (Pty) Limited sold the land which it had acquired 10
     years previously and it was unanimously decided that the  profit  of
     R100 000 on its sale would be treated as an extraordinary item.
(7)  Net current assets include:

     19x4  bank balance  R225 000
     19x3  bank overdraft R16 000.


<u>YOU ARE REQUIRED TO</u>:

(i)   to prepare the income statement for the year ended 30 June 19x4 from
      NET INCOME BEFORE EXTRAORDINARY ITEMS. Comparative figures are not
      required. Taxation is to be ignored.  Notes are not required.

(ii)  to prepare a cash flow statement for the year ended 30 June 19x4.

# M13

The financial statement data for the Perkerson Supply Company Limited, for the years ending December 31, 19x1 and December 31, 19x2 are as follows:

PERKERSON SUPPLY COMPANY LTD.

BALANCE SHEETS

| | December 31 | |
|---|---|---|
| | 19x1 | 19x2 |
| CURRENT ASSETS | | |
| Cash | R179 000 | R162 000 |
| Accounts receivable | 473 000 | 526 000 |
| Stock | 502 000 | 604 000 |
| | 1 154 000 | 1 292 000 |
| | ========= | ========= |
| FIXED ASSETS | | |
| Land | 297 000 | 315 000 |
| Buildings and machinery | 4 339 000 | 4 773 000 |
| Accumulated depreciation | (1 987 000) | (2 182 000) |
| | 2 649 000 | 2 906 000 |
| | R3 803 000 | R4 198 000 |
| | ========= | ========= |
| CURRENT LIABILITIES | | |
| Accounts payable | R206 000 | R279 000 |
| Taxes payable | 137 000 | 145 000 |
| Other short-term payables | 294 000 | 363 000 |
| | 637 000 | 787 000 |
| LONG-TERM LIABILITIES | | |
| Bonds payable | 992 000 | 967 000 |
| | 1 629 000 | 1 754 000 |
| SHAREHOLDERS' EQUITY | | |
| Ordinary shares | 836 000 | 852 000 |
| Retained income | 1 338 000 | 1 592 000 |
| | 2 174 000 | 2 444 000 |
| | R3 803 000 | R4 198 000 |
| | ========= | ========= |

Additional information:

(1)   Net income after taxation of R216 000 for the year was R324 000.
(2)   Dividends paid totalled R70 000 and interest of R130 000 was paid.
(4)   Depreciation expense for the year was R305 000 on buildings and machinery.
(4)   Machinery originally costing R125 000 and with accumulated depreciation of R110 000 was sold for R15 000.


YOU ARE REQUIRED TO:

Prepare the cash flow statement of Perkerson Supply Company Limited for the year ended 31 December 19x2.

# M14

You are given the following information regarding Equus (Pty) Limited:

(a) <u>INCOME STATEMENT FOR THE YEAR ENDED 30 JUNE 19x5</u>

| | | |
|---|---:|---:|
| Turnover | | R115 000 |
| | | ======= |
| Net income after allowing the following items – | | R40 000 |
|   Audit fees | R2 000 | |
|   Debenture discount written off | 500 | |
|   Depreciation of fixed assets | 750 | |
|   Directors' emoluments | 12 000 | |
|   Leasing charges | 750 | |
|   Loss on sale of motor vehicle | 1 000 | |
| SA taxation | | 21 000 |
|   Current | 20 000 | |
|   Underprovision in prior year | 1 000 | |
| Net income after tax | | 19 000 |
| Dividend | | 5 000 |
|   Interim | 2 000 | |
|   Final | 3 000 | |
| Retained income | | 14 000 |
| Retained income at beginning of year | | 16 000 |
| Retained income per balance sheet | | R30 000 |
| | | ====== |

(b) <u>NOTES</u>

(1) 100 R100 debentures were issued during the year at a discount of 5%.
(2) The final dividend of R3 000 was paid on 31 July 19x5.  The dividend of R4 000, declared on 30 June 19x4, was paid on 29 July 19x4.
(3) The motor vehicle has always been depreciated using the straight line method at 10% per annum on cost.  On 2 January 19x5 the motor vehicle purchased exactly 6 years before was traded in.  The company was allowed R3 000 off the purchase price of a new smaller vehicle.
(4) During the year the company issued a further R20 000 shares at a premium of 10%.
(5) The motor vehicle is the only fixed asset owned by the company.
(6) Other than those mentioned above, there are no long-term or current liabilities.
(7) Bank is the only current asset.
(8) The amount paid to the Receiver of Revenue during the year amounted to R21 000.

<u>YOU ARE REQUIRED TO</u>:

prepare the cash flow statement for the year ended 30 June 19x5.

The following lists of balances were extracted from the accounting records of Woodhouse Limited at 30 September 19x6 and 19x7.

|  | 19x6 | 19x7 |
|---|---|---|
| Bank (debit balances) | R20 000 | R31 000 |
| Creditors | 55 000 | 50 000 |
| General reserve | - | 15 000 |
| Debtors | 80 000 | 92 000 |
| Distributable reserve - retained income | 30 000 | 48 000 |
| Debentures 5% | 40 000 | 20 000 |
| Debentures 10% | - | 50 000 |
| Listed investments - non-current assets | 40 000 | 30 000 |
| Land and buildings | 55 000 | 130 000 |
| Non-distributable reserve arising on revaluation of land and buildings | - | 60 000 |
| Plant | 30 000 | 45 000 |
| Accumulated depreciation - plant | 5 000 | 7 000 |
| Share capital - ordinary - R1 shares | 100 000 | - |
| Share capital - redeemable preference - R1 shares | 50 000 | 25 000 |
| Share premium - ordinary shares | 25 000 | - |
| Stated capital account - ordinary shares | - | 150 000 |
| Stock | 80 000 | 97 000 |

All adjusting and closing entries have been recorded except the one referred to in (f) below.

Notes

(a)   No fixed assets were sold except plant, which was two years old at date of sale, which had originally cost R10 000 and was being depreciated at 10% p.a. on cost.  The income statement showed a profit on disposal of this plant of R3 000.

(b)   (i)   Listed investments costing R10 000 were purchased during the year.
      (ii)  Certain listed investments were sold during the year at a profit of R2 000.
      (iii) The directors had decided to write down the value of the listed investments on hand at 30 September 19x7 to market value.  This necessitated an adjustment of R3 000 in the income statement.

(c)   The 10%  redeemable  preference  shares  were  redeemed at  par  on 30 September  19x7.  The  preference  dividend  for  the year was paid on 30 September 19x7.

(d)   S.A. Normal tax for the year amounted to R26 000.

(e)   At 30 September 19x6 R5 000 owing by the Receiver of Revenue was included in  debtors.  R7 000 owing  to the  Receiver  of  Revenue  at 30 September 19x7 in respect of tax has been included in creditors.

## M15 CONTINUED

(f)     The    directors  declared    an  ordinary  dividend  of  R15  000  on  30
        September 19x7, but no entries have been made to record this dividend.
        No interim dividends  were paid.

(g)     Interest  paid  during  the  year  amounted  to  R6  000  and  dividends
        totalling R8 000 were received from investments.


<u>YOU ARE REQUIRED TO</u>:

prepare the  cash  flow  statement  of  Woodhouse Limited for the year ended
30 September 19x7.

The following are the trial balances of Berkley Limited at 31 December:

|  | 19x8 | 19x7 |
|---|---|---|
| Creditors | R53 000 | R26 000 |
| Accumulated depreciation |  |  |
|    -     plant | 7 000 | 75 000 |
|    -     motor vehicles | 16 000 | 10 000 |
| Capital redemption reserve | 5 000 | - |
| Debentures | - | 12 000 |
| Non-distributable revaluation reserve | 80 000 | - |
| Ordinary share capital - R1 shares | - | 80 000 |
| 10% preference share capital - R1 shares | - | 15 000 |
| Retained income | 223 000 | 210 000 |
| Ordinary shareholders for dividend | 11 000 | 8 000 |
| Stated capital account | 120 000 | - |
| Receiver of Revenue (creditor) | 12 000 | 6 000 |
| Debtors | 62 000 | 45 000 |
| Cash at bank | 1 000 | 5 000 |
| Loan levy | - | 12 000 |
| Land and buildings | 310 000 | 180 000 |
| Motor vehicles | 35 000 | 34 000 |
| Plant | 95 000 | 81 000 |
| Investments | - | 4 000 |
| Stock | 94 000 | 81 000 |

Additional information:

1. On 1 February 19x8 the company made a capitalisation issue whereby the ordinary shareholders received one additional share for every four held.

2. On 1 March 19x8 the company first converted its ordinary share capital to shares of no par value and then issued an additional 5 000 shares of no par value at R1,50 per share.

3. The preference shares were redeemed on 1 May at a premium of 4%, the dividend being paid to date.   The redemption was financed partly out of the proceeds of the company's investments (which were sold at a profit of R1 000) and partly out of the proceeds of an issue of 5 000 ordinary no par value shares which were issued on 30 April 19x8 at R2,50 per share.

4. The liability for taxation was correctly reflected at 31 December 19x7 and was paid on 28 February 19x8.   During the year ended 31 December 19x8 the company made 2 provisional tax payments of R8 000 each.

5. During the year ended 31 December 19x8 the company acquired additional land and buildings, after which all the company's land and buildings were revalued by a sworn appraiser and restated in the company's books at the new valuation.   No land and buildings were sold during the year.

6.      During June 19x8 plant which had originally cost R28 000 and which had been depreciated by R24 000 was traded in at a loss of R3 000 in part payment of a new machine.

        At the same time a motor vehicle was traded in at its book value of R2 000 on a new vehicle costing R6 000.

7.      There were no other fixed asset disposals or scrappings apart from those mentioned above.

8.      An interim ordinary dividend of 5 cents per share was paid on 30 June 19x8 to all shareholders registered on 15 June 19x8.

9.      Interest paid during the year amounted to R2 000 and income of R4 000 was received from the investments.

<u>YOU ARE REQUIRED TO</u>:

prepare, in accordance with generally accepted practice, the cash flow statement of Berkley Limited for the year ended 31 December 19x8.

The following are the trial balances of Berne Limited at 31 October:

|  | 19X9 | 19X8 |
|---|---|---|
| Bank | - | R 7 600 |
| Debtors | R106 000 | 89 200 |
| Goodwill (extraordinary item) | - | 4 800 |
| Investments at cost | - | 12 000 |
| Land and buildings | 240 000 | 190 800 |
| Motor vehicles at cost | 40 000 | 36 000 |
| Plant at cost | 96 400 | 73 600 |
| Preliminary expenses | - | 3 400 |
| Share issue expenses - preference shares | - | 1 000 |
| Stock | 52 000 | 47 600 |
|  | R534 400 | R466 000 |
|  | ======= | ======= |
| Accumulated depreciation |  |  |
|     - motor vehicles | R14 000 | R8 000 |
|     - plant | 46 000 | 36 400 |
| Creditors | 49 200 | 64 000 |
| Current portion of long term loan | 4 000 | - |
| Bank | 2 000 | - |
| Long term loan | 16 000 | 20 000 |
| Ordinary share capital - 140 000 shares of 50c each | - | 70 000 |
| Receiver of Revenue | 28 000 | 36 800 |
| 12% redeemable preference shares of R1 each | - | 16 000 |
| Retained income | 239 800 | 205 200 |
| Shareholders for dividend | 3 200 | 2 400 |
| Stated capital - ordinary shares | 113 000 | - |
| Revaluation land and buildings | 19 200 | 7 200 |
|  | R534 400 | R466 000 |
|  | ======= | ======= |

Additional information

1.    The preference shares were redeemed on 1 November 19X8 at a premium of 10%.  The redemption was financed out of the proceeds of the sale of the company's investments.

2.    The investments, acquired some years ago, were sold for R20 800.

3.    On 1 January 19X9 the company issued 52 000 ordinary shares to the public at a premium of 10 cents per share.  Share issue expenses of R800 were paid.

4.    On 28 February 19X9 the company made a capitalisation issue of 1 share for every 6 held.

5.    On 1 August 19X9 the company converted all its par value shares to shares of no par value.

6.     On 31 October 19X9 the company wrote off all the preliminary and share issue expenses in such a way as to maintain distributable reserves at the maximum amount.

7.     The long term loan was raised on 1 January 19X7 and is repayable in 5 equal instalments commencing 1 January 19Y0.

8.     In addition to the final ordinary dividend declared 31 October 19X9, an interim dividend of R4 000 was paid on 31 March 19X9.

9.     The company's estimated tax liability for the year ended 31 October 19X9 was R68 000.  Two provisional payments of R20 000 each were made during the year ended 31 October 19X9.  R40 000 was paid to the Receiver in  settlement of the 19X8 assessment.

10.    During August 19X9 the company sold some of its land,  that had cost R5 200, at a profit of R6 000.

11.    In September 19X9 an item of plant which had originally cost R11 600 and which had been depreciated by R9 600 was traded in at a profit of R800 in part payment on a new machine costing R40 800.  At the same time a machine with a book value of R1 200 was scrapped.

12.    During October 19X9 the company sold a motor vehicle at a loss of R600 and acquired 2 new vehicles for R5 000 each.

13.    The total depreciation charge for plant and motor vehicles for the year ended 31 October 19X9 was R34 800.

14.    Interest paid during 19X9 amounted to R3 200 and dividends of R1 200 were received from investments.


<u>YOU ARE REQUIRED TO PREPARE</u>:

A cash flow statement for Berne Limited for the year ended 31 October 19X9.

# M18

Most of Wildebeest Limited's books and records were destroyed during the year under review.

You have managed to salvage some of the records and last year's balance sheet and by diligent enquiry have ascertained the following information:

1) <u>Balance at 31 December 19x8</u>

|  |  |  |
|---|---|---|
| Capital employed |  |  |
|   Share capital |  | R75 000 |
|   Non distributable reserve |  | 15 000 |
|   Distributable reserve |  | 65 000 |
|     Retained income |  |  |
| |  | 155 000 |
| Long term loan |  | 100 000 |
| |  | R255 000 |

| | | |
|---|---|---|
| Employment of capital | | |
|   Fixed assets | | |
|     Land and buildings | | R25 000 |
|     Motor vehicles | | 56 000 |
|     Plant | | 73 000 |
| | | 154 000 |
|   Investments | | 8 500 |
|   Net current assets | | 92 500 |
|     Current assets | | |
|       Stock | R27 000 | |
|       Debtors | 74 000 | |
|       Bank | 42 000 | |
| | R143 000 | |
|     Current liabilities | | |
|       Receiver of Revenue | R11 000 | |
|       Creditors | 39 500 | |
| | R50 500 | |
| | | R255 000 |

2) The creditors in the above balance sheet include the current portion of the long term loan. The loan bears interest at 18% per annum payable six monthly on 30 June and 31 December. Repayments of capital are to be made on 30 June each year commencing on 30 June 19X9 at the rate of R10 000 per annum.

3) A review of the bank statements reveals the following:

(a) The bank balance at 31 December 19x9 was R67 000.

(b) At no time during the year was the account in overdraft.

(c) A cheque for R16 000 deposited on 1 May 19x9 was in respect of the sale of a car. This car had a book value of R19 000 on 1 May 19x9.
Part of the proceeds of the sale i.e. R10 000 was used as a trade in on a new car purchased for R39 200. The balance of the purchase price was paid a few days later.

(d) The deposit of a cheque for R6 000 was the difference between the purchase of 200 Duiker Ltd shares at R5 each and the sale of 4 000 Steenbok Ltd shares.

(e) The following payments inter alia were noted:

| | | | |
|---|---|---|---|
| 31 January 19x9 | Receiver of Revenue ('88 assess.) | R11 000 |
| 28 February 19x9 | Plant Co. (plant purchased) | 24 000 |
| 30 June 19x9 | Broker & Co (shares purchased) | 30 000 |
| 30 June 19x9 | Receiver of Revenue (prov payment) | 3 000 |
| 31 December 19x9 | " (prov payment) | 3 000 |

4) Stock was counted on 31 December 19x9 and stock costing R21 500 was on hand.

5) Debtors terms are 60 days. The credit controller informs you that 80% of debtors pay within the credit terms, 15% pay within 90 days and 5% are not collectable and are fully provided for at the year end. Cash collections from December debtors during January and February 19y0 were R14 800 and R10 000 respectively.

6) Creditors statements at 31 December 19x9 totalled R25 100.

7) Land and buildings costing R120 000 were purchased during the year. This was financed by a 100% bond raised on 1 August 19x9. The property was independently revalued at R136 000 on 31 December 19x9 and it was decided to show this amount in the books. Interest at the rate of 20% p.a. is payable each month and capital is repayable in equal annual instalments over six years, repayment commencing on 30 June 19y0.

8) Fixed asset depreciation policy is as follows:-
Land and buildings - not depreciated
Motor vehicles    - 15% on reducing balance
Plant             - 10% on reducing balance
The tax value of assets is the same as the book value and no assets are fully depreciated.

9)    No dividends were received, declared or paid during the year.

<u>YOU ARE REQUIRED</u>:

To prepare a cash flow statement for Wildebeest Limited for the year ended
31 December 19x9.

# M19

Powerline Limited is a public company engaged in the manufacturing of electronic components. The following are the unclassified balance sheets of Powerline Limited:

|  | 31 December 19X2 | 31 December 19X1 |
|---|---|---|
| Stated capital - ordinary shares | R810 000 | R750 000 |
| Creditors | 525 000 | 600 000 |
| Shareholders for ordinary dividend | 45 000 | 37 500 |
| Retained income | 1 965 000 | 1 632 000 |
| Accumulated depreciation |  |  |
|    - plant | 472 500 | 375 000 |
|    - motor vehicles | 52 500 | 33 000 |
| Capital redemption reserve fund | 75 000 | - |
| Bank overdraft | 30 000 | - |
| Mortgage debentures | - | 75 000 |
| Long term loan | 270 000 | 300 000 |
| Non distributable reserve |  |  |
| - revaluation of land and buildings | 180 000 | - |
| 8% redeemable preference shares | - | 150 000 |
| Receiver of Revenue | 270 000 | 300 000 |
|  | R4 695 000 | R4 252 500 |
|  | ========= | ========= |
| Debtors | R802 500 | R870 000 |
| Stock | 585 000 | 517 500 |
| Bank | - | 60 000 |
| Preliminary expenses | - | 52 500 |
| Land and buildings | 2 250 000 | 1 800 000 |
| Unlisted investments | 22 500 | 22 500 |
| Listed investments | - | 75 000 |
| Motor vehicles | 120 000 | 120 000 |
| Plant | 915 000 | 735 000 |
|  | R4 695 000 | R4 252 500 |
|  | ========= | ========= |

The following additional information is also available:

1) The 8% preference shares were redeemed on 30 June 19X2 at a premium of 2%. The redemption was financed partly out of the proceeds of an issue of 60 000 no par value ordinary shares issued on 29 June 19X2 at R1,25 per share and partly out of the proceeds of the sale of the company's listed investments. (See notes 5 & 11)

2) Share issue expenses amounting to R4 500 were incurred in issuing the no par value shares. The preliminary expenses at 31 December 19X1 were correctly written off partially against the stated capital account and partially against retained income.

3) As the long-term loan is repayable in 10 equal instalments of R30 000 from 1 January 19X3, R30 000 of the long-term liability was transferred to creditors.

# M19 CONTINUED

4)   The company received income from investments amounting to R8 750 and
     paid interest of R22 500.

5)   An interim ordinary dividend of R37 500 was declared and paid on
     10 July 19X2.  The preference dividend for half a year was paid when
     the shares were redeemed.

6)   The balance on the Receiver of Revenue account on 31 December 19X1 was
     paid on 16 February 19X2.  In addition two provisional tax payments of
     R135 000 each were made during the year ended 31 December 19X2.

7)   The total depreciation charge for the year ended 31 December 19X2 was
     R172 500.

8)   In January 19X2 a motor vehicle was sold at a profit of R3 000.  At the
     same time a new vehicle costing R18 000 was acquired.

9)   The company acquired new plant costing R255 000 during August 19X2.
     During the same month an item of plant which had cost    R36 000 and
     which had been depreciated by R24 000 was sold at a profit of R3 000,
     while another item of plant with a book value of R18 000 was scrapped.

10)  Land and buildings which had cost of R570 000 were sold for R675 000 in
     March 19X2.

11)  The listed investments were sold for R90 000 in July 19X2 to finance
     the redemption of preference shares.

<u>YOU ARE REQUIRED TO:</u>

prepare the cash flow statement of Powerline Limited for the year ended
31 December 19X2 in compliance with the requirements of the Companies Act and
generally accepted accounting practice.

**M20**

The following trial balances were extracted from the books of Prague Limited
at 31 July:

|                                            | 19x0      | 19x1      |
|--------------------------------------------|-----------|-----------|
| Bank overdraft                             | R12 750   | -         |
| Capital redemption reserve fund            | -         | R90 000   |
| Cash at bank                               | -         | 45 000    |
| Creditors                                  | 378 750   | 333 750   |
| Debtors                                    | 616 250   | 702 500   |
| Goodwill                                   | 25 000    | 25 000    |
| Investments                                | 37 500    | -         |
| Land and buildings                         | 1 125 000 | 1 425 000 |
| Long term loan                             | 112 500   | 90 000    |
| Plant and machinery                        | 435 000   | 570 000   |
| Accumulated depreciation                   |           |           |
|   - plant                        | 213 750   | 270 000   |
| Preliminary expenses                       | 7 500     | -         |
| Receiver of Revenue (credit balances)      | 217 500   | 165 000   |
| Retained income                            | 1 056 000 | 1 507 500 |
| Share capital - ordinary                   | 412 500   | 465 000   |
|     - 8% redeemable preference | 90 000 | - |
| Shareholders for dividends                 | 15 000    | 18 750    |
| Stock                                      | 262 500   | 307 500   |
| Short term portion of loan                 | -         | 22 500    |
| Surplus on revaluation of land and building| -         | 112 500   |

All adjusting and closing entries have been made except the one referred to
in (4) below.

<u>NOTES</u>

1) The ordinary share capital is made up of 25 cents par value shares. On
   1 November 19x0 the company issued a further 210 000 ordinary shares to
   the public at a premium of 5 cents per share. On 15 November 19x0 the
   preliminary expenses were written off in such a way as to maintain
   distributable reserves at the maximum amount.

2) On 31 January 19x1 the preference shares were redeemed at a premium of
   10%. The redemption was financed out of the company's liquid resources
   which included the proceeds of R42 500 on disposal of the investments.
   The premium on redemption was provided for partly out of the balance on
   the share premium account.

3) The long-term loan is repayable in 5 equal annual instalments of
   R22 500 commencing on 31 January 19x2.

4) The company has been amortising goodwill at R5 000 p.a.  No entries have been made in respect of the amount to be amortised for the current year.

5) During the year the company purchased additional land and buildings for R225 000 and sold some of its land at a profit of R11 250.

6) During January 19x1 a machine which had originally cost R67 500 and on which depreciation of R56 250 had been provided was traded in at a profit of R3 750 in part payment of a new machine costing R240 000.  In March 19x1 a machine with a book value of R3 000 was scrapped.

7) The amount owing to the Receiver of Revenue was correctly reflected at 31 July 19x0 and was paid to him on 30 November 19x0.  In addition provisional payments totalling R165 000 were made during the current year.

8) In addition to the ordinary dividend declared at 31 July 19x1, an interim dividend of R15 000 was paid on 31 January 19x1.

9) Interest amounting to R13 500 was paid during the year and a dividend of R4 500 was received.


<u>YOU ARE REQUIRED TO PREPARE</u>:

the cash flow statement of Prague Limited for the year ended 31 July 19x1 in accordance with generally accepted practice.

## M21

"The cash flow statement is prepared to provide information which is not provided in the balance sheet or income statement".

<u>YOU ARE REQUIRED TO</u>:

discuss this statement.  Your answer must include a discussion of the importance of the operating activities figure in the cash flow statement.

# M22

The following balances were extracted from the ledger of W Ferreira Limited.

| | 30 September 19x2 | 30 September 19x1 |
|---|---|---|
| Accounts payable | R133 000 | R160 000 |
| Accounts receivable | 265 000 | 231 000 |
| Accumulated depreciation | | |
| - motor vehicles | 35 000 | 20 000 |
| - plant | 115 000 | 91 000 |
| Bank overdraft | 5 000 | |
| Bank balance | - | 19 000 |
| Deferred taxation | 32 000 | 20 000 |
| Goodwill at cost | - | 12 000 |
| Investments at cost | - | 30 000 |
| Land and buildings at valuation | 600 000 | 477 000 |
| Long term loan | 40 000 | 50 000 |
| Motor vehicles at cost | 100 000 | 90 000 |
| Ordinary share capital | | |
| 350 000 shares of 50c each | - | 175 000 |
| Plant at cost | 241 000 | 184 000 |
| Preliminary and share issue expenses | - | 11 000 |
| Provision for taxation | 70 000 | 92 000 |
| Redeemable preference shares - 12% p.a. | - | 40 000 |
| Retained income | 570 000 | 493 000 |
| Shareholders for dividend | 8 000 | 6 000 |
| Stated capital | 280 000 | - |
| Stock | 130 000 | 111 000 |
| Surplus on revaluation of land and buildings | 48 000 | 18 000 |

The following additional information must be taken into account:

1.  The preference shares were redeemed on 31 October 19x1 at a premium of 2%. The redemption was financed out of the proceeds from the disposal of the company's investments.

2.  The investments were sold on 16 October 19x1 for R52 000.

3.  On 21 December 19x1 the company issued a further 130 000 ordinary shares to the public at a premium of 10c per share. Share issue expenses of R2 000 were incurred. The directors then decided to write off the preliminary and share issue expenses so as to retain the maximum balance in the retained income account. The necessary accounting entries were made.

4.  On 15 January 19x2 the company made a capitalisation issue of one share for every six held to existing shareholders.

5.  On 1 June 19x2 the company converted all its ordinary par value shares to no par value shares.

# M22 CONTINUED

6.     The long term loan was raised on 1 December 19x9 and is repayable in 5 equal annual instalments, commencing on 1 January 19y3.

7.     In addition to the amount owing in respect of the final ordinary dividend  proposed on 30 September 19x1, an interim ordinary dividend of R10 000 was paid on 16 April 19x2.

8.     The taxation note to the financial statements at 30 September 19x2 reflected the following information:

```
SA Normal taxation
   Current taxation                      R170 000
   Underprovision in previous year          8 000
   Deferred taxation                       12 000
                                         R190 000
                                         =======
```

9.     During July 19x2 the company  sold a piece of land which had cost R13 000, for a profit of R15 000.

10.    During August 19x2 some obsolete plant was scrapped and new plant costing R102 000 was purchased.

11.    During September 19x2 the company sold a motor vehicle costing R14 000 for R1 500. A loss of R1 500 was incurred.

12.    The total depreciation charge for plant and vehicles for the year ended 30 September 19x2 was R87 000.


<u>YOU ARE REQUIRED TO:</u>

prepare (in accordance with generally accepted accounting practice) the cash flow statement of W Ferreira Limited for the year ended 30 September 19x2.

**SECTION N**

**ANALYSIS AND
INTERPRETATION OF
FINANCIAL STATEMENTS**

The following summarised balance sheet at 30 September 19x5 (with comparative figures at 30 September 19x4) and income statement are presented to you:

BANGERS LIMITED

BALANCE SHEET AT 30 SEPTEMBER 19x5

|  | 19x5 | 19x4 |
|---|---|---|
| Share capital |  |  |
| Authorised 10 000 redeemable preference shares | R10 000 | R10 000 |
| 50 000 ordinary shares of R1 each | 50 000 | 50 000 |
|  | R60 000 | R60 000 |
|  | ====== | ====== |
| Issued |  |  |
| 10 000 redeemable preference shares of R1 each | - | R10 000 |
| 45 000 ordinary shares of R1 each | R45 000 | 45 000 |
| Capital redemption reserve | 10 000 | - |
| General reserve  R14 000 |  |  |
| Redemption of preference shares  11 000 | 3 000 | 14 000 |
| Retained income | 8 880 | 6 400 |
|  | 66 880 | 71 400 |
| Creditors | 35 650 | 21 600 |
| Bank overdraft | 22 470 | 6 400 |
|  | R125 000 | R99 400 |
|  | ======= | ====== |

|  | 19x5 |  | 19x4 |  |
|---|---|---|---|---|
| Goodwill, at cost less amounts written off |  | R1 000 | R2 000 |  |
| Land and buildings, at cost |  | 10 000 | 10 000 |  |
| Plant and machinery at cost | R78 000 |  |  | R60 000 |
| Accumulated depreciation | 45 000 | 33 000 | 20 200 | 39 800 |
| Furniture and fixtures, at cost | 8 100 |  |  | 7 850 |
| Accumulated depreciation | 3 100 | 5 000 | 5 050 | 2 800 |
| Motor vehicles, at cost | 4 000 |  |  | 4 000 |
| Accumulated depreciation | 3 200 | 800 | 1 600 | 2 400 |
| Stock |  | 42 400 | 33 100 |  |
| Debtors | 34 150 |  |  | 28 250 |
| Provision for bad debts | 1 350 | 32 800 | 27 450 | 800 |
|  |  | R125 000 | R99 400 |  |
|  |  | ======= | ====== |  |

# N1 CONTINUED

<u>INCOME STATEMENTS</u>

|                                         |       | 19x5   |       | 19x4    |
|-----------------------------------------|-------|--------|-------|---------|
| OPERATING INCOME                        |       | R13 330 |      | R8 680  |
| TAXATION                                |       | 4 350  |       | 3 000   |
|                                         |       | 8 980  |       | 5 680   |
|                                         |       |        |       |         |
| DIVIDENDS PAID - PREFERENCE SHARES      | R250  |        | R500  |         |
|     - ORDINARY SHARES - INTERIM | 2 250 |  | 2 250 |     |
|     - ORDINARY SHARE - FINAL | - | 2 500 | 4 500 | 7 250 |
| RETAINED INCOME FOR THE YEAR            |       | 6 480  |       | (1 570) |
| RETAINED INCOME AT BEGINNING OF YEAR    |       | 2 400  |       | 3 970   |
| RETAINED INCOME PER BALANCE SHEET       |       | R8 880 |       | R2 400  |

In order to increase the capacity of the factory new plant was purchased during the year for R20 000 while certain plant, which was obsolete, was sold as scrap for R100. The plant scrapped had originally cost R2 000 and at date of disposal depreciation of R1 800 had been provided in respect of it. In addition fixtures costing R250 were installed. The following information is available:

|                                         | Year ended 30 September 19x5 | Year ended 30 September 19x4 |
|-----------------------------------------|------------------------------|------------------------------|
| Net sales                               | R200 000                     | R150 000                     |
| Cost of sales                           | 160 000                      | 120 000                      |
| Gross profit                            | 40 000                       | 30 000                       |
| Sundry expenses (including depreciation and goodwill written off) | 26 670 | 21 320 |
| Net income                              | R13 330                      | R8 680                       |

<u>YOU ARE REQUIRED TO</u>:

(a) prepare a cash flow statement for the year ended 30 September 19x5.
(b) calculate and interpret six significant ratios, and
(c) comment on the liquid position of the company, on how that position has developed and on how it might be improved.

Mr Pep of Pill Agencies gives you the following trading accounts and informs you that he suspects that a storekeeper employed by him from 1 June 19x4 has been stealing.  He is satisfied that no goods were stolen prior to this date as his previous storekeeper had been with him for many years.

TRADING STATEMENTS FOR THE YEARS ENDED 30 SEPTEMBER 19x3 AND 19x4

|  | 19x3 | 19x4 |
|---|---|---|
| Stock at beginning of year | R8 500 | R8 670 |
| Purchases | 36 000 | 43 624 |
| Duty | 9 000 | 10 906 |
| Importing charges | 6 000 | 7 000 |
|  | 59 500 | 70 200 |
| Stock at end of year | 8 670 | 9 600 |
|  | 50 830 | 60 600 |
| Gross profit | 25 415 | 27 006 |
| Sales | R76 245 | R87 606 |

He gives you the following information:

(a)    The firm imports a particular pharmaceutical commodity which it supplies to local retailers.

(b)    On 1 January 19x4 the overseas price of the commodity increased by 4% and on 1 May 19x4 it increased by 2% of the price ruling after 1 January 19x4.

Purchases for the year were as follows:

| 1 October 19x3 to 31 December 19x3 | R10 500 |
|---|---|
| 1 January 19x4 to 30 April 19x4 | 14 560 |
| 1 May 19x4 to 30 September 19x4 | 18 564 |

(c)    The import duty had remained constant at 25% _ad valorem_.  Importing charges have always been calculated on the basis of weight.

(d)    Severe competition has prevented the firm from passing all the increased costs on to its customers but on 1 July 19x4 the selling price had been increased by 3%. Sales for the year were as follows:

| 1 October 19x3 to 30 June 19x4 | R65 255 |
|---|---|
| 1 July 19x4 to 30 September 19x4 | 22 351 |

(e)    Stock on hand at 30 September 19x4 consists entirely of goods received during the last three months of the financial year.  It has never been found necessary to write stocks down below cost.

(f)    Previous years trading accounts reveal that the rate of gross profit to turnover has remained constant at approximately 33 1/3%.

<u>YOU ARE REQUIRED</u>:

(i)   to state whether or not the trading results for the year ended 30
      September 19x4 indicate that stock has been stolen, and
(ii)  if they do, to estimate the amount of the discrepancy.

Calculations to be made to the nearest R.

Grant's Electronic Company, a closely held family manufacturer of electric components, has, since the death of its founder/president two years ago, been managed by her nephew John, formerly a company salesman.  The manager at the firm's bank has received from the family numerous complaints about John's actions and has asked you to evaluate John's performance.  The company's most recent financial statements are:

GRANT'S ELECTRONIC COMPANY
BALANCE SHEET AT 30 JUNE 19x8

| CAPITAL EMPLOYED | | |
|---|---|---|
| Share capital and reserves | | R2 010 |
| Long term liabilities | | |
|   9% loan | | 880 |
| | | 2 890 |
| Current liabilities | | 1 110 |
|   Creditors | R730 | |
|   Bills payable (11%) | 380 | |
| | | R4 000 |

| EMPLOYMENT OF CAPITAL | | |
|---|---|---|
| Fixed assets | | R1 130 |
| Current assets | | 2 870 |
|   Stock | R1 190 | |
|   Debtors | 1 550 | |
|   Bank | 130 | |
| | | R4 000 |

INCOME STATEMENT FOR THE YEAR ENDED 30 JUNE 19x8

| | |
|---|---|
| Sales | R6 200 |
| Cost of sales | 4 750 |
| Gross profit | 1 450 |
| Expenses | 1 020 |
| Net operating income | 430 |
| Interest | 121 |
| Net income before tax | 309 |
| Taxation | 123 |
| Net income for the year | R186 |

# N3 CONTINUED

The following are the industry average ratios:

Current ratio:  2,2
Quick ratio:    1,0
Debt interest assets:  50%
Times interest earned:   5,2 times
Stock turnover:  3,8 times
Average collection period:  52 days
Fixed assets turnover: 9,25 times
Total assets turnover: 1,85 times
Net income on sales: 3,19%
Return on total assets: 5,90%
Return on net worth: 10,8%


<u>YOU ARE REQUIRED TO</u>:

a)    Calculate the relevant financial ratios for this analysis.

b)    Evaluate John's performance and list specific areas that need
      improvement.

# N4

You are furnished with the following information relating to P Limited, a manufacturing company for the years ended 31 December 19x5 and 19x4.

|                                                  | 19x5 (R000's) | 19x4 (R000's) |
| ------------------------------------------------ | ------------- | ------------- |
| Ordinary share capital (R1 shares)               | 500           | 400           |
| Preference share capital (R1 shares)             | 100           | 100           |
| Distributable reserves (including current earnings) | 150        | 130           |
| Long-term borrowings                             | 200           | 200           |
| Stock on hand                                    | 497           | 344           |
| Debtors                                          | 510           | 430           |
| Cash at bank                                     | -             | 90            |
| Creditors                                        | 490           | 480           |
| Bank overdraft                                   | 40            | -             |
| Net income before interest and taxation          | 160           | 130           |
| Interest paid on long-term borrowings            | 20            | 20            |
| Preference dividends paid                        | 10            | 10            |
| Rate of taxation                                 | 50 cents/R    | 50 cents/R    |
| Ordinary dividends paid                          | 40            | 30            |

## NOTES:

1. There are no arrears on interest payments or preference dividends.
2. The share issue took place on 1 July 19x5.   There had been no other share issues since incorporation.
3. The net income of the company corresponds with its taxable income.

YOU ARE REQUIRED TO:

(a) Calculate the earnings per share for 19x5 and 19x4, and show how this information should be presented in the income statement.

(b) Analyse the return of equity (including the effect of gearing) of the company and comment thereon.

(c) Analyse the liquidity position of the company and comment thereon.

(d) Comment upon the dividend policy of the company.

NOTE:  You may ignore the effect of inflation.

# N5

(a)    While most users would be interested in all the ratios and percentages
       yielded by a set of financial statements, certain types of ratios may
       be said to be of more importance to particular users.

<u>YOU ARE REQUIRED TO</u>:

Indicate the ratios in which the following categories of users would be
specifically interested.    Support your selection of ratios with reasons.

(i)    Management
(ii)   Investors
(iii)  Long term lenders
(iv)   Short term creditors

(b)    A ratio on its own may be a meaningless figure, it acquires
       significance when a comparison is made.

<u>YOU ARE REQUIRED TO</u>:

Indicate the three major areas against which a particular company's financial
ratios may be compared and to explain what may be inferred from such
comparison.

The following is an extract made from a detailed comparative statement of ratios for the four years ended 30 June 19x5 calculated from the annual financial statements of Reliable Retailers Limited.   The managing director is of the opinion that the information given below indicates that the company will have to tighten up on credit allowed to customers.

|  |  | 19x2 | 19x3 | 19x4 | 19x5 |
|---|---|---|---|---|---|
| 1. | Number of average day's credit sales outstanding at the end of the year (basis 300 working days) | 90 | 85 | 80 | 75 |
| 2. | Bad debts to debtors | 10% | 12% | 15% | 15% |
| 3. | Debtors outstanding at 30 June | R5 100 | R5 525 | R7 000 | R8 500 |

YOU ARE REQUIRED TO STATE, giving full reasons, whether or not you agree with the managing director.

## N7

The following information in respect of Z Limited is given to you:

<u>SUMMARISED INCOME STATEMENT</u>

| | | |
|---|---:|---:|
| Sales (net) | | R1 520 400 |
| Cost of sales | | 905 000 |
| | | 615 400 |
| Expenses | | |
| Selling and administration | R265 360 | |
| Depreciation | 4 000 | 311 320 |
| | | 304 080 |
| Taxation | | 152 040 |
| Net income for the year | | R152 040 |

<u>STATEMENT OF NET CURRENT LIABILITIES</u>

| | | |
|---|---:|---:|
| Current liabilities | | R446 100 |
| Current assets | | 380 100 |
| Stock | R226 250 | |
| Debtors | 141 904 | |
| Bank | 11 946 | |
| Shortage of working capital | | R66 000 |

Additional information:

1. All sales are made on credit.
2. The only assets other than current assets were fixed assets with book values of R705 900.

<u>YOU ARE REQUIRED</u>:

Assuming that Z Limited operates for 360 days per annum to compute the following ratios in the most meaningful way given the above information.

1. Debtors to sales (net) ratio. (Average number of days outstanding.)
2. Stock turnover ratio.
3. Number of days cash flow from operations required to cover the shortage of working capital.

## N8

The financial statements of Eroica Limited for the year ended 30 September
19x9 contain the following information:

| | |
|---|---|
| Current ratio | 1,75 to 1 |
| Liquidity ratio (Acid test) | 1,25 to 1 |
| Ratio of purchases to cost of stock sold | 1,125 to 1 |
| Percentage of fixed assets to issued share capital | 60% |
| Net profit percentage to issued share capital | 15% |
| Percentage of dividend paid on 19 December 19x8 to shareholders' funds at beginning of year | 25% |
| Annual rate of stock turnover, based on stock at 30 September 19x9 | 4,16 times |
| Gross profit percentage to turnover | 20% |
| Average age of outstanding debts, based on a year of 52 weeks | 7 weeks |
| Net current assets | R37 500 |
| Issued share capital in ordinary shares of R1 each | R50 000 |

The company only sells goods on credit.

On 30 September 19x9, there were:

(a)     no assets or debit balances other than fixed and current assets,
(b)     no current assets other than stock, debtors and bank balances,
(c)     no liabilities other than creditors,
(d)     no reserves other than retained income.


<u>YOU ARE REQUIRED</u>:

To prepare, in as much detail as possible,

(i)     the summarised balance sheet at 30 September 19x9, and
(ii)    the income statement for the year ended 30 September 19x9.
        Ignore taxation.

The following figures were extracted from the final accounts of Sellers Limited for the years ended 30 June 19x3, 19x4 and 19x5. From them you are required to prepare a comparative statement of ratios and to comment on the results.

|  | 19x3 | 19x4 | 19x5 |
|---|---|---|---|
| Sales - wholesale:  credit (net) | R40 000 | R42 000 | R40 000 |
| Sales - retail:  credit (net) | - | 10 000 | 30 000 |
| Sales - retail:  cash (net) | - | 3 000 | 10 000 |
| Cost of sales | 32 000 | 41 400 | 56 000 |
| Stock at commencement of year | 7 500 | 8 500 | 9 500 |
| Stock at end of year | 8 500 | 9 500 | 12 500 |
| Bad debts incurred - wholesale customers | 400 | 450 | 420 |
| Bad debts incurred - retail customers | - | 200 | 900 |
| Selling and distribution expenses (other than bad debts) | 4 000 | 6 800 | 12 000 |
| Discount allowed | 800 | 960 | 1 040 |
| Net income | 600 | 2 600 | 6 100 |
| Debtors - wholesale customers | 3 700 | 4 000 | 3 800 |
| Debtors - retail customers | - | 2 000 | 5 850 |
| Creditors | 5 000 | 8 000 | 12 000 |
| Share capital | 20 000 | 20 000 | 20 000 |
| Reserves (including retained income) | 2 000 | 4 600 | 6 700 |
| Dividend paid on 31 December 19x4 | - | - | 4 000 |

Discount terms to all credit customers were 2 1/2% one month. The management informs you that the gross profit on wholesale sales has remained constant. The debts written off as bad were all of small amounts.

The reserves (including retained income) amounted to R1 400 at 30 June 19x2. There has been no alteration in the share capital since the inception of the company. Profits prior to 19x3 have never exceeded R1 000 per annum. There were no long term loans.

The following are the summarised income statements for the year 19x3 and the balance sheet at 31 December 19x3 of Exe Limited and Wye Limited:

<u>SUMMARISED INCOME STATEMENTS</u>

|  | Exe | | Wye | |
|---|---|---|---|---|
| Sales (all credit) | | R360 000 | | R360 000 |
| Cost of sales | | 315 000 | | 320 000 |
| Stock 1 January 19x3 | R48 000 | | R8 000 | |
| Purchases | 319 000 | | 324 000 | |
| | 367 000 | | 332 000 | |
| Stock 31 December 19x3 | 52 000 | | 12 000 | |
| Gross profit | | 45 000 | | 40 000 |
| Expenses | | 16 000 | | 18 000 |
| Retained income for the year | | 29 000 | | 22 000 |
| Retained income at 19x2 | | 31 000 | | 2 000 |
| Retained income per balance sheet | | R60 000 | | R24 000 |

<u>SUMMARISED BALANCE SHEETS</u>

|  | Exe | Wye |  | Exe | Wye |
|---|---|---|---|---|---|
| Share capital - issued | R100 000 | R100 000 | Fixed assets | R127 000 | R107 000 |
| General reserve | 80 000 | 16 000 | Stock | 52 000 | 12 000 |
| Retained income | 60 000 | 24 000 | Debtors | 40 000 | 24 000 |
| Creditors | 63 000 | 40 000 | Bank | 84 000 | 37 000 |
| | R303 000 | R180 000 | | R303 000 | R180 000 |

No shares were issued and no dividends were paid during the year.

<u>YOU ARE REQUIRED</u>:

(a)   to calculate the following ratios:
 (i)   Rate of stock turnover
 (ii)  Debtor ratio (in months)
 (iii) Current ratio
 (iv)  Liquid (Acid Test) ratio
 (v)   Gross profit as percentage of sales
 (vi)  Net profit as percentage of sales
 (vii) Return on capital employed.

 The stock of each company has been built up at an even rate during the year.

(b)   to describe briefly the conclusions to be drawn from a comparison of the above ratios and percentages relating to Exe Limited with those relating to Wye Limited.

 Both companies sell the same kind of products in similar markets.

 All calculations should be correct to two decimal places where necessary.

The following incomplete balance sheet is presented to you:

<u>X LIMITED</u>

<u>BALANCE SHEET AT 31 MARCH 19X9</u>

| | | | | |
|---|---|---|---|---|
| SHARE CAPITAL | R600 000 | FIXED ASSETS | | R588 000 |
|   Authorised and issued | | | | |
|   600 000 ordinary shares | | CURRENT ASSETS | | ....... |
|   of R1 each | |   Stock | R...... | |
| ACCUMULATED LOSS | ....... |   Debtors | ...... | |
| SHAREHOLDERS' FUNDS | ....... |   Bank | <u>50 000</u> | |
| LONG TERM LIABILITY | | | | |
|   10% Secured debentures | <u>.......</u> | | | |
| | | | | |
| CURRENT LIABILITIES | | | | |
|   Trade creditors | R...... | | | |
|   Taxation | <u>50 000</u> | | | |
| | R | | | <u>R864 000</u> |
| | ======= | | | ======= |

Additional information:

| | | |
|---|---|---|
| 1. | Current ratio at 31 March 19x9 | 1,5:1 |
| 2. | Total liabilities to shareholders' funds | 0,8:1 |
| 3. | Stock turnover based on sales and closing stock | 15 times |
| 4. | Stock turnover based on cost of sales and | |
| | closing stock | 10,5 times |
| 5. | Gross profit for year ended 31 March 19x9 | R630 000 |

<u>YOU ARE REQUIRED TO:</u>
To prepare a balance sheet of X Limited at 31 March 19x9 using the above information.

# N12

The following financial data relate to Ying Tong (Pty) Limited and are extracted from the company's income statement for the year ended 31 December 19x9, and from the balance sheet at that date:

| | |
|---|---|
| Issued share capital (R1 shares) | R500 |
| Turnover | R100 000 |
| Gross profit % on sale | 15% |
| Turnover to investment in assets | 1,60:1 |
| Net income before interest and after tax to turnover | 6% |
| Return on total assets | 9,6% |
| Working capital | R30 000 |
| Current ratio | 2,5:1 |
| Quick ratio | 1,3:1 |
| Debt ratio | ,56:1 |
| Dividends paid and proposed | R4,40 per share |

Taxation is calculated at 50% of accounting net income before taxation. Interest expense is 40% of net income after taxation.

<u>YOU ARE REQUIRED TO</u>:

Prepare the income statement of Ying Tong (Pty) Limited for the year ended 31 December 19x9 and the balance sheet at that date.

You need only give the necessary details which you are able to extract from the information supplied above.

# SECTION O

# JOINT VENTURES

**Ol**

Cohen of Vryheid and Jonker of Johannesburg enter into a joint venture in drums of chemicals sharing profits and losses equally.

Show the ledger accounts in Cohen's books recording the following transactions and rule them off at 31 March 19x4, the date of Cohen's balance sheet:

19x4
Feb.  1       Cohen buys 1 000 drums for R500 and pays cash
 "   18      Jonker pays railage on drums received, R200
 "   25      Jonker sells 500 drums for R2 per drum cash
Mar.  3       Cohen buys 1 200 drums for R600 and pays cash
 "    3      Cohen pays railage on drums forwarded, R240
 "    8      Jonker sells 800 drums for R1 600 and sends Cohen the cheque he receives
 "   31      Cohen buys 600 drums for R300 and pays cash

H Brown of Piet Retief and S White of Johannesburg enter into a joint venture to purchase cattle in Piet Retief and sell them in Johannesburg.  Profits are to be share equally.

The following transactions take place:

```
19x4
July 11      Brown buys 10 cattle for cash at R250 each
  "   12      Brown pays railage on 10 cattle to Johannesburg R150
  "   20      Brown buys 20 cattle for cash at R270 each f.o.r. Johannesburg
  "   25      S White sells 5 cattle to B Pink on credit at R300 each
Aug.  4      S White sells 15 cattle for R4 600 cash
  "    8      S White sells 10 cattle for R3 200 cash
  "    9      Brown buys 15 cattle for cash at R280 each
  "    9      Brown pays railage on 15 cattle to Johannesburg R225
  "   30      S White sells 10 cattle for cash at R315 each
  "   31      S White pays H Brown R11 000
```

Show these transactions in White's ledger and rule if off at 31 August 19x4.

S Clarke of Maritzburg and J McKenzie of Durban entered into a joint venture, in which the former purchased 500 pigs at R130 each, f.o.r. Maritzburg, and sent them to McKenzie, at Durban, who was to sell them to the best advantage. The transport, amounting to R800, was paid by Clarke. McKenzie successfully tendered for a certain contract to supply 700 pigs at R150 each, intending to use the pigs sent by Clarke. To complete this contract, he purchased for account of the joint venture 200 pigs at R140 each, and duly delivered the 700 animals. McKenzie paid delivery charges amounting to R200 for the 500 pigs and R100 for the others, and charged the joint venture R300 rent for keeping the pigs until sold. McKenzie in turn purchased 100 head of cattle at R300 each, and forwarded them to Maritzburg for sale by Clarke. Clarke paid the railage amounting to R500 and delivery and storage charges amounting to R140 and sold 70 head of cattle for R25 000 and the remainder for R11 000 and was allowed commission at 1% on the sale price of all the cattle. Clarke drew on McKenzie at sight for R48 000 and McKenzie drew at sight on Clarke for R6 000.

The profits on these ventures were to be shared equally by Clarke and McKenzie.

Show the ledger accounts in Clarke's books. Separate joint venture accounts should be kept for pigs and cattle.

No journal entries are required.

# O4

R Gain of Postmasburg enters into a joint venture with L Hay of Cape Town for the purchase and sale of mineral ore.   It is agreed that the profits of the venture shall be shared equally.

From the following particulars, write up the ledger accounts in Gain's books, showing the division of profits to 30 June 19x2.

1.   January 3, Gain bought 10 tons of ore for R2 500, and railed same to Cape Town, paying railage R50.
2.   January 10, Gain bought 5 tons of ore at R255 per ton, f.o.r. Cape Town.
3.   January 15, Hay sold 10 tons of ore at R365 per ton.
4.   January 20, Hay paid sundry assay fees and selling expenses, R110.
5.   February 11, Gain bought 15 tons at R250 per ton and sold them to another agent in Postmasburg for R3 900 net.
6.   February 19, Hay sold 5 tons for a net amount of R1 750.
7.   April 12, Gain bought 20 tons at R260 per ton, and paid railage to Cape Town, R5 per ton.
8.   April 15, Hay remitted to Gain R2 500.
9.   April 15, Hay sold 15 tons for R4 875.
10.   May 10, Hay sold 5 tons for R1 625.
11.   May 14, Hay paid expenses, R300.
12.   June 5, Gain bought 10 tons at R265 per ton f.o.r. Cape Town.
13.   June 10, Hay received R400 adjustment on previous sales.

Spick and Span of Johannesburg enter into a joint venture, sharing profits in the ratio of 3:2, to send paint on consignment to Spruce of Cape Town.   They enter into an agreement with Spruce, the terms of which are as follows:

(a)   Ownership of the goods is to remain with Spick and Span.
(b)   Spruce is to receive a del credere commission of 7 1/2% of the sales.
(c)   Spruce is to be liable to Spick and Span for the value of the goods as and when they are sold, and is to render an account sales each month. A remittance of the amount due by Spruce is to be forwarded to Spick at the end of each month.

The following are the transactions for the month of February 19x2:

(a)   On 1 February Spick sends R800 worth of paint to Spruce and pays railage of R40.   Span sends goods worth R1 200 to Spruce, and he pays railage amounting to R60.   Span also pays R20 delivery charges.
(b)   On 15 February Spick draws a bill on Spruce for R600 for two months, and then discounts the bill with his bankers at 5% per annum, and the proceeds are divided between Spick and Span in the profit-sharing ratio.
(c)   The account sales is received from Spruce on 28 February, and it is ascertained that all the goods have been sold for R3 000.   The following expenses have been incurred by Spruce, who has deducted all of them from the amount due (together with the commission) and has forwarded his cheque for the balance to Spick.

| Advertising | R25; | Delivery charges | R130; |
|---|---|---|---|
| Bad debts | R50; | Discounts | R10. |

(d)   Spick and Span settle with each other at the end of February 19x2.


<u>YOU ARE REQUIRED TO</u>:

to show how the profit is calculated and to give the entries in the books of Spick in the form of ledger accounts.

Brown of Durban and Green of Johannesburg enter into a joint venture in fresh fruit sharing profits and losses in the ratio of 2:1 respectively.

Show ledger accounts, excluding the bank account, in Green's books recording the following transactions and rule them off at 31 October - his financial year end.

| Oct. | | |
|---|---|---|
| | | Brown buys 120 cases for R480 and pays cash. |
| " | 5 | Green pays railage of R60 in cash. |
| " | 6 | Green pays selling expenses of R75 in cash. |
| " | 8 | Green sells 90 cases for R720 to Red of Cape Town. |
| " | 13 | Green sells 30 cases for R240 cash. |
| " | 15 | Brown draws bill at 30 d/s on Green for R600. |
| " | 18 | Green accepts the bill on presentation. |
| " | 18 | Green receives cash from Red. |
| " | 21 | Brown buys 60 cases for R600 and pays cash. |
| " | 21 | Brown pays railage of R60 in cash. |
| " | 25 | Green pays selling expenses of R45 in cash. |
| " | 27 | Green sells 45 cases for R900 cash. |
| " | 27 | Green remits R500 to Brown. |

# O7

Du Toit and Van Breda enter into a joint venture, the agreement regarding which provides:

(a)   A separate bank account is to be opened for the venture.
(b)   A special set of books for the venture is to be kept.
(c)   The purpose of the venture is to speculate in pigs and sheep.  Du Toit is entitled to two-thirds of the profit on pigs and one- third of the profit on sheep, while Van Breda is entitled to two-thirds of the profit on sheep and one-third of the profit on pigs.
(d)   Van Breda is entitled to a salary of R800 per month, but in respect of the month of January 19x4 he is to receive R600 only.  This salary is to be charged equally to pigs and sheep.
(e)   Any entertainment expenses are to be charged equally to pigs and sheep.
(f)   Profits are to be ascertained at the end of each month and distributed to the venturers.  At the same time, adjustments are to be made in respect of any moneys received or paid by the venturers from their private funds.

The following transactions are entered into:

19x4
Jan. 12     Each contributes to the joint bank account the sum of R5 000
  "   14     They buy 100 pigs for R8 000 f.o.r. Nelspruit and pay the amount from the joint bank account.
  "   15     They pay from the joint bank account railage on the pigs to Johannesburg amounting to R450.
  "   18     They sell 80 pigs for R7 700 and bank the proceeds in the joint bank account.
  "   24     They buy 200 sheep for R4 400 f.o.r. Cradock and pay the amount from the joint bank account.
  "   24     They pay from the joint bank account railage on the sheep to Johannesburg amounting to R500.
  "   31     They sell 100 sheep for R3 000 and bank the proceeds in the joint bank account.
  "   31     Entertainment expenses to date paid by Du Toit from his private funds amount to R80.
Feb.  2     They sell 20 pigs for R2 150 and bank the proceeds in Du Toit's private bank account.
  "   12     They buy 50 pigs for R4 800 f.o.r. Kaapmuiden and pay the amount from the joint bank account.
  "   14     Van Breda pays from his private bank account R230 in respect of railage on pigs to Johannesburg.
  "   21     Two sheep die.   The carcasses are valueless.
  "   25     They sell 50 sheep for R1 500 and bank the proceeds in the joint bank account.
  "   28     Entertainment expenses for the month paid by Du Toit from his private funds amount to R120.

Give the necessary ledger accounts in the books of the venture.

L Louis, a cattle speculator, of Klawer, entered into a joint venture which the A B Livestock Co. (Pty) Limited of Cape Town.   Louis purchased 600 cattle at R180 each at Klawer and railed them to Cape Town, paying railage amounting to R2 000 and insurance amounting to R600.   The A B Livestock Co. (Pty) Limited, on behalf of the joint venture, successfully tendered for a contract to supply 750 cattle at R200 each.    To complete this contract, the A B Livestock Co. (Pty) Limited purchased for account of the joint venture 150 cattle at R190 each.    The A B Livestock Co. (Pty) Limited paid delivery charges on the 600 cattle amounting to R400 and R80 on the 150 cattle. Grazing-rent charges paid by the A B Livestock Co. (Pty) Limited amounted to R200.     The A B Livestock Co. (Pty) Limited duly delivered and received payment for the 750 cattle.   Louis drew at sight on the A B Livestock Co. (Pty) Limited for R100 000.

The profits on this venture were to be shared equally by Louis and the company.

Prepare the joint venture account as it will appear in the ledger of each party, and draft a memorandum account showing the result of the venture. Dates may be omitted.

L Lloyd of London entered into an agreement with D Davis of Durban for the shipment of certain cotton goods to South Africa.  Davis is to receive a commission of 2% on sales.  The profit or loss resulting from their dealings in these goods is to be shared equally.

Lloyd took goods, valued at  8 100 from his stock, and shipped them to Davis, paying freight and insurance  500 thereon.  He purchased further goods for 5 410 cash, and goods for  9 200 on credit, all for shipment to Davis. Carriage on these goods totalled  290, and freight and insurance  1 020.

Certain of the goods were damaged in transit, and in response to a claim by Davis the insurance company's Durban office accepted liability to the extent of R8 000.

The balance of the goods, on which Davis had paid landing charges amounting to R4 320 were sold by him on credit for R54 000.

Each party recorded in his books only the transactions in which he was directly concerned.

Davis had sent a cheque to Lloyd in settlement.  Prepare the main ledger account kept by each party.  Show also how you determine the amount of profit or loss resulting from these transactions.

Work at R2 to the  and ignore bank charges on the remittance.

# SECTION P

# MISCELLANEOUS TOPICS

## P1

A company has an authorised capital of R100 000 divided into shares of R1 each.  All the shares have been issued and are fully paid.

The manager is entitled to commission of 10% of the profits after charging his commission and taxation and after allowing for a dividend of 10%.  A dividend of 10% has been paid during the year.

Taxation at the rate of 40c in the R of the profits after allowing manager's commission must be provided.

The profits, before allowing for any of the above items, amount to R34 334.

How much commission will the manager be entitled to?

Calculations should be made to the nearest rand.

**P2**

Given below is the trial balance of Stout and Thin Limited at the close of the financial year 30 June 19x2.    The managing director is entitled to a commission of 5% of the profits after charging his commission and after allowing for taxation.

Provision for SA normal tax should be made at the rate of 40c in the R.

A dividend of 5% is proposed by the directors.

From the information given, prepare the income statement for the year ended 30 June 19x2 and show separately details of the calculation of the manager's commission (calculations to be made to the nearest R).   Comparative figures may be omitted.

TRIAL BALANCE AT 30 JUNE 19X2

| | | |
|---|---:|---:|
| Share capital - authorised and issued | | |
|   in R1 shares | | R1 100 000 |
| Retained income at 30 June 19x1 | | 25 000 |
| Land and buildings at cost | R1 138 000 | |
| Creditors | | 50 000 |
| Rent received | | 117 000 |
| Staff salaries (including managing director's | | |
|   salary of R15 000) | 36 000 | |
| General expenses | 22 000 | |
| Bank | 106 000 | |
| | R1 292 000 | R1 292 000 |

No depreciation is provided on buildings.

No directors' fees are payable.

The audit fee of R420 has been included in general expenses.

**P3**

'Carol Ann' cosmetics are manufactured in Cape Town by Carol Ann Preparations Limited.

Ladye Faire, an equal partnership between Carol Ann Preparations Limited and A Aarons, acts as distributor in the Transvaal, selling direct to the public.

Carol Ann Preparations Limited invoices supplies to the partnership at cost plus 25%.  Carol Ann Preparations Limited also allows the partnership a special commission of 5% of the amount by which the turnover of the partnership in any financial year exceeds R250 000.  The partnership has a constant mark-up on all goods.

The following is the income estimate of Ladye Faire for the year ending 31 December 19x2:

| | | |
|---|---:|---:|
| Sales | | R280 000 |
| Cost of sales | | 56 000 |
| | | 224 000 |
| Special commission | | 1 500 |
| | | 225 500 |
| Advertising | R50 000 | |
| Bad debts | 35 000 | |
| Other expenses (not variable) | 95 000 | 180 000 |
| Net income | | R45 500 |

Divided:
|  |  |
|---|---:|
| Carol Ann Preparations Limited | R22 750 |
| A Aarons | 22 750 |
| | R45 500 |

Note: The figure for estimated sales reflects the maximum possible under existing economic conditions.  Ladye Faire has been allowing indiscriminate credit.  It is estimated that it will cost R6 000 per annum to introduce a satisfactory system of credit control.  Bad debts could then be reduced to R1 000 per annum.

On the assumption that these estimates are accurate, make an estimate of the effect of introducing a satisfactory system of credit control for the year under review as far as both Carol Ann Preparations Limited and A Aarons are concerned.  Ignore taxation.

Carol Ann Preparations Limited's production costs are not affected by the volume of output.

# SECTION Q

# PROGRESS TESTS

# Q1

1.

Goodwill is shown at R6 000 in the books of A and B who were sharing profits in the ratio 2:1.

A died and in accordance with the terms of the original partnership agreement the goodwill was assessed at R9 000.

B admitted C to a fifth share of the partnership.   Goodwill was assessed for purposes of the admission of C at R12 000.

B and C agreed that goodwill was to be written down to a nominal value of R1 000.

Assuming that no entries have been made in the books since immediately prior to the death of A the following entry should be passed to give effect to the above:

| | | | |
|---|---|---|---|
| A | Capital B | R5 000 | |
| | Goodwill | | R5 000 |

| | | | |
|---|---|---|---|
| B | Capital B | 5 400 | |
| | Capital C | 1 600 | |
| | Goodwill | | 5 000 |
| | Capital A | | 2 000 |

| | | | |
|---|---|---|---|
| C | Capital B | 4 800 | |
| | Capital C | 2 200 | |
| | Goodwill | | 5 000 |
| | Capital A | | 2 000 |

| | | | |
|---|---|---|---|
| D | Capital B | 600 | |
| | Capital C | 2 400 | |
| | Capital A | | 3 000 |

E    <u>Some other entry</u> viz.,

|  |  |
|---|---|
| .................................... | Dr. ..... |
| .................................... | Dr. ..... |
| .................................... | Cr. ..... |
| .................................... | Cr. ..... |

583

2.

A trial balance was taken out at 31 December 19x6 and it did not balance.
The bookkeeper of the firm made it balance by entering the difference on an
account he called a "suspense account".    When the list of creditors was
extracted its total did not agree with the balance on the creditors' control
account in the general ledger.   The bookkeeper made the control account agree
with the list by transferring the difference to an account in the general
ledger that he called a "creditors' suspense account".

Subsequently, the following was discovered:

A payment to X, a creditor, was made by endorsing to him a bill for R200 which
had previously been received from D, and the receipt of which had been
correctly recorded in the books.   To record the transaction the bookkeeper
had put through the following journal entry:

```
    Bills receivable                        R200
    X (Creditors' ledger)                    200
      Creditors' control                             R400
    ___________________________________
```

The following journal entry is necessary to correct the books:

```
A    Creditors' control account            R600
       Bills receivable                            R400
       Suspense account                             200
     ___________________________________

B    Creditors' control account             600
       Bills receivable                            400
     ___________________________________

C    Creditors' suspense account            400
     Creditors' control account             200
       Bills receivable                            400
     ___________________________________

D    Creditors' suspense account            600
       Bills receivable                            400
       Suspense account                             200
     ___________________________________

E    Suspense account                        200
     Creditors' suspense account            200
       Bills receivable                            400
     ___________________________________
```

# Q1 CONTINUED

3.

The following mistakes were made in writing up a set of books:

(i)   The bills receivable book for one month had been overcast by R10 and in addition the incorrect total of R1 533 was posted to the Sundry Debtors Control as R1 523.

(ii)  The posting of an amount of R23 from the sales day book to Adams's account in the debtors' ledger had been omitted.

(iii) The total of the returns outwards book for one month was R123 but it had been posted to purchases account as R213.

(iv)  A supplier had been paid twice for goods costing R62 and both cheques had been debited to purchases account from the cash book.  The amount had been deducted from a payment to the supplier in the new year.

(v)   The credit side of the postage account in the general ledger had been overcast by R1.

(vi)  The sales day book for one month had been undercast by R100.

(vii) The wages paid column on the credit side of the cash book had been brought forward to the last page of the cash book as R119 instead of R191.   There were no other entries effecting this column on the last page.   The credit side of the cash book failed to cross cast by this difference between R191 and R119.   The total amount of the wages column was posted to the General Ledger as R119.

There were no other mistakes.

The general ledger trial balance must have shown an excess of:

A     debits over credits of R173
B     debits over credits of R261
C     credits over debits of R83
D     debits over credits of R7
E     ..... over ....... of R.....

# Q1 CONTINUED

4.

At 31 December 19x5, A, B and C were in partnership sharing profits and losses in the proportion 3:3:2.   At that date the total of their combined capital accounts was R17 600.   Goodwill did not appear as an asset in the books.

On 1 January 19x6 D was admitted to the partnership and paid R5 000 as capital and R4 000 for a one-fifth share of the business.   The total amount was retained in the business.

Under the new partnership agreement goodwill was not to be shown in the books and the profit sharing ratio of A, B, C and D was to be 3:3:2:2 respectively. Salaries of R8 000;  R5 000;  R4 000 were to be credited annually to B, C and D respectively.

Drawings for the year ended 31 December 19x6 were:

A   R1 600;       B   R8 000;       C   R7 000;       D   R6 000.

At 31 December 19x6 the balances on capital accounts were:

A   R12 400;     B   R10 000;     C   R6 800;       D   R5 800.

Therefore the total profit credited to the partners at 31 December 19x6 must have been:

R ..........

5.

A of Durban and B of Johannesburg entered into a joint venture for the purchase and sale of arms and ammunition.   Profits and losses were to be shared, A 2/3, B 1/3.

The following transactions took place during the quarter ended 30 September 19x8.

1.    On 1 July 19x8 a shipment of 150 revolvers costing R6 750 c.i.f. arrived in Durban where A paid importing charges amounting to R540. The amount of R6 750 was paid to the overseas supplier by B.

2.    A sent 60 revolvers to B who paid railage of R120.

3.    A sold 60 revolvers at cost plus 50% and B sold 45 revolvers at cost plus 50%.   All sales were made for cash.

4.    At the end of each quarter a settlement is made between A and B so that neither party need refund any amount received.

The amount remitted by A to B on 30 September 19x8 must have been

R ............

# Q1 CONTINUED

6.

A, B and C were in partnership sharing profits and losses in the ratio 6:3:1.
Their balance sheet at 31 December 19x5 was as follows:

```
Capital - A            R18 000              Assets              R40 000
          B              2 000
          C             18 000   R38 000
Creditors                          2 000
Contingent liability -
  Bill due on 1 July 19x6
  discounted           R4 000
                       ======
                                 R40 000                        R40 000
                                 ======                         ======
```

They agreed to dissolve partnership and agreed to distribute cash received
from the sale of assets immediately it had been received.  This was, however,
to be done on the basis that while the maximum distribution was to be made to
the partners under no circumstances would a partner ever be required to refund
to the partnership any amount he had received.  It was also agreed that if
the situation arose the rule of Garner vs. Murray was to be used.

Assets were sold as follows for cash:

```
31 January 19x6 assets of book value   R12 000 for R16 000
28 February 19x6 assets of book value   20 000 for   4 000
31 March 19x6 assets of book value       8 000 for  16 000
                                        R40 000     R36 000
                                        ======      ======
```

It was known that no expenses would be incurred in selling the assets or
dissolving the partnership.

The amount paid to C on 28 February 19x6 was, therefore:

```
A       R13 000
B       R1 000
C       R14 000
D       R3 000
E       Some other amount, viz., R ..........
```

# Q1 CONTINUED

7.

Gamma Trading Company allows you 5% cash discount on all purchases made in any one calendar month provided payment is received by them or or before the 25th of the following month.

The balance due to Gamma Trading at 31 December 19x6 in respect of purchases made in that month was according to their statement R337, but upon reconciling the statement with your ledger you find that:

(a)    An invoice for R23 had been omitted from his statement.

(b)    An invoice for R29 correctly shown in his statement had been entered in your ledger as R92.

(c)    He had omitted to deduct 20% trade discount from an invoice correctly entered in your ledger as R160.

(d)    The return of goods on 22 December 19x6 amounting to R30 had not been shown on his statement.

(e)    His statement had been undercast by R10.

(f)    A cheque dated 20 November 19x6 for R190 (after deducting the 5% discount) had not been received by Gamma Trading.  On investigation it was found to have been posted to an incorrect address and had not yet been returned.

(g)    An invoice for R50 had been entered in your books as a credit note.

The amount of the cheque sent to Gamma Trading Company to reach them before 25 January 19x7 to settle their account in full should be:

A    R95,00  
B    R85,50  
C    R285,00  
D    R295,00  
E    Some other amount viz., R .........

# Q1 CONTINUED

8.

The owner of W and M stores informs you that a fire occurred in the store on the night of 31 January 19x7.  He requests you to assist him in preparing a claim for the insurance company who had agreed to insure the stock for R20 000 the policy being subject to the "average clause".

The following figures were produced:

| | | |
|---|---|---:|
| (i) | Stock 1 July 19x6 | R15 500 |
| (ii) | Purchases 1 July 19x6 - 31 January 19x7 | 63 300 |
| (iii) | Gross sales 1 July 19x6 - 31 December 19x6 | |
| | (including the post Christmas sale) | 61 500 |
| (iv) | Gross sales January 19x7 | 12 400 |
| (v) | Returns outwards 1 July 19x6 - 31 January 19x7 | 1 000 |
| (vi) | Returns inwards 1 July 19x6 - 31 December 19x6 | 750 |
| (vii) | Trade discount received 1 July 19x6 - 31 January 19x7 | 1 500 |
| (viii) | Discount allowed 1 July 19x6 - 31 January 19x7 | 750 |
| (ix) | Stock salvaged and unsoiled | 5 500 |

<u>Note</u> Purchases are stated above after deducting the trade discount.  There were no returns inwards during January 19x7.

Goods have always been marked up by adding 50% to the cost price to arrive at the normal selling price.  All goods were sold at the marked selling price except those during the period 28 December 19x6 - 31 December 19x6 when a post Christmas sale was held.  During the sale all marked prices were reduced by 33 1/3%.  No sale goods are returnable. Turnover during the sale was R12 000. On 2 January the owner decided that in an effort to increase his turnover to reduce his markup in such a way that in future a gross profit of 25% on sales would be achieved.

Based on the information supplied the insurance company claim should be:

| | |
|---|---|
| A | R17 000 |
| B | R18 500 |
| C | R14 167 |
| D | R10 500 |
| E | Some other amount viz., R .......... |

# Q1 CONTINUED

9.

The Happy Ride Bus Company Limited whose financial year ends on 30 April provides depreciation on buses on the basis that each bus will have a life of 4 years and that the residual value will amount to 20% of the cost price. The Company makes all calculations to the nearest rand in preparing its annual financial statements.

<u>Purchases of buses were made as follows</u>:

| | | |
|---|---|---|
| 1 February 19x3 | - | R25 000 |
| 31 July 19x4 | - | R20 000 |
| 1 May 19x5 | - | R15 000 |
| 1 October 19x5 | - | R25 000 |

<u>Sales and Disposals of buses</u>:

1 May 19x5 — Bus purchased 1 February 19x3 at a cost of R12 500 was sold for R10 000.

30 September 19x5 — Bus purchased 31 July 19x4 at a cost of R10 000 was sold for R6 000.

1 January 19x6 — Bus purchased 1 February 19x3 at a cost of R6 250 was scrapped as it had been involved in an accident and the insurance company felt it would be uneconomical to repair. The insurance company refunded an amount based on the book value of the bus at 31 December 19x5.

The balance on the Provision for Depreciation Account for buses at 30 April 19x6 must, therefore, have been:

A     R16 849
B     R16 328
C     R13 480
D     R14 313
E     Some other amount, viz., R .........

10.

A Limited bought all the shares in X Limited on 1 January 19x6.   At 30 June 19x5, after all the closing entries had been made, the following balances appeared in the ledger of X Limited:

| | |
|---|---:|
| Share capital | R20 000 |
| Share premium | 1 000 |
| General reserve | 10 000 |
| Appropriation account | 8 000 |

At 30 June 19x7, after all the closing entries had been made, the following balances appeared in the ledgers of the two companies:

| | A Limited | X Limited |
|---|---:|---:|
| Share capital | R100 000 | R20 000 |
| Share premium | 10 000 | 1 000 |
| General reserve | 12 000 | 17 500 |
| Appropriation account | 20 000 | 8 500 |

Since 30 June 19x5 X Limited had been making a profit.   It is known that the profits had been earned at a constant rate during the two years to 30 June 19x7 and that no dividends other than one of 20% declared and paid on 2 January 19x6 had been declared or paid by X Limited.   The transfer of R7 500 to general reserves was made on 30 June 19x7.

The distributable reserves appearing in the consolidated balance sheet of A Limited and its subsidiary at 30 June 19x7 should, therefore, total:

| | |
|---|---|
| A | R38 000 |
| B | R39 000 |
| C | R40 000 |
| D | R41 000 |
| E | Some other amount, viz., R ......... |

1.

The bank overdraft according to a cash book was R60.   There were cheques
outstanding of R170.   A deposit of R70 was entered in the cash book but the
amount was not credited by the bank until the following month.   Bank charges
of R7 appeared in the bank statement but they had not yet been entered in the
cash book.   The credit side of the cash book had been undercast by R5.

The balance according to the bank statement was, therefore:

A        R28 credit
B        R38 debit
C        R98 credit
D        R35 debit
E        Some other amount, viz., R .......... debit/credit


2.

Maggie and Jiggs were in partnership, their profit/loss sharing ratio being
8:2.

At 31 July 19x7 their summarised balance sheet was as follows:

| Capital – Maggie | R15 000 | Stock | R18 000 |
|---|---|---|---|
| Capital – Jiggs | 6 000 | Debtors | 3 900 |
| Creditors | 4 500 | Bank | 3 600 |
| | R25 500 | | R25 500 |

They decide to dissolve the partnership and during the first two weeks of
August 19x7 stock standing in the books at R12 000 was sold for R13 500 cash.
R2 700 was collected from debtors and expenses amounting to R750 were paid.

It was known that the maximum further expenses which could be incurred in
connection with the dissolution could not exceed R450.

At 14 August 19x7 each partner wishes to draw the maximum possible amount from
the firm but under no circumstances do they wish to risk having to make a
refund.   In view of these circumstances, Maggie may withdraw:

A        R4 620
B        R9 480
C        R9 840
D        R9 930
E        Some other amount, viz., R .........

## Q2 CONTINUED

3.

The income statement of Garth Limited showed a net profit before tax for the year ended 31 July 19x7 of R36 600.

During the year ended 31 July 19x7:

1.   Fixed assets were purchased for R20 000.
2.   Fixed assets, the depreciated value of which was R2 200 were sold for R2 800.
3.   Depreciation of R6 000 was provided on fixed assets.
4.   A dividend of R10 000 was declared and paid.
5.   Provisional tax payments amounting to R12 000 were paid.  The tax payable for the year amounted to R13 900.

There were no other relevant changes.

On comparing the working capital of the company on 31 July 19x6 and 31 July 19x7 it was found that it had:

A    Increased by R900
B    Increased by R1 500
C    Decreased by R900
D    Decreased by R2 800
E    Increased by R ..........
     Decreased by R ..........

# Q2 CONTINUED

4.

Dr Pug, a veterinary surgeon, does not keep proper books.

1.      The following is a summary of Dr Pug's balance sheet at 30 June 19x6:

| Capital | R9 200 | Surgery equipment | R3 000 |
|---|---|---|---|
| Creditors for practice | | Debtors | 6 000 |
|    expenses | 800 | Bank | 1 000 |
| | ===== | | ===== |

2.      The following information has been extracted from the bank statements of the practice for the year ended 30 June 19x7:

| Deposits | R40 000 |
|---|---|
| Cheques drawn for | |
|    practice expenses | 12 000 |
| Cheques drawn for | |
|    personal use | 24 000 |
| Bank charges | 70 |

3.      Dr Pug deposits intact all cash received.

4.      Depreciation of R200 is to be written off surgery equipment.

5.      At 30 June 19x7 debtors totalled R8 500.   Bad debts of R799 had been written off during the year.

6.      At 30 June 19x7 creditors for practice expenses amounted to R1 080.

7.      Cash of R800 received from debtors and recorded on 30 June 19x7 was deposited at the bank on 1 July 19x7.

The excess of income over expenditure earned by the practice for the year ended 30 June 19x7 was:

A       R30 950
B       R29 920
C       R29 120
D       R30 750
E       Some other amount, viz., R .........

# Q2 CONTINUED

5.

A and B were in partnership sharing profits and losses in the ratio 3:2.  At 30 June 19x7 their balance sheet was as follows:

| Capital Accounts | | | Fixed Assets | |
|---|---|---|---|---|
| A | R6 000 | | Goodwill | R2 400 |
| B | 4 000 | R10 000 | Other | 9 600 |
| Reserve | | 12 000 | | 12 000 |
| Creditors | | 7 400 | Current assets | 17 400 |
| | | R29 400 | | R29 400 |
| | | ====== | | ====== |

C purchased a fifth share in the business for cash on 1 July 19x7 on the following terms:

1. Goodwill was agreed to be worth R12 000 and was to be shown at this amount in the books.
2. Other fixed and current assets were agreed to be fairly stated in the books.
3. The reserve was to appear in the books of the new partnership.
4. A and B were not to contribute any cash and the profit sharing ratio between them was to remain unaltered.
5. A, B and C agreed that the balances on their capital accounts after all adjustments caused by the admission of C had been made, would be fixed. Profits and losses were to be shared by the three partners in proportion to their capital accounts.

The amount of cash brought in by C must therefore have been:

A    R4 900
B    R5 500
C    R7 900
D    R8 500
E    Some other amount, viz., R .........

6.

X Co. Limited was incorporated with a capital of 200 000 shares of no par value.

The subscribers to the memorandum subscribed for 10 000 shares and paid R10 000.   90 000 shares were offered to the public at R1,20 per share. The offer was fully subscribed.

Preliminary and share issue expenses amounting to R4 000 were paid in cash.

During the first year the company made a net profit after taxation of R35 000. At the end of the first year the directors decided to write off the preliminary and share issue expenses but they required that the distributable reserves be maintained at the maximum amount.

Two years later the company agrees to offer a further 50 000 shares to the public.

The minimum amount at which these shares can be issued without a special resolution is:

A  R1,00 per share
B  R1,14 per share
C  R1,18 per share
D  R1,20 per share
E  Some other amount, viz., R .......... per share

7.

On 1 July 19x4 A Limited purchased certain plant for R10 500.   The plant is expected to have a life of 10 years and a scrap value of R500.

It was decided to depreciate this asset by the sinking fund method.   The company's financial year ends on 30 June.   R0,069029 per annum at 8% compound interest will produce R1 in 10 years.

The balance (to the nearest Rand) on the Depreciation Fund Account at 30 June 19x7 must therefore be:

A  R2 071
N  R2 207
C  R2 241
D  R2 389
E  Some other amount, viz., R .........

8.

At 31 July 19x7 X extracts a list of debtors balances totalling R4 976,41. This amount did not agree with the amount of the balance on the debtors control account in the general ledger.

On checking, the following mistakes were discovered:

1. An invoice for R42,20 entered in the sales journal had not been posted to A's account in the debtors ledger.
2. An amount of R6,70 had been posted twice from the returns inwards book to B's account in the debtors ledger.
3. The debit balance on D's account in the debtors ledger had been brought down as R14,81 instead of R18,14.
4. The credit side of the debtors control account had been overcast by R100.
5. A receipt for R76,21 had been posted to D's account in the debtors ledger but had not been entered in the cash book.
6. The returns outwards book had been undercast by R10.

If these were the only mistakes, the balance on the debtors control account in the general ledger, before the errors were discovered, must have been:

A    R4 947,97
B    R4 994,85
C    R5 028,64
D    R5 204,85
E    Some other amount, viz., R .........

9.

X of Johannesburg entered into a joint venture with Y of Cape Town for the sale of imported electric drills on the following terms:

1.      X and Y would be allowed a commission of 10% calculated on the total proceeds of the sales made by each of them.
2.      Interest on all transactions would be charged and allowed at the rate of 6% per annum.
3.      X and Y would share profits and losses in the ratio 2:3.

Note: The commission payable on sales made by X and Y is to be calculated at the end of the accounting period 30 June 19x7.

The following transactions took place:

19x7
March 31      Y Imported 1 000 drills at a cost of R20 000 and paid importing charges of R5 000 on the same day.
April 30      X received 600 drills from Y and paid railage of R600.
April 30      Y sold all the drills he had kept in Cape Town at a gross profit of 20% on sales.
May   31      X sold half the drills received by him for R11 200.
June  30      X sold a further 200 drills for R6 400.
June 30      Settlement was effected between X and Y so that no amount received by either party would every have to be repaid.

The amount paid by X to Y on 30 June 19x7 was therefore:

A      R14 645
B      R14 774
C      R14 956
D      R15 034
E      Some other amount, viz., R ..........

# Q2 CONTINUED

10.

On 1 January 19x8 A Limited acquired 60% of the shares in B Limited.   The share capital of B Limited was divided into ordinary shares of R1 each. There were no reserves other than retained income.   At that date all the assets and liabilities of B Limited were considered to be fairly valued except for stock which was valued at R10 000 less.   B Limited did not adjust its books for the change in the value of stock.

The following is a summary of the retained income of B Limited.

| | |
|---|---:|
| Balance 1 January 19x8 | R40 000 |
| Net income for the year | 60 000 |
| | 100 000 |
| Dividend paid 31 December 19x8 | 80 000 |
| Balance 31 December 19x8 | R20 000 |

All the stock at 1 January 19x8 was disposed of before 31 December 19x8.

On 1 January 19x9 B Limited made a capitalisation issue at par of 1 share for every 6 held out of existing profits.   A Limited did not make an adjustment to the value of "Investment in B Limited" account on receipt of these shares.

If the balance on "Investment in B Limited" account at 1 January 19x9 was R48 000, the number of shares received by A Limited on the capitalisation issue was therefore  .......... shares.

# Q3

1.

The partnership deed of X and Y provides the follows:

1.    Interest at the rate of 5% per annum was to be allowed on their respective capital account balances at the beginning of each year. No interest was to be charged on drawings.
2.    X was to be entitled to a salary of R10 000 per annum and Y R8 000 per annum.
3.    Remaining profits/losses were to be shared by X three fifths and Y two fifths.

The profit for the year ended 31 December 19x1 after allowing for interest and partners' salaries was R25 000.

X had drawn R12 000 and Y R11 000 during the year. At 31 December 19x1 after allowing for interest, salaries, profit and deduction of drawings, the balances on their capital accounts were:

    X    R44 500;        Y    R32 200

The amount of interest credited to X in respect of the year ended 31 December 19x1, must have been:

A    R2 700
B    R1 701
C    R1 200
D    R1 500
E    Some other amount, viz., R ..........

2.

A Limited increased its selling prices by 4% on 1 January 19x2. As from the same date suppliers increased the prices of goods purchased for resale by A Limited.

The following are relevant figures for the years ended 31 December 19x1 and 19x2:

|  | 19x1 | 19x2 |
|---|---|---|
| Cost of sales | 200 000 | 203 300 |
| Gross profit | 100 000 | 93 100 |
| Sales | R300 000 | R296 400 |

The total increase in cost of sales, due to the increased prices of goods purchased for resale, for the year ended 31 December 19x2, taking into account the volume of goods sold, must have been:

A    R13 300
B    R3 300
C    R8 550
D    R16 400
E    Some other amount, viz., R ..........

600

## Q3 CONTINUED

3.

Department C of a large wholesale business sells a variety of articles to small retailers on credit.  Stocks are valued at cost and goods sold are normally marked up to realise a gross profit of 33 1/3% on selling prices, except during sales periods.

Due to stocktaking in other departments on 31 March 19x8, physical stock was taken in Department C at the close of business on Saturday, 25 March 19x8, and amounted to R86 400 at cost.

The following information relates to the period 27 - 31 March 19x8:

1.  On 27 and 28 March a clearance sale was held during which the selling prices of all goods were reduced to half the marked prices.  Sales totalling R15 510 were made, but goods sold to a customer for R360 were returned by him as defective.  These goods were returned to the supplier on 30 March and were replaced free of charge by him on 5 April 19x8.  A credit note had been passed on receipt of goods from the customer.
2.  Sales at normal selling prices on 29, 30 and 31 March amounted to R14 700.
3.  Purchases of goods for resale during the period 27 - 31 March totalled R8 040.
4.  Goods sold and invoiced on 23 March 19x8 were not delivered to the customer until 28 March but were included in the stock count on 25 March.

Stock on hand at cost in Department C on 31 March 19x8, must, therefore have been:

A    R60 150
B    R63 920
C    R63 960
D    R107 880
E    Some other amount, viz., R .........

4.

B Limited purchased plant and machinery costing R1 000 000 on 1 January 19x1 and during the year ended 31 December 19x2 further plant costing R100 000 was purchased.   On 30 June 19x3, plant which had cost R200 000 when purchased on 1 January 19x1 was sold at the written down book value at that date.

Depreciation has consistently been provided at the rate of 10% per annum on the reducing balance method.

The following is an extract from the financial statements in respect of plant and machinery:

|  |  | Cost | Accumulated depreciation | Net book value |
|---|---|---|---|---|
| at 31.12.19x1 | Plant and machinery | R1 000 000 | R100 000 | R900 000 |
| at 31.12.19x2 | Plant and machinery | 1 100 000 | 195 000 | 905 000 |

The net book value of plant and machinery shown in the financial statements for the year ended 31 December 19x3 must have been:

A      R610 000
B      R622 600
C      R668 700
D      R822 600
E      Some other amount, viz., R ..........

5.

A, B and C were in partnership sharing profits/losses in the ratio 5:3:2. The following is their summarised balance sheet at 31 December 19x7:

| Capital - A | R8 000 | Assets | R35 400 |
|---|---|---|---|
|      - B | 7 000 | Bank balance | 2 000 |
|      - C | 4 400 | | |
| Loan A | 10 000 | | |
| Creditors | 8 000 | | |
| | R37 400 | | R37 400 |

It was decided to dissolve the partnership on 1 January 19x8 and to realise the assets at the best prices over a period of three months. A agreed that his loan would only need to be repaid at the end of the third month together with interest at the rate of 12% per annum (i.e. R100 per month), provided repayment was not jeopardised by cash distributions to partners. Such cash distributions were to be made monthly if possible but in such a way as to ensure that no partner would be called upon to make a refund.

Assets sold and expenses incurred were as follows:

| | Book value | Amount realised | Realisation expenses incurred |
|---|---|---|---|
| At 31 January 19x8 | R16 200 | R12 000 | R500 |
| At 28 February 19x8 | 12 400 | 9 900 | 400 |
| At 31 March 19x8 | 6 800 | 6 000 | |

The cash distribution made to B on 28 February 19x8 must have been:

| | |
|---|---|
| A | R2 590 |
| B | R2 500 |
| C | R2 680 |
| D | R2 830 |
| E | Some other amount, viz., R .......... |

6.

During the first half of the year ended 31 December 19x1, CD added a fixed percentage to the cost of goods sold to arrive at selling prices, except during his winter sale held during June 19x1 when he reduced all selling prices by 25%.   During the winter sale he sold goods costing R25 000 for R30 000.   Sales at normal selling prices from 1 January to 30 June 19x1 amounted to R160 000.

In the second half of the year the cost of all goods which he sells was increased by 10% from 1 July 19x1 and to arrive at selling prices he added the same percentage mark up as he had done during the first half of the year. His sales during the second half of the year amounted to R224 400.   No sales at reduced selling prices were held during this half of the year.   There was no stock on hand at the beginning of the second half of the year.

CD's gross profit for the year ended 31 December 19x1 must, therefore, have been:

A     R161 900
B     R157 400
C     R150 000
D     R141 950
E     Some other amount, viz., R ..........

7.

A bill for R90,65 received from debtor A Black in March 19x8 was incorrectly entered in the Bills Payable book, the total of which is posted monthly to the relevant ledger accounts in the general ledger.  The individual amount of R90,65 was, however, incorrectly posted to an account "A Black" in the creditors ledger as R9,65.

When the list of creditors was extracted from the creditors ledger it was found that the total of the list did not agree with the balance in the creditors control account in the general ledger.  A journal entry was then passed which made the control agree to the list by transferring the difference to a creditors suspense account opened in the general ledger.

The journal entry necessary to correct the relevant accounts in the general ledger (i.e. excluding any entries in the debtors or creditors ledger) must be:

A    Bills payable                            R90,65
       Bills receivable                                    R90,65

B    Bills payable                            R90,65
       Creditors suspense                                  R90,65

C    Bills payable                            R90,65
     Bills receivable                          90,65
       Debtors control                                     R90,65
       Creditors suspense                                   90,65

D    Bills receivable                         R90,65
     Bills payable                             90,65
       Debtors control                                     R90,65
       Creditors control                                     9,65
       Creditors suspense                                   81,00

E    Bills receivable                         R90,65
     Debtors control                           90,65
       Bills payable                                       R90,65
       Creditors control                                     9,65
       Creditors suspense                                   81,00

8.

A of Durban entered into a joint venture with B of Johannesburg for the importation and sale of bicycles upon the following terms:

1. A and B would each be entitled to 5% commission on the sales effected by them individually, such commission to be calculated at the end of each accounting period, viz., 28 February.
2. Thereafter, remaining profits/losses to be shared by A three fifths; B two fifths.

The following transactions took place:

19x7
Sept. 1   A remitted R30 000 to the manufacturers in England in payment of the f.o.b. invoice price of 1 500 bicycles.
Oct.  4   The 1 500 bicycles arrived intact at Durban and A paid R6 000 importing charges.
Oct. 10   A railed 900 bicycles to B who paid railage charges amounting to R900.

19x8
Jan. 31   A sold 300 bicycles at a gross profit of 25% on selling price.
Feb. 15   B sold 650 bicycles for R21 400.
Feb. 28   All payments in respect of sales had been received and settlement was made between A and B by cheque, so that neither party would ever have to make a refund.

The amount of the cheque remitted by B to A at 28 February 19x8 must have been:

A     R23 280
B     R22 485
C     R22 410
D     R25 100
E     Some other amount, viz., R .........

9.

AB started business on 1 January 19x7 with the following assets:

      Cash paid into business bank account - R20 000;
      Land - R10 000;
      Buildings - R5 000.

He did not keep complete accounting records but you are able to ascertain that:

During the year ended 31 December 19x7:

1. Deposits paid into the business bank account totalled R130 500. This amount included the R20 000 paid in to start the business and R10 000 in respect of a loan obtained for the business.
2. Payments by cheque were made to creditors, and for shop fixtures purchased for R7 000 on 1 January 19x7 and R5 100 (of which R100 represents interest) part repayment of the loan.
3. Business expenses amounting to R1 878 and personal drawings of AB totalling R4 800 were paid out of cash collections.

At 31 December 19x7:

1. Stock at cost amounted to R16 710.
2. Debtors outstanding totalled R1 270 of which R123 was considered irrecoverable.
3. Amounts owing to creditors for goods purchased for resale totalled R3 780.
4. The credit balance on the bank statement was R5 300 but cheques amounting to R2 150 had not yet been presented at the bank for payment.
5. Cash on hand was R334.

The total of goods purchased for resale during the year ended 31 December 19x7, must have been:

A      R119 030
B      R115 250
C      R112 252
D      R126 030
E      Some other amount, viz., R..........

10.

On 1 January 19x1 A Limited entered into a ten year lease of a factory building and on the same date paid R80 000 the amount due under the lease. The company has decided to write the lease off over the life of the lease by the annuity system of depreciation, taking interest at the rate of 10% per annum.

The amount required to write off R1 by the annuity method over ten years with interest at 10% per annum is R0,16275.

Making all calculations to the nearest rand, the value at which the leased property will be shown in the annual financial statements at 31 December 19x3 will be:

A     R80 000
B     R40 980
C     R63 384
D     R69 458
E     Some other amount, viz., R ..........

## Q4

1.

The financial year end of XL Sports Club is 31 December.  The following
information in respect of subscriptions has been extracted from the club's
books:

|  | Year ended<br>31 December 19x7 | Year ended<br>31 December 19x8 |
|---|---|---|
| Arrears for 19x7 | R348 |  |
| Advance for 19x8 | 284 |  |
| Arrear 19x8 |  | R212 |
| Advance 19x9 |  | 432 |
| Written off during year (19x7 arrears) |  | 60 |

The Income and Expenditure Account for the year ended 31 December 19x8 was
credited with an amount of R4 572 in respect of subscriptions.

The amount of cash received during the year ended 31 December 19x8 in respect
of subscriptions must have been:

A     R4 796
B     R4 856
C     R5 008
D     R4 732
E     Some other amount, viz., R .........

2.

The financial year end of Power Tools Limited is 28 February.  The company
works a five day week.  It was decided to count physical stock on Saturday
and Sunday, 25 and 26 February 19x8.  All goods purchased have been
consistently marked up by 25% on cost to arrive at selling prices.

The following information is given:

| | |
|---|---|
| Stock per stock sheets - at cost | R101 480 |
| Purchases at cost - 27, 28 February 19x8 | 7 340 |
| Sales - 27, 28 February 1978 | 11 500 |

**NOTES:**

1.    Credit notes amounting to R1 500 were issued on 27 February 19x8 to
      customers in respect of goods sent to them prior to stocktaking.
      These goods were collected by the company's delivery vans on 7 March
      19x8.
2.    Goods invoiced to customers at R750 on 24 February 19x8 were delivered
      on 3 March 19x8.  These goods had not been set aside or wrapped until
      2 March 19x8.
3.    Goods purchased for resale totalling R480 had been properly entered in
      the books of account on 24 February 19x8 but were not received by the
      company until 8 March 19x8.

# Q4 CONTINUED

The amount to be shown in the balance sheet in respect of stock at 28 February 19x8 must be:

A      R101 300
B      R101 900
C      R100 220
D      R100 700
E      Some other amount, viz., R ..........

3.

AJ did not keep proper books and records but you are able to ascertain the following:

At 28 February 19x7 he had R400 in the bank, whereas at 28 February 19x8 he had an overdraft of R800. Stock had increased by R4 800 at 28 February 19x8 compared with the previous year and debtors (after deducting the provision for bad debts) had increased by R2 400. Creditors at 28 February 19x8 were R4 400 more than at 28 February 19x7. During the year ended 28 February 19x8 fixed assets had increased by R2 880 before accounting for depreciation for the current year. At 28 February 19x8 the provision for bad debts had been decreased by R100. Depreciation in respect of fixed assets for the year ended 28 February 19x8 amounts to R1 560.

You ascertain that AJ drew R21 600 during the year for personal expenses.

AJ's net profit for the year ended 28 February 19x8 must, therefore, have been:

A      R25 320
B      R24 920
C      R26 480
D      R24 820
E      Some other amount, viz., R ..........

4.

Hoe Limited was incorporated on 1 June 19x4 with the following authorised share capital:
>       100 000 10% Preference shares of R1 each
>       200 000 Ordinary shares of R1 each.

The following issues and allotments were made:

1 June 19x4 - Subscribers to memorandum - 5 000 ordinary shares at par
30 November 19x4 - 25 000 Preference shares at a premium of 5% and 50 000 ordinary shares at par.   Share issue expenses amounted to R7 500
1 July 19x5 - 50 000 Ordinary shares at a premium of 10%.   Share issue expenses amounted to R2 500.

On 1 June 19x7 the ordinary shares were converted into shares of no par value and on 30 June 19x7 the remaining unissued ordinary shares were issued at R1,75 per share.

On 1 December 19x7 R50 000 12% debentures were issued at a discount of 10%.

The policy of the company has been to write off share issue expenses during the financial year in which they were incurred in such a way as to leave distributable reserves at the maximum amount possible.   This policy has been carried out since incorporation and the company has made substantial profits each year ending on 28 February.

The balance on the stated capital account at 28 February 19x8 must, therefore, have been:

A       R298 750
B       R267 500
C       R268 750
D       R273 750
E       Some other amount, viz., R .........

# Q4 CONTINUED

5.

The net current assets of X Limited at 30 June 19x7 were R25 000 and at 30 June 19x8 were R31 000.

The following information relates to the year ended 30 June 19x8:

1.  Net profit after tax per the income statement was R34 000.
2.  Depreciation amounting to R18 600 was provided in respect of fixed assets.
3.  Land and buildings were sold during the year for R25 000.   In terms of the articles the profit of R10 000 is not available for distribution as dividend.
4.  Taxation for the current year has been accurately estimated at R26 000, and two provisional payments totalling R28 000 were made.
5.  A dividend of R30 000 has been recommended by the directors.
6.  A loan of R25 000 received in 19x3 was repaid during the year. Interest amounting to R2 000 had been paid to date of repayment.

There were no other changes during the year ended 30 June 19x8 except for the purchase of new plant and machinery.   Depreciation on the new plant and machinery has been provided and is included in the amount of R18 600 per Note (2) above.

The amount spent on the acquisition of new plant and machinery must, therefore, have been:

A    R8 400
B    R8 600
C    R5 400
D    R16 600
E    Some other amount, viz., R .........

# Q4 CONTINUED

6.

The directors of ABC Limited throughout the year ended 30 June 19x8 were:

P managing director, Q chairman, R financial director, S production manager. T the company secretary was appointed alternate to R on 1 January 19x8, and U the factory manager was appointed alternate to S during the latter's absence on company business during the last quarter of the financial year.

The following salaries were paid during the year ended 30 June 19x8:

     P  R15 000;   R  R12 500;    S  R12 000;    T  R12 000;    U  R11 000.

All directors, including alternates, receive fees of R50 per meeting attended. Other than S no directors were absent from any of the meetings which they were eligible to attend.   Meetings were held on the fifth day of each month.

The chairman and managing director each received an entertainment allowance of R1 200 during the year, and with the exception of D each director and alternate director had the use of a company car, the benefit of which is assessed  at R400 per annum.   During the absence of S his car was used on company business.

The total directors remuneration which must be disclosed by way of note to the financial statements for the year ended 30 June 19x8 amounts to:

A       R61 250
B       R55 000
C       R45 250
D       R54 750
E       R45 500

7.

A, B and C were in partnership sharing profits/losses in the ratio 4:4:2.
Their summarised balance sheet at 31 December 19x7 was as follows:

| | | | | |
|---|---|---|---|---|
| Capital A | R11 900 | | Goodwill | R5 000 |
| B | 6 005 | | Fixed assets | 20 000 |
| C | 4 095 | | Stock | 7 000 |
| | 22 000 | | | |
| Creditors | 5 200 | | | |
| Loan - C | 2 000 | | | |
| Bank overdraft | 2 800 | | | |
| | R32 000 | | | R32 000 |

It was agreed that the partnership be dissolved with effect from
1 January 19x8 and that the assets were to be sold at best prices over a
period of three months.  Available cash was to be distributed to the partners
at the end of each month ensuring that no partner would ever be called upon
to make a refund.  In the event of a deficiency in the capital account of a
partner, the other partners were to share the deficiency in their profit
sharing ratio.

It was found that interest on capital accounts had been incorrectly credited
at the rate of 5% instead of 10% per annum on the balances of their capital
accounts at 1 January 19x7 which were as follows:

| | |
|---|---|
| A | R9 000 |
| B | R4 500 |
| C | R4 500 |

The adjusting entries were made on 15 January 19x8.

You obtain the following additional information:

1. The partners had taken out a joint life policy the premiums on which
   had been debited to profit and loss account.  The insurance company
   agreed to cancel the policy and paid the surrender value of R4 200 on
   28 February 19x8.  The amount was banked in the business bank account.
2. The partners occupied business premises under a lease which was due to
   expire on 31 December 19x8.  The monthly rental is R300.  The lease was
   taken over by a chain store as from 1 March 19x8 upon payment of R2 000
   to the partnership for the right to use their name.  The R2 000 was
   paid on 28 February 19x8.

3. The tangible assets were disposed of as follows:

| | Book value | Amount realised |
|---|---|---|
| By 31 January 19x8 | R7 000 | R4 000 |
| By 28 February 19x8 | 10 000 | 6 000 |
| By 31 March 19x8 | 10 000 | 6 000 |

4. Costs of realisation were nil.

  The total amount distributed to A by 28 February 19x8 must have been:

  A  R7 430
  B  R4 970
  C  R3 600
  D  R7 830
  E  Some other amount, viz., R ..........

8.

A of Durban and B of Johannesburg entered into a joint venture for the purchase and sale of arms and ammunition. Profit and losses were to be shared in the ratio 2:1.

The overseas supplier was to receive a commission of 10% of the turnover for each quarter.

The following transactions took place during the quarter ended 30 September 19x8:

1. On 1 July 19x8 a shipment of 150 revolvers costing R6 750 c.i.f. arrived in Durban where A paid importing charges amounting to R540. The amount of R6 750 was paid to the overseas supplier by B.
2. A sent 60 revolvers to B who paid railage of R120.
3. A sold 60 revolvers at cost plus 50% and B sold 50 revolvers at cost plus 50%.
4. A remitted the commission due to the overseas supplier on 30 September 19x8.
5. At the end of each quarter a settlement is made between A and B so that neither party ever need refund any amount received.

The amount remitted by A to B on 30 September 19x8 must have been:

A  R3 010,70
B  R3 710,37
C  R3 658,70
D  R3 055,70
E  Some other amount, viz., R ..........

# Q4 CONTINUED

9.

PQR Limited uses a single raw material in the manufacture of goods which it sells.    Stock records are kept and issues made to the factory on the first in first out method.

The company constantly achieves a gross profit of 10% on sales.    Any increase in the price of raw materials is not reflected in the price of the finished product until the old stocks of raw material have been used up.

On the night of 31 July 19x8 all stocks of raw materials, except those kept in a store away from the factory, were destroyed by fire.    The stock of raw materials in the store at 31 July 19x8 had cost R9 900.

The following relevant information is given:

1.      Stocks
|  |  |
|---|---:|
| Raw materials at 28 February 19x8 | R96 000 |
| Finished goods at 28 February 19x8 | 177 000 |
| Finished goods at 31 July 19x8 | 162 000 |
| Work in progress at 28 February 19x8 | 000 |
| Work in progress at 31 July 19x8 | 66 000 |

2.      During the five months 1 March 19x8 to 31 July 19x8:
|  |  |
|---|---:|
| Raw material purchases | R477 000 |
| Direct wages earned | 129 000 |
| Factory overheads incurred | 69 000 |
| Sales | 750 000 |

You ascertain that the gross profit percentage of 10% was maintained during the period up to the date of the fire and that the stock of raw materials had been insured for R90 000 at replacement value, subject to an average clause in the insurance policy.    There had been an increase of R3 per ton in the purchase price of raw materials (from R30 to R33) on 30 June 19x8.    Only one purchase of 1 000 tons had been made during July 19x8 at the increased price.

The amount which the insurance company will pay in respect of a claim for the raw materials destroyed will be:

A       R90 000
B       R89 100
C       R81 000
D       R81 290
E       Some other amount, viz., R .........

# Q4 CONTINUED

10.

X and Y were in partnership sharing profits/losses in the ratio 2:1.   On 1
January 19x8 they admitted Z to the partnership. Z was to pay   R24 000 into
the business bank account and become entitled to a one-third share in the
partnership.   X and Y were to continue to share profits/losses between
themselves in the same ratio as before.   X, Y and Z would each be entitled
to a salary at the rate of R8 000 per annum.   At 1 January 19x8 it was agreed
that the assets and liabilities of the partnership of X and Y were fairly
valued except goodwill which stood in the books at R4 000.   At the same date
there was a reserve of R10 800.

The summarised balance sheet of X, Y and Z at 30 June 19x8 was as follows:

| | | | |
|---|---:|---|---:|
| Capital X | R24 400 | Goodwill | R4 000 |
| Y | 12 000 | Furniture, at cost, less | |
| Z | 17 200 | depreciation | 8 000 |
| Reserve | 18 000 | Current assets | 69 600 |
| Creditors | 10 000 | | |
| | R81 600 | | R81 600 |
| | ====== | | ====== |

<u>Notes</u>:

1.   The net profit for the six months ended 30 June 19x8 amounted to R28
     800 after allowing for partners salaries but before making the transfer
     to the reserve.
2.   An amount of R7 200 was transferred to reserve.
3.   Partners drawings were:

           X  R10 800;     Y  R7 600;     Z  R9 600.

The value placed on goodwill on 1 January 19x8 upon Z's admission to the
partnership must have been:

A     R14 400
B     R18 400
C     R4 800
D     R6 133
E     Some other amount, viz., R .........

# SECTION R

# HIRE PURCHASE

SECTION R

HIRE PURCHASE

## R1

An engineering company commencing business acquires machinery, the cash price of which is R6 000.  The company's liquid position, however, makes it impossible to pay at once. Accordingly, the sellers agree to payment by three instalments of R2 412,69 each, at the end of the first, second and third years trading.  The difference between the prices represents an addition of 10% on the balance outstanding at the commencement of each year.

Show the relative accounts in the books of the engineering company, calculating depreciation at 10% on the diminishing balance each year.

Taxi Company Limited bought a fleet of 3 motor cars from the Car Sales Limited.  The sale was made on 1 October 19x1 and it was agreed that payment should be made in four annual instalments of R1 500 each payable on 30 September each year.  The first payment was made on 30 September 19x2, and all other payments were made on due date.

The effective rate of interest charged by the Car Sales Limited is 12% per annum and the cash price is R4 556.

Show the relative accounts in the ledger of the Taxi Company Limited for the four years ended 30 September 19x5.

Depreciation was calculated at 20% per annum on cost.

All calculations are to be made to the nearest R1.

## R3

Benoni Bottlers Limited buy 2 lorries under a hire purchase agreement from Car Distributors Limited on 31 March 19x3. The debt is to be liquidated by the payment of a deposit of R1 000 and five instalments of R1 200 each payable on 31 March each year, the first instalment to be paid on 31 March 19x4.

You are informed that the effective rate of interest is 10% per annum and the cash price is R5 549.

All payments were made on due date.

Depreciation is to be calculated at the rate of 15% per annum on cost.

(1) You are required to show the relative ledger accounts (including interest suspense account) in the books of Benoni Bottlers Limited for the financial years ended 31 March 19x4 and 19x5.

(2) Show the relative sections of the balance sheet of the company at 31 March 19x5.

All calculations are to be made to the nearest R.

# R4

The Riverside Trading Company Limited buys 5 motor lorries under a hire purchase agreement from the Canadian Motor Company Limited.  It pays a deposit of R5 350 on 1 April 19x1 and  agrees to  pay six quarterly  instalments of R2 500 each, the first instalment being due on 1 October 19x1.

The cash price of each motor lorry purchased is R3 800.

Give the journal entries (cash entries should be journalised) in the Riverside Trading Company Limited's books to 31 December 19x1 assuming the instalment is paid on due date.

Show the relative parts of the Riverside Trading Company Limited's balance sheet at 31 December 19x1 assuming that depreciation is calculated at 10% per annum on cost.

# R5

A company buys four tractors under a hire purchase agreement.  It pays a
deposit of R2 500 on 1 January 19x2 and agrees to pay five quarterly
instalments of R1 200 each, the first instalment being due on 1 July 19x2.
The cash price of the tractors is R2 000 each.

Give the journal entries in the company's books to 30 September 19x2 assuming
the instalment is paid on due date.  Cash entries should be journalised.

Show the relative parts of the company's balance sheet at 30 September 19x2
assuming depreciation is calculated at the rate of 12% per annum on cost.

# R6

On 1 April 19x1 the Transvaal Transport Company Limited bought 2 motor lorries under a hire-purchase agreement from P Black Limited for a deposit of R2 500 and eighteen instalments of R250 each, payable on the last day of each month, starting from 30 April 19x1.

The list price of each lorry was R3 250 of which it is customary to allow a discount of 10% if the transaction is for cash.

The company paid the first three instalments on 30 April, 2 June and 1 July.

It was decided to calculate depreciation at the rate of 20% per annum.

Show the relative entries in the Transvaal Transport Company Limited's books from the date the lorries were purchased to 30 June 19x1 and show how the transaction would be reflected in a detailed balance sheet at that date.

# R7

Xavier Girault, whose financial year ends on 31 December, obtained hairdressing equipment from Hairdressing Supplies Limited on hire purchase on the following terms:

(a)    Deposit of R155, payable on 1 January 19.4 when the equipment was delivered.

(b)    Four instalments of R150 each, payable on 30 June and 31 December of each year.

The cash price of the equipment was R710.

Three accounts were opened in Girault's ledger in respect of this transaction, namely an asset account, a creditor account and an interest suspense account.

Interest was written off to profit and loss account each year on the basis of the amount due to Hairdressing Supplies Limited during each of the six-monthly periods.

Depreciation on the asset was written off at 10% per annum on cost.

Show the above three accounts as they would have appeared in the ledger of Xavier Girault at 31 December 19.5 and show details of the interest calculation.

**R8**

On 1 July 19.4 Excelsior Mills Limited entered into a hire purchase agreement with A.B.C. Motors Limited for the purchase of five motor vans on the following terms.:

> List price per van - R2 475
> Deposit - R4 725 (included in the deposit is an allowance of R1 125 on an old van traded in).  This van stood in the books of Excelsior Mills Limited at R675.
>
> Finance charges - R1 260
> Terms of repayment - 18 equal monthly instalments payable on the first of each month and commencing on 1 August 19.4.

Depreciation is to be calculated at the rate of 20 per cent per annum.  Show the following ledger accounts in the books of Excelsior Mills Limited for the six months ended 31 December 19.4.

> 1.   Motor vans account
> 2.   A.B.C. Motors Limited
> 3.   Finance charges account
> 4.   Accumulated depreciation - motor vans.

Also show the disclosure of these accounts in the balance sheet at 31 December 19.4.

# R9

The Earthworm Contractors Limited buys 3 bulldozers under a hire purchase
agreement from Langley Industrial Machines Corporation.  The agreement
provided for the payment of a deposit of R4 000 payable on 30 June 19.4 and
four annual instalments of R3 000 each, payable on 30 June each year, the
first being  due on 30 June 19.5.   The cash price of the 3 bulldozers  is
R13 510.

In fixing the amount of the instalments, Langley Industrial Machines
Corporation added compound interest at the rate of 10% per annum to the cash
price of the bulldozers.

All payments were made on due date.


<u>YOU ARE REQUIRED TO</u>:


Show the relative ledger accounts in the books of Earthworm Contractors
Limited for the financial years ended 30 June 19.5 and 19.6.  Depreciation is
to be calculated at the rate of 15% per annum on cost.

All calculations to the nearest R.

# R10

A manufacturing company requires a new machine which will cost R30 000 cash.

It will be possible to acquire the machine by hire-purchase, paying a deposit of R7 500 and eight quarterly instalments of R3 100 each, the first of which is due three months after purchase.

Assuming the machine was acquired by hire purchase on 2 January 19.4 record the transactions in the ledger of the company up to the end of its financial year on 30 June 19.4.

Depreciation is to be calculated at 10% per annum.

# SECTION S

# DEFERRED TAXATION

# S1

Alpha Limited acquired plant on 1 January 19x5 for R800 000 and brought it into use in a process of manufacture on the same day.

The company provides depreciation at the rate of 10% per annum on the straight line basis.

The tax allowances granted were;

|  |  |
|---|---|
| initial | 25% |
| wear and tear | 15% p.a. reducing balance. |

On 31 December 19x9 the plant was sold for R405 000.

Assume a tax rate of 40c in the Rand.

YOU ARE REQUIRED TO:

prepare the deferred tax account for the 5 years ended 31 December 19x5 to 19x9.

# S2

Beta Limited purchased new manufacturing plant for R500 000 on 1 January 19x1.

The tax allowances granted were;
|  |  |
| --- | --- |
| initial allowance | 40% |
| wear and tear | 15% p.a. reducing balance. |

Depreciation is to be provided at the rate of 15% p.a. on cost.

Net income before taxation, depreciation and profits or losses on the sale of plant, is expected to be R600 000 in 19x1, increasing by R20 000 thereafter.

The company's financial year end is 31 December.

Assume a tax rate of 40c in the Rand.


<u>YOU ARE REQUIRED TO</u>:

give the relevant portions of the income statements and the tax notes thereto for the years ended 31 December 19x1 to 19x5 assuming that the plant is sold on 31 December 19x5 for R100 000.

## S3

The following information relates to Delta Limited at 31 December 19x4, the
company's financial year end:

| | |
|---|---:|
| Share capital (authorised and issued R1 shares) | R600 000 |
| Retained income - 1 January 19x4 | 144 000 |
| Net income before depreciation and tax | 375 000 |
| Deferred taxation - 1 January 19x4 | 50 000 |
| Plant - cost 1 January 19x4 | 625 000 |
| Accumulated depreciation - 1 January 19x4 | 187 500 |
| Purchase new plant - 2 January 19x4 | 100 000 |
| Tax value old plant - 1 January 19x4 | 312 500 |
| Depreciation | 107 500 |
| Wear and tear and initial allowances | 102 500 |
| Tax rate | 40% |

<u>YOU ARE REQUIRED TO</u>:

prepare an extract of the balance sheet of Delta Limited at 31 December 19x4
and the income statement for the year ended on that date in accordance with
Schedule 4 and generally accepted accounting practice.

The extract should be as complete as the information given will allow.

## S4

Eta Limited purchased manufacturing plant on 1 January 19x1 for R200 000 in its first year of trading.

The company provides depreciation at the rate of 10% p.a. on the straight line basis.

The tax allowance granted were:

|  |  |
|---|---|
| initial | 25% |
| wear and tear | 10% reducing balance. |

The  company's financial year end is 31 December and it  made a profit of R160 000 each year before depreciation, any profit or loss on sale of plant and tax.

The plant was sold on 31 December 19x4 for R105 000.

The tax rate is 40c in the Rand.


<u>YOU ARE REQUIRED TO</u>:

prepare the income statement and notes thereto of Eta Limited for the years ended 31 December 19x1 to 19x4.

# S5

The annual financial statement of Gamma Limited for the year ended 31 December
19x5 are:-


<u>BALANCE SHEET</u>

CAPITAL EMPLOYED
| | |
|---|---|
| Share capital | R200 000 |
| Distributable reserve | 600 000 |
|   Retained income | |
| | R800 000 |

EMPLOYMENT OF CAPITAL
| | |
|---|---|
| Plant at cost | R1 000 000 |
| Accumulated depreciation | 200 000 |
| | R800 000 |

<u>INCOME STATEMENT</u>
| | |
|---|---|
| Net operating income | R200 000 |
| Depreciation | 100 000 |
| Net income before tax | 100 000 |
| Taxation | 56 000 |
| Net income after tax | R44 000 |

The taxation value of the plant at the above balance sheet date was R480 000.
Wear and tear granted by the tax authorities for 19x5 was R60 000.

The tax rate is 40c in the Rand.


<u>YOU ARE REQUIRED TO</u>:

a)      calculate the deferred taxation which should have appeared in the
        balance sheet at the beginning and end of 19x5.

b)      calculate the amount which should be shown as deferred tax in the
        income statement for the year ended 31 December 19x5.

c)      state the underlying principles which govern the provision of deferred
        taxation.

Bunting Limited acquired plant costing R400 000 on 1 July 19x4.  The plant is to be depreciated over its useful life of five years with no residual value using the straight line method.

The Receiver of Revenue will allow wear and tear at the rate of 20% p.a. using the straight line method and an initial allowance of 25%.

The net income before taxation of the company for the years ended 31 December 19x4 to 19x7 is as follows:

|  | <u>19x4</u> | <u>19x5</u> | <u>19x6</u> | <u>19x7</u> |
|---|---|---|---|---|
| Net income | R320 000 | R360 000 | R410 000 | R480 000 |

The plant was scrapped on 31 December 19x7.

Assume a constant tax rate of 40%.


<u>YOU ARE REQUIRED TO GIVE</u>:

a)    the journal entries for taxation and related matters for the years ended 31 December 19x4 and 19x7.

b)    the deferred tax account for the years 19x4 to 19x7.

On 1 January 19x1 Crow Limited started manufacturing operations.  On that day it purchased plant costing R300 000.

The Receiver of Revenue advised the company that in addition to the initial allowance of 25% he would allow wear and tear at the rate of 20% p.a. using the reducing balance method.  The directors decided to allow for depreciation at the rate of 15% p.a. on cost.

The taxable income for the year ended 30 June 19x2 was R300 000 and provisional tax paid was R111 000.  On 31 December 19x2 the company paid the amount owing to the Receiver of Revenue.

The taxable income for the year ended 30 June 19x3 was R360 000 and provisional tax payments amounted to R140 000.

The retained income at 30 June 19x1 was R235 000.  The company paid dividends of R100 000 on 30 June 19x2 and R150 000 on 30 June 19x3.

Assume a constant tax rate of 40%.


**<u>YOU ARE REQUIRED TO</u>:**


prepare extracts of the balance sheets of Crow Limited at 30 June 19x2 and 19x3 and income statements and notes to the financial statements for the years ended on those dates in accordance with Schedule Four and generally accepted accounting practice.

On 1 January 19x3 Dove Limited started trading and purchased plant for R250 000. The Receiver of Revenue agreed to allow the company an initial allowance of 25% and a wear and tear allowance of 20% p.a. on the reducing balance method.

The directors decided to provide for depreciation at the rate of 15% p.a. on cost.

The net income before tax was as follows:

     Year to 31 December 19x3  R75 000  
     Year to 31 December 19x4   140 000  
     Year to 31 December 19x5   225 000

The plant was sold on 31 December 19x5 for R130 000.

Assume a constant tax rate of 40%.

<u>YOU ARE REQUIRED TO GIVE</u>:

(a)    the journal entries relating to taxation in the company's books for the 3 years. (Ignore provisional payments).

(b)    the income statements and notes thereto for the years ended 31 December 19x3 to 19x5 in accordance with the Schedule Four and generally accepted accounting practice.

**S9**

At 30 June 19x6 the balance sheet of Eagle Limited included an item of deferred tax amounting to R11 152.

The following particulars are supplied:

| | Year ended 30 June | |
| --- | --- | --- |
| | 19x8 | 19x7 |
| Net income before tax | R282 000 | R252 000 |
| Wear and tear allowed on plant | 40 000 | 50 000 |
| Depreciation on same plant provided for in the financial statements | 48 000 | 48 000 |

Assume a constant tax rate of 40%.

<u>YOU ARE REQUIRED TO</u>:

prepare extracts of the balance sheets of Eagle Limited at 30 June 19x7 and 19x8 and income statements and notes to the financial statements for the years ended on those dates in accordance with Schedule Four and generally accepted accounting practice.

# S10

The following balances were extracted from the ledger of Finch Limited at the 30 June 19x7, the company's financial year end:

| | |
|---|---:|
| Share capital (authorised and issued R2 shares) | R500 000 |
| Retained income - 1 July 19x6 | 125 000 |
| Net income before tax | 210 000 |
| Deferred taxation - 1 July 19x6 | 37 500 |
| Plant - cost 1 July 19x6 | 468 750 |
| Accumulated depreciation - 1 July 19x6 | 140 625 |
| Purchase new plant - 1 July 19x6 | 75 000 |
| Tax value old plant - 1 July 19x6 | 234 375 |
| Depreciation | 80 650 |
| Wear and tear and initial allowances | 76 900 |
| Tax rate | 40% |

<u>YOU ARE REQUIRED TO</u>:

prepare an extract of the balance sheet of Finch Limited at 30 June 19x7 and the income statement and notes to the financial statements for the year ended on that date.

The extract of the balance sheet should be as complete as the information given will allow.

# S11

The net income before taxation of Highveld Limited for the year ended 31 March 19x3 amounted to R35 000.  Provisional payments totalling R10 000 were made during the year.

The company purchased plant and machinery on 1 April 19x1 for R120 000.  This plant and machinery is being depreciated at 20% p.a. straight line by the company.  The Receiver of Revenue is allowing wear and tear over 3 years using the straight line method.

The plant was sold on 31 March 19x3 for R60 000.

The tax rate has remained unchanged at 40%.

<u>YOU ARE REQUIRED TO</u>:

show the effect of the above in the financial statements and notes of Highveld Limited for the year ended 31 March 19x3 after all the necessary entries regarding taxation have been passed.

# SECTION T

# FINANCE LEASES

SECTION 7

FINANCE LEASES

# T1

Ashton Limited entered into a lease agreement with Boston Limited on 2 January 19x3, the terms of which were as follows:

a)   Asset to be leased - motor vehicle - cost  R40 000.

b)   Payments to be made - R11 600 p.a. on 31 December each year, except the first payment of R11 600 which is to be made on 2 January 19x3.

c)   Effective rate of interest - 23%.

d)   On payment of R11 600 on 31 December 19x6 ownership of the asset will lodge with Ashton Limited.

e)   The estimated useful life of the asset is four years with no residual value.

f)   The financial year end of Ashton Limited is 31 December.


<u>YOU ARE REQUIRED TO GIVE</u>:

a)   the journal entries for the above transactions in respect of the two years ended 31 December 19x3 and 19x4 assuming

  (i)   the company does not use an interest suspense account
  (ii)  the company uses an interest suspense account.

b)   the necessary disclosure in the financial statements of Ashton Limited for the year ended 31 December 19x4.

# T2

Caxton Limited entered into a lease agreement with Dalton Limited on 2 January 19x1, the terms of which were as follows:

a)      Assets to be leased - motor vehicles - cost  R90 000.

b)      Payments to be made - R40 250 p.a. on 31 December each year.

c)      Effective rate of interest - 16,269%.

d)      On payment of R40 250 on 31 December 19x3 ownership of the asset will lodge with Caxton Limited.

e)      The estimated life of the assets is three years with no residual value.

f)      The financial year end of Caxton Limited is 31 December.


<u>YOU ARE REQUIRED TO GIVE</u>:

a)      the ledger  accounts of the above in respect of the three years ended 31 December 19x1, 19x2 and 19x3 assuming

        (i)    the company does not use an interest suspense account
        (ii)   the company uses an interest suspense account.

b)      the necessary disclosure in the financial statements of Caxton Limited for the year ended 31 December 19x1.

# T3

Eaton Limited entered into a lease agreement with Felton Limited on 2 January 19x5 the terms of which were as follows:

a)   Asset to be leased - plant - cost  R387 500.

b)   Payments to be made - R105 000 p.a. on 31 December each year, except the first payment of R105 000 which is to be made on 2 January 19x5.

c)   Effective rate of interest - 17,992%.

d)   On payment of R105 000 on 31 December 19x8 ownership of the asset will lodge with Eaton Limited.

e)   The estimated useful life of the asset is four years with no residual value.

f)   The financial year end of Eaton Limited is 31 December.

<u>YOU ARE REQUIRED TO GIVE</u>:

a)   the journal entries for the above transactions in respect of the  year ended 31 December 19x5 assuming

   (i)   the company does not use an interest suspense account
   (ii)  the company uses an interest suspense account.

b)   the necessary disclosure in the financial statements of Eaton Limited for the years ended 31 December 19x6 and 19x7.

# T4

Gaston Limited entered into a  lease agreement with  Houston Limited on
2 January 19x4, the terms of which were as follows:

a)      Asset to be leased - plant - cost  R300 000.

b)      Payments to be made  - R75 000 p.a. on 31 December each year, except
        the first payment of R75 000 which is to be made on 2 January 19x4.

c)      Effective rate of interest - 12,5898%.

d)      On payment of R75 000 on 31 December 19x7 ownership of the asset will
        lodge with Gaston Limited.

e)      The estimate life of the asset is four years with no residual value.

f)      The financial year end of Gaston Limited is 31 December.


<u>YOU ARE REQUIRED TO GIVE</u>:

a)      the ledger accounts of the above  in respect of the four years ended
        31 December 19x4 to 19x7 assuming

        (i)   the company does not use an interest suspense account
        (ii)  the company does use an interest suspense account.

b)      the necessary disclosure in the financial statements of Gaston Limited
        for the year ended 31 December 19x4.

# T5

Jonton Limited entered into a lease agreement with Kelton Limited on 2 January 19x1, the terms of which were as follows:

a)  Asset to leased - plant - cost  R800 000.

b)  Payments to be made - R184 780 on 31 December each year.

c)  Effective rate of interest - 5% p.a.

d)  On payment of R184 780 on 31 December 19x5 ownership of the asset will lodge with Jonton Limited.

e)  The estimated life of the asset is five years with no residual value.

f)  The financial year end of Jonton Limited is 31 December.

<u>YOU ARE REQUIRED TO GIVE</u>:

a)  the journal entries for the above transactions in respect of the year ended 31 December 19x1 assuming

    (i)  the company does not use an interest suspense account
    (ii) the company uses a suspense account.

b)  the necessary disclosure in the financial statements of Jonton Limited for the year ended 31 December 19x2.

# T6

Kingston Limited entered into a   lease agreement with  Langton Limited on
2 January 19x4, the terms of which were as follows:

a)      Asset to be leased - plant - cost  R258 000.

b)      Payments to be made  - 2 January 19x4        R60 000
                                19x5          70 560
                                19x6          82 791
                                19x7          96 939

c)      Effective rate of interest - 12%.

d)      The term of the lease is four years.

e)      The estimate life of the asset is four years with no residual value.

f)      The financial year end of Kingston Limited is 31 December.


<u>YOU ARE REQUIRED TO GIVE</u>:

a)      the journal entries of the above  in respect of the year ended
        31 December 19x4

        (i)   the company does not use an interest suspense account
        (ii)  the company does use an interest suspense account.

b)      the necessary disclosure  in  the  financial  statements  of  Kingston
        Limited for the years ended 31 December 19x4 and 19x5.

## T7

Milton Limited entered into a  lease agreement with  Neston Limited on
2 January 19x1, the terms of which were as follows:

a)      Assets to be leased - motor vehicles - cost  R135 900.

b)      Three payments to be made  - R43 750 p.a. on 2 January each year,
        commencing on 2 January 19x1.  Final payment R43 735 on 2 January 19x4.

c)      Effective rate of interest - 20%.

d)      On payment of R43 735 on 2 January 19x4 ownership of the assets will
        lodge with Milton Limited.

e)      The estimate life of the assets is four years with no residual value.

f)      The financial year end of Milton Limited is 31 December.


<u>YOU ARE REQUIRED TO GIVE</u>:

a)      the  ledger  accounts  of  the  above  in  respect  of  the  year ended
        31 December 19x1 assuming
        (i)   the company does not use an interest suspense account
        (ii)  the company does use an interest suspense account.

b)      the necessary disclosure in the financial statements of Milton Limited
        for the year ended 31 December 19x1.

**T8**

Orton Limited entered into a lease agreement with Preston Limited on 2 January 19x5, the terms of which were as follows:

a)    Asset to be leased - plant - cost  R172 480.

b)    Payments to be made  - 2 January 19x5      R46 360
                                        19x6         50 126
                                        19x7         62 838
                                        19x8         70 349

c)    Effective rate of interest - 20%.

d)    On payment of R70 349 on 2 January 19x8 ownership of the asset will lodge with Orton Limited.

e)    The estimate life of the asset is four years with no residual value.

f)    The financial year end of Orton Limited is 31 December.


<u>YOU ARE REQUIRED TO GIVE</u>:

the necessary disclosure in the financial statements of Orton Limited for the years ended 31 December 19x5, 19x6 and 19x7.

## T9

Quinton Limited entered into a  lease agreement with  Ralston Limited on 2 January 19x6, the terms of which were as follows:

a)    Asset to be leased - motor vehicle - cost  R57 750.

b)    Payments to be made  -  2 January  19x6   R8 750
                             31 December 19x6   16 880
                             31 December 19x7   18 288
                             31 December 19x8   24 555

c)    Effective rate of interest - 9,9%.

d)    On payment of R24 652 on 31 December 19x8 ownership of the asset will lodge with Quinton Limited.

e)    The estimate life of the asset is three years with no residual value.

f)    The financial year end of Quinton Limited is 31 December.


<u>YOU ARE REQUIRED TO GIVE</u>:

a)    the ledger accounts of the above  in respect of the three years ended 31 December 19x6 to 19x8 assuming
      (i)    the company does not use an interest suspense account
      (ii)   the company does use an interest suspense account.

b)    the necessary disclosure in the financial statements of Quinton Limited for the year ended 31 December 19x6.

**T10**

On 1 May 19x1 Aviary Limited entered into a lease agreement with Starling
Limited.  The terms of the lease were as follows:

1)      Asset to be leased - plant  - cost  R46 000

2)      Payments to be made
            1 May 19x1        R10 000
            1 May 19x2         13 200
            1 May 19x3         17 280
            1 May 19x4         22 464

3)      Effective rate of interest 20%

4)      On payment of R22 464 ownership of the asset passes to Aviary Limited

5)      Estimated useful life of the asset - four years with no residual value

6)      The financial year end of Aviary Limited is 30 April.


<u>YOU ARE REQUIRED TO</u>:

give the necessary disclosure in the financial statements of Aviary Limited
for the year ended 30 April 19x2 in accordance with Schedule Four and
generally accepted accounting practice.

# T11

Stanton Limited entered into a lease agreement with Taunton Limited on 2 January 19x1, the terms of which were as follows:

(a)    Assets to be leased - motor vehicles - cost R300 000.

(b)    Payments to be made - five of R72 500 half yearly in arrears and a final payment of R72 444.

(c)    Effective rate of interest - 23.5% p.a.

(d)    On payment of R72 444 on 31 December 19x3 the ownership of the assets will lodge with Stanton Limited.

(e)    The estimated life of the assets is 3 years with no residual value.

(f)    The financial year end of Stanton Limited is 31 December.

<u>YOU ARE REQUIRED TO</u>:

give the necessary disclosure in the financial statements of Stanton Limited for the years ended 31 December 19x1 and 19x2.